Gorakhnāth and the Kānphaṭa Yogīs

Gorakhnāth and the Kānphaṭa Yogīs

George Weston Briggs

MOTILAL BANARSIDASS PUBLISHERS
PRIVATE LIMITED • DELHI

Reprint: Delhi, 1973, 1982, 1989, 1998, 2001, 2007, 2009
First Indian Edition: Kolkata, 1938

ISBN: 978-81-208-0563-7 (Cloth)
ISBN: 978-81-208-0564-4 (Paper)

MOTILAL BANARSIDASS
41 U.A. Bungalow Road, Jawahar Nagar, Delhi 110 007
8 Mahalaxmi Chamber, 22 Bhulabhai Desai Road, Mumbai 400 026
203 Royapettah High Road, Mylapore, Chennai 600 004
236, 9th Main III Block, Jayanagar, Bangalore 560 011
Sanas Plaza, 1302 Baji Rao Road, Pune 411 002
8 Camac Street, Kolkata 700 017
Ashok Rajpath, Patna 800 004
Chowk, Varanasi 221 001

Printed in India
By Jainendra Prakash Jain at Shri Jainendra Press,
A-45 Naraina, Phase-I, New Delhi 110 028
and Published by Narendra Prakash Jain for
Motilal Banarsidass Publishers Private Limited,
Bungalow Road, Delhi 110 007

To

Magdeja

PREFACE

THE cult of the Kānphaṭa Yogīs is a definite unit within Hinduism; but the ideas and practices of the sect reach a much wider distribution than the order. In this study of these Yogīs what may seem like undue attention is given to legend and folklore in general, and to the description of institutions, but this has been necessary in order to create the proper background for the understanding of the special Yoga of the sect. The study has been carried on in the midst of regular tasks, both in India and in this country, over a long period of time. A good deal of the data supplied by others has been checked as the author has met with Yogīs in many places, and with some Gorakhnāthīs many times.

The analysis of the subject-matter of this study has been made so that the first two sections of the book may serve to illustrate the third. The assumption has been maintained throughout, that folklore and tradition are indispensable to an understanding of the growth and influence of the sect; and that popular views concerning Yogīs are as essential for an understanding of this phase of the religious life of India as are the formulated texts of the sect.

The use of various spellings of names and places corresponds with practice in different areas.

The Sanskrit text here presented has not been, so far as the author knows, heretofore translated into English. There are, in other works, quotations including in all practically every verse of the *Gorakṣaśataka*, but the English translations of those verses are often in very free renderings. The translation here offered has been checked with the extensive commentary by Lakṣmi Nārāyaṇa, attached to the 'Poona' copy of the *Gorakṣaśataka*. The translations of passages from other Sanskrit texts of the sect are also by the author.

The attempt has been made to present the whole matter objectively and without comment, reserving a few paragraphs in the last chapter for some personal opinions. When the study was begun, the author had little idea that it would lead where it has. He has had no desire to hold up to view any unpleasant aspects of Hinduism and can only plead that Hindus are much more realistic and thorough in their criticisms of some of the practices here described.

Special thanks are due to the *mahants* and *gurus* of the order, more particularly to those at Gorakhpur, Devī Pātan, Ṭilla and Dhinodhar; and to a few friends in this country for council and for reading certain chapters of the book.

The Reverend Daniel Buck and Pandit Brahmarṣa Jagatānand deserve separate mention, the one for his companionship, and as an interpreter in visits to Kānphaṭa institutions, the other for assistance in the reading of Yoga texts. The late Professor A. V. Williams Jackson of Columbia University, Professor Franklin Edgerton of Yale University, and the late Dr. George William Brown of the Kennedy School of Missions have given generously of time and council. To the late Dr. J. N. Farquhar is due the impulse which started this investigation. His successors, the Reverend E. C. Dewick, M.A. and Mr. L. A. Hogg have rendered assistance in the later stages of its progress.

The pictures reproduced in the book, with the exception of one, were taken by the author. The cut showing the cave-temple of Gorakhnāth was furnished by Messrs. Constable and Company, Ltd., of London, with permission of H.H. the Mahārāja of Nepāl. The picture first appeared in Mr. Perceval Landon's *Nepāl*, volume one, page sixty-six. The line drawings were made by George S. Briggs, a son of the author.

Grateful acknowledgement is made to the following publishers for permission to quote from the volumes listed below. All of the excerpts are noted in appropriate places in the text.

The Secretary of the Delegates, The Clarendon Press:

The Vedānta Sūtras with Commentary of Rāmanuja and *The Vedānta Sūtras with the Commentary of Shaṅkarāchārya*. By G. Thibaut.

The Oxford University Press of New York and London:

Hymns from the Ṛig-veda. By A. A. Macdonell.
The Sāṁkhya System. By A. B. Keith.
Popular Religion and Folklore of Northern India. By W. Crooke.
The Religion of the Rig-Veda. By H. D. Griswold.
Outlines of the Religious Literature of India. By J. N. Farquhar.
The Darvishes. By J. P. Brown.

The Oxford University Press, New York, and Professor R. E. Hume, Ph.D.:

The Thirteen Principal Upanishads.

Macmillan and Company, New York, and Macmillan and Company, Ltd., London:

Tribes and Castes of the Central Provinces. By E. V. Russell and Hira Lal.

Macmillan and Company, New York, and The Cambridge University Press:

The Cambridge History of India. Vol. I. By J. E. Rapson, Editor.
A History of Indian Philosophy. 2 Vols. By S. N. Dasgupta.

Macmillan and Company, New York, and George Allen and Unwin:

Indian Philosophy. 2 Vols. By S. Radhakrishnan.

Arthur Probsthain, London:

Indian Serpent Lore. By J. Vogel.
Mohenjo-daro and the Indus River Civilization. 3 Vols. By Sir John Marshall.

Luzac and Company, London:

The Serpent Power and other works on *Tāntra.* By Arthur Avalon (Sir John Woodroffe).
(Also for the reproduction of one of the plates from *The Serpent Power.*)

Edward Arnold and Company, London:

Hinduism and Buddhism. By Sir Charles Eliot.

Harvard University Press, Cambridge:

Religion and Philosophy of the Veda. 2 Vols. By A. B. Keith.

John Lane, The Bodley Head Limited, London:

The Gurkhas. By Major W. Brook Northey and Captain C. G. Morris.

D. B. Taraporevala Sons and Company, Bombay:

The Mysterious Kuṇḍalinī. By Dr. Rele.

The Superintendent of Government Printing, The Panjab:

A Glossary of the Tribes and Castes of the Panjab, and of the North-West Frontier Province. By H. A. Rose.

I am indebted to one of my students, the Reverend William L. Lancey, B.A., B.D., for the preparation of the Index.

Of readers, especially of Indians, the author desires generous consideration, for he has endeavoured to carry on this study not with bias or for controversy, but with the desire to understand what these Yogīs themselves believe and do.

Madison, N. J., G.W.B.
22 June, 1938.

TABLE OF CONTENTS

CHAPTER ONE

GORAKHNĀTHĪS

THE followers of Gorakhnāth are known as *Yogī*, as *Gorakhnāthī*, and as *Darṣanī*, but most distinctively as *Kānphaṭa*. The first of these names refers to their traditional practice of the *Haṭha Yoga*, the second to the name of their reputed founder, the third to the huge ear-rings which are one of their distinctive marks, and the fourth to their unique practice of having the cartilege of their ears split for the insertion of the ear-rings. In the Panjab, in the Himālayas, in Bombay, and elsewhere they are often called *Nātha*, which is a general term meaning 'master.' Women of the sect are similarly called *Nāthnī*. In Western India they are generally known as *Dharamnāthī* (or Dhoramnāthī), after a famous disciple of Gorakhnāth, by that name. In other parts of India the names Kānphaṭa and Gorakhnāthī are commonly used.

It is said that the practice of splitting the ears originated with Gorakhnāth,[1] and that the designation *Kānphaṭa* (literally, 'Split-eared') was a term of disrespect applied to these Yogīs by Musalmāns.[1]

The word Yogī is a general descriptive term, applied to many who do not belong to the Kānphaṭas. 'It 'has many shades of meaning, from that of saint to that of sorcerer or charlatan.'[2] It is also a general term for ascetics, particularly

---

[1] *IA*, vol. VII, p. 299.

[2] *BRI*, p. 215; *RTCCP*, vol. III; *BHCS*, pp. 319 ff., 402; *Wi*, p. 217.

The following quotation is from *RTCP*, vol. II, p. 389. In the Panjab the term *Yogī*, is used to cover a wider group, 'that miscellaneous assortment of low caste *faqīrs* and fortune-tellers, both Hindu and Musalmān, but chiefly Musalmān, who are commonly known as

for those who are endeavouring, by restraint and discipline of the body, to secure union with the Brahman. From the generalized point of view, the Gorakhnāthīs constitute the principal group and the better class of Yogīs, although some of the less desirable characters of ascetics bearing the name Yogī, may be found amongst them. They form a distinct order of Yogīs.[1]

Kānphaṭa Yogīs are found everywhere in India, being as widely scattered as any of the ascetic orders.[2] They are met with separately as mendicants and as hermits, and in groups, in the Northern Deccan, in the Central Provinces, in Gujarāt, in Mahārāṣṭra, in the Panjab, in the provinces of the Ganges basin and in Nepāl.[3]

It is not proper for Yogīs to live alone; and they are not supposed to wander, but to abide in monasteries, or at temples, and to meditate. The books prescribe as follows, for Yogīs:

The practice of the Haṭha Yoga should be carried out in a private cell, four cubits square, free from stones, fire and water, [situated] in a well-governed country, free from violence, where the law (*dharma*) is followed and where alms are abundant. [The cell] should

---

Jogīs. Every rascally beggar who pretends to be able to tell fortunes, or to practice astrological and necromantic arts, in however small a degree, buys himself a drum and calls himself, and is called by others, a Jogī. Those men include all the Musalmāns, and probably a part of the Hindus of the eastern districts, who style themselves Jogīs. They are a thoroughly vagabond set, and wander about the country beating a drum and begging, practising surgery and physic in a small way, writing charms, telling fortunes, and practising exorcism and divination; or, sitting in the villages, eke out their earnings from these occupations by the offerings made at the local shrines of the malevolent godlings of the Sayads and other Musalmān saints; for the Jogī is so impure that he will eat the offerings made at any shrine. These people, or at least the Musalmān section of them, are called Rāwal in the centre of the Panjab. Rāwal corresponds to Nāth. In Kāṭhiāwār they are said to exorcise evil spirits and to worship *Koriāl*. In Siālkot they pretend to avert storms from the ripening crops by plunging a drawn sword into the field or a knife into a mound, sacrificing goats and accepting suitable offerings.'

[1] See *Census Report, North-Western Provinces and Oudh*, 1891, pp. 225, 226; *ERE*, vol. XII, p. 833.

[2] *FORL*, p. 347; *BRI*, p. 213.

[3] Tessitori, *ERE*, vol. XII, p. 834; *BRI*, p. 213.

be neither too high nor too low, free from cracks, hollows and holes, [and should have] a small door. [It] should be well plastered with cow-dung, clean and free from all kinds of vermin. On the outside [surrounding it] it should be graced with a beautiful enclosure [garden] with sheds, a platform and a well. These are the marks, as described by adepts in the practice of Haṭha [Yoga], of a cell where the Yoga is to be practised. Having seated [himself] in such a cell, with his thoughts abandoned, [the Yogī] should practise Yoga in the manner indicated by his guru.'[1]

Yogīs go on pilgrimages, visiting shrines and holy places all over India.[2] In the rainy season of 1924, there were very few Yogīs at Gorakhpur, most of them being away visiting various sacred places.[3] However, they make their monasteries their headquarters. Some do live alone,[4] in the jungles,

---

[1] *Haṭhayogapradīpika*, ch. I, vv. 12–14. The *Gorakhbodh* allows otherwise (*ERE*, vol. XII, p. 832).

[2] In earlier times they may have travelled further. The following report, while it deals with another type of ascetic, illustrates the fact that Indian ascetics have known great areas in Asia. The following is the statement of an 'oordhbabu' (*ūrdhvabāhu*) who claimed to have travelled extensively in Asia. Setting out from Bithur, he visited shrines in Central, Western and Southern India. Thence he travelled east, and then visited the holy places of Ceylon. He then proceeded to Malaya, and thence returned to India. Following the west coast of the peninsula, he visited Dwāraka, and Hiṅg Lāj; thence to Multān, Attock (Aṭak) and eastward to Hardwār. Retracing his steps westward, he visited Kābul, Bāmiān, Khurāsān, Herāt and Astrābād, and continued to the western borders of the Caspian Sea, Astrakān and Moscow. Thence travelling through Persia, he visited Hamadān, Ispahān, Śīrāz, Kermānshāh and other cities. Sailing from Abushahr he visited cities, including Bahrein and Basrah. Unable to reach Baghdād, he sailed to Muscat and Sūrat. Then he visited Mokha and returned to Karāchī and Sind. He then journeyed to Balk, Bokhārā, Samarqand, Badakhshān. Thence he entered Kashmīr and moved on into the Himālayas to Gangotri. He then travelled in Oudh and Nepāl, visiting Kāṭhamāṇḍu and the mountain regions beyond. Returning to Kāṭhamāṇḍu, he set out for Tibet, reaching Lhāsa and Lake Manasorowāra. He then returned to India and finally settled at Benares. This record of the sādhu's travels was made by Jonathan Duncan, Esq., at Benares in 1792, and Mr. Duncan reported that the ascetic gave circumstantial details of things in cities as far away as Moscow and Astrakān to confirm his statements. See *Asiatic Researches*, vol. V, pp. 37 ff.

[3] Holy men, in general, are not supposed to travel during the rainy season; but modern means of transportation are changing these customs.

[4] *Bombay Gazetteer*, vol. IX, p. 543.

practising Yoga; but hermits of this kind are exceedingly difficult to find. The author was able to get track of but two adepts, Bābā Hīra Nāthjī at Kālī Mohīnī in Alwār, between Bhātinda and Bandikui, and Bāwā Tejnal, at Patañjali Āśrama in Hardwār; and was unable to find either. Some of these are considered to be real adepts.

Census figures dealing with Gorakhnāthīs are not satisfactory, because, in many instances, other Yogīs (or 'Jogīs') and mendicants are included in the enumerations.

The census returns for 1891[1] show 'Jogīs' under 'miscellaneous and disreputable vagrants,' and enumerate 214,546 for India. The figures for the Provinces of Agra and Oudh[2] were, Āughar, 5,319; Gorakhnāthī, 28,816; Jogī, including Gorakhnāthī and others, 78,387. This would indicate that the Gorakhnāthīs, including Āughars, constituted about forty-

---

[1] vol. II, p. 14 (Statistics):

Panjab	91,937
Rājputāna	49,262
Bombay	16,823
Central India	10,274

The Report, vol. I, Part. 1 (1911) gives the following comparative study:

Faqīr (1911)	979,293
(1901)	1,212,648
(1891)	830,430

Part 2, Tables (1911) give the following distribution of Religious Mendicants, etc.:

Bengal	47,666
Bihār and Orissa	16,388
Bombay	94,764
Central Provinces and Berār	94,933
North-West and Frontier Provinces	12,848
United Provinces	21,405
Rājputāna Agency	170,135
Hyderābād	33,743
Kashmir	31,614
Central Indian Agency	32,327
Bombay States	82,568

[2] Part 1, p. 225.

five per cent of the Yogīs.[1] The same report for Agra and Oudh[2] shows that the proportion of male to female Yogīs was about 42/35; that Āughars were 2,422 males and 1,895 females; and Gorakhpanthīs 6,955 males and 6,178 females. The figures are of special interest because these Yogīs are generally supposed to be celibates.[3] It is to be noted that many female Yogīs are widows. Of the Yogīs reported in the Panjab, 38,137 were Musalmāns.[4]

The Census of 1901[5] shows, for India:

Faqīr, Hindu	...	436,803	Male/Female	252/185
Jogī, Hindu	...	659,891	do.	385/325
Jogī, Muhammadan	...	43,139	do.	21/22
Nātha, Hindu	...	45,463	do..	25/21

There were 10,947 Yogīs in the Bombay Presidency.[6]

---

[1] *Census of India*, 1891, North-Western Provinces, Part 3, p. 52:

Division		Jogī		Āughar		Gorakh-panthī	
		Male	Female	Male	Female	Male	Female
Meerut	...	23,767	19,331	In some Divisions		In some Divisions	
Agra	...	2,584	2,258				
Rohilkhand	...	3,500	2,845				
Allahābād	...	2,962	3,109				
Benares	...	436	430				
Gorakhpur	...	5,811	4,952				
Kumaon	...	2,581	2,180				
Total		41,641	35,105	2,368	1,870	6,941	6,178
Total Oudh and N.-W. Provinces		42,562	35,822	2,422	1,895	6,955	6,178

[2] Part 3, p. 52. The largest number of Yogīs was found in the Meerut Division, the Gorakhpur Division being second.

[3] *Martin* (vol. II, pp. 484, 485) reported that though they were not permitted to marry they were at liberty to communicate with whatever women they pleased.

[4] *Census of Panjab, Report*, 1891, pp. 113–8.

[5] *Census of India*, vol. I, Part 2, *Tables*, pp. 283, 288, 301.

[6] *ETCB*, vol. II, p. 103.

In 1911[1] there were enumerated in India 979,293 faqīrs, 814,365 Jogīs and 698,036 mendicants; there being 15,000 Kānphaṭas in the Central Provinces.[2]

The enumeration for 1921[3] was:

Jogī, Hindu	...	629,978	Male/Female	325/305
Jogī, Muhammadan	...	31,158	do.	16/15
Faqīr, Hindu	...	141,132	do.	80/61

Table XVII of the Imperial Census of India for 1931 shows under the headings of Aghorī, Faqīr, Jogī, Sādhu and Sannyāsī a total of more than a million persons, not far from half of whom are females, but does not so return ascetics as to show how many Gorakhnāthīs there are in India.

On the basis of the more detailed figures of 1891, the Gorakhnāthīs would still be very numerous. But no exact, or even approximate, statement can be made; simply, Kānphaṭas are very widely scattered and are exceedingly numerous.

The distinctive marks of the sect of the Kānphaṭas are the split-ears (*kān-phaṭa*) and the huge ear-rings. In the final stage of their ceremony of initiation a specially chosen *guru*, or teacher, splits the central hollows of both ears with a two edged knife (or razor).[4] The slits are plugged with sticks of *nīm*-wood; and, after the wounds have healed, large rings (*mudrā*) are inserted. These are a symbol of the Yogī's faith. Some explain that in splitting the ear a *nāḍi* (mystic channel)[5] in the cartilege is cut, thus assisting in the acquirement of yogic power.[6] The Yogī, wearing the mudrā, becomes immortal.[7] The rings worn in Western India are about seven inches in circumference and weigh two and a quarter ounces or more.[8] Weight is dependent upon the substance out of which the rings are made. In Kacch, where some of the wealthier Yogīs wear mudrās of gold, the strain of their weight is carried by a string, which is passed over the head.

---

[1] *Census of India*, vol. I, Part 1, *Tables*, pp. 192, 198, 309.
[2] *RTCCP*, vol. III, p. 250.
[3] *Census of India*, vol. I, Part 2, p. 154. [4] See *OMAS*, p. 165.
[5] See ch. xv. [6] Āipanthīs at Hardwār.
[7] *RTCP*, vol. II, p. 398. (See the story on p. 9, below.)
[8] *Bombay Gazetteer*, vol. V, p. 85.

Rings are of two general shapes, flat and cylindrical; the former called *darṣan*, the latter *kuṇḍal*. The word 'kuṇḍal' simply means 'round.' Darṣan is a term of extreme respect. The use of the word is sometimes explained as a sign that the wearer has had a vision of the Brahman.[1] The ring is sometimes called *pāvitrī*, 'holy,' 'sacred.'

Rings are made of various substances. The rule seems to be that the initiate first wears rings of clay. A legend relates how Gorakhnāth cut holes, three inches long, in Bhartri's ears and inserted ear-rings of clay. Some Yogīs continue to wear earthen rings. But, since these are easily broken, others of more durable substances are usually substituted. The element of value also enters into the use of more substantial rings.

Rhinoceros horn is a favourite substance for ear-rings. It is not easily broken. The practice goes back to an early period, for such rings are dug up, from time to time, in the oldest burial places of the sect, for example, at Ṭilla and in *old* Almora. The *mahant* (head of the monastery) at Ṭilla, in the Panjab, wore (1924) rings of rhinoceros horn covered with plates of gold. Rings of rhinoceros leather are not uncommon.[2]

A legend is available, explaining the use of rhinoceros horn, which accounts for the practice, not because the rings are not easily broken, but for the reason that the rhinoceros is a sacred animal. The story is as follows: As a result of the great war between the Pāṇḍavas and the Kāuravas (the ancient war which is the central theme of the *Mahābhārata*) the Pāṇḍavas, having slain their kinsmen, a most heinous sin, were thereby disqualified from performing the funeral rites for them. They appealed to Brahmā for absolution. In reply, the Creator commanded: 'First make the pilgrimage to Badrināth and Kedārnāth.' The Pāṇḍavas straightway set off upon the journey. Returning from the Himālayas, they reported to Brahmā and then again asked for permission to perform the funeral rites for their slain kinsmen (ancestors). Brahmā gave instructions: 'Kill a rhinoceros, make a vessel of its skin, and with that offer water to your relatives. They

---

[1] So explained to the author at Purī.

[2] The author once saw especially fine ones at Gorakh Bansuri, Calcutta.

will receive the oblation and then will be able to proceed to Paradise.' So the Pāṇḍavas slew a rhinoceros, made a vessel of its skin and from it poured out water to their kinsmen. The *piṇḍa* was then offered (i.e. the funeral rites were performed) and the slain relatives attained Paradise. Since that time the rhinoceros has been considered a sacred animal, and that is why the Gorakhnāthīs make their ear-rings from its horn.[1]

Thin gold discs are sometimes seen. The pīr (abbot) and some important Yogīs of Dhinodhar, in Kacch, wear heavy rings of gold, darṣan-shaped, inlaid with precious and semi-precious stones. A mahant from Delhi, in 1924, wore rings of crystal with inlay of gold and precious stones. Other substances used are copper,[2] stag's and antelope's horn, ivory, agate, jade, glass (white and coloured) and wood. In Mewār many Kānphaṭas use rings of conch shell. The conch is their battle trumpet.[3]

The wearing of the ear-rings is of great importance. If, by accident, one is broken, a model in cloth, or the *siṅgnād*, must be substituted before the Yogī may partake of food, or perform his religious duties.[4] Or, he must bathe and procure another before he eats with his fellows or engages in conversation.

A Yogī must protect himself from having his rings torn out. In the old days he, whose ears had been mutilated, did not survive; he either died outright or was buried alive.[5] It is claimed in Kumaon that the practice still holds (1924).

---

[1] This story was obtained at Śrī Nagar, Garhwāl. The same reason is found to explain why followers of Guru Govind Singh use ear-rings made of the horn of the rhinoceros. There are many marks, in the lower Himālayas, showing where the Pāṇḍavas, with the dog, travelled in the course of their wanderings. At Deo Dhura may be seen great boulders said to have been thrown about in sport by the Pāṇḍavas; and near the temple of Devī there are two boulders cleft through by a fresh-looking fissure and there is a similar rift in the lower rock. The smaller, upper rock is said to be the weapon with which Bhīma cleft the great boulders. Holes in the rocks are still pointed out as his finger-prints. *Himalayan Gazetteer*, vol. III, pp. 201, 202.

[2] The author saw fine ones at Purī in 1924.

[3] *BCI*, vol. III, p. 198. [4] See *RTCCP*, vol. III, p. 250.

[5] *Bombay Gazetteer*, vol. VIII, p. 155.

Even now a Yogī with mutilated ears cannot face the world. He must flee from his brethren; he must never be seen again; he is excommunicated; no tomb is erected over his body when he dies;[1] others will not associate with him; and he is not allowed to share in religious ceremonies and he loses his *pūjārī* rights.

There is conflict of opinion concerning the origin of the practice of wearing the rings. As stated above, the institution of the custom is attributed to Gorakhnāth. However, Śiva is the great ascetic and he wears huge ear-rings.[2] Legend records that ear-rings (kuṇḍal), made from dirt off her body, were attached to the body which Śiva had left behind when he descended the lotus stalk in the form of an insect, by Śakti.[3] These ear-rings were later changed into mudrās. Śiva's ears were split at that time. By this means the body of Śiva became immortal. Some trace the practice to Macchendranāth, the guru of Gorakhnāth. The Āipanthīs of Hardwār say that Macchendranāth, when he began to preach the Yoga, by order of Mahādeo, saw that Śiva had his ears split and that he (Śiva) wore the great rings. Macchendra, thereupon, longed to have similar rings himself. He began to worship Śiva and so pleased the god that his desire was granted. Macchendranāth was then ordered to split the ears of all who should become his disciples. Another legend, which connects the practice with Macchendranāth, states that when he was born as a fish, he was discovered to have had rings in his ears.[4] At Purī, they say that the order to split the ears came from Macchendranāth.

But the origin of the practice of splitting the ears is traced to others as well. It is said that Bhartri asked his guru. Jālandharipā, for a distinguishing mark. So holes, three inches wide, were made in Bhartri's ears and rings of clay were inserted. Later, those rings were changed for others of wood, then of crystal-gilt and finally of ivory.[5]

Legends and traditions which refer the custom to Gorakh-

---

[1] *RTCP*, vol. III, p. 250. But, at Śrī Nagar, they reported to the author that he would have a *samādh*.

[2] *FORL*, p. 388. [3] *RTCP*, vol. II, pp. 391, 392.

[4] Told to the author at Nāsik. [5] *RTCP*, vol. II, p. 398.

nāth are numerous. It is said that Śiva ordered Pārvatī to split Gorakhnāth's ears[1] and that thus the practice arose. Again, Karkāi and Bhuskāi received consent from their guru, Gorakhnāth, to split each other's ears.[2] The agreement was made at a place on the road to Hiṅg Lāj, a shrine which every perfect Yogī must visit. Gorakhnāth is said to have split Bhartri's ears.[2]

Women who wear the mudrā are numerous. They are chiefly widows who have become Yogīs, and initiated wives of Yogīs. However, not all women whose husbands are Yogīs, have their ears split. Widows often take the vows, are initiated into the sect and then go on pilgrimage. Some of these are in charge of temples.[3] Married women who are Yogīs and who wear the mudrā are not uncommon in Kumaon and Garhwāl. But it is not according to rule that wives of householders wear the ear-rings.[4]

Āughars are followers of Gorakhnāth who have not undergone the final ceremony of having their ears split. A legend is current which serves to justify them in not completing initiation. Once two *siddhas* (perfect Yogīs) tried to split the ears of a candidate who had been at Hiṅg Lāj; but they found that the slits closed as fast as they were made. So they gave up the attempt. Since then Āughars have dispensed with the custom.[5] It will be seen, further on, that while many Āughars contemplate completing their initiation, there is a division of Gorakhnāthīs who always remain Āughars.

The Gūdara sometimes wears a ring, as do the Kānphaṭas.[6] These mendicants are Śāivites, so-called because they carry a pan of metal in which is kept a small fire for the burning of scented woods at the houses of persons from whom they beg. They cry out, '*Alakh, Alakh*!' Their peculiar garb consists of a large, round cap, a long ochre-coloured frock, and ear-rings like those of the Kānphaṭas,

---

[1] RTCP, vol. II, p. 390. [2] *RTCP*, vol. II, p. 398.

[3] For example, in Almora, the author met two such women and saw their temples.

[4] So they said in Almora. [5] *RTCP*, vol. II, p. 398.

[6] *Wi*, pp. 235, 236; *RTCB*, vol. II, p. 22.

or cylinders of wood passed through the lobe of the ears, which they term *khecharīmudrā*, the seal or symbol of the deity, 'of him who moves in the heavens.' The Gūdara belongs to the Āughar sect of Śāivites founded by a Dasnāmī by the name of Brāhmagīri, through the favour of Gorakhnāth, who is said to have invested the ascetic with his ear-rings. The Gūdara sub-sect wears the ring in one ear, and in the other a flat copper plate with the footprint of Āughar or Gorakhnāth. Other groups wear rings of copper or of pewter in both ears.

From the Nizam's Dominions it is reported that the various orders of Gorakhnāthīs are distinguished by the kind of materials from which they make their ear-rings.[1]

Both Āughars and Yogīs of the sect wear a *janeo*, or sacred thread, which is made by certain members of the order, who are taught the art. It is not made by all Yogīs nor by Brāhmans. The thread is spun from black sheep's wool[2] and consists of nine strands. It is worn around the neck.

To this thread is attached a ring, which may be flat or cylindrical, called *pāvitrī*. It is made of deer's horn, rhinoceros horn, of bone, of brass or other metal. Brass rings obtained from Nepāl have on their rim three images, that of Paśupati (Śiva) with the trident on one side of it and the bull on the other. The ring represents Pārvatī.

To the ring are attached, by means of a white cotton cord, a whistle, *siṅgnād*, and a single *rudrākṣa* berry. The siṅgnād is, as the name implies, a whistle made of horn, either of black-buck horn, of stag horn, or of rhinoceros horn. As a matter of fact, it may be made of wood or of jade. It is about two inches long. That of black-buck's horn is the most popular.

The use of horn is explained in a legend about a king Bhartri (Bhartṛhari). Once his seventy queens urged him to go hunting. While he was away he ran across a herd of seventy hinds and one stag; but was unable to overtake the stag. Finally, a hind asked the stag to allow himself to be

---

[1] *STCND*, vol. I, p. 278.

[2] In the hills of Kumaon many Yogīs use cotton for this thread.

shot, and he agreed, on certain conditions, one of which was that his horn should be used for the Yogī's whistle.[1]

The siṅgnād is blown before meals and before morning and evening worship.[2] It may be blown before the Yogī performs his offices of nature. The mahant (abbot) at Dhinodhar uses his whistle in returning a salute and before performing his duties. One of his chief privileges is to blow his whistle when he worships his gods. The use of the whistle was ordered by Śiva. It has a phallic significance, as has the pāvitrī which is associated with it.

Some attach a tooth pick of silver to the thread. This may have a protective use against evil influences.

Because the whistle is fastened to it, the thread is called *siṅgnād-janeo.*[3]

Some Yogīs wear around the loins, a special rope made of black sheep's wool to which they fasten the loin cloth, *laṅgoṭī*. It is called *ārband-laṅgoṭ-nāg*. As the last word in this name signifies, they, except for the rope, go naked. This cord, which is an inch or more in diameter, is made on a bobbin, and is finished with a loop on one end and a button on the other.[4] It is fastened in front. Most Yogīs use a strip of cotton cloth instead of this rope of wool.

A third 'thread' is worn by some Kānphaṭas. Special regulations go with its use. For example, while wearing this cord, and the other paraphernalia that go with it, the Yogī may neither sit nor stand still but must go out, as soon as he has put it on, and beg.[5] This cord is called *hāl maṭaṅgā*. It is made of three strands, each of eight threads, plaited with the twist to the right into a bobbin cord.[6] One end is finished with five tails, and the other has a bell, like a large,

---

[1] *RTCP*, vol. II, p. 404. The whole story is told in ch. vii.

[2] *RTCCP*, vol. III, p. 250. [3] Compare *BHC*, p. 403.

[4] Compare *RTCP*, vol. II, p. 399. The author saw an especially fine one at Devī Pātan in 1924.

[5] Dasnāmīs also, who are special devotees of Bhāiroṁ, wear this cord. One such had on his forehead a *ṭikā* consisting of two curved, horizontal marks, both red; with a black dot between them and a black line below them. Hanumān is indicated by the red lines and the black line and the dot are for Bhāiroṁ.

[6] *PNO*, vol. II, para. 126. Some say sixteen strands, some nine and some twelve.

brass sleigh-bell, attached to it. Sometimes strips of red cloth are woven into the cord. The 'thread' is reckoned of various lengths, nine, eleven and one-half[1] or twenty-three cubits;[2] and is of about the diameter of a lead pencil, although it may be considerably larger.

The cord may be worn as a sort of plaited net-jacket. In this case it is first doubled. The end, with bell attached, is hung down in front, the bell reaching to the knees; the cord is then thrown over the left shoulder and turned back under the right shoulder; then around the chest and under the left and over the right shoulder; it is crossed under the long section in front and then wound round and round the body, alternately under and over the front strands and plaited as it is wound about the chest. After the cord is adjusted, two rosaries are put on, one over each shoulder and under the opposite one. Smaller rosaries are put around the neck and on each forearm. 'Handkerchiefs' are fastened to the upper arms. The Yogī then takes his bowl, his bag and his fire-tongs and goes out to beg. The wearing of the cord is a matter of choice rather than of regulation.[3]

An occasional Gorakhnāthī wears the usual *janeo*, or sacred thread of the Hindu.

Yogīs are met with who do not wear the sacred thread, siṅgnād-janeo. A Yogī who has attained to unusual spiritual eminence may discard the use of the thread and the ear-rings, saying that he wears them invisibly,[4] or that he wears them underneath his skin. This is not an uncommon claim in legends about holy men.[5]

Although Kānphaṭa Yogīs wear no distinctive rosaries, they do use some that are of significance and of interest. One of these consisting of rudrākṣa berries is that commonly worn by Śāivites. It is hung around the neck and consists of thirty-two, of sixty-four, of eighty-four, of one hundred

[1] So they say at Devī Pātan. [2] So they say at Benares.

[3] This paragraph is based upon exhibitions of putting on the *hāl maṭaṅgā* by Yogīs at Cawnpore and at Benares.

[4] *RTCP*, vol. II, p. 402.

[5] Compare Rāe Dās, the Chamār, and his Brāhmaṇical cord.—*The Chamārs*, p. 209.

and eight, or even of more berries.[1] A smaller one having eighteen[2] or twenty-eight berries,[3] is worn on the wrist, or elbow. This is called *sumaraṇī*. The small rosary is often carried in the hand. Beads are used in worship and as a check on memory, while repeating the names of God. This is evident from the technical terms for rosary, *japa māla*, 'muttering chaplet' and *sumaraṇī*, 'remembrancer.' A Śāivite has to recite the 1,008 names of his god.[4]

Rudrākṣa berries (of the tree *elæocarpus ganitrus*[5]) are significant for the Yogī in many ways. The word 'rudrākṣa' means 'eye of Rudra (Śiva)' and may refer to the third, now invisible, eye of that god, which will be opened for the destruction of the world.[6] There is a mark on the seed that is said to resemble an eye. Or, the berries may refer to the tears, shed by Śiva[7] in rage when he set out to destroy the three cities, Tripura; for those tears became rudrākṣa berries. Again, some say that the string of 108 berries represents that many successive appearances of Śiva on the earth.[8] The size of the berries is of importance.

Rudrākṣa berries are found with faces ranging from one to twenty-one in number, and each kind has a special significance. The usual number of faces is five, and some say that this berry is sacred to Hanumān, or to the Pāṇḍavas. It also represents the five-faced Śiva.[9]

---

[1] Eighty-four beads make up the proper Śāivite rosary. It is interesting to note that $84 = 7 \times 12$ and symbolizes the number of the planets (7) and the signs of the Zodiac (12). $108 = 9 \times 12$ where the moon is counted in its three phases as increasing, full and waning to make-up nine (9). 'Consequently these Hindu rosaries symbolize the whole circuit of the hosts of heaven.' (See, in *Journal of the Royal Society of Arts*, vol. L. (1902), p. 275 f., a discussion, by Sir George Birdwood, of a paper on 'The History of the Rosary in all Countries' by the Rev. H. Thurston, S.J.) $108 = 2^2 \times 3^3$ and is, therefore, an auspicious number.

[2] So reported at Dhinodhar. [3] So reported in the 'hills.'

[4] Śāktas count up to one hundred, using the finger (joints) of the right hand, and keep score by joints of the fingers of the left hand. They use dead men's teeth and similar relics also, for beads.—*ERE*, vol. X, p. 848 f.

[5] Seeds of the *badar* or *jujuh*. *PNQ*, vol. II, p. 558.

[6] *NCS*, p. 83. [7] *ERE*, vol. X, p. 848. [8] So reported in Benares.

[9] *Bengali Religious Lyrics*, *Śākta*, p. 90. See *Brahmanism and Hinduism*, p. 82 f.

The number of faces is often merely of symbolic importance; for example, that of three faces represents the trident, or the triad; that of four, the four Vedas, or Brahmā; that of six, the six systems of philosophy; that of seven, the seven the worlds; that of eight, the eight-armed Durgā; that of nine, the nine Nāthas; that of ten, the ten *avtāras* (of Viṣṇu); while that of eleven is sacred to Mahādeva and is counted as the 'very best' and is worn by celibates only. It is referred to as *askand* [(?) not spilling, as of semen]. The two-faced berry is worn only by a Yogī who is accompanied by his wife.[1] A much valued berry is that which is double, that is, two berries naturally joined. If the total number of faces on the two be eleven, the double is called Gāurī-Śaṅkar, and it is sacred to Pārvatī (Gāurī) and Śiva. One-faced berries are very seldom found. It is said that kings only possess them, and that one who finds such a berry is set up for life in wealth, because it secures to the owner everything that he may wish. This rare type is often counterfeited.[2]

There is no rule as to the number of faces for the berry that the guru gives to his disciple at the initiation; and the one received at that time may be changed, later on, for one of another number of faces.

Two rosaries made of white 'stone' beads (really nummulities[3]) are greatly prized by Yogīs. Both are obtained on the difficult pilgrimage to the Vāmacāra Śakti Temple at Hiṅg Lāj.[4] That made of the smaller 'stone' beads is called *Hiṅg Lāj kā ṭhumṛā*; the other, made of larger beads, *Āśāpūrī*. The former is said to represent grains of millet (*jawār*), the latter, grains of rice, or *bājra*.[5] The former is the more commonly

---

[1] *RTCP*, vol. II, p. 399.

[2] A seed of this kind belonged to Kharak Sing, son of Mahārāja Ranjīt Singh, the only one of its kind ever seen; but it has been lost! —Crooke, *Religion and Folklore*, p. 289.

[3] Of the family *nummulinidœ*, a family of foraminifers having a calcareous, symmetrical, usually lentrical or discoidal, shell composed of numerous chambers concentrically arranged. Especially abundant in eocene and oligocene deposits of Eastern and Southern Asia.

[4] For the native accounts concerning these beads, see pp. 103 ff.

[5] *Jawār*, the larger millet, a common food-grain, *Andro pogon, sorghum* or *sorghum vulgare*. *Imperial Gazetteer of India*, Index Volume, Glossary, p. xiv. *Bājra*, bulrush millet, a common food-grain, *pennisetum typhoideum* (ibid., p. vi.)

worn, and is evidently the more prized. It consists of 500[1] or 1,000 beads.

Necklaces made of beads of glass, of china, and of other materials are worn by Yogīs, but, apparently, with no special religious significance.

All Yogīs use ashes, but the practice is not limited to them, for all ascetics observe the custom, which is very old. *Sabhasma-dṛja*, 'sprinkled with ashes,' is a generic term for Śāivite.[2] Kānphaṭas use ashes for the *tripuṇḍ* (*tripuṇḍra*) or triple mark drawn across the forehead, and on other parts of the body. This mark is to represent the half-moon drawn three times. They also cover the body with ashes, or with earth mixed with ashes. Those who go naked rub the whole body with ashes. The hair is also sprinkled with ashes. It is said that the practice serves to protect the user from vermin. Earth is often used instead of ashes.[3]

Ashes may be taken from the *dhūnī*, the Yogī's hearthfire. Ashes of burned cow-dung are also used. Śiva, as the Yogī *par excellence*, covers his body with ashes from the burning grounds.

Several reasons are given for the use of ashes.[4] They signify death to the world,[5] and, in this case, undoubtedly refer to the burning grounds; or, they may indicate that the

---

[1] Reported at Dhinodhar.

[2] *BRI*, p. 314, n. 3. *Bṛhat Saṁhitā*, 60, 19, p. 328. (Ed. Kern).

[3] Compare *Panjab Census Report*, 1891, p. 118.

[4] There are elaborate explanations of the practice as it relates to Śiva. For example: 'The sacred body of Śiva is covered with ashes naturally. In this form it is called 'the eternal ashes.' In the next place after he has, by a spark emitted out of his central eye, reduced the gods together with all animate and inanimate beings to ashes at the end of each *kalpa*, he rubs their ashes upon his sacred body. In this form it is called 'the original ashes,' and since the god thus adorns his sacred body, they only can be the true servants of Śiva who constantly wear the sacred ashes rubbed upon their person. The reward for so doing is declared in the *Āgamas* to be the blotting out of all the greater sins. They also teach that the ashes to have this effect must be made of cow-dung: and that there are three methods of preparing them, namely, *Kalpa*, *Anakalpa* and *Upakalpa*; and that no other ashes but such as are made in one of these three ways must be rubbed on the body.' Quoted by Murdock in his *Śiva Bhakti*, p. 17.

[5] *RTCP*, vol. II, p. 140.

body must be reduced to ashes ultimately,[1] or they may be a sign that the Yogī has abandoned the world.

Ashes protect from evil spirits as well.

The common mark placed upon the forehead by the Yogī is the tripuṇḍ, consisting of three horizontal lines, or of a broad band, made by the hand, with ashes, with ashes and clay, or with sandal-wood paste. Similar lines are drawn on other parts of the body, for example, on the arms and chest.[2] These are, strictly, Śāivite marks. The tripuṇḍ is sometimes said to represent the moon. Some Yogīs put on the forehead a mark consisting of a black, horizontal line with a black dot above it, representing Bhāiroṁ; and below it a red circle representing Hanumān (Mahābīr). A few put a single spot of sandal-wood paste on the forehead, when they are 'offering' the paste to Bhāiroṁ.[3] Still others put a black spot on the forehead when they are burning incense. Other forms of the *ṭikā* are the double square of sandal-wood paste:[4] a single spot of ashes on the forehead; a yellow, rounded rectangle with a red dot in the centre; a rounded rectangle of yellow with a single grain of rice in the middle, below a brush of ashes; two circles one above the other, the upper of sandal-wood paste, the other red;[5] a circle made of a mixture of sandal-wood paste and a red substance, for Bhāiroṁ; two spots one above the other, the upper red, the lower black; two elongated enclosures one above the other, in red, with a red dot below. In Benares it was explained that these marks have to do with the *iṣṭadeva*, or chosen god, of the particular Yogī. The examples given by no means exhaust the varieties of ṭikā employed.

All Yogīs who make the pilgrimage to Hiṅg Lāj stop at Koteśwar on their return journey and are there branded on the 'front' of their right fore arm with an image of the *yoni-liṅga*. The reason given for this practice will be found in chapter six.[6] The brand mark which is reproduced bears a phallic significance. It is generally claimed that Yogīs receive no other brand marks.[7]

---

[1] *B. and H*, p. 67, n. 1. [2] *NSC*, p. 83. [3] *E.g.*, in Almora.
[4] *E.g.*, at Kāma. [5] *E.g.*, at Devī Pātan.
[6] See also *PNQ*, vol. II, para. 345.
[7] So reported at Naini Tāl, Tulsipur and Gorakhpur.

At the time that a candidate is made a novice (Āughar), his head, including his scalp-lock (*cuṭiya*), is shaved. Aside from this, there seems to be no uniform practice with reference to the care of the hair. Apparently the hair on the head and face should all be shaved or none.[1] If a Yogī has his moustache and his beard shaved and not his head, or the reverse, he must pay a fine of one rupee and four annas.[2] Some allow their hair to grow long[3] and it is left unkempt or matted. Others shave their heads. Some braid black wool into their hair.[4] The photographs shown in this volume indicate a lack of uniformity in practice. It is claimed that those who have their heads shaved wear clothes, while others go scantily clothed (*naṅga*), or wear no clothes at all, and are obliged to sit on the ground.[5] But this assertion does not seem to hold good in general.

There seems to be no rule about the care of the finger-nails. They are trimmed in the usual way. It is reported that some allow the nails to go unpruned.[6] But this is denied.[7] The nails are not removed at death.

The 'yellow'[8] robe is the distinctive dress of the Yogī.

The ochre-coloured dress is worn because Śiva ordered it. The cloth of the Yogī was first dyed by Pārvatī who resorted to self-mutilation,[9] dyed a cloth with her blood, and gave it to Gorakhnāth.

In practice, the yellow robe is by no means commonly worn. Many dress in the ordinary garb of the Hindu, some-

---

[1] So reported at Dhinodhar, Devī Pātan, Gorakhpur.

[2] This is $1\frac{1}{4}$, or $\frac{5}{4}$ rupees, five being an auspicious number.

[3] *BHCS*, p. 403.

[4] *RTCCP*, vol. III, p. 251, quoting Maclagan; *OMAS*, p. 185.

[5] At Devī Pātan. [6] *BHCS*, p. 403. [7] At Gorakhpur.

[8] Yellow (and red) is a symbol of fertility and is the marriage colour. It is the colour of ripe grain, is lucky, and is connected with the cult of Gāurī. Turmeric as a sacred plant is used in the anointing of the bride and groom. The corpse is anointed with turmeric, since death is looked upon as a marriage. Yellow is also a protection against demons. (Crooke, *Popular Religion and Folklore of Northern India*, p. 295.) Some Rākṣases are yellow. (Keith, *Religion and Philosophy of the Veda*, vol. I, p. 237.) These notions may have some bearing upon the question of the use of yellow. But the explanation given in the text, below, probably has truth in it.

[9] *RTCB*, vol. II, p. 390.

times coloured with ochre, but very often simply white. Thin cotton is used in the warm weather and slightly heavier clothing in the cold weather. In the Panjab, in the cold season, heavy clothes of wool are worn, made after the common patterns of the people.[1] However, many Yogīs go scantily clothed, wearing only a loin cloth. Some add to this a scarf, or a jacket of the usual type. A girdle of wool (*ārband*)[2] is sometimes the only clothing. At Deoprayāg in the Himālayas there was (in 1924) a Nāga, who was absolutely naked. He lived in a cave, alone. He never crossed the river (Bhāgīrathī) into the town. He bathed three times a day and then rubbed his body with ashes. He performed his evening worship facing the east. Occasionally one sees a long, loose robe of orange colour, often drawn in at the waist with a cord.

The headdress varies greatly. Turbans (*pagṛī*) are common. These are either white or ochre-coloured, as a rule. Many wear a simple white cap, others a cap of patch-work.[3] This last is the characteristic headdress of the *Satnāthīs*.[4] while travelling. A conical cap of nine sections,[5] with ear-flaps, or a cap of black ribbons is worn.[6] Still others wear no head covering at all. The Āughars of Kirāna wear an ochre-coloured turban over which is twisted a net work of black thread, covered with gold. The head of the monastery at Kāma has a flat, or cylindrical, turban made of threads of black sheep's wool, for special occasions. But, commonly, he wore a white skull-cap of the ordinary 'Hindu' pattern.

Besides rosaries and other articles of dress and ornaments as already described, Yogīs wear certain objects for personal adornment. Bracelets of brass, of precious metals and of rhinoceros leather may be mentioned; brass bracelets obtained in Nepāl, like the *pāvitrī* of brass already described,

---

[1] See various photographs. [2] See p. 12 above.

[3] 'In Sind, Yogīs wear caps.' (Hughes, *A Gazetteer of the Province of Sindh*, p. 96). The cap is not described.

[4] This was reported at Purī. see *Wi*, p. 216; Conybeare, *Statistical and Historical Account of the North-Western Provinces of India, Bareilly*, p. 592.

[5] *PNQ*, vol. II, para 279.

[6] *SHTC*, p. 262; *BCI*, vol. II, p. 497.

having on the rim an image of Paśupati, with Nanda, the bull, on one side and the trident on the other; and armlets of copper from Kedārnāth and of iron from Badrināth. Some Yogīs wear anklets. *Kaṅgnas*, or wristlets and armlets made of thread are worn, likewise charms and amulets of the usual types. The mahant at Gorakhpur wore on his right arm two cylindrical cases of gold, containing charms.[1] Finger rings of various patterns and materials are common.

The dress of some notables of the Kānphaṭas may be described. The pīr of Dhinodhar wears very rich clothes. As described in 1839,[2] his dress of honour consisted of a gold-bordered silk turban, a scanty waist band, a sacred woollen neck thread, a *sheli*, a red, or brick-coloured scarf, and wooden pattens. He was allowed to wear neither an *aṅgarakhā* nor leather shoes.[3] Some of his ornaments were very valuable, and some were very old. His ear-rings were of gold, very large, and inlaid with gems. They were so heavy that they had to be supported by a string passed over his head. His finger rings were of gold, and of the 'Kacch' pattern, and his bracelets were broad and heavy. On the morning of the author's visit to Dhinodhar[4] the pīr was dressed much as was his predecessor in 1839. His turban was of black cloth and his waist-band of heavy, dark-red silk, rolled and wound about him. He wore in his girdle a two-handled dagger, finished in gold. This was a mark of distinction. He was dressed in white. His shawl was ochre-coloured. He wore the usual rosaries and had on much jewelry, including strings of beads, and a heavy, finely-wrought necklace of gold. His shoes were of the usual pattern, made of wood. The appointments of his *gaddi* (his cushion, or official seat), his *huqqa* (water-pipe), his box and other articles were of silver. His staff was trimmed with silver.

The mahant of Gorakhpur wore (1924) clothes of white, like those of ordinary Hindus. But he had for special occasions a heavy coat of gold-embroidered cloth and a turban. While he was attired in these garments his attendants carried heavy

---

[1] In the spring of 1924. [2] *JRAS*, 1839, p. 270.
[3] *IA*, vol. VII, p. 52.
[4] The author visited the pīr, on 29th March, 1924.

maces of bamboo covered with sheets of silver, and waved over him yak-tail fans.

The special dress which some Yogīs wear when they go out to beg is very elaborate. The whole process of dressing, as the author saw it, was as follows: First, the Yogī rubbed ashes on his body and face. Then, after putting on a *dhotī*, or loin-cloth, and a jacket, he proceeded to adjust his hāl maṭaṅgā.[1] He then fastened kaṁgas, arm bands, short rosaries and 'handkerchiefs' to his wrists and arms, slung threads over his shoulders, and put many rosaries around his neck. Then swinging his wallet (food bag) over his left shoulder he took up his fire tongs and his begging bowl and started on the round of houses from which he was accustomed to beg.[2]

Like most Indian ascetics, Kānphaṭas have a number of necessary accessories. Among these is the *dhūnī*, or fire, consisting of a smouldering log of wood (or more than one), sometimes in a hollow pit. Whenever he takes up his abode he lights his fire, provided there is not one already at the place. At all important shrines and monasteries such fires are found, some of which have been kept burning for long periods of time. The dhūnī at Dhinodhar, and those at Gorakhpur, Ṭilla and Pāe Dhūnī in Bombay are famous because of associations with Dharamnāth, Gorakhnāth and others. These have been kept burning for centuries. It is an interesting fact that the Forest Department of Government supplies two hundred and fifty bullock carts of wood annually for the dhūnī of Bhāiroṁ at the shrine of Devī Pātan. Householders of the Kānphaṭas keep a dhūnī in their houses.[3]

Kānphaṭa Yogīs carry a begging bowl, a wallet, fire-tongs, and a staff, and use a crutch. The begging bowl (*khappar*) may be of cocoanut shell. The most prized bowls of this kind are of large size, made of *dariya nārial*, the large variety of cocoanut found in the west. These are blackened, and are without a handle. Some use a bowl with a handle, but the

---

[1] See p. 12 above.

[2] An Āipanth Yogī donned all his clothes in the presence of the author one morning in November, 1923, in Cawnpore, preparatory to begging.

[3] So reported in Almora.

regulation pattern is as just described. A bowl with a handle, made of gourd, is also used. This is a common type and is often called *tomṛī*. A bowl of this shape, made of brass is often seen.

The wallet, or bag, which is made of red cloth, is square in shape. It is usually hung from the left shoulder, and is used to carry utensils and the supplies collected while begging. There is no prescribed length for the fire-tongs (*cimṭā*). All ascetics carry them. Tongs may serve as a weapon, and perhaps, incidentally as a protection against evil spirits. Occasionally the tongs take the place of a musical instrument. Sometimes a pair of tweezers is attached to the tongs. These are used to handle coals for the *cilam*, or pipe bowl. The tweezers may be attached to the pipe bowl by a chain.

The staff of the Kānphaṭas is of bamboo, or of *timur*, a stick covered with knots, or a trident of metal.[1] At Purī[2] a Satnāth Yogī of the monastery carried a club,[3] made of straw covered with cloth, called a *sudarṣan*. In Bombay and Belgaon the trident is carried by Yogīs while they are out begging.[4] Sticks of the ordinary kinds are also carried.

The crutch, *ācal*, is made of a horizontal stick about sixteen inches long, fastened to a short perpendicular support. It is used as a rest for the chin, or the arms, during meditation and at certain other times. Crutches are used to support the body prepared for burial.

The conch shell is used by Yogīs in worship, being blown at the time of service.

As a rule the hour-glass-shaped drum (*ḍholak*) is not used by Yogīs, although Śiva as Nātarāja carries one. But there are exceptions; e.g., in Almora. In Bombay there is a class of Yogīs who carry a drum (*dāur*), and who, therefore, are called Dāurī Gosāins.[5]

---

[1] The trident was formerly a weapon, and is well-known. It is connected with sun worship and with the solar race. (*JRAS*, 1891, p. 389.) Its use in India goes back at least as far as the Indus River Civilization.

[2] In 1924. [3] Reminiscent of Lakulīśa?

[4] *Bombay Gazetteer*, vol. XXI, p. 185; *PNQ*, vol. II, para 964,.

[5] *ERE*, vol. XII, p. 835.

Some Yogīs in Benares and elsewhere carry a fan made of peacock feathers (*han mocal*) used to keep off flies, and also in exorcism, to keep off evil spirits, and to relieve children suffering from the effects of the evil eye.[1]

Yogīs have a reputation for certain habits and practices which are not well thought of, some of which are quite common amongst them, and some of which are confined to the few. Not all that is said and written about Yogīs applies to the Kānphaṭa. But the following practices are found to a greater or less extent amongst the Gorakhnāthīs. They make charms for themselves, and some sell them to others;[2] they pronounce spells and practice palmistry and juggling,[3] tell fortunes,[4] and interpret dreams; they sell a woollen amulet to protect children from the evil eye;[5] and they pretend to cure disease,[6] muttering texts over the sick, and practising medicine and exorcism, and vending drugs. Russell says that Nandia Yogīs lay claim to supernatural and magic powers. This is, of course, involved in their practice of medicine and exorcism and belief in Yoga. Some are reputed to have transmuted base metals into gold or silver. There is a legend of such transmutation in the times of Altamsh.[7] Others, for fraud, impersonate members of families on pilgrimages.[8] Still others resort to gambling and swindling and the three card game. Some are said to be able to control hail storms. In Siālkot there was once a Yogī (*raṭhbana*) who could impose a check upon hail, or direct it into waste land.[9] There are Yogīs who are engaged in extensive commercial enterprises;[10] others, like those in Benares, were rich;[11] still others are enrolled in the armies of Hindu kings.[12] Others are engaged in trades; and some sell small wares and silk thread.[13] In Almora they are to be found as tailors and sellers of milk. In many parts of India Yogīs are found as weavers, and are rated as inferior Śūdras, illegitimate and semi-legitimate descendants of Yogīs of

---

[1] Compare *RTCCP*, vol. III, p. 253. [2] *IA*, vol. X, p. 146.
[3] *BRI*, p. 215. [4] *I.A.*, vol. X, p. 146.
[5] *RTCCP*, vol. III, p. 252. [6] *Wi.*, p. 217.
[7] *RTCP*, vol. II, p. 398. [8] *BRI*, p. 215.
[9] *RTCCP*, vol. II, p. 398. [10] *BHTC*, p. 404.
[11] *SHTC*, p. 262. [12] *BHTC*, p. 404. [13] *Wi*, p. 218.

Gorakhpur.[1] Some sell apron strings and lace. The author once found a Yogī in charge of a government rest house. Others are engaged in agriculture, their women helping them in sowing and weeding.[2]

Barth says that Yogīs were degraded and despised, and that there are evidences of their being dangerous characters. Legends show that large bands moved about the country. They must have been feared and their arrogant demands were undoubtedly granted. They had a sharp struggle with the Sikhs in the sixteenth century.[3] The walls about Dhinodhar are loopholed for defence, and these means of protection must have been needed. Their power in Kacch was broken about the middle of the sixteenth century, by Atīts of Junāgad.[4] Before that time they held several places and seized Atīts and other sādhus passing on pilgrimages and forcibly split their ears.[5] Sometimes there are struggles between Yogīs and other ascetics over priority in bathing privileges at certain *melas*. Some lead about trained, deformed cattle; others train monkeys, still others carry snakes, and others raise buffaloes, donkeys and dogs.

They often, especially Bhartri Yogīs, play musical instruments, including the *sāraṅgī*,[6] and sing cyclic songs,[7] or ballads, including those of Gopichand, Bhartri, Puran Bhagat, Rāja Rasālū, Hīr and Rāñjha, Gūgā Pīr, Gorakhnāth, Macchendranāth, Dharamnāth, Garībnāth, Rānī Piṅglā, Devī and Gaṇeśa.[8] They use also religious songs[9] and poems such as *The Praise of the Seven Gods* (*Sapta Deva Stotra*).[10]

---

[1] *HTS*, p. 236. See chap ii.

[2] *Bombay Gazetteer*, vol. XXI, p. 185.

[3] *Mac.*, vol. II, pp. 139, 140. [4] *IA*, vol. VII, p. 5.

[5] Atīts are degraded Dasnāmīs who reverence Dattatreya. *Wi.*, pp. 204–5. See also article, 'The Fighting Ascetics of India,' by J. N. Farquhar, *Bulletin of the John Rylands Library*, vol. IX, No. 2, July, 1925.

[6] *IA*, vol. X, p. 146. In Almora they say 'No.'

[7] *Martin*, vol. III, pp. 407, 408, 534.

[8] Compare *Crooke*, vol. III, p. 60; *Bombay Gazetteer, Nasik*, 1883, vol. XVI, p. 74.

[9] *IA*, vol. X, p. 146.

[10] The author saw a copy of this book with an Āipanth Yogī at Cawnpore, in November, 1923.

The Nandias, who keep deformed oxen for exhibit, sing songs of Zahir Pīr and Hīr and Rāñja.

People do homage to Yogīs, touching their feet with fingers dipped in holy water, and receive flowers, mangoes and pieces of cocoanut as charms and talismans. Sometimes a touch works a cure. Sometimes a chili is obtained from one as a remedy for sickness. On the other hand, their curse is feared and this in turn often works as an incentive to do homage.

CHAPTER TWO

THE ORDER

Gorakhnāthīs claim that they receive none but the twice-born into their order.[1] This position is not quite clear, however, for some Yogīs admit that Śūdras are received.[2] Oman reported low caste recruits[3] and said that they admitted every description of people.[4] Wilson made a similar report.[5] In some parts of the Panjab low castes are admitted and menials are called 'Camarwā.'[6] And it was reported in 1901 that they admit anyone, that even a Musalmān may become a Yogī.[7] At Dhinodhar, orphans, children of destitute persons, lazy and disheartened men, even old men, the indolent and those afflicted with domestic troubles are admitted;[8] but recruits are chiefly from the Shepherd (Rabarī) caste. The abbot in 1838 was Warnāth of that caste.[9] Formerly in Kacch *Ḍheḍs* were admitted to the order, and one pīr of the monastery was Meghnāth, of that caste; however, the practice was discontinued and Meghwāls, or Ḍheḍs, were denied admittance.[10] At Gorakhmandi they recruit from most Hindu castes, but ostensibly receive neither Christians, Musalmāns nor Ḍheḍs.[11] Kāṇṭhaḍnāthīs recruit from *Ahīrs*, *Rājputs* and others.[12] At Ṭilla candidates are drawn chiefly from *Khatris*, *Aroras* and *Brāhamans*.[13] It is probable that caste distinctions are to

---

[1] *RTCP*, vol. II, p. 400. [2] At Devī Pātan and Almora.
[3] *OMAS*, p. 185. [4] *OMAS*, p. 152. [5] *Wi*, p. 206.
[6] *RTCP*, vol. II, p. 404. [7] *Census of the Panjab, Report*, 1891, p. 117.
[8] See *Khakhar*, p. 10; *Bombay Gazetteer*, vol. V, p. 87; *IA*, vol. VII, p. 53.
[9] *JRAS*, 1839, p. 270. [10] *IA*, 1878, p. 51, n.
[11] *Bombay Gazetteer*, vol. VIII, p. 155. [12] *Khakhar*, p. 13.
[13] *District Gazetteer*, *Jhelum* 1904, p. 36.

a great extent ignored.[1] In some places they receive boys whom parents have promised to Yogīs in fulfilment of vows.[2]

At Gorakhpur each candidate is examined as to his family and caste before he is accepted. Besides, each candidate has to go to the police station and prove that he is not a criminal, and there he makes record that he is willing to become a Yogī.

Yogīs are casteless. Within the order there are no caste restrictions upon eating, drinking and smoking. But Hindu and Musalmān Yogīs do not eat together, the former refusing to eat with the latter.[3] Theoretical equality does not, however, extend to women, for Yogīs do not allow their women folk to eat with them,[4] although women of all *panths* eat together.[5]

Initiation is divided, roughly, into two stages:[6] the first, a probationary period, followed by ceremonies leading to preliminary discipleship; the second, during which the ceremony of splitting the ears, which leads to full membership in the sect, is performed. An initiate in the first stage is called an Āughar; in the second stage he becomes a full-fledged Yogī.

A candidate may be of almost any age. There are many boys, of varying ages, who are fully initiated Kānphaṭas.[7] In Gorakhmandi the rule is initiation in youth.[8]

The months most auspicious for the ceremonies are *Pūs*, December–January; *Māgh*, January–February; *Phāgun*, February–March; and *Cāit*, March–April; and initiations are almost entirely confined to these months.

Initiation usually takes place at a monastery, but it may be

---

1 Compare *BRI*, p. 213.

2 *Census of the Panjab, Report*, 1891, p. 118.

3 So reported at Tilla.

4 As reported to the author at Benares.

5 *RTCP*, vol. II, p. 400.

6 Some insist that there are three stages; but the distinction lies in a subdivision of what is set up here under the second stage, and deals with the rites that follow the healing of the ear-wound. See report of the case at Gorakhpur, below, p. 37.

7 See pictures.

8 *Bombay Gazetteer*, vol. VIII, p. 155.

performed at a place of pilgrimage,[1] or at a temple of Bhāiroṁ.[2]

The candidate is first closely confined for a period ranging from forty days[3] to from three to six months;[4] that is, for a period of testing satisfactory to the guru. During this time the candidate is tried as to his resolution and ability to carry through his undertaking. At the same time he is dissuaded from becoming a Yogī, the guru pointing out to him the hardships that his initiation and his life as a Yogī would entail.

When the guru is satisfied with the self-control and resolution shown by the candidate, a fast of two or three days may be prescribed. Then, on the day chosen for the initiation ceremony, the candidate bathes and appears before his guru, bringing with him a rupee and a quarter, a cocoanut, flowers, and sweets.[5] The latter are distributed amongst those present. A two-edged knife, with which the ears are to be split in the second stage of initiation, is presented to the candidate three times, and he is again dissuaded from proceeding with the ceremony.

The knife is driven into the ground, or is laid down before him and the candidate takes the necessary vows over it, swearing not to engage in trade, not to take employment, not to keep dangerous weapons, not to become angry when abused, not to marry, and to protect his ears. Like all other ascetics he takes the vow of *ahiṁsa* (non-injury). He then receives the mantra,[6] or initiatory verse, either from his guru, or from some other Yogī. Ochre-coloured clothes are then presented to him, and he is accepted as a disciple by his guru. A barber now shaves his head, including the scalp-lock (*cuṭiya*). In some places, however, his guru cuts off the cuṭiya.[7] In Almora it was stated that a special guru, not the

---

[1] The author saw a recently initiated Yogī at the Kumbh Mela at Allahābād, in 1918.

[2] So reported at Benares. This applies when there is no monastery at the place. At Kāma, it was said, that the ceremony is performed at a monastery.

[3] *BCI*, vol. II, p. 497.

[4] So reported at Almora.

[5] *Laḍḍu*, or similar sweets.

[6] Mantras are used with each act throughout the ceremony of initiation—Almora.

[7] So stated in Dhinodhar, Gorakhpur and Benares.

candidate's chief guru, cuts the scalp-lock. If the Ganges river is nearby, the hair is consigned to it; if not, the guru keeps the hair in his wallet until he and his disciple go to the river, when it is taken and offered to the Ganges. Or, the hair may be thrown into a tank.[1] A feast is then given.

Among the Ratannāth Yogīs the candidate is given, by his guru, a razor and scissors seven times, and he is urged not to proceed with the initiation. The scissors suggest the cutting of the scalp-lock, which entails the breaking of caste; the razor, the painful ordeal of having the ears split. But if the candidate persists, his guru cuts off his scalp-lock after which his head is shaved by a barber. He then bathes and is besmeared with ashes, and a *kafni* or shroud, a *laṅgoṭī* or loin-cloth, and a cap are given to him. The ashes and the shroud signify death to the world. After six months, or so, if his guru be satisfied, the candidate's ears are split.[2]

After the ceremony the novice allows his hair to grow, or at least his scalp-lock, until he pays a visit to some famous shrine, when he has it cut, places it before the deity, with offerings of food, and gives a feast.[1] This practice is denied however by the Yogīs of Gorakhpur. In Almora, they say that the cuṭiya alone is allowed to grow until a pilgrimage is made to some sacred place like Hardwār, when it is cut and offered to the Ganges.

After the barber has finished his work and the candidate has bathed, he seats himself before his guru, facing north, or east.[3] His teacher then puts around his neck the siṅgnād-janeo, or sacred thread of the order.

The candidate's body is then smeared with ashes.

He is now the accepted disciple of his guru and begins to serve his religious guide.[4]

The candidate may now add to his name the sect word, *dās*.[5] To this Almora Yogīs agree, but at Gorakhpur and at Devī Pātan it was contradicted. He may at this time, or during the final stage of the initiation, receive from his

---

[1] So Russell, *TCCP*, vol. III, pp. 250, 251.
[2] *RTCP*, vol. II, p. 401, n. 1. [3] So stated in Almora.
[4] Compare *CTC*, vol. III, p. 157.
[5] Compare *OMAS*, p. 85; *RTCCP*, vol. III, p. 250.

guru a new name, that of some saint, or of a plant, or of an animal.[1]

Those who have undergone the first stage of initiation are usually termed Āughars.

They wear, as a usual thing, the clothes of the ordinary Hindu. The one in charge of the shrine on the summit at Dhinodhar wore (1924) a very long, loose coat, of ochre-colour, reaching nearly to his ankles, and without a waist-band; and a turban of cotton of the same colour.

Some Āughars wear their hair long and unkempt.[2]

The Āughar serves his guru, attends his teaching, and performs certain duties about the establishment where he lives. At Dhinodhar the novice is made to repeat, twice daily, in the presence of his guru, the words, *oṁkār*, *updesh*, *adesh* and *oṁ* through his siṅgnād.[3] In Almora it was said that these words need not be repeated through the whistle.

The Āughar is not accorded equal rights with the Yogī. This is illustrated by the fact that at feasts and when gifts are distributed, the Āughar receives but half the portion of a Yogī. In Benares, however, Yogīs maintain that Āughars would share equally with them.

There is no stated period of service before which an Āughar may proceed with the final stage of initiation which will constitute him a Yogī.[4] At any time, when his guru is satisfied that he is ready, the disciple may proceed with the initiation. There are some, however, who wait for twelve years; and, according to Russell, the novice in the Central Provinces must remain such for twelve years, during which time he is expected to make two or three *parikramas* (that is, travel from the mouth of the river to its source on one bank, and return by the other) of the Narbada river. During each pilgrimage, he allows his hair to grow, and, at the end of the journey, shaves all but the scalp-lock, and offers the hair to the river.[5] In Benares, in Gorakhpur and

---

[1] Compare *PNC*, vol. II, para 562. [2] See pictures.

[3] *Bombay Gazetteer*, vol. V, p. 87; *IA*, vol. VII, p. 52. The *updesh mantra* is, 'Be wise, pious and useful.' *Oṁkār* is *Oṁ*.

[4] Sherring reported that the candidate was kept in a room under surveillance for forty days.—*SHTC*, p. 262.

[5] *RTCCP*, vol. III, pp. 250, 251.

in the Panjab, Yogīs assert that the parikrama is not obligatory. In Almora it was explained that an Āughar would make such a pilgrimage only as the companion of his guru, should the latter make the journey.

Āughars of all *panths* are constantly met with, who are old men, and who have no intention of ever having their ears split. They call themselves Gorakhnāthīs. At Kirāna, in Jhang, the Āughars are in good repute and are wealthy. They have their own pīr, or abbot, who, after his induction into office, is never allowed to descend the hill.[1] There are other monasteries of Āughars, for example, at Hardwār and at Bombay. Near the temple of Bālkeśwar on the sea-front at the latter place, is the residence of a group of Āughars who are followers of Bālaknāth. He has some followers in the Panjab. Rose says that he was a disciple of Gorakhnāth, who left his guru in childhood for the jungle where he used to suck unmilked cows. The *caran* (foot-prints in marble) of this saint is found there. These Āughars never become Kānphaṭas. They bear a rather bad reputation.

Āughars pretend to some magical powers, and some approximate the Aghorī.[2] Others say that they are followers of Kānipā, pupil of Jālandhar.[3] In the west, Āughars (Oghads) are an inferior class.[4]

When his guru is satisfied that the candidate is prepared to complete his initiation, the arrangements are made.[5] The chief tests of fitness are that the pupil has kept his vows, has been faithful in his service to his guru and is steadfastly resolved to proceed. First, the candidate bathes, is shaved, puts ashes on his body, and ties a cloth of cotton about his loins. Some say that he covers the upper part of his body with a cotton cloth dyed in ochre,[6] but others say not. He then presents himself, with two of his guru's disciples, before

---

[1] *RTCP*, vol. II, p. 402.

[2] *Census, North-western Provinces and Oudh*, 1891, Pt. 1., p. 226. *Gospel in Gonda*, p. 216.

[3] *Census of the Panjab, Report*, 1891, p. 115.

[4] *Bombay Gazetteer*, vol. VIII, p. 447.

[5] Compare *CTC*, vol. III, pp. 156, 157; *RTCCP*, vol. III, p. 251.

[6] An *āñchala, kafnī*.

his teacher.[1] The candidate is made to sit facing north. He draws his knees up and clasps his hands under them. Preparation for the splitting of the two ears is then made. A specially skilled Yogī is called to perform this service, for which he receives one and a quarter rupees.[2] The fee may be larger, two and a quarter or twenty-five and a quarter rupees. This guru is called *Kān Guru* (ear-guru) or *Cīra Guru* (the guru who splits the ears). The two edged knife is brought, and in front of Bhāiroṁ, mantras, or sacred texts, are pronounced over it. Slits, about three-quarters of an inch long, are then made in the cartileges of both ears. The mantra, '*Śiva Gorakṣa*,' being used.[3] Some claim that the effect of the mantra is to make the operation painless and bloodless. Plugs of *nīm* or of *bikua* wood are then inserted in the wounds. The gashes are washed daily with pure water or with nīm water. Some say that the plugs are removed daily when the wounds are dressed. The care of the wounds continues for forty days. It is said that the plugs fall out after nine days. In some instances the nīm sticks are covered with the soft, downy feathers of the peacock's quill and the wounds are kept wet.

According to one report the regular Yogī who slits the ears inserts the knife and then asks the novice whether he be willing to renounce the world or not; and if he is unwilling he withdraws the knife. If the novice says that he is willing to follow the precepts of the sect and become an ascetic, the ear-slitter moves the knife up and down, finishing the operation; pieces of a twig of nīm-wood, soaked in oil, are inserted in the wounds for three days, when ear-rings are inserted.[4] One of the pictures shows an initiate whose ears are not yet healed, wearing ear-rings.

---

[1] In some cases Yogīs are initiated by their fathers; e.g., in the Himālayas. There the practice has been handed down from father to son. In this case the cuṭiya, or scalp-lock, is cut by another Yogī and the ears split by still another.

[2] *RTCCP*, vol. III, p. 250; *RTCP*, vol. II, p. 401; *Census of the Panjab, Report*, 1891, p. 115.

[3] Compare *FORL*, p. 348.

[4] *Bombay Gazetteer*, vol. VIII, p. 447.

By the slitting of the ears the Āughar becomes a Yogī, and may add to his name the word Nātha, Lord. Often he takes a new name to which he adds the word, Nātha.[2] He may receive as a name that of a plant or animal; e.g. *Nīmnātha Kanahnātha*, *Nāgnātha*.[3] Kaṇṭhaḍnāthīs use the word Kaṇṭhaḍ, instead of Nātha.[4]

When the wounds have healed, the Yogī resumes his sacred thread, smears his body with ashes, and appears before his guru. From now on, he will 'remember' his teacher twice daily and appear before him. Ear-rings of clay, weighing about one-fourth of a pound, are now put on, the mantra, '*Oṁ svāham*,' being used.[5] In some parts of India the rings are of lacquered earthenware. After a period varying from fifteen to twenty, or forty days, or a year, rings of some other substance may be substituted for those of clay.[6]

When the rings are inserted, the following exhortation is whispered in the Yogī's ear; 'Be wise, pious and useful';[7] or, 'Be wise, perform your religious duties, keep yourself prompt in the service of your guru.'[8]

The ceremony of initiation is completed with the worship of the nine Nāthas, the eighty-four Siddhas and Bālasundarī. The goddess is represented by a twisted thread wick fixed in a ball of dough and lighted. This is placed in a square made on the ground with flour or rice. In this square a jar (*kalsa*) of water also is set. The light is worshipped with offerings of flowers, sweets (*laḍḍu, halwa*), cakes and a cocoanut. The latter is split with a knife before being offered.[9]

The duties of a Yogī are various. At Dhinodhar, for example, he repeats the name of Dādā, referring to the founder of the sect,[10] or Bābā, referring to his guru, serves his teacher, and performs such other tasks as are assigned to him. The disciple is considered as the adopted son of his guru and inherits from him.[11]

---

[1] *RTCP*, vol. II, p. 401. [2] *RTCP*, vol. II, p. 399.
[3] *PNQ*, vol. II, para 51. [4] *IA*, vol. VII, p. 53.
[5] *SHTC*, p. 14. [6] See under ear-rings, above, p. 7.
[7] The *updesh mantra*. [8] Compare *Bombay Gazetteer*, vol. V, p. 87.
[9] A substitute for human sacrifice? *CTC*, vol. III, p. 157.
[10] Compare *Bombay Gazetteer*, vol. V, p. 87.
[11] *IA*, vol. VII, p. 52.

After initiation a Yogī may elect to become a militant Yogī, vowed to celibacy. In this case he would be known as *Nāga*, *Nihaṅg*, or *Kānphaṭa*. On the other hand, quite contrary to supposed regulations, he may become a householder, or *gṛhasta*.[1]

The initiate becomes a member of the sub-sect of his guru; consequently, in choosing his guru, he chooses his sub-sect. He belongs, also, to the monastery of which his teacher is a member.[2]

Some women receive initiation. These are either married women, or those who enter the sect after the death of their husbands. In Almora, in 1924, there was one, Sarasvatī (Nāthnī), a widow whose husband had been a landlord. After his death, she was initiated into the Satnāth sub-sect at Almora. She had been on pilgrimages as far as Hiṅg Lāj. She was *pūjārī* at a temple of Bhāiroṁ in her own house. On her arm was a brand mark received at Koteśwar, and she wore the usual beads from Hiṅg Lāj. Her cocoanut begging-bowl (*darya nārial*) was from Bhūj in Kacch. In her rosary of thirty-two beads she wore a *tāwīz*, or amulet; black stones from Badrināth; and large, white stones from Hiṅg Lāj, set in silver. Another widow, at Kāma, who had made the pilgrimage to Hiṅg Lāj, was a member of the same sect.

The Kānphaṭas possess many monasteries, of which there are a number of importance.[3] Some of these occupy very old religious sites whose history undoubtedly long antedates the rise of the Gorakhnāthīs. There is no fixed rule of superiority amongst the monasteries; but that at Ṭilla, in the Panjab, is generally considered to be the chief seat of the Gorakhnāthīs. The abbot at Gorakhpur claims authority over the establishments in the United Provinces, and regions to the south look to this place as their chief authority. This monastery claims to supervise some 360 lesser establishments. However, the

---

[1] That he need not remain in the monastery is allowed by the *Haṭhayogapradīpika*, 1, 12 f. See *Wi*, p. 216 n. and Tessitori, *ERE*, vol. XII, p. 834.

[2] For the specialized functions of gurus and mahants, or pīrs, see below, pp. 38, 39.

[3] Baines calls attention to the fact that those with monasteries have the right to be called Yogīs. (*Ethnology*, p. 41.)

nearby monastery at Tulsipur is related to that at Sawārikot in Nepāl and is independent of Gorakhpur. The head of the Gorakhpur establishment was, in 1924, of the Dharamnāth sub-sect, while that at Tulsipur belonged to the Ratannāth branch of Gorakhnāthīs. There may be some relation between Gorakhpur and Dhinodhar where the Yogīs are known as Dharamnāthīs. Yet, the pīr at Dhinodhar belongs to the Santnāth sect of the Panjab and Nepāl. The chief monasteries seem to be more or less independent of each other. The chief seats of the Yogīs exercise wide influence.

There is an organization, called the *Bhek Bārah Panth* which has general supervision over the monasteries, and which is consulted when mahants are elected, and which deals with disputes arising from various causes, or where the deposition of a mahant is desired. The Bhek is composed of representatives from the twelve Panths of the Gorakhnāthīs, one from each. The elections are made at the Kumbh Mela, held at Hardwār once in every twelve years. At this time thousands of Yogīs from all of the *maṭhas* (monasteries) are assembled. Special elections may be made to supply vacancies when the Bhek is convened to settle questions, at local monasteries, or at great melas, such as those held at Ujjain and Allahābād. The head of this organization is chosen in turn from each of the twelve panths. This is a desirable office, with tenure of twelve years, for which the incumbent pays a fee of twelve hundred rupees. He is considered as Jogeśwar and ranks as head of all the Gorakhnāthīs. The Bhek has a monastery at Hardwār. On two occasions, when the author visited it, there was no one in residence. It is reported that the committee was not re-elected at the last Kumbh Mela.[1]

The monasteries (*maṭha*, *asthāl*, *akāṛā*) vary in structure and extent according to the wealth of the Yogīs who reside in them, or the extent of their endowments. They comprise a set of chambers, or cells, for the resident mahant, or abbot, his permanent pupils, and other members of the order. There are always in residence a number of disciples as well as vagrants. The older disciples usually have young

[1] See references to the trial at Gorakhpur, below, p. 37.

followers to whom they are teaching the elements of their doctrine and practice.[1] In connection with the monastery will be found a temple of Śiva, of Devī, or of Bhāiroṁ, or temples of all these deities and others; the *samādh*, or shrine, of the founder of the monastery, or of some other eminent teacher; tombs (*samādhs*) of numerous other Yogīs; and one or more *dharamśālas*, or rest-houses for the accommodation of the mendicants and other travellers who are constantly visiting the place. Ingress and egress are free to all.

The buildings of the Kānphaṭas vary from substantial halls, some two storeys high, like those at Dhinodhar, to less pretentious structures, like those at Tulsipur, and to rude, mud huts with roofs of thatch, like those at Purī.

The monastery is under the control of an abbot, called mahant, or pīr. The functions of the mahant are to direct the worship at the temple and elsewhere in the establishment and to appoint *pūjārīs* and assistants for this purpose; to instruct and to direct instruction in Yoga and in the duties of Yogīs; to administer the funds of the monastery and to keep the property in repair.

The mahant at Gorakhpur nominates his successor, invariably choosing a member of his own sub-sect. However, Sundarnāthjī, who was head of the monastery in 1924, died without naming a successor. A dispute immediately arose as to whether a brother guru (that is, a brother of the same sub-sect) or a *cela* (personal disciple) should succeed to the gaddi. The matter was taken to the civil courts for decision. Sundarnāthjī was of the sub-sect of Dharamnāth. The rule as stated at Gorakhpur is that, upon the death of the mahant, representatives of the twelve sub-sects of the Gorakhnāthīs meet to choose a successor. They invariably elect the person named by the late mahant. The law suit referred to above shows that the election is not wholly within the power of the residents of the monastery.

An interesting point in the dispute at Gorakhpur was that

---

[1] The maṭha is more particularly the residence of teachers. Their pupils frequent the establishment and may become semi-residential; but the inmates are not a permanent body following a fixed rule of life.

one Nanhoo Singh, who was involved in the suit, and who hoped to win the gaddi, was not a Yogī at all. He stated that if he had won his case at law, he had intended to undergo initiation, become a Yogī and have his ears split.[1] It seems that in this particular case the *guru bhāi* had died previously to the mahant and the dispute involved the question of cela. According to the opinion of the judge in the Gorakhpur case the succession would be (1) *cela*, (2) *guru bhāi*, (3) *caca guru;* e.g., disciple, guru of the same panth as the mahant, and brother of the brother guru.

After a mahant has been chosen, the electors proceed to the District Officer of Gorakhpur and announce their decision. The officer takes the signature of the twelve Yogīs on a declaration that the newly-elected mahant is their choice. After his election, it is said, the mahant is not allowed to leave the monastery. Sundarnāthjī had made the various pilgrimages from Nepāl to Kacch and from Badrināth to the south of the peninsula before he was elected head of the monastery. The mahant is inducted into office with the usual form of worship, the *prasād* and a feast which includes the giving of food in charity to all who may come to the ceremonies, whether they be Yogīs or not. The installation is concluded with fire-works. Part of the services of installation take place while the mahant is seated in a niche in the wall of the main shrine. The Yogīs worship him, present him with a new garment and mark his forehead with the ṭikā. Afterwards he is seated on the *rāja gaddi*, or royal seat, outside the veranda of the main shrine. Then the priest at the monastery gives him a garment and marks his forehead with the ṭikā, and makes other presents. There is, of course, a large number of Yogīs and others including prominent men of the community present. In connection with the ceremonies there is a protracted worship of *Pātar Deo*, covering seven days.[2]

The abbot at Dhinodhar, in Kacch is called pīr. The head

---

[1] Reported by the Rev. E. C. Dewick, M.A., in a letter to the author, dated 27 March, 1928. Nanhoo Singh won his suit, and is now mahant of Gorakhpur.

[2] See trial cited above. Pātar Deo = Patel Deo (?) the spirit of the ancient (village) proprietor. See Sleeman, *Rambles and Recollections*, Oxford edition, p. 221.

of that monastery, in March, 1924, was Pīr Śrī VII, Somnāthjī. The pīr is chosen, from among the Yogīs at the monastery, by the Rāo of Kacch and holds office for life. He is not allowed to go outside of the bounds of the state. The pīr is installed in office by the Rāo, who invests him with a dress of honour, and seats him on the gaddi, or cushion of authority, as chief of the Kānphaṭas. The pīr is held in high honour. He does not have to return the salute of anyone, not even of the Rāo; and he need not rise when the Rāo pays him a visit.[1] In 1924, the pīr had a small boy as his much beloved cela, or pupil. Evidently he hoped to provide for succession through him. It would seem that the succession is through adoption and that the Rāo's choice is only nominal. This view is upheld by the fact that, in the west, outside of Dhinodhar, the pīr, or bābā, is allowed to marry, and, failing issue, to adopt one of his disciples, thus providing for the succession at his establishment.

The mahant of Tulsipur (Devī Pātan) is chosen by vote of twelve Yogīs representing the twelve sub-sects of the Gorakhnāthīs. He is placed upon the gaddi, given a janeo and a special dress, and offerings of prasād are made before him. The mahant (in 1924) was Harināth. He did not initiate nor did he make disciples.

The mahant at Ṭilla occupies the most important seat of the Kānphaṭas; in other respects he does not exercise peculiar functions. His establishment is in good repair, except for the very old remains on the site, even though the income of the institution has been much curtailed in recent times. The records show that, once inducted into office, he should never descend the hill. However, in 1924, the author met him in Amritsar under circumstances related below. This fact, however, might be the very important exception which proves the rule.

It may now be stated that the office of mahant is either (1) *Māurūsī*, hereditary, by succession, (2) *Pañchayatī*, by decision of a council, or (3) *Hākimī* by authority or right. No definition of the third case has been discovered.

Next in order after the mahant is the guru or teacher in the

---

[1] *JRAS*, 1839, p. 270.

order. He usually has a group of students about him who are receiving instruction preparatory to initiation, or who are Yogīs under instruction in Yoga.

Yogīs and Āughars make up the rank and file of the order. As indicated above, a candidate chooses his guru in the first instance; but the choice may be decided finally by the mahant.

Life in the monastery follows a fairly close, but not very exacting routine. There is the early worship at the samādhs, and the later offerings as well; the time given to teaching and to meditation; the midday worship at the various shrines and the evening worship. Begging may form part of the day's work. There is plenty of time for conversation. Visitors are constantly coming and going. Every Yogī returning from a pilgrimage has much to report about all sorts of things. There is the business of administration. Each Yogī has his own room, where he may enjoy some privacy, but much of the life of the establishment is open to public view. Further details of activities may be noted in the accounts of the various establishments.

Gorakhnāthīs bury their dead,[1] rarely, if ever, employing the services of Brāhmans, the rites being performed by fellow-Yogīs.[2] A legend is sometimes given which accounts for the practice. There was once a dispute between Hindus and Musalmāns as to who were masters of the earth. To disprove the claims of the latter, Gorakhnāth sat on the ground, placing his food and belongings beside him, and called upon the earth to yield to him if he had a share in her. The earth opened and he sank below the surface of the ground.[3] The practice of burial is not confined to Kānphaṭas, being followed by some other ascetic orders.

Thy dying Yogī, especially if he be an adept in Yoga, is made to sit cross-legged, as in meditation.[4]

After death the body is prepared for burial. It is washed by Yogīs, rubbed with ashes of cow-dung, or with ashes from

---

[1] See *RTCP*, vol. II, pp. 399, 400.

[2] Compare *OBTM*, p. 264; *Wi*, p, 196; *SHTC*, p. 262.

[3] *RTCP*, vol. II, p. 400. [4] *RTCP*, vol. II, pp. 399, 400.

the dhūnī,[1] sometimes with sugar also, and dressed in new garments of everyday life.[2] Or, the body may be covered with an ochre-coloured shroud. A new sacred thread, with the nād, ring and rudrākṣa berry, and a new rosary are hung around the neck. Some say that the ear-rings are removed and replaced by earthen[3] ones. A ṭikā of sandalwood or of red lead is drawn on the forehead. Five things are put into the mouth—gold, silver, a pearl, a charred wick from a lamp (*cirāg*) used in the worship of Devī, and incense (*kesas khuṣbhu*).[4] The body is then placed in a posture of meditation (a sitting posture) on a seat, and is supported by one crutch, or by three. Under the body sugar, and sometimes earth, but not salt, are placed.[5] Flowers also may be put on the seat. A potsherd is placed on the head, but for this a black silk cap or a turban may be substituted.

The grave is a pit, dug deep, three and one half hands (*hāth*), and circular. In the south wall a niche is cut for the reception of the body which is set facing north. Under the seat one rupee and four annas or five and one-fourth rupees and sugar are deposited. The platform is made of 'wool, grass, etc.'

At the right end in front of the body is placed a gourd full of water; and at the left a *roṭ* (a thick loaf of unleavened bread), a saucer of rice and milk, and another of water. A loin cloth and a staff (*kanak*) are laid in front of the body. The begging bowl is filled with milk and is placed in the wallet which is hung from the right shoulder.[6] Rose says that the nails are removed and taken to Hardwār, but at Gorakhpur this was denied. Sugar and gold are put into the grave. It is then filled in with earth, and a mound is raised over it. Later, a masonry platform, or a tomb may be erected over the grave, in which case it will be surmounted with the *yonī-liṅga*.

---

[1] *PNQ*, vol. II, para 464. [2] *CTC*, vol. III, p. 158.

[3] *Census Report, Berār*, 1881, p. 60.

[4] Reported by the Āipanthīs at Hardwār.

[5] In Sind, sugar is placed under and above the body. (Aitken, *Gazetteer of the Province of Sind*, p. 184.) See note in *Śiva Saṁhitā*, p. 50, where it is pointed out that after beginning the practice of the Hatha Yoga, a Yogī may not use salt.

[6] Compare *CTC*, vol. III, p. 158.

The *pāduka* (*caran*) of the deceased may be put on the samādh.[1]

If the deceased had been a rich Yogī, or if he had been the disciple of a guru who owned land, his body would be placed in a chair shaped like a *doli*, it would be adorned with flowers, and he would be carried to the grave in a procession lead by musicians. In Berār, according to Kitts, the body is carried to the grave in a large wallet.[2]

The grave is called samādh or samādhi.

In some places, especially in Benares and in Almora, Yogīs were formerly buried in their own houses. But municipal regulations have put a stop to the practice. However in the outlying places about Almora the practice still continues. At Almora their burial grounds are at Pātal Devī, outside of the town. There are some, manifestly old, samādhs in Almora which consist of four slabs of stone making a box with a fifth slab for a cover. There are now no liṅgas on them.

If the Yogī was a poor man, or if he had been the disciple of a man without landed property, his body might be placed on two poles and sunk in a river.[3] This practice was acknowledged at Benares, but Gorakhpur Yogīs insisted that all are buried.

For ten or twelve days after the death offerings are made to the deceased. *Bel* leaves and flowers are placed on the grave and upon it a lamp is kept burning.

After the disposal of the body, all the Yogīs bathe with water supplied by the deceased's disciples, and then sweets (laḍḍu) are distributed. There is no further ceremonial impurity.[4] However, some say that clothes are washed on the tenth day after death.[5] A council of all the Yogīs at the place where death occurred is held, and in case the deceased had not chosen a successor, a guru, if this was his rank, is chosen to take his place. The clothes of the dead are given to degraded Yogīs or are divided among those present. Food and money also are distributed.

---

[1] This applies in the case of disciples of Matseyendranāth and of Dattatreya also. See Enthoven, *Folklore of Bombay*, p. 150.

[2] *Census Report, Berār*, 1881, p. 60.

[3] Compare *CTC*, vol. III, p. 158.

[4] See *CTC*, vol. III, p. 158.

[5] At Almora.

On the third day cakes (*roṭ*) cooked rice, milk and *cūrmā* are offered on the grave and then are consumed by the worshippers. If the deceased were not well off, cūrmā only is offered. Some wash their clothes on the third day, but this is not considered necessary.

On the twelfth day turmeric powder is sprinkled.[1] And worship of Bahrām Deo and Mārī Māī is performed on a kettle drum (*ḍanka*).

On the thirteenth day a conch shell is blown and the *kṛya karna* is completed and the spirit of the deceased departs. At Dhinodhar a feast is given on the thirteenth day and alms are distributed.[2] In Berār, on the Śivrātri, the pāduka of the deceased is worshipped.[3]

After a year (*bārsī*), or a year and a half, the *śrāddha*, or funeral rite is performed.[4] The Yogīs keep vigil all night and in some places the ceremony known as bharad, the beating of drums for Devī, is kept up. In the watch before dawn fish, or *pakāuṛī*, or *khīr*, or *palāu* or flesh is distributed. Six or seven thrones (gaddi) are erected; to the pīr, to Joginīs, to Śākhya (or witness), to Bīr, to Dhandāri (cook of Guru Gorakhnāth), to Gorakhnāth and to Neka or Ant (reported at Almora). Mantras are recited, clothes and coins of gold, silver and copper are distributed, and a cow or some other gift is made to the pīr. Gifts are made also to Yogīs. The silver goes to Śākhya, copper to Bīr, the cow to the pīr, water to Gorakhnāth.

Formerly all classes attended this ceremony, now only Yogīs.

Householders also are buried, and in some cases their families likewise. Kitts reported that ceremonies for the widow of a Yogī are the same as for a member of the order, but that her shroud would be of red or green, not of ochre colour.[5]

Worship is continued at the samādhs indefinitely and is

---

[1] Kitts, *Berār Census Report*, 1881, p. 60.
[2] *Bombay Gazetteer*, vol. V, p. 87.
[3] *Census Report, Berār*, 1881, p. 60.
[4] Compare *RTCP*, vol. II, pp. 399, 400.
[5] *Census Report, Berār*, 1881, p. 60.

performed twice a day. In the early morning,[1] after bathing, the pūjārī offers Ganges water, sandalwood, rice, bel leaves, flowers, sweets and incense at each samādh connected with the monastery; or at least some of these things are offered. The food is then thrown away. In the evening milk and sweets are offered, a lamp is lighted and incense is burned. The poor before consuming their food offer it at the samādhs.

The buried Yogī is supposed to remain in trance indefinitely.[2]

---

[1] The Āipanthīs at Hardwār said 'four o'clock.'

[2] *Modern India and the Indians*, p. 73.

CHAPTER THREE

VOWS

Yogīs vow not to engage in trade and not to take employment. So they are supposed to beg for their food. But this is by no means the universal practice. It is estimated that but one in one hundred begs; and at monasteries and at shrines where offerings and income are sufficient, the inmates do not have to go out to beg at all. Very often all that a Yogī may ask for is brought at once by willing devotees. Most of those who bring gifts are not immediate followers of the Yogīs. Certain Yogīs, called Darṣanīs, do not beg but remain in definite places, in the forest, at temples, in caves or at monasteries, where they are visited and worshipped.[1] While away on pilgrimage, it may be necessary for a Yogī to beg. If food is not available, they eat fruit and roots; and in some instances, if food is not given them they mix ashes from the dhūnī with water and drink it as a substitute.

As beggars they go from house to house crying, '*Alakh, Alakh*,'[2] but they do not sing. Some put on special clothes when they go out to beg.[3] In Belgaon both men and women beg, carrying a begging bowl, and often a trident as well.[4] They take both money and food.

There is a difference of opinion amongst writers on the question of food; and Yogīs themselves do not agree about the matter. Sherring[5] says that they accept food from all

---

[1] *RTCCP*, vol. III, p. 250.

[2] Compare *Census of the Panjab, Report*, 1891, p. 118.

[3] See above, p. 12.

[4] See *Bombay Gazetteer*, vol. XXI, p. 185; *PNQ*, vol. II, paras, 404, 964.

[5] *SHTC*, p. 262.

houses and all castes. Russell says that they beg only from Hindus.[1] Crooke,[2] on the other hand, said that they would not take food from lower castes, from whose hands respectable Hindus would not take food. Sherring[3] says that they eat flesh. Tessitori and Crooke[4] report that Kanphaṭas accept food other than beef and pork. Moshan Fani reported that they ate beef and pork, and that they killed and ate men.[5] The practice evidently varies. In Kāṭhiāwār[6] there are no restrictions on food and they will eat with any strangers who care to join them.

Their food consists of millets, rice, vegetables, fruits, fowls, goat's flesh, mutton, fish, beef and pork. But not every one accepts all these articles of diet. By some the cow is considered sacred and the pig unclean.[6] At Dhinodhar the chief food consists of millet and pulse. And these commoner foods of the people in general are the usual articles of diet.

One of the marks of the sect is the practice of charity. This is followed in Nepāl, in the United Provinces, in the Panjab and at Dhinodhar and in other places in the west. It is said that Dharamnāth began the practice at Dhinodhar in reaction to the neglect with which he was treated in Kacch.[7] Begging was undertaken to secure means for feeding the sick and the suffering of every caste. Then, grants of land were made to the monasteries with this purpose in view.[8] At present their income is used in entertaining strangers of all castes and creeds. At Dhinodhar two meals a day are served to all who come. High caste visitors receive their food uncooked; but low caste persons are served in the large dining hall, and Musalmāns and degraded castes in the garden.[9] Special caldrons are provided for preparing the food. At Gorakhmandi, in Kāṭhiāwār, when the meals are ready, a servant of the abbot goes out and calls twice in a low voice: 'Whoever is hungry, come. The abbot's table is

---

[1] *RTCCP*, vol. III, p. 252. [2] *CTC*, vol. III, p. 158.

[3] *SHTC*, p. 262.

[4] *CTC*, vol. III. p, 158; *ERE*, vol. XII, p. 834.

[5] *Dabistan*, vol. II, p. 129.

[6] *Bombay Gazetteer*, vol. VIII, p. 155. [7] See legend below.

[8] See *IA*, vol. VII, p. 51.

[9] Compare *Bombay Gazetteer*, vol. III, p. 86.

spread.'[1] The ordinary food served is millet and red pulse. On special days, in August, *Gokal Atham*, and at *Nāurātri*, in October, rice and *lapsi* (wheat flour and molasses cooked in butter), and opium are distributed.[2] Oman[3] reported that the throngs of men, women and children going to Ṭilla to the great festivals, are supplied with accommodation, food and coverings there. At Ṭilla they pride themselves on their practice of charity.

Gorakhnāthīs are under a vow of celibacy. At Dhinodhar the rule is strictly enforced. It was reported in 1880,[4] that women were not allowed to enter the precincts of the monastery. In 1924, the author saw women doing menial work of various kinds there; but there was no reason to believe that the rule of celibacy was broken through their presence. At Devī Pātan and at Gorakhpur the rule is enforced that Āughars and Yogīs are not allowed to marry. And probably at most monasteries of the Gorakhnāthīs celibacy is enforced. At the maṭha in Benares, however, the residents were (1924) married men who had their wives with them. And Kāśināth, who attended the temple of Kāl Bhāiroṁ (in Benares), lived in his own house in the city.

It is possible that the rule of celibacy does not require absolute continence for, to cite one exception, Yogīs acknowledge the practice of *śākta* rites. It is difficult to state just how far the rule of continence is enforced. The reputation of Yogīs is not above reproach. Buchanan reported that though they were not permitted to marry, they were at liberty to communicate with whatever woman they pleased.[5] Celibates are sometimes called *maṭhadāṛīs*, i.e. those who live in a monastery.[6]

Reports from various areas show that marriage is common amongst Kānphaṭas,[7] and Census returns confirm this.[8] The so-called secular Yogīs are numerous. In some instances Brāhmans are employed to perform their marriage cere-

---

[1] *Bombay Gazetteer*, vol. VIII, pp. 155, 156, 446 f.
[2] *Bombay Gazetteer*, vol. V, p. 86. [3] *OMAS*, pp. 264, 265.
[4] *IA*, vol. VII, p. 51. [5] *Martin*, vol. II, pp. 484, 485.
[6] *Bombay Gazetteer*, vol. VIII, p. 185.
[7] E.g. *Bombay Gazetteer*, vol. XXI, p. 185. [8] See pp. 4 ff.

monies. Even in monasteries of repute the practice has been known. Buchanan, before 1838, reported married Yogīs living and teaching in the maṭha at Gorakhpur.[1]

At Gorakhmandi, both celibates (maṭhadārīs) and householders (*gharbārīs*) are found.[2] Married Yogīs are called also *Bindi-nāgi*, *saṁyogī* and *gṛhasta*. In the Himālayas many householders are found, and in some instances the pūjārī rights at their temples are kept in the family, being handed down from father to son.

While the regulation that Yogīs who marry are not allowed to live in a monastery is not universally enforced, still, in many places gṛhastas are allowed neither to live at nor to eat in the monastery. At Tulsipur a well-known gṛhasta had his house, where (1924) he lived with his wife, adjoining the grounds of the monastery at Devī Pātan. Yogīs who marry are held in contempt by others, and, in some instances have to pay a fine before they are permitted to smoke with celibates.[3] Married Yogīs continue to wear the ear-rings, the sacred thread, the clothes and other articles of the sect, and they may continue to practise Yoga.

In marriage, Yogīs hold to the caste from which they have come, in choosing a wife, and avoid marriage in the same sub-sect.

In Almora there are householders of the Dharamnāth and Satnāth sub-sects. No rules require sons of gṛhastas to become Yogīs, but this happens; and such instances were discovered by the author in Naini Tāl and Almora. In the latter case a second son became a Yogī in order to secure his father's rights and property in a temple and a house belonging to the family, the eldest son being a *munshi* in the Cantonment in Almora. The third son was an Āughar.

Householders engage in secular employments. In Almora are to be found milkmen, tailors and agriculturalists. In various parts of India Yogīs are engaged in weaving, cultivation, in peddling, as soldiers, and as money-lenders.[4] In

---

[1] *Martin*, vol. II, p. 484.
[2] *Bombay Gazetteer*, vol. VIII, p. 155.
[3] *RTCP*, vol. II, p. 410.
[4] See Tessitori, *ERE*, vol. XII, p. 834.

the Simla Hills, Yogīs burn the dead, and for every corpse receive four *annas* in money together with a plate of brass and a woollen or cotton cloth. They also receive grain at each harvest.

The *Śiva Saṁhitā* allows success to householders. The last three verses of that work read: Therefore the Yoga should be performed by master Yogīs according to the prescribed rules. He who is satisfied with whatever he receives, self-controlled and unattached (to household affairs), even though he be an householder, is released through the practice of Yoga. Success for the masterful householders, who are attached to the practices of the Yoga, must arise by means of *japa*. Therefore, let the householder exert himself. Established in the house, with ample household, having renounced attachment and engaged in Yoga practice secretly, the householder sees (increasingly) the wonderful marks of success, and, having carried out my instructions, should enjoy (bliss).

Women who have been initiated into the sect are numerous.[1] Those who are wives of Yogīs are of two classes, those who are themselves Yoginīs and those who are not. Both classes are common. In Kumaon and in Garhwāl, in 1924, the author saw women of both classes. Women may be initiated before or after their marriage. A woman who, before her marriage, has had her ears split is not married by the usual Hindu rites; the marriage in such cases being by purchase, a formal agreement having the sanction of the sub-sect. A feast is always given. On the other hand, the marriage of a woman, before she has been initiated, is by the usual Hindu ceremony (*śādī*). At Kāma, in Kumaon, in 1924, the mahant said that such a woman could not be initiated. From Rāwalpindī female Yogīs are reported.

A number of castes trace their origin to Yogīs. The records, however, are not always clear as to whether the Yogīs reported trace their origin to Gorakhnāthīs.[2]

In the Simla Hills, Yogīs form a sort of occupational caste,

---

[1] For an account of women who have been initiated into the sect as widows see above, p. 34.

[2] For the origin of Yogī castes see J. N. Farquhar's paper, 'The Fighting Ascetics of India.'

as just stated, burning the bodies of the dead and receiving certain perquisites for the service. From the fact that they take offerings made at death, Kanets and higher castes will not drink with them. They wear ear-rings, but rank below Kānphaṭas.[1]

The Nāthas in the higher hills, where the worship of Śiva is prevalent, correspond very closely to the Yogīs of the plains. They practise little asceticism, but grow vegetables and perform certain semi-sacerdotal functions, taking the place of the *acrāj* (a class of Brāhmans) of the plains in the funeral ceremonies of Kanets and receive the clothes of the dead. They consecrate new houses and purify them when they have been defiled. They are a true caste. One or more in nearly every Nātha household has his ears pierced in honour of Śiva and is called Kānphaṭanāth. They are unclean and uncanny.

In the Panjab, secular Yogīs are called Rāwal. They make their living by begging, fortune-telling, singing and similar means; they were originally, probably, Yogīs.[2] The Saṁyog of the Panjab is a true caste. In Kulu they are Nāthas; in Ambāia, Jogī Pādha; in Nābha, they are teachers of the children of Hindus; in Laharu they are of the Jāṭu tribe, part being secular, part celibate. Among them widow marriage is practised. The Saṁyog of Ambāla has twelve sections. (The Barahnāth sub-group.)[3] In the Karnāl they are Hindus. They receive offerings made to impure gods, and form the lowest of all castes; they practise witchcraft and divination and are musicians.[4] In Kāṅgra there are two groups, the *Andarlā* who are both Ḍarṣanīs and Āughars and the *Bāhirlā*, all Āughars.[5] These connect with Gorakhnāth through a legend concerning the sons of Macchendranāth. Once Gorakhnāth gave the boys each a goat to be sacrificed at a place where no one could

---

[1] *RTCP*, vol. II, p. 399 n.; vol. III, p. 165.

[2] *RTCP*, vol. II, p. 389.

[3] Some of the names are Āi, Dhaj, Sahaj, Hāit, Kaṇṭhar, Pāgal, Pāśupanthī, Rāwal. The third is apparently a remnant of a Vāiṣṇavite movement.

[4] *RTCP*, vol. II, p. 389.

[5] For sub-divisions see Rose, *RTCP*, vol. II, pp. 402, 403.

4

see them. One actually performed the sacrifice; but the other reported that he could find no place where either man or bird or sun or moon would not be a witness. Gorakhnāth praised him and placed him close to himself, while the first was expelled from his presence. Thus arose the appellations 'Andarlā' and 'Bāhirlā.' Both of these divisions observe the usual Hindu customs, except that at death ceremonies the Bāhirlā give Brāhmans food but do not feast them; and at funerals blow a *nād* instead of a conch. Of the Darṣanīs some go clothed; others, unclothed, use ashes. The Naṅgas eat flesh and drink liquor, while the others do not.

The Yogī castes of the Central Provinces[1] rank as Hindus of the menial group, from whom no good Hindu would take either food or water. They accept cooked food from respectable castes; permit the marriage of widows, using their own priests[2] in the ceremonies; allow divorce and follow the social customs of the cultivating castes of the locality. They are divided into sub-sects which are determined according to occupation or profession, as follows: Barwa or Gārpagārī who ward off hail storms from the standing crops; Maṇihārī, pedlars who travel about to bazaars, selling various small articles such as hand mirrors, spangles and dyeing powder, coral beads, imitation jewelry, pens, pencils and other articles, securing pearls and coral from Bombay to sell in the villages; Rītabikanāth, who prepare and sell soap-nut; Patbina, who make hempen thread for gunny bags used in carrying grain on bullocks; and Ladāimār, who hunt jackals and sell and eat their flesh.[3]

Reports on the Yogī castes of Bengal, who, as do those of Assam also,[4] trace their origin to Kānphaṭas, are quite extensive. Buchanan[5] traces the origin of this group in Bengal to one of two causes: either they belonged to the priesthood of the country during the reign of Gopicand, or,

---

[1] *RTCCP*, vol. III, pp. 252, 253.
[2] Those who are not Kānphaṭas employ Brāhmans.
[3] *RTCCP*, vol. III, pp. 252, 253.
[4] *District Gazetteer of Eastern Bengal and Assam*, 1910, p. 41.
[5] *Martin*, vol. III, p. 408.

they were Śūdras dedicated to the religious life, degraded by Śaṅkara, who came with the Pālas from western India. Buchanan reports a tradition in North-eastern Bengal[1] to the effect that the Yogīs were formerly pupils of the great Śaṅkara, and that they took to drinking and were degraded. The legend of Gopicand[2] gives evidence pointing in this direction. For the Yogī, Hāḍī by name, who figures in that story was a sweeper (*Ḍom*) by caste. In Rangpur, Buchanan found low-caste Yogīs who were itinerant bards, who sang songs of Gopicand, who were descendants of the priesthood of the time of Gopicand.[3] The same writer[4] reported two divisions of Yogīs who did not intermarry. One were the Helayas, weavers and cultivators. Their women dyed thread and retailed turmeric, capsicum and other seasonings. The other division were the Theyayas, idle beggars who burned shells for lime. Some of these were cultivators. Both groups were eaters of impure food and drunkards who buried their dead. They were said to have been disgraced by Śaṅkara. They were illiterate. Elsewhere,[5] Buchanan wrote that in eastern Bengal there was a caste of Yogīs who were weavers, lime burners, unskilled labourers, beggars and wandering singers. Some of them are now engaged in agriculture, some are goldsmiths, and some are found in the subordinate grades of Government service. In Rangpur they sing the cyclic songs of Gopicand.

According to Risley[6] there are in Eastern Bengal two sub-castes of Yogīs, the Māsyas and the Ekadasīs. Between these two sections no marriages are arranged, and they do not accept cooked food from each other. But they drink from each other's water vessels. Their division is based upon differences in their funeral rites. The period of mourning

---

[1] *Martin*, vol. III, pp. 408, 536.

[2] *JASBe*, vol. XLVII, Pt. 1, pp. 139 ff.

[3] *Martin*, vol. III, p. 408. [4] *Martin*, vol. III, pp. 535, 536.

[5] *Martin*, vol. III, pp. 408, 534. cf. Hunter, *Statistical Account of Bengal*, vol. I, p. 69.

[6] *RTCB*, vol. I, pp. 355–61. Māsya Jogīs belong to South Bikrāmpur, Tipperah and Nookhale; Ekadasīs to North Bikrāmpur and Dacca. Those of Tipperah number some 68,000. See also, *District Gazetteer, Eastern Bengal*, Webster, 1910, p. 26.

for one group is thirty days (*māsa*), for the other, eleven (*ekadasa*) days. The division is based upon the further fact that some live upon an island and others upon the mainland.[1] The cultivating members of the caste form a distinct group called Hālwa Jugī. It is said that they were out-casted for abandoning the traditional occupation of weaving. There are legends accounting for the origin of these castes. The Māsyas were born from the unions of eight Siddhas with eight Śaktis created by Mahādeo. Another legend makes the Māsyas descendants of unions between Sannyāsīs from Benares and Vāiśya women. Again it is said that these Yogīs are descendants of pupils of Nāthas (Yogīs) and Brāhman widows, the latter being of the Nātha group, the former of the Śiva gotra (family, stock).

Ekadasīs are descendants of Sannyāsīs from Benares and Brāhman women, or descendants of pupils of Nāthas (Yogīs) and Brāhman widows. The legends in both cases seem to be the same and to point to the Yogī-origin of the caste. Both groups bury their dead, the lips of the corpse being touched with fire by the son, or grandson. Both worship female ancestors at weddings, perform ancestral worship in their homes, wear the sacred thread, and read the Vedas. These Yogīs are weavers by caste, but are now taking up agriculture, lime-burning, goldsmith's work and subordinate grades in Government service.

According to Crooke[2] the Māsya Yogīs, of the United Provinces, are found chiefly in Brindaban, Mathūra and Gokul; and their principal places of pilgrimage are Benares, Gāya and Sītākund in Chittagong.

The family of Dalāl Bazaar in the Koakhali district in Eastern Bengal, is now considered as the head of their race. In the middle of the eighteenth century Braja Ballabh Rāi, a Jogī, of this family was a broker (*dalāl*) and his brother Rādha Ballabh Rāi was appraiser (*jashandār*) of the English factory of Carpata on the Meghan River. The son of the former so proved a man of business that the Company, in 1765,

---

[1] The Sandīp division live on the island of Sandīp; the Bhuluānāth division on the mainland. This is a local distinction.

[2] *ERE*, vol. II, p. 494, article 'Bengal.'

bestowed on him the title and rank of Rāja and gave him a rent-free estate still in the family.[1]

The Dharmagharī Jugīs of Western Bengal are looked down upon by others. They 'worship Dharma, Śitalā and other aboriginal deities.'[2] They are beggars. They trace their origin to Siddhas. Some of their sub-caste names are Matsyendra, Gorkṣa and Bṛbhāirab. The first two of these names are significant in pointing to relationships with Gorakhnāthīs. These Jugīs practise infant marriage, employ ing a caste member as priest; and allow neither the marriage of widows nor divorce. They worship Śiva for the most part, Viṣṇu to some extent. Some are Śāktas. They practise samādh-burial. Their social position is low. In 1881 the Jugīs in Bengal numbered more than 350,000.

In the Nizām's Dominions[3] two divisions of the Gorakhnāthīs are found, the Davre and the Rāvals. Both were originally recruits from Marāṭha Kunbis, but now form independent castes. The Davre, who are of the Navanāth sect, derive their name from the drum (*dabara*) which they use in singing the hymns of Bhāirava. They are also known as Kumar Bharadī, from the name of a dance which they perform at the commencement of the marriage ceremony of their Kunbi (an agricultural caste) disciples. They admit only married Kunbis and others of higher caste. The recruits are mostly children, dedicated by parents to Bhāirava in fulfilment of vows. The initiation of the boy (or girl) takes place in the temple of Bhāirava at Sonārī, at about the ages of twelve. The lobes of the ears are split and brass rings are worn. The division consists of three exogamous sections. Marriage is usually early, widow remarriage is allowed, polygamy is practised and divorce is permissible. Brāhmans officiate at their weddings. Their gurus are Kānphaṭa Yogīs. They are buried in a sitting posture facing east, and are carried to the grave in a cloth bag. The procession is accompanied by musicians. The body is smeared with ashes of cowdung; and bel leaves and flowers are offered. Water is poured into the mouth. Gāñja, tobacco, spirits and the

---

[1] *RTCB*, vol. I, p. 356. [2] *RTCB*, vol. I, p. 357.
[3] *SCTND*, vol. I, pp. 278 ff.

food of the kind the deceased was fond of are placed in the grave. The chief mourner first throws in earth, and offerings of bel leaves and flowers three times and the grave is then filled up. Upon return to the home of the deceased, the mourners chew nīm leaves, wash their mouths and then go to their own homes. Davres rank just below Marāṭha Kunbis. They eat fish, fowl or mutton and drink spirits. There are mendicants amongst them.

The Rāval Jogī (Rāul, Śivjogī, Kaniālanāth Rāval) are very numerous, and like the other branch of the Gorakhnāthīs, recruit mostly from Marāṭha Kunbis, but from Mālīs, Rājputs and others as well.

For the ceremony of initiation a square of limestone powder is traced on the ground and about it are placed nine burning lamps made of wheat flour. The novice, after having bathed, takes a seat in the square, on a low wooden stool, and has his head shaved. His body is then covered with ashes of cowdung. A sacred thread of black wool consisting of nine threads and a rosary of one hundred and eight rudrākṣa beads are hung about his neck. His guru gives him a trident, a piece of cloth and an alms bag, and whispers in his ear a mantra. Ear-rings of conch shells are inserted. Their social customs resemble closely those of the Davre. The notable exception is the funeral rites. While following the practices already described, they dress the body in ochre-coloured clothes and burn camphor and incense before it. Four men carry the body, while a fifth holds his scalp lock. At the grave salt is thrown over the body. After the grave is filled up a mound is raised. A member of the funeral party stands over the mound, blows a conch and recites mantras for the benefit of the deceased. With the last syllable of the verse, each member of the party throws a handful of earth on the mound and then all return home. They mark their foreheads with ashes of cowdung. No śrāddha is performed. On the third and eleventh days a garland is hung from the roof of the house and over the water pot and a dough lamp is fed with ghī. A goat is killed and offered and a feast is held. They worship souls of ancestors on Nāgpañcamī.

Both groups worship Bhāiroṁ and other Hindu gods, attend the Hindu festivals, follow Macchendranāth and Gorakhnāth and use the trident and the liṅga. They keep images of deceased ancestors. They rank below Kunbis. Only low, unclean castes will accept food cooked by Rāvals. They accept *kacca* food from Kunbis, eat flesh, except beef and pork, and drink spirits. They are mendicants, but some are cultivators, weavers and tailors.

In Bombay[1] the Yogīs, also called Nāthas, have two divisions; the Gujarāt Jogīs, who are ascetics; and the Marāṭha Jogīs, including Karnāṭaka and Kanāra Jogīs, who are both regular and secular. The secular groups are husbandmen and labourers. Some breed buffaloes and dogs, while others make and sell black stone vessels. The Marāṭhas have twelve endogamous divisions, Balgār, Berak, Bhorpi, Bombāri, Dawarjī, Jogār, Ker, Kindri, Kurub, Mendār and Murād. These twelve clans are named each after one of the twelve orders said to have been founded by Gorakhnāth, and no marriages between members of the sub-castes are permitted. Widow marriage is allowed. Polygamy is practised. They bury their dead, mourning for twelve days; otherwise they do not differ much in customs from those of the surrounding cultivating castes. They eat goats, sheep, hares, deer, wild pig and fowls and use spirituous liquors, smoke gāñja and eat opium. Boys are initiated at the age of twelve years. They are a wandering class, who carry their huts, made of matting set on bamboo poles, and goods from camp to camp on ponies and buffaloes. The men dress in ochre-coloured clothes, wear large, thick ear-rings of ivory, clay, bone, or fish-scale in the lobes of their ears and use rosaries of rudrākṣa beads. Their women wear petticoats and bodices and braid their hair, allowing it to hang down their back. Their favourite song is the legend of Gopicand.[2] Their chief gods are Gorakhnāth and Matsyendranāth. They practise sorcery and witchcraft.

Nātha Gosavīs of Sāvantvādi (Kāṅkān) are allied to the Kānphaṭas. They slit the ear, wear pewter ear-rings and call upon Śrī Gorakh in connection with the blood sacrifice at weddings.[3]

---

[1] *ETCB*, vol. II, pp. 103 ff.
[2] *Bombay Gazetteer*, vol. VIII, pp. 456, 457.
[3] *Bombay Gazetteer*, vol. X, p. 419 and n. 1.

Householders of certain villages in the Poona district wander from place to place carrying their huts and goods on ponies and buffaloes. They eat fish and the flesh of sheep, goats, hares, deer, wild pig and fowls, drink liquor and eat opium. They wear large thick ivory, clay, bone or fish-scale rings in the lobes of their ears, put on rudrākṣa rosaries, and sing songs of Gopicand. They bury their dead and exhibit other traits pointing to Gorakhnāth. Their chief gods are Gorakhnāth and Matsyendranāth.

In Belgaon, wives of Yogīs wear a short-sleeved bodice and a cloth the corner of which is not passed back between the legs, a gold nose ring, a necklace of glass or of metal beads, a small, central gold brooch, and three sorts of ear-rings. While their husbands are living with them they have red lead in the parting of their hair and wear glass bangles and a lucky necklace. They are clean but lazy.[1] These Yogīs are really a caste, bound together by a social organization through which disputes are settled. Besides begging, they are engaged in cultivation, in which they are skilled. Their women help in sowing and weeding. They raise buffaloes and dogs.[2]

In Berār[3] the Nāthas comprise eighteen divisions, of which the recognized or regular sub-sects are Āudhut, Kānphaṭiya and Gorakhnāth. Among the heterodox are Udāsī, Kalbelī and Bharadī. They know seven other divisions, each identical with a Hindu deity, known as the nine Nāthas, *Navanāthas*. They trace their origin to Ādināth through Gorakhnāth and Matsyendranāth. Gorakhnāthīs are considered of a higher order than the Kānphaṭiyas, for at a feast given by Gorakhnāth and Matsyendranāth each guest was given what he desired. The chosen dishes were all produced through the miraculous powers of the two Yogīs. Kānipā asked for cooked snakes and scorpions and was promptly hooted from the feast. (But Kānphaṭiya is not derived from Kānipā.) Kānphaṭiyas split the lobe of the ear, Gorakhnāthīs the cartilege. The marriage ceremonies of Gṛhastas resemble those of neighbouring Hindus. The marriage dowry is one

---

1 *Bombay Gazetteer*, vol. XXI, p. 185.
2 *Bombay Gazetteer*, vol. XXI, p. 155.
3 See Kitts, *Census Report, Berār*, 1881, pp. 58 ff.

and one-fourth rupees. The married Yogīs are called saṁjogī, the celibates Yogī, or Jogī. They eke out their living by weaving coarse cloth, *nawār*, and blankets. They carry a bunch of peacock feathers with which they make magic passes over the sick, and act as fortune-tellers and makers of charms. Others keep on exhibition small performing bulls. The householders are followers of Gorakhnāth and Matsyendranāth. Their chief objects of worship at the Śivrātri are the carans of those two saints. The Bharadīs perform a ceremony in honour of Devī in which they beat drums and remain awake all night, hence their name. These Nathās recruit from all castes.

Thurston[1] reports as Yogīs for South India, jugglers and beggars, mostly householders, who sell beads and keep pigs. They are snake charmers, who have no restriction as regards food, and cultivators, scavengers, robbers and destroyers of dogs. They keep widows in concubinage. Some of their women are professional tattooers. Like those in Berār, they wander about, carrying on donkeys the materials for their rude huts which they set up on the outskirts of the villages. They account for their condition as resulting from a curse that was imposed because of some slighting remarks made regarding Pārvatī's breasts. These Yogīs claim superiority to Mālas and Mādigās. The caste is divided into exogamous sects. They will eat crocodile, field rats and cats. They carry a bag containing snakes. The Pāmula (the word means 'snake') is a Jogī.

In their betrothal ceremony, a small sum of money and a pig are given to the bride's party. The pig is killed and a feast held, with much consumption of liquor. In the marriage ceremony the *Kaṅgnas*, which are tied by the maternal uncles to the wrists of the bride and groom, are made of human hair and to them are attached leaves of the *Alangium Lamarckii* and *Strychnos Nux Vomica*. On the way to the bride's hut for the ceremony of the marriage, the groom's party is stopped by a rope or a bamboo screen, which is held by relatives of the bride and others. After a short struggle, money is paid and the company proceeds. The marriage badge, a string of black beads, is tied around the bride's neck, the bride and

[1] *TTCSI*, vol. II, pp. 494 ff.

groom sometimes sitting on a pestle and mortar. Rice is thrown over them and they are carried beneath the marriage booth on the shoulders of their maternal uncles.

Widows may remarry up to seven times.

At puberty a girl is secluded in a hut made by her brother or her husband; and, on the last day of her isolation, her clothes and the hut are burned. The dead are buried, the corpse being carried to the grave wrapped in cloth. Before it is lowered into the grave all throw rice over the eyes and a man of a different sect places four annas in the mouth. Fire is also carried to the grave by the son and food is left there. Some place a chicken and a small portion of salt in the armpit of the corpse.

The Jogī Puruṣa[1] is a recently formed caste that speaks Marāṭhi and Tulu. Their head monastery is at Kadiri but they have several other establishments. The individuals of the caste are disciples of the various maṭhas, and worship Bhāiroṁ and Gorakhnāth. There are both celibates and householders amongst them. The former wear rings of rhinoceros horn or of clay. The householders do not split the ears but put pieces of clay over the cartilege where it is usually split in initiation. They use the sacred thread to which is attached a whistle of brass, or of copper, or of silver. The whistle is used when the worshipper offers prayer to Bhāiroṁ. Brāhmans are employed for their marriages. The dead are buried in a sitting posture and a funeral feast is held on the twelfth day, a Brāhman priest officiating. Food is offered to crows and gifts are made to Brāhmans. The purificatory rites for the deceased initiate of Bhāirava (Bhāiroṁ) include worship (*pūjā*) at the grave each day from the third to the twelfth day. Some of these Jogīs are mendicants, others follow menial occupations, serving as coolies, peons and the like.

Bhaddaṛī[2] Yogīs and Nandī Jogīs in the west of the United Provinces, work as tailors and silk-spinners, and have several gotras with Rājput names (e.g. Chāuhān, Kucchwāha, Gahlot).[3] There is also a caste known as Ḍomjogī

[1] *TTCSI*, vol. II, p. 500.
[2] Often Musulmāns. *CTC*, vol. III, p. 59.
[3] *CTC*, vol. III, p. 61.

who are beggars. The Ṭhārus, who live below the Nepalese hills, are divided into clans, one of which is known as Jogī.

The tale goes that a Jogī once kept a Ṭhāru woman as his mistress. Their descendants are known as Jogī-Ṭhāru. They bury their dead, using a samādh. There is a group in Gorakhpur known as Kānphaṭa Ratannāth (Rathināth). Rathināth is worshipped by the Jogī-Ṭhārus.[1]

Another interesting group of Jogīs, who trace their origin to Gorakhnāth are the Sepalas. The following description of them is based upon a visit to one of their camps in the rainy season of 1924: The Yogīs, or Jogīs, who were encamped on the open plain, were protected from the weather by very poor, thin tents of country-made cloth. These shelters were pyramidal in shape, and were erected something like American Indian wigwams. The edges of the tents were about two feet from the ground, and the space below the edges was open on all sides. Furniture was scanty, and, altogether, conditions were of poverty. About the camp were a large number of donkeys, the Sepalas deriving most of their income from the sale of these animals. These Jogīs keep fowls and dogs also.

But it is as snake charmers that they are of special interest. They go about in the cities and villages in the neighbourhood of their camps taking their snakes with them. These they charm with the music of their queer, gourd pipes (*bīn*). One of the first things that the Jogīs did, when the visitors reached their camp, was to show their snakes. They brought out their round, flat baskets, took off the covers and prodded the snakes with their fingers to drive them out. They had a good many black cobras, all very large and splendid specimens. One had been caught only the day before in the jungle. Soon after snakes are captured they are drugged and their fangs are removed. The men showed snakes of other kinds as well, one of a large variety, well marked, and another 'two headed' snake. This, they assert, has a head at either end of its body, one of which it uses one year, and the other the next. Some of the customs of these Jogīs are of interest.

---

[1] Knowles, *The Gospel in Gonda*, p. 213; *CTC*, vol. IV, pp. 386, 399.

They wear in their ears very large rings. These are set in the lower part of the ears, contrary to the practice of the Gorakhnāthīs, and the holes for the rings are made with a large needle. All sorts of rings are worn, but the ones most valued are made of the bone of a certain 'snake found in the hills,' the *sālu sāṁp*. They make offerings to Gorakhnāth at the time of the piercing of the ears. These Jogīs wear all sorts of beads, but especially the rudrākṣa, and the small, white ones obtained at Hiṅg Lāj. These latter they purchase in Hindustan, rather than undertake the long and difficult journey to the west. They do not wear a sacred thread; they allow their beards to grow long, twist them in two coils and wind the ends around their ears, much as Sikhs of the Panjab do; they wear their hair in a knot and over it wind a turban in a peculiar way, so that it looks as if it were going to topple over forward. They do not practise Yoga. Like other Yogīs, they bury their dead, placing the body in a sitting posture. They claim to worship Gorakhnāth, and are disciples of Kānipā, or Kānipāo, whose teacher was Jālandharipā.[1] It is said, however, that Kānipā was the son of Kinwār, who caught the fish from which Matsyendranāth was born. They are, as the above description indicates, householders, keeping their families with them in camp. While Yogīs of this class seem to be included among 'the criminal tribes,' who are under constant police surveillance, this particular group had, evidently, earned a good reputation; for, although they had many notes from officials showing that they had been under observation in the past, they were then free to go where they pleased. It is claimed that these Jogīs do not thieve. Their papers showed that they are great travellers and that they had been over many parts of India. Some of the gotras, family names, of the Sepalas are Gādaṛia, Tāṅk, Pheṅkṛa, Linak, Cāuhān, Tahliwāl, Athwāl, Sohtra and Bāṁna.[2] They rank lower than Hindu Yogīs because they will take food from Musalmāns, and eat the flesh of the jackal. At Devī Pātan it was said that Sepalas eat snakes. These Jogīs are an unclean and ignorant people despised by almost every class of

[1] See *RTCP*, vol. II, p. 405.
[2] E.g. so the Yogīs in Almora asserted.

Indians, but feared and dreaded by many. Sepalas are sometimes, as 'Kānipāos,' reckoned as 'halfpanth' of the Gorakhnāthīs.[1]

It is of interest to compare descriptions of the Sepalas with those of castes of Yogīs in Bombay, Berār and the Nizām's Dominions and in the south where many hints of relationship appear. In the account of the feast given by Gorakhnāth and Matsyendranāth, which determined the rank of sub-sect castes in Berār, Kānipā, whose disciples the Sepalas claim to be, asked, it will be remembered, for cooked snakes and scorpions, and was promptly hooted from the assembly.

---

[1] See *RTCP*, vol. II, p. 409.

CHAPTER FOUR

DIVISIONS OF THE ORDER

THE problem of the sub-sects of the Kānphaṭas and of the relation of their founders to Gorakhnāth is a difficult one to solve. Traditionally there are twelve sub-sects, each organized by a disciple of Gorakhnāth. But, while some of these sub-sects were formed soon after the death of Gorakhnāth, still others were later brought into line with the general scheme of the order. One, at least, of the sub-sects is often considered as but a half division and in some places is denied even such a place of respectability. But this sub-sect claims descent from Gorakhnāth. The whole number of sub-sects named in the various lists far exceeds twelve;[1] some names, however, are not those of major divisions, but of schools, or of individual gurus with a following, but belonging to some more comprehensive group.

The author, after compiling the various lists, and collecting names of sub-sects from all available sources, visited Ṭilla and Amritsar in December, 1924, where he discussed the whole matter with the mahant, Pīr Kalla Nāth, of Ṭilla. This mahant, who is generally held to be at the head of all the Kānphaṭas, together with a few other Yogīs, went over the list of names, making frequent reference to his records. The results of this conference are included in the following account of the sub-divisions of the Gorakhnāthīs. Reference to the names arranged in the tables attached to this chapter will show that not all of the sub-sects of the order are traceable to Gorakhnāth himself. Jālandharpā (Jālandharipā) was made by Ādināth, while Kānipā and perhaps Bhartṛhari were disciples of Jālandhar. Furthermore, Mat-

[1] See comparative Table A at the end of this chapter.

syendranāth made some disciples, besides Gorakhnāth, who in turn, made disciples and formed sub-sects; and Gorakhnāth was associated with Matsyendranāth in making others. The *paramparās* show, further, that either Gorakhnāth and Matsyendranāth were closely related in the formation of the sect of Kānphaṭas, or that Gorakhnāth was greater than his teacher; for all the tradition bears the clearer impress of the former. In Chart D, at the end of this chapter, the order is traced back to Śakti. This would agree with the *teaching* of the Yogic doctrine of the sect and is, apparently, a matter of theory.

Before making a final analysis of the lists, it may be well to record a tradition, reminiscent of the earlier Śāivite sects, which they relate at Ṭilla.[1] There were formerly eighteen panths of Śiva and twelve of Gorakhnāth. These two groups fought each other; and, as a result, twelve of the former and six of the latter were destroyed. The remaining twelve *panths* of the two sects constitute the order of the Kānphaṭas, or Gorakhnāthīs. Those which were derived from Śiva are: (1) Kaṇṭharnāth of Bhūj, in Kacch; (2) Pāgalnāth of Peshāwar and Rohtak; (3) Rāwal of Afghanistān; (4) Paṅkh; (5) Ban of Mārwār; (6) Gopāl, or Rām ke.

Those of Gorakhnāth which survived are: (1) Hethnāth; (2) Colināth of the Āi-panth of Devī Bimla (Bombay); (3) Cāndnāth, Kaplāni; (4) Bāirāg, Ratadhonda Mārwār, Ratannāth; (5) Pāonāth, of Jāipur, of whom Jālandharpā, Kānipāo and Gopicand; (6) Dhajjanāth (Mahābīr) whose members are all foreigners. This tradition most probably suggests a new alignment of Śāivite sects under the influence of the great Gorakhnāth, in which many older Śāivite panths disappeared. The Yogī at Purī, with his club, is reminiscent of the Lakulīśas and the tradition from Ṭilla holds that the Satnāth is related to the Paṅk, one of the older sects of Śiva.

The principal panths, or sub-sects of the order may be described as follows:

1. *Satnāth.* This division is reported in nearly all of the lists. It is related to the Paṅk, the fourth of the sects surviving from the Śiva panths. They have a gaddi at Purī and other

[1] Told to the author in December, 1924.

establishments at Bhewa, Thānesar and Karnāl. According to the mahant at Purī, the patch-work cap, coat and quilt are a mark of this sub-sect. From this line sprang the Dharamnāthīs; and Garībnāth, who accompanied Dharamnāth to Kacch, was of this division. This panth is said to follow Brahmā.

2. *Rāmnāth* (Rām ke), sometimes wrongly identified with Rāmcandra. This sub-sect is related to the Śiva group called Gopāl. It traces its origin to Santokhnāth, who did not himself form a panth. Their chief gaddi is at Delhi. Dās Gopālnāthīs are reported from Jodhpur.

3. *Dharamnāth*. This sub-division traces its origin to Rāja Dharam who became a Yogī of the line of Satnāth. Their headquarters are on the Godāvarī; and they have a famous and important monastery at Dhinodhar in Kacch. Dharamnāth is also said to have been a disciple of Matsyendranāth, and is counted as one of the nine Nāthas.[1] But the previous statement is in closer accord with traditions concerning him.

4. *Lakṣmannāth*. Lakṣmannāth succeeded Gorakhnāth at Ṭilla. This panth has two divisions, or schools, Natesrī and Daryā. The distinctive characteristics of these two are that the former reside on the hill at Ṭilla, while the latter live on the plains. Daryā is also considered as a separate panth having its origin at Ṭilla. The other sub-sect is known as Natesrī in Amritsar, and as Darbārī Ṭilla Bāl Gondal in Hoshiārpur. This is the Heth, or Hethnāth, panth of the original Gorakhnāthīs. To this division belong the Hāith of the Ambāla and Jhelum districts and Bāljāti of the Karnāl. Rāñjha belonged to Natesrī. The Jāfir Pīrs (see below) follow Rāñjha.

5. *Daryānāth*. Although now a separate panth, this division belongs to the Heth panth of the original Gorakhnāthīs. Members of this panth are found all through North India and the Panjab. Many are found in Sind.[2] Beyond the Indus this division has establishments at Makhad, Kohāt and Quetta. Their sacred seat is at Uderolāl in Sind, where is found the

---

[1] *IA*, vol. VII, p. 47.

[2] Aitken, *Gazetteer of the Province of Sind*, Part A, p. 164.

tomb of an infant who transformed himself into an armed horseman and emerged from the Indus to rebuke the Muslim Mahammad Yusuf of Taṭṭa. He is known also as Ūderolāl, Dulanlāl, Amarlāl, Zinda Pīr and Daryā Shāh. He is also called Shekh Tāhir at Ūderolāl and Khwāja Khizr at Sukkur. At his temple in Ūderolāl a lamp is kept burning perpetually and at the new moon he is worshipped at the river, or at a canal or by water, with rice, sugar-candy, spices, fruit and lighted lamps. He left the world by disappearing into the ground. There was a dispute between Hindus and Muslims as to the disposal of his body by cremation or burial. He reappeared and commanded them to use the two methods. Consequently, there are both a tomb and a temple at the place. About 50,000 attend the annual religious feast at Ūderolāl.

6. *Gaṅgānāth.* This sub-sect was founded by Gaṅgānāth, who followed Kapalmuni. From this division some trace the Kāyanāthīs. There is some connection with the Ratannāth sub-division, reported under the next number.

7. *Bāirāg* (Bhartṛhari, Bāirāg Catri). This is the fourth of the original panths of Gorakhnāth. It traces its origin to Bhartṛhari who was initiated by Jālandharipā; but who is said to have been a disciple of Gorakhnāth.[1]

He is said to have abdicated the throne of Ujjāin to become a Yogī. One tradition makes him the son of Rāja Bhoj. Although he was initiated by Jālandharipā, he is said to have been a disciple of Gorakhnāth; and the Āipanthīs of Hardwār say that he was initiated by Gorakhnāth. His chief associates were of the Kaplāni panth, also sprung from Jālandharipā's sub-sect. Another tradition affirms that the panth is traced to Māināth, an orphan who was brought up by the Meos and who later became a disciple of Gorakhnāth.[2]

An important name in this division of the Gorakhnāthīs is that of Premnāth, who is sometimes said to have founded a panth.

Another famous disciple of Bhartṛhari was Ratannāth of Peshāwar. Beyond the frontier, and in Peshāwar, these followers of Ratannāth do not wear the mudrā. To account for

---

[1] *Gazetteer of the Province of Sind*, vol. II, p. 56.
[2] *RTCP*, vol. II, p. 404.

this it is reported that once at Ṭilla when Ratannāth was taken to task for not having ear-rings he opened his breast and showed them in his heart. Once his rings were taken away from him as a punishment for some offence, and he showed them in his mouth. Musalmāns revere him. Ratannāth is famous for having created a boy out of the dirt of his body. This boy was afterwards known as Kāyanāth, and as Qaim ud Dīn. When Kāyanāth died, both Musalmāns and Hindus claimed his body; but it disappeared, only the clothes remaining. Hindus built a samādh for him, and Musalmāns a tomb. Another group of Yogīs related to Ratannāth is the Mekhla Dhārī. In Ambāla they wear a *taṛāgī*. In Nābha there are secular Yogīs who trace their origin to Ratannāth. They belong to the Puniya gotra (a Jāṭ gotra). The founder of this group of householders was Māīnāth. After he had become a Yogī, the Jāṭs compelled him to marry a girl of the juggler Yogīs. The Bharat in Dera Gazi Khan belong to this division.

Ratannāthīs are counted as Daryānāthīs as well. There are shrines connected with the name of Ratannāth in Kābul and Jalālābād. Even Musalmāns believe in the powers of these Yogīs.

8. *Rāwal* or *Nāgnāth*. This is the third of the original Śiva group. The Rāwals, who are the most important of the Musalmān Yogīs, are great wanderers. In the western districts of the Panjab 'they are occultists and quacks.' There are two main groups of them: (1) the Madia, said to have been founded by Gorakhnāth; and (2) the Gal who are referred to Śiva and who are known both as Pāgalpanthīs and as Rāwal Galla. Those of the second division are found in Peshāwar, and the Bohar monastery in Rohtak belongs to them. The chief seat of the Rāwals is at Rāwalpindī, and members of the panth are found in Hajāro and in Afghanistan. Not all recognize the Rāwals as one of the twelve sects of the Gorakhnāthīs, although they are widely reported as such.[1]

According to one account they form 'half' of one of the twelve orders, the other half being the Pārasnāthīs. Rāwals are also Kaphlāin. Rāwals are found in the Nizām's Dominions.

---

[1] See Table A.

9. *Jālandharipā.* These belong to the Pāonāth panth, the fifth of the original Gorakhnāthīs. But the paramparās agree that Jālandharipā belongs to an earlier branch of the sect.[1] He was the founder of the 'Pā' panths as over against the 'Nāth' panths. Pā is Tibetan for *wāla*,[2] and illustrates Eastern influence within the Kānphaṭas. In some Gorakhnāthī lists are included, within this division, Kānipā and Gopcand. The Pāpnāth, also known as Pānāth, are said to be a sub-division of Jālandharipā and followers of Mahādeo (Śiva). Jālandharnāth (and Kāṁphnāth) are sometimes identified with the Āughar, while Gorakhnāth and Matsyendranāth are known as Kānphaṭas. The sphere of activity of the former was Bengal and Bihar, that of the latter two was the United Provinces and the Panjab.[3]

This panth has an establishment at Jāipur.

10. *Āipanth.* This panth is related to Colināth of the original Gorakhnāthī group,[4] and is connected with both Bhushtāi and Karkāi, disciples of Gorakhnāth. Karkāināth is also known as Kanaknāth and Kaṅkhnāth. The followers of the two Yogīs last named are said to belong to schools of the Hethnāth. The Āipanthīs of Hardwār say that they were followers of Pīr Pārasnāth, and that they separated from them through the worship of Āidevī. They trace their origin back to a female disciple of Gorakhnāth, now known as Bimlā Devī. They explain this by saying that 'Āi' means 'Māi' (Mother, Goddess). They used to use 'āi' instead of 'nāth'[5] in their names, but five generations after Narmāijī they resumed the name of 'nāth.' Māināthīs probably sprang from this group. Five generations after Narmāijī, who himself lived several generations after Gorakhnāth, came Mastnāth, and from his time the members of this panth have been called 'Nāthas.' Narmāijī was born in Khot, now in Jīnd State. As a disciple of Gorakhnāth, then, Mastnāth cannot be considered as a contemporary of the great Yogī. Followers

---

1 See Tables B and D.
2 *Census Report, Panjab*, 1891, p. 117; *CTC*, vol. III, p. 59.
3 *Census Report, Panjab*, 1891, p. 114, note 1.
4 *Coli* is, according to Swātmārāma, member twenty-one after Gorakhnāth.
5 *RTCP*, vol. II, p. 404.

of Mastnāth are not very respectable, and only recently have they been recognized by the rest of the order. They carry a crooked stick which they use as an arm crutch.[1]

The Bāwās are of the Āipanth through Mastnāth.

The Āipanth was included in the twelve when the order of Kānphaṭas was organized.[2] This would suggest that the order of Gorakhnāthīs was consolidated a considerable time after the death of Gorakhnāth.

The story is told that once, when Mastnāth was engaged in meditation (*jog*), one of his disciples who came before him wearing only a loin-cloth, was cursed with the necessity of remaining naked forever. For this reason the followers of this unfortunate Yogī are called 'Nāgas.' There are two divisions of the followers of Mastnāth: (1) the Baṛī Dargāh, who avoid flesh and liquor and (2) the Chhoṭī Dargāh, who indulge in both. The latter group was founded by a Camār, a disciple of Mastnāth. Menials of this panth are called Camarwā.[3] The chief monastery of this panth, at Bohar in Rohtak, was founded by Narmāijī. There are no idols at this place. The Āipanthīs have a large and important establishment at Hardwār. Other seats of the Āināthīs are found at Ranpat, Madhata and Camār, in the Panjab. The Āipanth is mentioned in the *Dabistan* (vol. II, p. 128).

11. *Kaplāni*. This division, included in the Cāndnāth sub-sect of the old order of Gorakhnāthīs, traces its origin to Kapalmuni, a disciple of Gorakhnāth, and was founded by Ajāipāl. This panth is also called Kapil, or Kapil Deo ke. A group belonging to this sub-sect is the Nīmnāthī, also called Gaphlāni, or Khiskāi. But see (5) below.

The headquarters of the panth are at Gaṅgā Sāgar.[4]

12. *Dhajjanāth*. This panth, the sixth of the old Gorakhnāthī list, is associated with the name of Mahābīr (Hanumān). At Ṭilla, and in two of the lists, this is counted as one of the twelve sub-sects. The statements that the members of this sub-sect carry a flag, and that some of them

---

[1] *Census of Panjab, Report*, 1891, p. 116.

[2] So reported by the Āipanthīs of Hardwār.

[3] *RTCP*, vol. II, p. 403 and note.

[4] So a Yogī at Nāini Tāl declared.

are found at Peshāwar and Ambāla are not accepted at Ṭilla. It is asserted that they are to be found in Ceylon.[1]

13. *Kānipā.* While Jālandharipā was confined in the well at Ujjāin,[2] from which he was finally rescued through the help of Gorakhnāth and Matsyendranāth, his disciple, Kānipā occupied his teacher's place as mahant. He afterwards founded a panth. From this line came Gopicand (Candra) otherwise known as Siddh Saṅgarī, who became one of the eighty-four Siddhas. Gopicand is sometimes given as the name of a panth; and Gopicand is considered also as a disciple both of Kānipā and of Jālandharipā.

From Siddh Saṅgarī is traced the Spādhā of Bengal, keepers of snakes. One of this group initiated Ismael, founder of a panth. The Kālbeliyas are said to be his disciples.

To this line belong, also, the Sepalas, who keep snakes[3] Some of this division wear the rings as do the Kānphaṭas, others wear them in the lobes of the ears.

Strictly speaking, the Kānipā are not considered as one of the twelve panths, but as a half sub-sect. Even this statement is not universally accepted.

A tradition traces the Bāmārg sect (the 'Left-Hand' sect) to Kānipā.[4] It is of interest at this point to note that the development of erotic elements in Śakti worship was in Bengal and Assam. The list of names given by Sen[5] is: Mīnanāth, Gorakhnāth, Hāḍīpā, Kalupā. Hāḍīpā was the teacher of the mother of Gopicand. Jālandharipā is also known as Hāḍi or Hāḍipā. This list belongs to eastern Bengal. Another name apparently belonging to this cycle is Kālepā (Kāripā, or exactly Kānipā).

Both Jālandharipā and Kānipā are placed in the Pāonāth division brought down from the Gorakhnāthīs. Some identify the Jālandharipā and the Kānipā.

Two of the original panths of Śiva are not accounted for in the above enumeration, the Ban of Mārwār and the Kaṇṭharnāth of Bhūj. The latter is mentioned in a descrip-

---

[1] *PNQ*, vol. II, para. 279. [2] See chap. nine.
[3] See above, pp. 59 ff. [4] *RTCP*, vol. I, p. 329.
[5] *History of Bengali Language and Literature*, p. 28.

tion of Yogī establishments,[1] but the connection of the Kaṇṭharnāthīs with recognized sub-divisions is not clear.

A number of names remain to be considered; but they are not of wide enough significance to warrant their inclusion in the larger divisions of the Kānphaṭas. In all probability they represent minor divisions within the more important groups or the names of important personages or alternate names of some already recorded. They are as follows:

(1) The Hāṇḍī Pharaṅg (Bharaṅg, Śaraṅgnāth, Hāṇḍī Bhiraṅg, Cand Bharaṅg [?]) The explanation of this name is given in the following legend. Śakkarnāth, disciple of Gorakhnāth, in his wanderings, came to a land ruled by a low-caste rāja, who seized him and ordered him to cause a rain of sugar, on pain of torture. Śakkarnāth performed the miracle and then buried the rāja alive. Twelve years later the Yogī returned and found thc king a skeleton, but restored him to life and made him his disciple and cook. (Another version of the story states that the rāja was struck blind, and that after twelve years Śakkarnāth restored his sight.) The rāja, however, was not reformed as the result of his punishment. One day he took out some of the pulse he was cooking and tasted it. Bhāiroṁ chanced to appear that day in person and refused the food. The reason was discovered and the rāja was punished by having the pot (*haṇḍī*) hung about his neck. He was obliged to wander the livelong day, getting food out of the pot. His punishment lasted four years, after which he was pardoned, but his followers still bear the name, Hāṇḍī Bharaṅg.[2] A most interesting version of this story is told at Trimbak. At that place Yogīs show a stone samādh, said to be that of Aurangzeb. The legend is that Aurangzeb became a disciple of Gorakhnāth, but that the other Yogīs refused to eat with him; so he buried himself alive. After twelve years he came out of his tomb as Mṛtaknāth (Lord of Death). He was only a skeleton when he came forth, but after his reappearance flesh came upon his bones. Afterwards, Gorakhnāth ordered him to cook food for the Yogīs present. He did so, but, when the food was ready, he tasted it to see if it were properly seasoned.

---

[1] See p. 110. [2] See *RTCP*, vol. II, pp. 395, 396.

The food was declared unclean and the pot was hung over his head. Therefore, he is called Siddha Hāṇḍī Pharaṅg Nāth. He went off to Poona, where to this day this sect reside, at Hāṇḍī Paraṅg Nātha.

Śakkarnāth had no disciples, so, on his deathbed, he called a Musalmān, Jāfir by name, made him his disciple, and advised him to take only uncircumcised Muslims into his following. These Yogīs are employed as Hindu cooks, and belong to the Santnāth sect.[1] The order today recognizes only Musalmāns and they do not eat with other Yogīs.

At Ṭilla it was stated that these Yogīs are not counted as one of the twelve panths.

Cānd Bharaṅgīs are said to be found in the west, near Dwāraka. And, as stated above, members of this sub-division are found in Poona.

(2) The Jāfir Pīrs are Musalmāns. They are well known in the Panjab. Although they are Kānphaṭas, Hindu Yogīs do not eat with them. They are followers of Rāñjha and disciples of Bālkeśwarnāth. These Yogīs are not counted as one of the twelve sects. Some trace them to Santoknāth, who is Viṣṇu. The Pīr Jogīs, who are also Musalmāns, perhaps of the same panth, will eat the food of other Yogīs, but others will not eat their food. At Ṭilla it was affirmed that these Yogīs are not found at Siālkot.

(3) Mānnāth (Mānmanthī, Mānāthī). To this line belongs Arjannāga, or Arjannaṅga (Paṅgalnāth [?]) who is now in Kāilās as a Siddha. There is an establishment belonging to this sub-sect at Jawālamukhi. These Yogīs trace their origin to Rāja Rasālū whose follower Mānānth was. They are found in Peshāwar and Jhelum.

(4) Aghorī (Ghorī). It is possible that there are some Aghorīs among the Yogīs. There are none at Ṭilla, but the Yogīs of that place said that sometimes the recently-buried corpse of a child might be dug up and eaten by Jogīs of this group. It is acknowledged that an occasional Kānphaṭa belongs to this panth. It was reported repeatedly by Yogīs and at different places, that an occasional Āughar becomes an Aghorī.[2]

---

[1] See *RTCP*, vol. II, p. 408.

[2] Hughes, *Gazetteer of the Province of Sind* (1876) says that the Āughar is a Yogī. Henry Balfour, *Jr. Anth. Inst. of Gt. Br. and*

(5) Nīmnāth and Pārasnāth. These two persons were sons of Matsyendranāth, begat, according to one tradition, in Ceylon. They were slain and afterwards restored to life by Gorakhnāth. Later, they were initiated by their father and then founded new sects. They are Jains.[1] However, there are groups under both names that are included in Yogī *panths*. The Nīmnāthīs who are distinct from the Pārasnāthīs, are also called Gaphāin (Gaphlāni) or Khiskāi. The Sartoras, Nīmnāthīs, always wear a cloth over the mouth and take the utmost precautions against the destruction of life. They are wanderers and receive food cooked by others. They use a *cilam*, not a huqqa. The Pārasnāth Pūj sub-division are celibates, but they live in houses. The interesting legend concerning these two persons is as follows. After Matsyendranāth left the queen in Ceylon taking with him his two sons, because Gorakhnāth had called him to his senses, they fell under the anger of the latter, and he put them to death and hung their skins on a tree. Later, for the sake of their father, he restored them to life. Some time afterwards, the boys were sent to a village to beg. They were ordered by a man to drag

---

Ireland, vol. XXVI (1897), pp. 340 ff., has collected data on the Aghorī under the title, *Life History of an Aghorī Fakīr*, in which he supplies the information which follows. They trace their origin to the Gorakhpanth and Gorakhnāth. The movement was started by Motināth. There are three divisions of them: Oghar, Sarbhuṅgī and Ghure. The Oghar is the branch to which the faqīr (whose history is recorded) belonged. All persons are eligible for admission to the sect. Ogharnāth used a fresh skull, from which he had eaten the flesh, as a drinking bowl. The faqīr (Kallu Siṅgh) claimed that some members of the order ate human flesh and were then able to make it live again. He did not claim these and other magical powers himself. In general the Aghorī eat the flesh of all dead animals except the horse, and the food of any sect or caste. Any skull will do for a begging bowl. (But the ghoulish practices which this man describes were known long before the time of Gorakhnāth. See chapter ten).

[1] There are other hints at Jain connections. The Jains have a temple near Pāe Dhūnī (Paidhoni) which shelters an idol of Ghorajīnāth, decked with gems.—S. M. Edwards, *Bombay City Gazetteer*, vol. I, p. 177. Paidhoni is the seat of the Kānphaṭas in old Bombay. The books on Bombay refer to a certain place in the old city as Pāe Dhonī and explain the name as meaning 'The-Place-of-Feet-Washing.' It is correct, however, to say that the name of this locality is derived from that of a famous establishment of a sect of the Yogīs.

away a dead calf, before he would give them alms. They did as he requested, and in return he gave them food. By the time that they had reached their teacher the food had turned to blood and worms. Then Matsyendranāth cursed the village. The sons later separated and formed new panths, the Pūj and the Sartora, with which other Yogīs have no concern.[1]

In a variant to this story Gorakhnāth goes with the boys to beg alms at a merchant's (*bania*) shop, and they are made to take away a dead calf. When Gorakhnāth sees the food transformed, he catches them by the hand, takes them to the merchant's house, and there puts them to death. Thereupon all the merchants complain that he has polluted all their sacrifices by this murder; and he retorts that they had polluted his disciples. He agrees, however, to restore the two boys to life if the merchants will henceforth worship him and no other. They agree and Gorakhnāth left Pārasnāth, one of the two boys, with the merchants, and the Jains deem him an incarnation of God.[2]

(6) Kaṇṭharnāth (Kaṇṭhaḍnāth). Some say that this group trace their origin to Gorakhnāth, others to Ganeśa. In Ambāla they are an endogamous panth of householders.[3] At Kāṇṭhkot they worship Ganeśa and Kaṇṭhaḍnāth, using the latter name while telling their beads. Here Kaṇṭhaḍnāth is worshipped twice a day. His followers take the vow of celibacy. In almost all of their customs they resemble the Dhinodhar Kānphaṭas.[4] However, in the west Kaṇṭhaḍnāthīs often marry; but the fathers do not eat with their children until their ears have been split and other dedicatory rites have been performed.[5]

Other names, for which no relationship can yet be assigned are, Kāiknāth; Pāyalnāth; Udāināth, identified with Paśupati, probably one who preceded the founding of the order,[6] second of the Nine Nāthas, founder of the panth of Yogīs;[7] Ārayapanthī of Bor Bosan near Kābā Pīr, Thānesar; Revnāth; Tājnāth; Fīlnāth; Sarpatnāth (Carpatnāth, Carpat, or Darpat-

---

[1] See *RTCP*, vol. II, pp. 394, 395. [2] See Table D.
[3] *RTCP*, vol. II, p. 406. [4] *Bombay Gazetteer*, vol. V, p. 88.
[5] *Bombay Gazetteer*, vol. V, p. 88, note.
[6] *RTCP*, vol. II, p. 395, note. [7] See *RTCP*, vol. II, p. 393.

nāth) tenth from Gorakhnāth in Svātmārāma's list; Gāininākh, teacher of Jñāneśvar; Narañjannāth; Barañjogī; Ādhnāth, Ādhināth (?); Pāpank; Kāmdhaj; Kaśyapa; Ardhanārī; Nāyari; Amaranāth; Kambhīdās; Tarnaknāth; Abhapanthī, of whom Abhangnāth is mentioned in the *Tahqīqāti Chīsthī.*[1]

The Pathsana of Karnāl and the Patsiana of Jīnd are a school of Yogīs.

A number of ascetic movements refer their origin to Gorakhnāth. One of these is traced to Śaraṅgnāth[2] or Śringnāth, who reached the height of his power after the death of the great guru. His *panth* is sometimes called the *Bāwājī kā panth*. He introduced new rules and made his disciples bore their ears and insert ear-rings of wood. After his death ten sects were founded, all growing out of his order. They are the (1) Girināth, (2) Pūrināma, (3) Sāṁsia, (4) Militant Nāgas, (5) Ajāipāl, (6) Gwālibāsada, (7) Ismāil Jogīs, (8) Āgamnāth, (9) Nīmnāth and (10) Jālandharnāth. There must be some confusion in this list, or there are duplicate names in this and the panths of the Kānphaṭas. Numbers five, six, seven, nine and ten have been discussed already. Of the others the author has seen members of the first only. At Kedārnāth, just outside of the town of Dwārahāt, in Kumāon, there is a small temple of Bhāiroṁ. This is situated below the gate of the main temple and the *pūjārī* at the shrine was a woman of the panth. These Yogīs marry. They do not split their ears. The famous witch, Nona Camārī, belonged to the panth of Ismāil Jogīs.[3]

Lāl Pādrīs[4] are not Goraknāthīs, although they are often found in close association with them. They are followers of Dattatreya, who was eminent in the practice of Yoga and who is held in high esteem by Yogīs. He is considered by some to have been an incarnation of Kṛṣṇa.[5] In the *Dabistan*, he is described in a contest of Yogic power with Gorakhnāth.[6] Dattatreya was probably a deified Brāhman of the tenth

---

[1] *RTCP*, vol. II, p. 404. [2] See p. 70, above.

[3] See the *Chamars*, pp. 26, 27, 179, 183, 185 for notes on Nona Chamārī.

[4] This is also a general term for Yogī, or ascetic, referring to the 'yellow' robe.

[5] *Wi*, pp. 205, 240. [6] vol. II, p. 140.

century, to whom the famous story of the testing of the virtue of the wife of Atri has been attached.[1] His shrines are scattered here and there in the districts about Poona,[2] and in one place his image has three heads to represent the Hindu Triad.[3] He was an Aghorī.

CHART B

PARAMPARĀ: as given by Pāngārkar, based on Nāmdev:

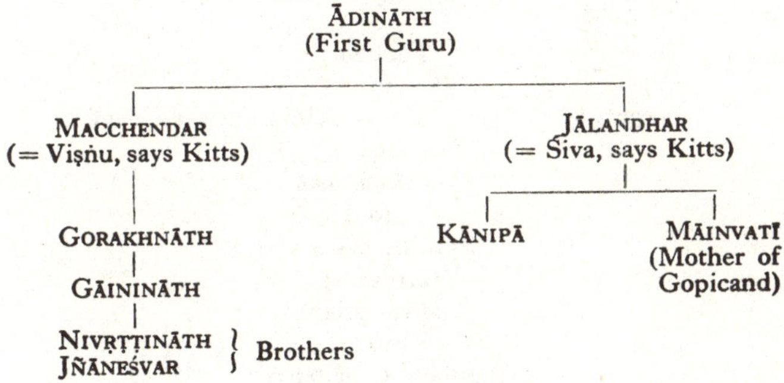

[1] *Hindu Religious Year*, pp. 98, 163, 165, 168, 175; *MWB*, p. 267.

[2] His appearance to Eknāth is described in *Eknāth* as translated by Abbott, pp. 18 ff.

[3] *MWB*, p. 267.

CHART C

Paramparā of Bahiṇā Bāī. (See Dr. Abbott's translation, p. 1.)

Ādināth (Śiva) (taught the Yoga to)
Pārvatī
Matsyendra (who heard it as Śiva taught it to Pārvatī)
to
Gorakhnāth
to
Gahini
to
Nivṛttināth (while N. was a child but yet a Yogī)
to
Dnyāneshvara
to
Satchidānanda
further on
Vishvambhara
to
Rāghava (Chāitanya)
to
Keshava Chāitanya
to
Bābāji Chāitanya
to
Tukobā (Tukārām)
to
Bahiṇā Bāī (b. 1628; d. 1700)

CHART D

PARAMPARĀ[1]

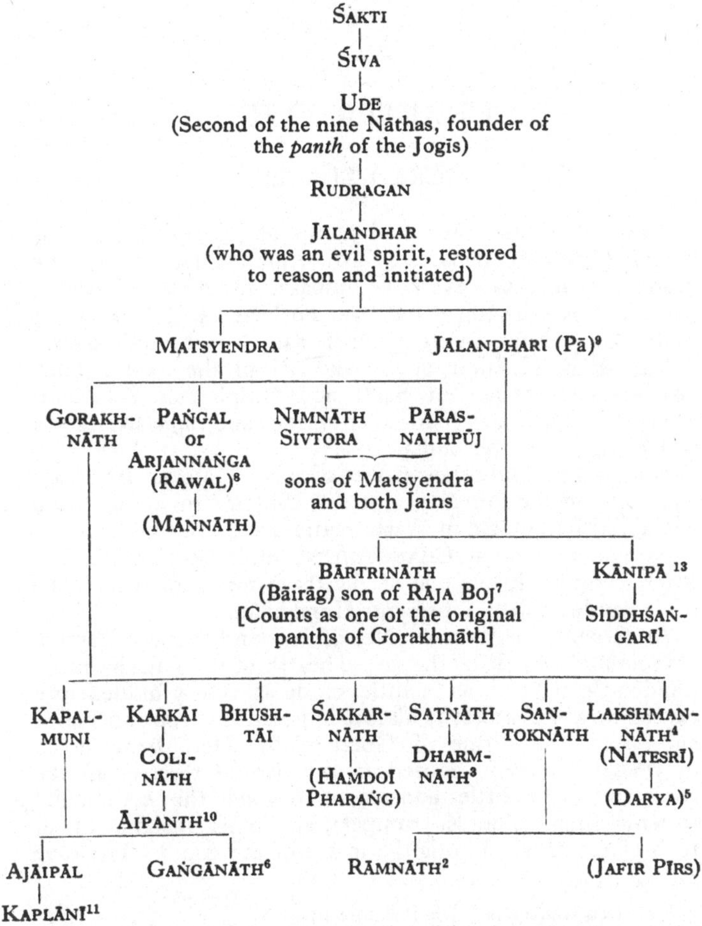

The figures refer to the order in text. The twelfth (Dhajjanāth) is not accounted for.

---

[1] *RTC* vol. II, p. 393 with modifications.

CHAPTER FIVE

SACRED PLACES

KĀNPHAṬAS visit the usual places of pilgrimage such as Prayāg (Tribeni), Benares (Kāśī), Ajudhya (Ayodhya), the source of the Godāvarī (Trimbak), Dwāraka, Hardwār, Badrināth, Kedārnāth, Brindaban, Pushkar, Rāmeśvar in the south, Darjeeling[1] in the north-east, Nepāl and Assam, Amarnāth in Kashmīr, and Hiṅg Lāj in the west. They visit certain shrines of Śakti and temples of Śiva and Bhāiroṁ. Their own particular shrines and monasteries are widely scattered over India.

It is best to study their places of special interest by areas; e.g. those in the Himālayas, in the United Provinces, in the Panjab, in Rājputāna, in Western India and elsewhere.

In a monastery at CHANGCHILING, in Sikkim, there is a black, complex image one of the three forms of which, the more gaudily robed, represents Gorakhnāth.[2]

At GORKHA in Western Nepāl, is found the cave temple of Gorakhnāth.[3] It is 'the sacred hearth of the Gurkha race.' Landon describes it as 'a little, crude sanctuary hidden in a cavern to which access is almost impossible except on hands and knees—the shrine of Gorakhnāth. Here beneath an overhanging stream, housed in the natural recesses of the rock and with little adornment beyond the ceremonial tridents, flags, halberds, trumpets, and other insignia of all such places of worship, is the image of the god.'[4] The cave

---

1 Kamru Kanaccha [?] is it Kāmarūpa?

2 Temple, *Hyderabad, Kashmir, Sikkim and Nepāl*, vol. II, p. 212.

3 For a picture of this temple, see Landon, *Nepāl*, vol. I, p. 66 It is reproduced as the frontispiece in this volume.

4 ibid., vol. II, p. 26.

and the town get their names from Gorakhnāth who is said to have resided there. Hence the national name of Gurkhas.[1]

About Kāṭhmāṇḍu centre a number of interesting places and shrines associated with the names Matsyendranāth and Gorakhnāth. The word Kāṭhmāṇḍu stands for 'Kaṭh Mandir,' or 'Temple of Wood,' a shrine built about 1600 A.D., by Lakṣmi in honour of Gorakhnāth.[2]

At BĀGMATI, about three miles from Pātan (Kāṭhmāṇḍu), there is a temple of Matsyendranāth which is recognized by Gorakhnāthīs.[3] There is also here a temple of Śiva Paśupatināth which appertains to the Kānphaṭas.[4] It is said that pilgrims to this place are never again born as a lower animal. The Nepalese Śaivite temples of Śambhunāth, Paśupatināth and others belong to the same sphere of interest as that of Matsyendranāth.[5] At Kistipur there is a temple of Bhāirab and at Kāṭhmāṇḍu one for Kāl Bhāirab.[6]

At the temple and monastery of Ratannāth at SAWĀRI KOṬ, 'Cangra Tāṅg Pahār,' is an image, or stone, which is supposed to contain the spirit of Gorakhnāth. The Kānphaṭas of this place have an intimate relation to those of Devī Pātan, the monastery at the latter place being under the authority of the former.[7]

In the Kumaun and Garhwāl Hills Kānphaṭas are found at various shrines of Bhāiroṁ. Such places of worship are often connected with the residences of particular Yogīs.

At ŚRĪ NAGAR, in Garhwāl, Gorakhnāth is worshipped as an incarnation of Śiva, and there is an establishment of Kān-

---

[1] See article, 'Tribes, Clans and Castes of Nepal,' by Capt. E. Vansittart, *JASBe*, vol. LXIII (1894) pp. 213 ff.

[2] *The Gurkhas*, p. 25.

[3] See Oldfield, *Sketches from Nepal*, vol. II, pp. 325, 326; *IA*, vol. IX, p. 169, note. For descriptions of these temples and places see also Kirkpatrick, *Kingdom of Nepal*, chap. vi and pp. 188 ff. For pictures and description see also Landon, *Nepal*.

[4] Oldfield, *Sketches from Nepal*, vol. I, p. 89., vol. II, p. 247; *BHCS*, p. 403. For description see also *IA*, vol. IX, p. 166, note; and Levi, *Le Nepāl*.

[5] See *Asiatic Researches*, vol. XVI, p. 471, note.

[6] See Landon's volumes on Nepāl. His pictures of the various temples are most excellent.

[7] See below, p. 95.

phaṭas at that place.[1] At this town the author (1924) found nothing of consequence. There were a few gṛhastas scattered about in the neighbourhood. Below Śrī Nagar there is a cavern dedicated to Gorakhnāth, which contains his image, gilded. The figure is about six inches high. The yoni-liṅga is also found in the cave, and in front is a temple of Bhāiroṁ. The pūjārī there claims that the cave used to be an important temple of Gorakhnāth; but that it was filled with river-sand during the Gohnā Lake flood of 1894; and that, although it was dug out later, it has ceased to attract as much attention as formerly. The shrine consists of three recesses in the rock. It is evidently neglected by pilgrims. The panth is Rām ke.

In Nāini Tāl, at the temple of Nandi Devī, where there is also a temple of Bhāiroṁ, Kānphaṭas are sometimes found. A Yogī there in September, 1924, whose name was Siṅghārnāth, was of the Kaplāni panth. He claimed to have been born in a family of gṛhastha Yogīs.

In Almora, above the temple of Nandi Devī, is the residence of a gṛhastha Yogī of the Dharamnāth panth. Attached to his residence is a small temple of Bhāiroṁ. The Yogī, Devnāth by name, who (1924) was pūjārī at this place, also served in the same capacity at the adjoining large temple to Mahādeo. This temple of Bhāiroṁ is a small, square building with a low, flat roof, surmounted by a small pinnacle, such as is common in these hills. The building contains a number of trisules and images of Ganeśa and Bhagavatī.

Another Yogī, Rāmnāth of the Dharamnāth panth, has a house and shop in the bazaar, to which is attached a temple of Bhāiroṁ. The place is two or three hundred years old. The temple contains an image of Bolanāth,[2] the head only,

---

[1] *Aitkin*, vol. II, p. 808.

[2] 'One of the rājas of Almora, in the lower Himālaya, had two sons, one of whom fell into evil ways, and when he was disinherited his younger brother, Gyān Chand, succeeded. Many years after, the elder brother appeared in the guise of a religious mendicant and Gyān Chand procured a gardener to slay him and his pregnant Brāhmani mistress. The dead man became a Bhūt or evil spirit, and is now worshipped as Bholanāth, 'innocent lord,' a title of Śiva, of whom, by and by, he will become a manifestation. His mistress and

with a similar image of Bhāiroṁ by its side, and an image of Ganeśa. These and many trisules painted red, as are the images, rest on a platform. Here also are a conch shell and the usual brass lamps. Many flowers are offered before the images. In the temple are found also a fan of peacock feathers, a yak-tail brush, several conch shells and a *śāligrām*. In the veranda is the usual temple bell. The building, which is not very large, has a flat roof and is surmounted by a pinnacle. By the side of the temple, at the right, are two ancient samādhs, both square, with pyramidal tops, surmounted by the yoni-liṅga symbol. They date from the reign of the Chānd Rājas. Behind the temple and to the left are two very old, low samādhs, on which the yoni section only, of the symbol, remains.

Near the Dāk Bungalow, in Almora, is another private establishment. The temple contains small images, about a foot high, of Bhāiroṁ and Pārvatī, carved in a slab of stone, and one of similar size of Gorakhnāth; the latter exhibiting the large ear-rings greatly exaggerated. The temple contains the usual collection of objects. One liṅga is arranged with a water jar above it so that water may fall continually upon it. The jar was empty. Here the father, though still alive, has been superseded by his son, also a Yogī, as pūjārī. These Yogīs are of the Satnāth sect. The endowment consists of one village.

KĀMA, a village not far from Dwārahāt, is the seat of the pīr of the Almora district. His name was (1924) Pīr Gopināth, and he belonged to the Dharamnāth panth. The village in which he lives is the property of the sect. The temple, which is in the house of the pīr, is dedicated to Nāgnāth. The pūjārī is a brother of the pīr. A section of the village is occupied by the families, not Yogīs, who cultivate the fields. The tradition at Kāma is that when the Gorkhālīs conquered Almora they built the fort and levelled the parade ground at the town of Almora. This was done on the site occupied by

---

her unborn child also became bhūts and are particularly dangerous to gardeners. A small iron trident, the emblem of Śiva, represents him, and it is placed in the corners of the peasants' huts to guard them against any sudden calamity.'—Crooke, *Religion and Folklore of Northern India*, p. 160.

the monastery and cemetery of the Gorakhnāthīs. In the process of levelling, many of the graves of the Yogīs were destroyed and many ear-rings and other emblems of the sect were unearthed.[1] A new cemetery was provided outside the town for the Yogīs, and their establishment was moved to the royal village of Kāma.

HARDWĀR has a number of places belonging to the Gorakhnāthīs. A cave, or subterranean passage, is associated with the Kānphaṭas.

The establishment of the Āipanthīs is large and, apparently, wealthy.

The monastery of the Daryāpānth has some ten or twelve Yogīs in residence. In 1924, the mahant was a minor in charge of a guardian. The author saw a large gathering of many classes of ascetics at this establishment, who had come to a distribution of gifts and food by a rich man, on the full moon of December.

The members of the Twelve-Panth organization have an establishment with good buildings in Hardwār.[2]

In the jungles about ṚIṢIKESH (Hṛṣīkeśa, Lord of the Senses) on the Ganges, above Hardwār, where Rāma underwent penance to wipe out the sin of having slain Rāvaṇa, adepts are supposed to live as hermits.

Among the lesser places of interest in the United Provinces may be mentioned the shrine of the Bhartṛharīs in the fort at CHŪNĀR.[3]

There is a small, evidently decaying establishment of the Gorakhnāthīs at ALLAHĀBĀD. It consists of two temples of Bhāiroṁ, one of Mahādeo, a small monastery and one samādh. During the rainy season of 1924 there were one Rāwalpanthī and one Bhartṛpanthī in residence. The monastery is subject to Gorakhpur.

The old town of Jhausi, opposite Allahābād on the Ganges, preserves an old tradition concerning Gorakhnāth, and Nevil says that Rāja Harbong of that place owed his downfall to

---

[1] But the Gurkhas revere Gorakhnāth.

[2] See chap. two for an account of this organization.

[3] *CTC*, vol III, p. 60. It is said that the saint spends part of each day there and the remainder of his time at Benares.

the Yogī and his teacher. An older account states that the kingdom was in great disorder. Harbang had ordered that both valuable and ordinary articles should be sold at the same price. 'This induced the great Gorukhnāth when on his travels to take up his abode for a time at Harbongpur, although his teacher, Muchhander, counselled retreat. Not many days after their arrival a murderer was to be executed but escaped, whereupon the rāja, in a rage, ordered that the two largest men in the crowd should be hung in the place of the criminal. The two largest men happened to be Gorukhnāth and Muchhandernāth; who took counsel together, and, when brought to the gallows, quarrelled for precedence. The rāja, struck with the strangeness of this proceeding, inquired the cause, and was informed by Muchhander that they had ascertained from books and learned paṇḍits that whoever should first be hanged that day would go immediately to Paradise. "If that be the cause," said the rāja, "the fate is too good for either of you. I'll hang first, if you please," and he was hanged at his own request. The devotees, shocked at the atrocities which took place in Harbongpur after his death, reduced it to ruins.'

Important monasteries and shrines of the Gorakhnāthīs are situated in Gorakhpur, Tulsipur and Benares. Those at the two former places are in a flourishing condition; but the Kānphaṭas of Benares seem to be losing ground.

Three places in Benares are connected with the name of the Gorakhnāthīs; the famous Lāṭh of Bhāiroṁ, the temple of Kāl Bhāiroṁ and Gorakhnāth kā Ṭilla.

At the Staff, or Lāṭh, of Bhāiroṁ, Kānphaṭas used to officiate as priests of Śiva. The Lāṭh is no longer in the possession of the Yogīs, having been sold about sixty years ago. The report is that the mahant kept a *mālin* (a woman of the gardener caste) and was addicted to gambling. Through his loss of character, and debt, he had finally to dispose of the shrine. Worship at the place is now in the hands of a widow who does not belong to the sect. The Lāṭh is situated in the Adampura ward in the northern part of the city. It consists of a huge, copper-covered stone liṅga, painted red. It is about eight feet high and about two and one half feet in diameter, is situated on a large, high, stone platform and is surrounded by a wall. Eight small platforms surround the liṅga. To the south of the main platform is a tank. On the west of the Lāṭh is a small, red bull. The copper-covered shaft which constitutes the liṅga is the portion of a broken Aśokan pillar which remains above ground. The pillar was thrown down during the riot of 1809.[1] This liṅga is visited by Yogīs, especially at the *Puran Māsa* of *Badan Śudi.*

The temple of Kāl Bhāiroṁ in the city is an important place of meeting for Yogīs, and is a famous shrine.

The third place of interest is the old Gorakhnāth kā Ṭilla, situated near the municipal gardens in the city. This place was built by Rāja Mān of Jodhpur,[2] and was well endowed. But, along with the Lāṭh of Bhāiroṁ, the endowments were nearly all lost through gambling and profligacy, and there now belong to it but a few inferior Yogīs, some married. The pūjārī in 1924 was Bastināth. The whole establishment, which is on a hill, or elevation, fully one story high, is reached by a flight of steps and is surrounded by rooms on all four sides. Below the level of the platform on two sides are houses or rooms. The principal temple faces east. The platform is made of stone slabs.

The temple, with its veranda, is built of red sandstone. In the room of the veranda there is a bell. In the temple veranda, which is surmounted by a dome, octagonal in shape, is a bell. And on each side of the veranda are four fluted pillars. The two next to the temple doors are painted white. The temple itself is square with a composite pyramidal roof surmounted by a trident. On the wall on both sides of the door are pictures, that on the left being of a woman, that on the right of Śiva as a Yogī, with the big ear-rings. Over the door are an image of Ganeśa and tridents painted red. In the inset of the wall on each side of the door is a picture of Bhāiroṁ, that on the left being of White Bhāiroṁ, that on the right of Black Bhāiroṁ. Both have large ear-rings. Inside of

---

[1] Smith, *ERE*, vol. II, p. 466; Crooke, *ERE*, vol. VI, p. 701; Nevill, *Benares*, p. 253; Wilkins, *Modern Hinduism*, p. 94; Mukerji, *Aśoka*, p. 85.

[2] c. 1748 or 1803 (?). Or by Rāja Mān Sinh, of Gwālior, who died in 1518?

the temple, on the platform, are ten conch shells of various sizes, besides the caran of Jālandharnāth. Behind this is a picture of Kālī. The platform in the temple is three feet high. There are also on the platform a fan of peacock feathers and a red cushion with white beads upon it. In front of the platform are two tall horns of bronze and a small brass stand supporting brass bells, small stone liṅgas and śālagrāmas, and a stone from the Narbada with a caran painted upon it. A peacock-feather fan is found in a niche in the wall on the left, and a lamp similarly on the right. There is also a lamp on a tall, wooden stand.

Built against the temple on the north side is a small shrine containing the yoni-liṅga. It is about four feet high, including the spire. On the south side is a somewhat larger shrine, about ten feet high, dedicated to Śiva.

Behind the temple are quarters in which a single gṛhasta Yogī lives. South of the temple is the well, and beyond that, the kitchen. In the row of rooms to the north of the temple is the dhūnī, under a veranda.

On the platform of the temple, at the south-east, close to the temple is a *sthān* of Bhāiroṁ with trisules, and a small image in relief on a stone slab, painted red.

On the front, or eastern border of the platform are four small shrines of red sandstone. The one at the south-east corner is a samādh containing the yoni-liṅga. A bell is hung in the roof. The next shrine contains the caran of Gorakhnāth. There is a bell in the roof. In the third is a bull and a yoni-liṅga. There is a bell in the roof. Fourth, in the north-east corner, is a samādh containing a yoni-liṅga and a black liṅga on a stone slab with a snake over it. The roofs of the corner shrines are dome-shaped, of the other two, pyramid-shaped.

North-east of the principal temple, but down a flight of steps, is a temple of Mahādeo. It has a flat roof.

There is a samādh in the street outside the boundaries of the monastery.

The whole elevated area is faced with stone slabs and is substantial.

The number of Yogīs in the establishments in Benares is decreasing. Formerly they were powerful and respected. In

1884, they numbered 159, of whom 63 were women.[1] They had two *akhāṛās*, one at Gorakhnāth kā Ṭilla (in Benares), and one at Kāl Bhāiroṁ.[2] They owned the Kāl Bhāiroṁ temple also. Their present low estate is due to disintegrating conditions which were allowed to creep in amongst them.[3]

The most important centre of the Kānphaṭas in the United Provinces is at GORAKHPUR,[4] a city named after the shrine of Gorakhnāth.[5] It was to this place, as they say, in the *Tretā* age, that Gorakhnāth came from the Panjab.[6]

The shrine is old. The first temple is said to have been built there in the Tretā age and it was dedicated to Śiva.[7] Tradition has it that Gorakhnāth found there an old shrine of Gorakṣa, a deity of great renown in Nepāl, and made it famous.[8] Popular report puts the founding of the city by Gorakhnāth in A.D. 1400. It is also said that when Gorakhnāth came to this place he found only a tank, *Mānsorāwar*, in a jungle with fine trees all about it. He remained there a long time. It is possible that both the name and the fame of Gorakhnāth may be traced to this place.

It is claimed by some that Gorakhnāth was buried in Gorakhpur.[9] Others say that he was buried in the Panjab. Still others insist that he never died, but that he is now living with Siddhas and Nāthas on Mount Kāilāsa.

The original shrine was converted into a mosque by Ala-ud-Din (1296–1316). Then a shrine was built in a nearby place by Gorakhnāthīs. Aurangzeb (1659–1707) converted this also into a mosque. Afterwards, on the present site, a

---

[1] Fisher and Hewett, *Statistical, Descriptive and Historical Account of the North-Western Provinces of India*, vol. XIV, Pt. I (*Benares*), p. 56.

[2] Nevill, *District Gazetteer, Benares*, p. 93.

[3] Information based upon a letter from the Tahsīldār of Benares, dated November 25, 1924.

[4] *Wi*, p. 215; Nevill, *District Gazetteer, Gorakhpur*, p. 239; *FORL*, p. 347.

[5] Compare, *Imperial Gazetteer*, vol. XII, p. 342.

[6] *Wi*, p. 215. [7] *BIC*, vol. II, p. 1,235.

[8] Alexander, *Statistical, Descriptive and Historical Account of the North-West Provinces of India, Gorakhpur*, p. 371.

[9] Tessitori, *ERE*, vol. XII, p. 835.

third shrine was built by Buddhnāth.[1] According to tradition, Gorakhnāth himself gave the specifications. The present buildings were erected about A.D. 1800. The shrine has recently been enlarged. In the summer of 1924, the roof of the shrine was raised. Photographs show it both as it appeared before the alterations, and as it is today.

The present site occupies an area of about five acres. There are, besides the grounds containing the shrine, two gardens and a cattle-shed (*gāo-śāla*). The shrine is situated west of the city of Gorakhpur, in Purāṇa Gorakhpur, north of the railway.

The place of chief interest at this holy site is the shrine of Gorakhnāth. This is a rectangular building with a veranda all around it. The parapet, both around the veranda and around the flat roof (before the alterations were made) of the main structure, is finished in open work. The veranda supports are rounded, double pillars with rounded arches, scalloped. The whole building is whitewashed and is decorated in colours. The plinth, which rises about two feet above the ground, has a front of fifty-one and one-half feet and a depth of thirty-eight feet. The veranda is about eight and one-half feet wide. The shrine faces east. It is not a tomb. It contains the gaddi of Gorakhnāth on which rests his caran. This is covered with flowers daily. Beside the gaddi are peacock-feathered staves wound with red and white cloth, and hand bells. There is generally a group of *Ṭhākurs* at the right of the gaddi. The lamp at the right has been burning for a long time, they say since Gorakhnāth's day. There is no liṅga in the shrine. In the veranda are the usual temple bells.

On the west face of the shrine is an image of Kālī.

In front of the shrine and at the right of the door is a liṅga, painted red. Stuck up in a line on each side of this and clustered around it are tridents, the arms of Bhāiroṁ, whose station, as guardian of the shrine, is here. The tridents are painted red. Many tridents are buried beneath the platform. They were offerings to Bhāiroṁ. Behind this

---

[1] *Wi*, p. 215.

armoury of tridents is the block of wood where goats are sacrificed.

Worship is conducted at the shrine three times a day. During the midday worship, to the beating of drums and the ringing of the temple bells, the pūjārī circumambulates the shrine, walking in the veranda, with his right side towards the inner shrine. He then opens the door and the worship is completed before the caran.

There is a large number of buildings in the enclosure that contains the shrine of Gorakhnāth. They are all in good repair, attesting the prosperity of the monastery. North of the shrine is a temple of Mahādeo. Directly east of this is a thatched shed housing the dhūnī of Gorakhnāth. East of this is a temple of Paśupati containing a four-faced liṅga; and still further east is a temple of Hanumān; and then a large pipal tree with a platform built around it. North-east of the main enclosure is a temple of Haṭh Devī, a śakti shrine, in front of which, under a tree, is a platform where the hair of the first shaving ceremony of infants is offered.

Directly in front of the shrine of Gorakhnāth is a covered samādh with a liṅga in it; and in front of this a platform, having three liṅgas and a covered liṅga, all samādhs. Still further east is a square building, with coloured pictures on its walls, containing three samādhs, each having a liṅga. The pictures on the walls are of both Śaivite and Vaiṣṇavite significance; Kṛṣṇa and the gopīs and the hooded serpent are represented.

At the south-east corner of the main shrine is a stone platform, or throne, where mahants are 'made'; and where they sit in state once a year, at the time of the Ḍasehra Festival, to receive offerings.

Further to the south-east of the shrine in another samādh, with a liṅga[1] in it; still further east is a temple to Mahādeo; then comes a decorated building containing a samādh; and beyond this, eastward, the samādh of Gambīrnāth.

South of the shrine, on the southern boundary of the area, is the monastery.

Behind the shrine, in the south-west corner of the enclosure,

[1] As in each instance above this is the usual yoni-liṅga.

is the stable. In the rear of the shrine is another samādh; and the whole area north-west of the shrine is taken up with samādhs, some of which are of masonry work, four being covered, but most of which are rounded mounds of earth covered with a plaster of cow-dung and clay.

Just outside of the grounds, to the south-east, is a huge, recumbent figure of Bhīmsen.

West of the compound which encloses the shrine of Gorakhnāth is a large garden with a residence in it. There is also on the south side of the compound a garden with a resident in it. During the litigation, which began in the summer of 1924, concerning the succession to the gaddi these residences were occupied by rival claimants to the pīr-ship.

Worship is performed on some of the samādhs in the evening, when lamps are lighted and incense is burnt.

The monastery is important, since its establishment is traced back to Gorakhnāth. Pāṅgārkar says that Gorakhnāth placed his guru *bhāi*, a fellow teacher, in charge of Gorakhpur.[1] There are connected with the establishment about one hundred Yogīs and a few Āughars. This is the headquarters of the sect in the United Provinces. The mahant is chosen by vote after the nomination of the previous pīr has been announced.

At present all the residents of the monastery are celibates. Martin reported that several teachers living in the establishment were married and that they lived there with their families. In his day, the prayers of the mahants were considered especially efficient in restoring children to health. This belief still prevails. The Yogīs now use a large nummulite, obtained at Nagar Ṭhaṭha, in Sind, to insure easy delivery to women. The 'white stones' are washed in water and the liquid is then given to the women to drink.[2] Martin reported that inmates of the monastery acted as sages for a few Śūdras in the worship of Śiva.

The endowment of the establishment at Gorakhpur consists

---

[1] *Śrī Jñāneśvaramahārāja Carita*, p. 60.

[2] The mahant, in 1924, presented the author with a 'white stone,' or nummulite, which he had used for this purpose.

of eight villages together with parts of others. Their grounds and their villages are held rent-free.

There is still another important establishment of the Gorakhnāthīs in the United Provinces.

The Devī Pātan temple, and the monastery adjoining it, both under the control of the Kānphaṭa Yogīs, are situated on a small hill close to the town of TULSIPUR, in the Balrāmpur State. It is not far from the foothills of the Himālayas and the borders of Nepāl.

The site of the temple of Devī Pātan is one of the fifty-one[1] *pīṭhas*, or places celebrated as spots on which the dismembered limbs of Durgā (Sati) were scattered.[2] When Viṣṇu cut her to pieces, and her dismembered body was strewn over the world, as Śiva, distracted, carried her body about, her right hand fell at this place and sank into the ground. The word, Pātan, refers to this event, for the word is derived from the Sanskrit *pāt*, from the root *pat*, meaning to fall, to sink. Pātāla, from the same derivation, is the name of the regions under the earth, the lower regions. The word also means a hole in the earth. Pātāla is the abode of the Nāgas or dragons. The Devī Pātan is also called Pātaleśvarī. Another legend makes this the place where Sītā disappeared into the earth. After Rāma had rescued her from Rāvaṇa, she was accused of unfaithfulness. Her purity and fidelity were attested by the

---

[1] Some of the *pīthās* are as follows (see Sen's *Saṭi*, pp. 104, 105):
Devī Pātan, where her right hand fell.
Valley of Jawālamukhi, where her tongue fell.
Sugandha in South Bengal, her nose fell.
Labhpur, her lips fell.
Janasthāna in the Deccan, her cheeks fell.
Hiṅg Lāj in the West, her forehead (crown of her head) fell.
Benares, her ear drops fell.
Ujjāin, her elbow fell.
Kāmākhyā in Assam, her organs of generation fell.
Calcutta (Kālighāt), her great toe (left foot) fell.
Faljur (Jaintia Parganas), her left leg fell.
Somewhere in 'Sylhet (or Kashmir?)' her neck fell.
Ukule Ghāt (or Kālighāt?), her fingers fell.

[2] For the story read *Sati, A Mythical Story*, etc., (1916) by C. D. Sen. There are many accounts of this event in the literature of India. More exactly the members were scattered over Assam and Bengal.

ordeal of fire. She then returned to Ayodhya with Rāma. Later, at the clamour of the crowd, Rāma sent her into exile under the old accusation. There, in the hermitage of Vālmiki, she bore two sons to Rāma. They grew up in the forest and there learned the *Rāmāyaṇa*, the epic of Rāma's deeds, which Vālmiki had composed. Years after he had exiled Sītā, Rāma performed the great horse sacrifice. During the ceremonies, hermit youths recited this poem, over a period of twenty-five days, in the presence of Rāma and his court. At last Rāma recognized the youths as his sons. He, therefore, sent for Sītā, asking her to re-affirm her innocence and to return to the palace. She came before the great assembly, where with clasped hands, bending low her face, and speaking in a voice choked with sobs, she said: 'As I, even in mind, have never thought of any other than Rāma, so may Mādhavī, the Goddess of the Earth, grant me a hiding place.' Thereupon, 'suddenly cleaving the earth, a divine throne of marvellous beauty rose up, borne by resplendent dragons on their heads; and, seated on it, the Goddess of the Earth, raising Sītā with her arm, said to her, "Welcome to thee!" and placed her by her side. And as the queen, seated on her throne, descended to Rasātala, a continuous shower of flowers fell down from heaven on her head.'[1]

The hillock on which the temple stands is a very ancient religious site, undoubtedly one of the oldest seats of Śāivite worship in northern India.[2] The oldest cycle of legends referring to the place relate to characters of the *Mahābhārata*, especially to Karna. A shrine to 'Rāja Karan' still exists on the slope of the hill. Another group of legends refers to the dishonouring of Devī at the hands of a rāja of the Panjab. After her body had been dismembered, her right hand fell at this spot and sank into the ground. In this story there is, evidently, a confusion of the older story, about the dis-

---

[1] Quoted in Griffith, *The Rāmāyāna of Valmīki*, vol. V, p. 326, from E. B. Cowell in *Academy*, No. 43, but using the word *Rasātala* (Receptacle of the Waters) for Hades. The word rendered 'dragon' is 'nāga.' It may be of interest to note that Janaka, father of Sītā, is spoken of as a master Yogī and as a man intimately connected with the origin of Yoga. See *Bhakta Mālā*.

[2] See *Gazetteer of Oudh*, 1877, pp. 367–70.

membering of the Devī's body, and later elements, possibly Musalmān. A temple was erected here by Ratannāth, a disciple third in descent from Gorakhnāth. The site is still under the authority of the monastery Ratannāth at Sawārikot in the Nepalese Hills.

In the time of Aurangzeb, or in the fifteenth century as some say, the temple was despoiled by a Musalmān officer. The avenging of the death of this soldier is the basis of the legend explaining the practice of spilling the blood of suckling pigs on the grave of a Musalmān, near the site of the temple of Devī Pātan. It is said that two temple guards, Sumer Dhar and Mūl Cand, brought the despoiler to his death.

The site of the temple is extensive, and the elevation on which it stands was once occupied by a fort. Tradition connects this with the name of Rāja Karan, Karna of the *Mahābhārata*. There are here also an ancient temple and a very old well.

The two places of interest, both of which are objects of attention at the annual fair, or mela, held toward the end of the spring season, are the temple of Devī Pātan, with its monastery, and the grave of the Musalmān referred to above.

The present temple, is, in a general way, built around the older building said to have been erected by Ratannāth. And on a block of red sandstone enclosed in the present edifice is an inscription containing the name of Gorakhnāth.[1]

The core of the temple is of red sandstone. It is probably a portion of the older temple. It may be seen from the doorway, and at various places in the shrine. But the present temple which is built around the older one is white. The spire is of white marble, surmounted by a gilded umbrella, The temple faces east. It is rectangular in shape, and the central shrine is surrounded by a wide veranda. In front of the temple is a broad platform of stone. The interior is dark, there being no windows and only one door, which is small and made of brass. Within is an image of Devī, painted red, before which offerings, including the heads of sacrificed goats, are made.

---

[1] See Nevill, *District Gazetteer, Gonda*, subject 'Devi Patan.'

In the west face of the temple is an image of Bāl Devī, the goddess who grants children. Here the hair of the first shaving of a child's head is offered. And it was here that, in 1924, the young prince of Balrāmpur was brought. Before the goddess, his head was shaved, and the hair was then offered to her. On the walls about the image, as in similar shrines and in other places generally, small figures resembling children are drawn in black. These pictures are drawn, ceremonially, by women desiring children; or, in cases where all of a mother's children are girls, in the hope that she may obtain a son. Some of the figures are ornate.

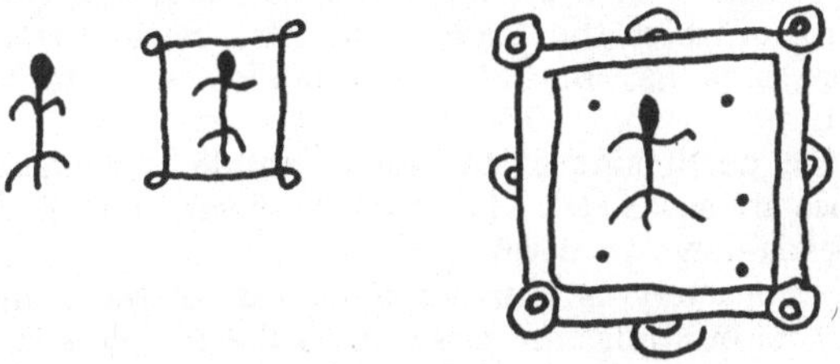

In the veranda on either side of the door of the temple are the large kettle drums which are used in the daily worship. Several large bells are hung in the veranda.

In front of the temple, on the stone platform, is the block where goats are sacrificed;[1] and a pit where a *hom*, or fire, is kept burning on special occasions. On the edge of this platform are two large, stone lions, facing the temple. At the left, but behind these, is a long rack on which are hung temple bells, six in number, some of considerable age. Behind the bells, to the east, is a shed used for rest and as an eating place. At the north-east corner is a spot sacred to Nāgnāth. On it are a small image of a hooded serpent, a fragment only, and some other bits of broken images. Worship is conducted here, especially at the Nāgpañcamī festival.

Close to the temple on the east and south, and scattered

[1] Knowles, *Gospel in Gonda*, p. 116, says that the priests who sacrifice the goats and buffaloes are Yogīs of *Ṭhāru* origin. Ṭhārus are a jungle people living in the forests on the borders of Nepāl. They are particularly clever in using the cleaver with which the heads of animals for sacrifice are severed at a single stroke.

over the site at various distances, are numerous samādhs or tombs of Yogīs. Some are old and out of repair. Over most of these graves are masonry platforms surmounted by the yoni-liṅga symbol. These very numerous graves attest the age and importance of the monastery.

On the east side of the temple, beyond the shed, is a huge pipal tree with a platform around it. On its south side is a small, raised platform sacred to Kāl Bhāiroṁ, with a large number of tridents (*triśul*) beside it. Close by this shrine is the small, domed structure called Rāja Karan's building, and containing an image of that ancient hero.

Still further east is a temple of Śītal Mātā, the goddess of smallpox, of which the Yogīs are pūjārīs. Beyond this temple are more samādhs. Beyond this is an old temple to Mahādeo or Śiva.

On the north side of the main temple is a stake where buffaloes are sacrificed. Towards the north, a long flight of steps leads down to an ancient tank.

The monastery is situated north-east of the temple, and some of its buildings are close up to the temple site. There are between thirty-five and forty Yogīs in residence as a usual thing. The dhūnī, or Yogī's fire, is housed north-east of the temple, in a portion of the monastery. The Government Forest Department makes an annual grant of 250 wagon-loads of wood for this dhūnī.

South of the temple site a road leads through a bazaar to the grave of the Musalmān.[1] In front of the tomb, under a tree, is an oval stone on which pilgrims dash out the brains of suckling pigs and then carry the bleeding animals into the tomb to let the blood drip on the Musalmān's grave. The pigs for this purpose are purchased in the bazaar near the tomb. Hindus of caste, even Brāhmans, it is said, perform this rite.

Near the tomb is a platform in which a broken stone is set erect. This is the place of Hulikā Devī, the goddess of the Holi. The pujārīs of the goddess are Yogīs. In fact, in all the places of worship round about the temple of Devī Pātan, as well as in the temple itself, the pūjārīs are Gorakhnāthīs.

There are samādhs in this neighbourhood also.

---

[1] His name was Mirza.

There is an approach to the main temple from the east by a low flight of steps.

Great interest at Devī Pātan centers around the annual mela, or religious fair, which occurs early in April. Then the desecration of the tomb of the Musalmān is carried on with feverish haste by many people. Suckling pigs are purchased, carried to the tank at the north of the temple, and dipped three times in the water. The worshipper then receives a ṭīkā or mark, from a priest, and carries the pig to the round stone in front of the tomb, going around the site of the temple, not crossing the temple area. At the round stone the act described above is performed, and the bleeding pig is carried into the tomb. However, the mela is not the only occasion when pigs are thus sacrificed, for it is a regular practice at the tomb.

The mela is an occasion of special worship at the temple. The sides of the stairway on the east are lined with stalls in which are sold the sweets and flowers which make up the simple offerings to Devī. Besides these, offerings of cocoanuts goats and buffaloes are made. It was reported that in 1871, 20 buffaloes, 250 goats and 250 pigs were sacrificed daily during the fair.[1]

Across the small stream to the west of the temple site is the large bazaar where horses and other animals are brought for sale. This fair is especially noted for the Nepalese ponies that are brought to the market. On the east of the temple hill is laid out a large, temporary bazaar where wares of all kinds, from beads and trinkets to pots and cloth, are sold. The usual holiday group of merry-go-rounds, 'ferris' wheels, snake-charmers, and other entertainers is found at the fair.

The rājas of Balrāmpur are patrons of the fair and of the temple. The State levies a tax on all sales in both bazaars. As many as 75,000, even 100,000, attend the fair.[2]

The annual fair at Devī Pātan opens with the arrival of the pīr, or abbot, from the monastery of the Kānphaṭa Yogīs

---

[1] *Gazetteer of Oudh*, vol. I, p. 370. Knowles, *Gospel in Gonda*, p. 173, estimated that 22,000 animals were sacrificed there in 1886. 'It was calculated that one animal a minute was sacrificed from sunrise to sunset every day for a week.'

[2] Nevill, *District Gazetteer, Gonda*, p. 193; *Gazetteer of Oudh*, vol. I, p. 370.

at Sawārikot, or Dāṅg Cangra, in Nepāl. This place is sixty miles from the temple.[1] At the Ratannāth monastery each year a mahant, or pīr, is chosen, who with the pīr chosen the previous year, goes in procession in Devī Pātan. The former goes in front, carrying a stone liṅga, said to contain the spirit of Gorakhnāth. Attendants carry a large, red umbrella, with a handle covered with sheet-silver, silver maces, tridents with flags, a kettle-drum covered with a red cloth, and yak-tail fans. A long peculiarly-shaped horn is also carried in the procession. The pīr stops from time to time to receive the offerings that the crowd have to make. At such times the stone liṅga is garlanded again and again. All along the way the people cast offerings of all sorts in their path, and the pīrs are under a constant bombardment of sweets. It is considered fortunate to secure bits of the offerings that have been made. Consequently there is a great scramble for the offerings, as well as to make them. Chickens, sweets, flowers and other articles are 'presented,' and then carried away as possessing special sanctity and magic powers, by those who have brought them.

On the outskirts of Tulsipur, about a mile from the temple, the procession is met, in the early morning of the first day of the mela, by a company of soldiers and a military band belonging to the State of Balrāmpur, and a little farther on by a company of village watchmen, in uniform. Besides the escort, a large crowd follows the visiting pīrs.

At the foot of the steps leading to the temple from the east, the visitors are met by the local mahant, or abbot, of Devī Pātan, and the pīrs and their attendants are conducted to the temple and are seated on the platform on its eastern side. Their arrival is greeted with the blowing of horns, the ringing of bells and the beating of drums. The visiting company remains four days. Each evening of their stay an elaborate ceremony is performed when prasād, food offered to the pīrs, is distributed. This exercise is preceded by the regular beating of drums and the ringing of bells for about half an hour. During this ceremony, the two pīrs sit opposite to each other, on the eastern platform, the

[1] These bits of information are based upon local statements.

recently appointed one having charge of the stone liṅga from Sawārikot. The umbrella, the maces, the tridents and the horn are in use. The constantly changing crowd casts a continuous shower of sweets on the carpet where the pīrs and attendants are sitting. The chief pīr wears a two-handled knife in his girdle (a symbol of distinction) and carries a carved bamboo staff in his hand. All about the temple are Kori-Camārs playing musical instruments (*saraṅgī*) and beating drums. These are temple attendants. There are many men about, dressed as women, who carry trays and beg.

In the veranda of the temple, worshippers make the circuit of the shrine, going with their right hand next the temple. Men and women, in the excitement of the crowd, become 'possessed' by the Devī, called Bhagavatī, and dance, clap their hands and 'prophesy' what should be offered to the goddess. Whatever is thus suggested is presented to her.

But the temple is not without worshippers at other times.

Worship is carried on with great regularity on the temple site. Very early in the morning and again in the evening a simple service is held when a visit is paid to each samādh in the place. In the morning, after bathing, the pūjārī offers Ganges water, sandalwood, rice, bel leaves, flowers and milk at each grave. He may add sweets and burn incense. In the evening milk is offered, with incense and sweets, and a lamp is lighted.

In connection with the noon-time worship of Bhāiroṁ, the guardian of the temple, the pūjārī, goes around the platform and shrine of the god, his right hand towards it. Then after pouring out water, he offers to the god a plate heaped with rice, afterwards throwing the food to dogs. (Bhāiroṁ is accompanied by a black dog).

The evening worship and prasād at the temple is preceded by the regular beating of the kettle-drums and the ringing of the temple bells for about half an hour. The temple doors are then thrown open and the offerings are made.

The monastery at Devī Pātan has been famous for its adepts in the Haṭha Yoga. It owns, besides its own site, nine villages which are tax-free. It has a considerable income from offerings. The mahant, in 1924, was Harināth of the Bāirāg Panth to which the Ratannāth pīrs belong.

CHAPTER SIX

SACRED PLACES (*Concluded*)

TURNING now to the north-west, the temple of AMARNĀTH, in Kashmīr, is to be noted. Yogīs visit the shrine of their master which is situated in a cave. Formerly all danced before Śiva, here, naked. Women now wear a single garment. Śiva is here represented by a liṅga which is a block of ice.

Besides the important monastery at Gorakh Ṭilla, there are a good many places in the Panjab connected with the Gorakhnāthīs. GORAKHṢETRA, or Gorkhatṛi, in Peshāwar was once a haunt of Kānphaṭa Yogīs and is mentioned by Bāber and Abūl Fazal. Traditionally this is the place where Gorakhnāth lived in the *Satya Yuga*.[1] In the north-west the chief saint of the Kānphaṭas is Ratannāth of Peshāwar. These Yogīs do not wear the rings in their ears because they claim to wear them in their hearts.

There are Yogī shrines at Kohāt, Jalālābād and Kābul.

SIĀLKOT is famous as the home of Puran Bhagat, the well-known disciple of Gorakhnāth. The well where Puran was found by that Yogī is situated two miles north of the Cantonment.[2] A legend connected with the place relates how a Khatrānī woman, while bathing in the Āik river, was wooed by Bāsak Nāg (the King of Serpents), and bore a son, Śālavahan, who rose to be a man of great power and wealth, and who, through the assistance of the serpent (Nāg) became a king. To Śālavahan were born two sons who became Yogīs, the older of whom was Puran Bhagat, on whose account the well is still

[1] *Martin*, vol. II, p. 484; *BHCS*, p. 403.

[2] See *Sialkot Gazetteer*, 1904. Also *Archæological Report*, vol. II, pp. 21, 22; vol. XIV, pp. 44–47. The whole story is given in chap. nine.

famous. The well is noted for its very cold water and its healing qualities. Hindu women go there to bathe, in order to be cured of barrenness; especially on Sunday and on the new moon, do they come from all parts of the Panjab for this purpose.[1]

In Gūgā's temple at SULTĀNPUR, which belongs to the Chamārs, Gūgā and his *wazīr* are mounted on horses, Gogrī on a mare, but Narsiṁh, Kāila Bīr and Gorakhnāth are on foot.[2]

At BATRA there is a comparatively new shrine to Gūgā, erected by one who had obtained a son in his old age. Beside it is a shrine to Gorakhnāth, facing east.

There is a shrine of Birāg Lok near PALAMPUR with a legend connected with Gorakhnāth. The founder of the shrine, when a boy, once, while herding cattle, met a gosāin (said to be Gorakhnāth himself) who told him never to disclose the fact of their friendship, else he would no longer remain in his palace. Keeping the secret, however, made him ill, and so, at last he told his parents about the gosāin. They gave him *sattu* for the holy man. But, when about to cook it, the boy complained that he had no water, whereupon the gosāin touched the ground with his *gaja* (iron staff) and a spring appeared, which still exists. The gosāin did not eat the food, saying that his hunger was satisfied by its savour. The boy then caught the holy man by the arm, upon which the latter struck him with his hand and turned him into stone. A few days later a Bhaṭ Brāhman became possessed and saw all that had occurred. Then a temple was erected and the spot called Birāg (Gosāin) Lok (corrupted from '*ālop*,' 'disappearance') As Birāg Lok had been a herdsman, he became peculiarly the guru of cattle and now fulfils vows made regarding cattle. A fair is held at the shrine on Har the third. He-goats and corn are offered. An image of Gorakhnāth was placed in the temple in Sikh times.[3] This is a Siddh temple. There are

---

[1] Based on a report by A. H. Daula (June 22, 1925) which he made after hearing Ganga Ram Parshad, B.A., LL.B., President of the Ārya Samāj of Siālkot, read from an account in Hindi. Forwarded to the author by Dr. H. D. Griswold.

[2] *RTCP*, vol. I, p. 183.

[3] *IA*, 1903, p. 378 and note; *RTCP*, vol. I, p. 246.

in it three images—of Gūgā, of Gorgī and of Guru Gorakhnāth—each about three feet high and mounted.[1]

The Āi-panth monastery at the Takṣala Gate in LAHORE is a rambling place. It contains a few samādhs and a temple to Śiva. In front of this temple is a large, rounded slab of stone painted black, which contains an image of Kāl Bhāiroṁ, painted black, with a large trident. The mahant of this place is the pūjārī of the temple. He was the only Yogī present at the time of the author's visit (December 10, 1924). The compound of the monastery is used as a sort of *sārāī* (caravanserai). The Yogī's ear-rings were of crystal.

At AMRITSAR, at the temple of Bhāiroṁ, at Durgiāna, there is an image of Bhāiroṁ and a large cubical platform, about five feet high, painted red, with a cloth over it, in which is a niche and a lamp. Beside this there is a temple of Śiva. It is a place of meeting for the group known as the twelve Panths. It was here that the author had his audience with the pīr of Ṭilla.

Near LĀDWA, in the Ambāla district, there are places where two shrines are found close by each other, the one on the right and the other on the left of that of Gūgā, the one on the left being dedicated to Gorakhṇāth. The explanation of this is that Gūgā was the disciple[2] of Gorakhnāth.[3]

At BOHAR, in Rohtak, there is a fine block of buildings which belongs to Yogīs who follow Mastnāth.[4] An annual fair of a disreputable character is held there.[5] In the *Tārīkḥ-i-Sher Shāhi* (date about 1579) there is mention of Bālnāth of the Yogīs near the fort of Rohtas.

There is, at KIRĀNA, a famous monastery with a large landed endowment. The residents are Āughars, and their chief is called pīr. They wear an ochre-coloured turban over which is placed a network of black thread covered with gold. The pīr, when once elected, may never again descend

---

[1] *RTCP*, vol. I, p. 188.

[2] See chap. nine.

[3] *IA*, vol. XXVI (1897), p. 84, referring to Ibbetson's *Karnāl Settlement Report*.

[4] Elliot, *History of India*, etc., vol. IV, p. 301.

[5] *Census Report, Panjab*, 1891, p. 116.

the hill on which the establishment is situated.[1] This monastery was moved from Ṭilla under circumstances related below.

The most famous establishment of the Kānphaṭas in the Panjab, and in fact in all India, is at GORAKH ṬILLA.[2]

Ṭilla, or Gorakh Ṭilla,[3] is situated about twenty-five miles north-west of Jhelum, on the highest point of an isolated line of hills in the Salt Range, at an elevation of 3,242 feet. The hill is rugged and difficult to ascend. There is a steep, almost perpendicular, cliff on one side of it. This is accounted for by the following legend. Lakṣmannāth, the Jogī of Ṭilla, was once visited by Siddhvacārnāth (Bhartṛhari), and was unable at the moment to provide food for his guest. So Bhartṛhari carried off part of the hill to Kirāna Bar, threw it down, and founded a new monastery. This explains the steep ascent at Ṭilla.[4] The view from the monastery is a very fine one. In ordinary weather the snows of the Himālayas make a splendid sight. Nearby and below are the remains of decaying hills; and the course of the Jhelum is plainly seen.

The old buildings at Ṭilla were destroyed by Shah Durrani in 1748, and the establishment was rebuilt by Rāja Mān (of Jodhpur?)

Ṭilla is one of the oldest religious sites in northern India,[5] and its use for religious purposes antedates by millenniums the coming of Gorakhnāth.[6] Tradition affirms that Gorakhnāth settled there in the *Tretā Yuga*, after Rāmcandra, and adopted Bālnāth as his disciple.[7] The place was once known as Ṭilla Bālnāth, a name derived from a temple on the summit dedicated to the sun as Bālnāth.[8] It was here that

---

[1] *Census Report, Panjab*, 1891, p. 116.

[2] A good picture of Ṭilla is to be found in *OMAS*, opposite p. 266. On Ṭilla see *Census Report, Panjab*, 1891, pp. 115 ff; *OMAS*, pp. 264 ff.

[3] Also known as Jogī Ṭilla, Ṭilla Gorakhnāth.

[4] *Census Report, Panjab*, 1891, p. 117.

[5] *Jhelum District Gazetteer*, 1904, p. 34.

[6] *Census Report, Panjab*, 1891, p. 117.

[7] *RTCP*, vol. I, p. 389.

[8] *Ain-i-Akbari*, vol. II, p. 315, note 1. Cunningham (*Ancient Geography of India*, p. 164) considered this name, Bālnāth, older than the time of Alexander; but this may be doubted.

Bālnāth underwent his penance, and it was from him that Bhartṛhari learned the practice of austerities. The samādh of Bhartṛhari is at Ṭilla[1] and the cave there is named after him. The monastery is now in charge of the Lakṣman, or Daryā, or Hethnāth panth of the sect, and they have disciples beyond the Afghan frontier.

It is undoubtedly true that Gorakh Ṭilla, or Jogī Ṭilla, was one of the first centres of the Kānphaṭa Yogīs. Panjab legends make repeated reference to the place as one of the stations to which Gorakhnāth often retired.[2] In the story of the marriage of Vālmīk's daughter reference is made to Ṭilla. 'In the pond where a Brāhman at the Kumbh Mela was cured of leprosy, Gorakhnāth will bathe, who will make his temple on Ṭilla.'[3] From a remote period all other centres of the Kānphaṭas in the Panjab have been under Ṭilla. At Gorakhpur, Yogīs stated that Ṭilla is now the chief seat of the sect. The pīr of Ṭilla is the head of all the Gorakhnāthīs. (But the committee of the Twelve Panths seem to have some superior supervisory power. See chapter two.)

The establishment is situated on the top of the hill and is enclosed by a wall. One of the principal temples in the main enclosure is to Hanumān. The elevated portion to the west, within the enclosed wall, contains samādhs in three corners and a temple of Śiva to the east of the centre of the platform. In front of this and at the north is the caran of Lakṣman. By itself, in the platform, north-west of the temple, is a large trident. North of the temple is a small shrine of Bhāiroṁ, and just to the east of this is an old tree under which is a niche marking the place where Gorakhnāth used to sit. They say that Ṭilla will stand as long as this tree lives. On the lower level to the east, within the walls, are the storerooms and the residence of the mahant and some other Yogīs. Attached to the main enclosure is a cow shed, and to the south-west of it are a large tank and some very old samādhs, mostly in ruins. There is a great number of

---

[1] *Jhelum Gazetteer*, 1904, p. 35.

[2] *E.g.*, *Temple*, Nos. 13, 20; vol. II, pp. 275, 375, 429, 549, 551, 554, 555, 557, 559, 566; *Synn*, p. 51.

[3] *IA*, 1907, pp. 23, 24.

samādhs about. A stone slab at this place marks the spot where Rāñjha used to sit and where he was initiated after he was driven away from the home of Hīr. Gorakhnāth pierced his ears. Thirty or forty Yogīs are usually in residence. At the time of the author's visit to Ṭilla (December, 1924) the mahant and many of the Yogīs were at Amritsar in the interests of the monastery at that place. For there had been a serious disturbance in the city and a number of Yogīs were under arrest. The mahant had gone to effect a settlement.

A special mela is held at Ṭilla in March.

The monastery is in possession of a deed granted by Akbār confirming earlier grants.[1] The endowments are now reduced to one village, owing to serious charges brought some time ago against one of the mahants.[2] The Āughars of Kirāna are more wealthy.

At Sargoda, about four miles distant, there is a branch of the Ṭilla monastery.

Several places in Sindh, and one shrine beyond the western boundary of India, are of interest in the study of the Yogīs, although they do not belong to the Kānphaṭas. These are Nagar Ṭhaṭha, Pīr Arr,[3] Koteśwar and Hiṅg Lāj.

Nagar Ṭhaṭha (Nangar Ṭaṭṭa)[4] is situated about seventy miles from Karāchī, on a plateau in the Makli Hills, overlooking the Indus. The town, which covers a very large area, was the ancient capital of Sind. It is now a famous Musalmān burial ground. It was noted for its scarves and waist-cloths of mixed silk and cotton and of silk and gold, and for its famous educational institutions. The importance of the place for the Gorakhnāthīs is that beads which they greatly prize are obtained there. The plateau around Ṭhaṭha is strewn thick with pebbles and nodular lumps of hard, yellow limestone which are sometimes quite speckled with little

---

[1] See *Jhelum District Gazetteer*, 1904, p. 35.

[2] *Census Report, Panjab*, 1891, p. 117.

[3] A note on this place will be found under the description of Dhinodar. See p. 118, below.

[4] See *Imperial Gazetteer of India*, vol. XXIII, pp. 254 ff.; *Gazetteer of the Province of Sind, Karachi District*, 1919; Burton, *Scinde, or the Unhappy Valley* (1851); Burton, *Sind Revisited* (1877); Hughes, *A Gazetteer of the Province of Sindh.*

nummulites These become detached, and lie on the ground in such quantities that it has become a trade to collect and string them for sale to pilgrims on their way to Hiṅg Lāj. They are called *ṭhumrā*.[1] The two rosaries of white beads which are made from these nummulites differ chiefly in the size of the 'stones' of which they are composed. That of the smaller beads is called Hiṅg Lāj ka ṭhumrā; the other, made of slightly larger beads, *Āśāpūrī*. The beads of the former are said to be petrified grains of the larger millet, the latter of the smaller millet, or of rice. The former rosary is more commonly worn, and is, evidently, the more prized. It consists of 500 or 1,000 beads. Like other pilgrims, Yogīs purchase these beads at Nagar Ṭhaṭha, and, upon reaching Hiṅg Lāj offer them to the goddess. The ṭhumrā is then put on. When the pilgrim reaches Āśāpūrī[2] Devī's shrine at Nagar Ṭhaṭha on his return journey, he offers the other rosary to her and then puts it on.

The Yogīs explain the presence of the substance out of which the beads are made and their reason for prizing them by the following legends. Śiva and Pārvatī, on their way to Hiṅg Lāj, stopped in the jungles of Āśāpūrī. There Śiva asked his consort to prepare him a dish of *khichri*, cooked millet and rice, while he went away into the jungle. Śiva then drew around her and her cooking place a magic circle of ashes, explaining to her that a giant (*asura*) would in his absence come to molest her; but that she would be perfectly safe so long as she remained within the circle, since the demon would be burnt to ashes should he venture to cross the magic line. Śiva then left with her his trident and went into the jungle. While he was away, the giant came and Pārvatī slew him with the trident. The demon's blood ran all about the place, defiling everything, including the fire place and the food which she was preparing. Soon afterwards Śiva returned. From his body the demon immediately appealed to Śiva for release, or *mukti*. Śiva granted the request and the demon's spirit ascended to Kailās,

---

[1] *Gazetteer of the Province of Sind, Karachi District*. See also chap. one.

[2] Āśāpūrnā, 'She who fulfils desires.'

Śiva's heaven. The giant's body became dust and this is still used as incense powder. Seeing how everything had been defiled by the giant's blood, Śiva ordered Pārvatī to throw the food away. The grains of the khichri turned into the 'stones' out of which the beads for the famous rosaries are made.

These nummulites are also thought of as petrified grain which the creator left on earth to remind him of his creation.[1]

The efficacy of the ṭhumrā is attested by the following tale. During their fourteen years' exile, Rāma and Sītā wandered into the neighbourhood of Āśāpūrī. There Sītā begged Rāma to go to Śiva and beg for a ṭhumrā. Rāma's sin of having killed a Brāhman (Rāvaṇa) was forgiven when he offered the rosary to Hiṅg Lāj Devī.

The sacredness of Āśāpūrī is due to the fact that Rāmcạndra, on his way to Hiṅg Lāj, left his staff at her shrine.

Another legend records that formerly at Nagar Ṭhaṭha Musalmān faqīrs in large numbers persecuted the followers of the Hindu faith. One day the Devī appeared to the Hindus riding on a lion and slew the faqīrs. She then went on to Hiṅg Lāj and made that place her abode. For this reason Yogīs visit both Nagar Ṭhaṭha and Hiṅg Lāj.

In these legends well-known elements of the Śiva-Pārvatī mythology are united with the pilgrimage of the divine Yogī, Śiva, to ancient shrines. It is noteworthy that Vaiṣṇavite elements mingle freely in these stories.

HIṄG LĀJ,[2] the last holy place of the Hindus towards the west, is visited by Gorakhnāthīs. They consider that a pilgrimage to this place is necessary for all who wish to perfect themselves and to become adepts in Yoga.[3]

Hiṅg Lāj is situated on the Makrān coast, about eighty miles from the mouth of the Indus, and some twelve miles from the sea. The shrine stands below a peak of the same

---

[1] Barnes, *Travels in Bokhara*, vol. I, p. 29.

[2] See *RTCP*, vol. II, p. 398; Barnes, *Travels in Bokhara*, 1834, vol. III; Masson, *Narrative of Various Journeys in Baluchistan, Afghanistan, the Panjab and Kohat*, 1844.

[3] *RTCP*, vol. II, p. 398.

name, on the banks of the Hiṅgol River, in the Las Bela State.[1] The river breaks through the mountains in a gorge, about two hundred yards wide between cliffs, about a thousand feet high. Above the gorge the country is rich and wild. Below the gorge the river is called Aghor.[2] Masson reported, in 1844, that he saw figures of the sun and moon hewn on the rocks in an inaccessible place.[3]

Hiṅg Lāj is one of the fifty-one pīṭhas,[4] or places celebrated as spots where the dissevered limbs of Sati were scattered. Here the crown[5] of her head fell. The shrine is dedicated to the terrific Agni Devī, of Hiṅg Lāj,[6] known also as the Hiṅj Lāj Devī, Hiṅguda Devī, and the Red Goddess. She is known as Bībī Nānī by Musalmāns and as Pārvatī, Kālī or Mātā by Hindus.[7] Bībī Nānī is celebrated from the Ganges to the Euphrates and is probably the Chaldean Nāna who was very old, dating perhaps a 'thousand years before Abraham.'[8] She is probably Nanaia of the Persians and Bactrians.[9] Hiṅg Lāj is the best known place of pilgrimage in Baluchistan. The Devī is the family goddess of many tribes in western India. Even in Mirzapur, in the United Provinces, she is worshipped by Kharwārs.[10] She is known and revered throughout India.

The shrine, which is of the *vāmacāra* or *cakrapūja* type, has long been in the hands of Musalmāns and formerly the woman in charge of the place made Muslims of all Hindu pilgrims who went there. The attendant who did

---

[1] Eighty miles, *Imperial Gazetteer of India*, vol. XIII, p. 143; 150 miles, Postan's *India*.

[2] Hart, *An Account of a Journey from Karāchī to Hiṅg Lāj*, etc., 1840.

[3] *Narrative*, vol. IV, p. 391.

[4] See above, chap. five, under 'Devī Pātan.'

[5] Sen, *Sati*, says 'forehead.'

[6] *Tod*, vol. III, p. 1,511.

[7] *Imperial Gazetteer of India*, vol. XIII, p. 82.

[8] Holdich, *India*, p. 45; Holdich, *The Gates of India*, pp. 162–3. His account of the Mekrān is on pp. 295 ff.

[9] Masson, *Narrative*, vol. IV, p. 390. At Lagash there was a Goddess Nina and her daughter Ninmar c. 3000 B.C. Baikie, *The Life of the Ancient East*, p. 200.

[10] Crooke, *ERE*, vol. VI, p. 716.

this was Caṇḍāla Māī.[1] Her descendants claim to be so intimate with the goddess as to play chess with her.

Pilgrims to the shrine follow the Karāchī-Miāni-Hiṅg Lāj road along the Makrān coast. The distance is one hundred and fifty miles, but the way is so difficult that the journey occupies twenty-four days. Pilgrims go from Karāchī in bands of from forty to fifty, each conducted by a Brāhman known as *agua*. At Karāchī he obtains a pass for the party. This is shown at Miāni where fees are collected by a *bhārti*, or hereditary examiner, from all except devotees and unmarried girls. In all, on the journey, there are fifteen places where offerings are made, all of which go to the agua.

Each pilgrim takes with him a stick of oleander, sometimes mounted with gold or silver; and each must choose a *dharam bhāi*, or 'brother by duty or faith.' This relationship is made binding at Kharinadī where each takes the other's used took-stick. Upon reaching Hiṅg Lāj, they offer their beads to the goddess and then exchange them.

Widows, and women with their children and husbands make this pilgrimage.[2]

Goldsmid,[3] who visited Hiṅg Lāj in 1861, while following the river, saw a place of sacrifice, a hollow in the hill, sacred to the goddess, smeared with the blood of animals offered to her; and rocks decorated with sectarian marks, in red. From this place up to the temple, about one-fourth of a mile, the stones under foot were smeared with blood.

The shrine itself lies in a verdant valley surrounded by mountains. Far below is the abode of Nānī, a castellated, mud edifice with a rude wooden door. A flight of steps leads down a deep, semi-circular cleft through which pilgrims creep on all fours to reach the building. To enter this is a test of chastity, for the sin-laden cannot so enter. The shrine is a level, mud surface upon which a lamp is kept burning.

---

[1] This name, 'Mother Caṇḍāla,' is very interesting. A Caṇḍāla is the lowest of the outcaste Hindus.

[2] The author has seen, e.g. at Almora, women belonging to the sect, both widows and married women, who had brought rosaries from Hiṅg Lāj and who had the brand-marks of Koteśwar on their arms. See chap. two.

[3] Crooke, *ERE*, vol. VI, p. 715.

There is here a dhūnī of Gorakhnāth, Gorakhjī kī dhūnī.

Into a tank, Alāil Kuṇḍ, those who can swim jump from an overhanging rock. A cocoanut and a piece of red-cloth are offered. A cocoanut cast into the water will exhibit the nature of the pilgrim's career. If, when the cocoanut is thrown into the tank, the water bubbles up, the pilgrim is assured that his life has been and will continue to be pure. If no bubbles appear, he will have to do penance to remove his sins.[1]

Close to the shrine is a well, said to be of unfathomable depth, from which pilgrims carry away water. Hājī Abdula Nabī describes the well as follows. The water 'rises up at times with a bubbling noise, discoloured like a river fresh swollen after rain, and carrying mud in suspension. The Hindu pilgrims, when this takes place, throw in betel-nuts, cloves, cardamoms and cocoanuts. Should there be delay in the rising, pilgrims in the most abject manner will call on Mātā to give them a sight of herself, exhorting each other to reveal their sins and inwardly repent. When the water rises, they *salaam* with both hands joined, and throw in their offerings, which, after some time, on a second rise, are brought back again, where they are collected and formed into large cakes which they bake near the spot.'[2]

Near the village of Khajūrī is a pit, or hollow, where the brother of Hiṅg Lāj Devī, on being pressed by Gabars and Zoroastrians, sank into the ground. A spring gushed forth, caused by the brother, who is called Gāib Pīr (i.e. disappeared) by Musalmāns and Mahādeo by Hindus.

There is a legend which deserves record at this juncture. While Śiva was at Āśāpūrī, Hiṅg Lāj Devī, in the form of a fly, settled in his hair. When he and Pārvatī, after wandering in search of Devī for twelve years, could not find her, Śiva, in rage, determined to disappear into the ground, to go to Pātāla. Thereupon the Devī came out of his hair, and, appearing in her proper form, said, 'Why be angry? I am with you.' The hollow in the ground marks the pit into which Śiva was about to disappear. Here a sound, 'Bam, bam,' is frequently heard. Those pilgrims who hear it are

---

[1] Barnes, *Travels*, vol. III, p. 33.
Crooke, *ERE*, vol. VI, p. 716.

assured of being freed from sins; but those who do not hear it, are thought to be great sinners, and are urged by attendants and others to confess their sins, their companions even offering to share them. Then the sound comes again.[1]

Boons are often granted by the Devī. Ugra Prabhu, grandson of Nāin Pāl, who obtained the kingdom of Mārwār in A.D. 470, made a pilgrimage to Hiṅg Lāj. The goddess was so pleased with the severity of his penance that she caused to ascend from the foundation of the shrine the sword with which he conquered the southern countries.[2] Another, Rāna Hamīr, who had a leprous spot on his hand, made the pilgrimage to Hiṅg Lāj and obtained a cure.[3]

On the return journey from Hiṅg Lāj, pilgrims stop at a temple of Mahādeo (Śiva) at KOTEŚWAR ('Grove of Śiva'). This is a celebrated and ancient Tīrtha, which, at one time, lay on the borders of India. It is situated in Sind, not far from Karāchī, on the Lakpāt River, ten or twelve miles from its bar or entrance. At this place a peculiar stone, of the size of a shilling, resembling a worn down liṅga is found in vast numbers.[4] Does this explain the meaning of 'Koteśwar'? Here Gorakhnāthīs are branded on the upper part of the right fore-arm with the yoni-liṅga, emblem of Śiva-Śakti. The reason for this practice is that on this pilgrimage Yogīs pass beyond the confines of India, and that the shrine at Hiṅg Lāj is in the keeping of Musalmāns. Hence pilgrims must be reconstituted Hindus when they return to India. In a legend explaining the practice it is related that there was formerly at Hiṅg Lāj a Musalmānī who was able to tell by magic when Yogīs were among the pilgrims coming to the shrine, and that she could by the same means recognize them when they reached the place. She used to mark their foreheads with a ṭika, thus making them Musalmāns. Consequently, on their way back from the shrine, they stopped

---

[1] These accounts may involve some confusion concerning the well, the pit and the tank.

[2] *Tod*, vol. II, p. 934. [3] *Tod*, vol. III, p. 1,656.

[4] See Capt. McMurdo, article, 'Dissertation on the River Indus,' *JRAS*, 1834, pp. 20–40. Koteśwar was the seaport of Lakpāt. See General G. Le Grand Jacob, C.B. in *Transactions of the Bombay Geographical Society*, 1862, article nine.

at Koteśwar and received there the brand mark of Mahādeva, as proof that he had remade them Hindus. The practice continues. The brandmark is as follows:

The stories centring around Nagar Ṭhaṭha, Hiṅg Lāj and Koteśwar show that Western India had its very ancient holy places, as old as those in the Himālayas and at Benares: and that early contacts were common between India and Western Asia, through some of them, notably Hiṅg Lāj. They also make it plain that Muslims in due time took possession of the holy places, but that pilgrimages continue as of old. Gorakhnāthīs lost Koteśwar to the Atīts in the sixteenth century.[1]

There are three sees of the Kānphaṭas in Kacch, in Vāgad, at Bhūj, and at Dhinodhar.[2] That at the latter place is the most important.

The monastery of Kaṇṭhaḍnāth at MANPHARA, near Kaṇṭhkot, in Vāgad,[3] traces its origin, says Khakhar[4] to Kaṇṭhkot about A.D. 844. But the monastery is not old. Yogīs at this place call themselves Kaṇṭhaḍnāthīs. They are celibates and depraved. But some of their members are allowed to marry.[4] Their power in Kacch was broken about three hundred years ago.[5] Descendants of the Yogīs of this place became herdsmen. Kaṇṭhaḍnāthīs worship Ganeśa and Kaṇṭhaḍnāth, repeating the latter's name in telling their beads. Kaṇṭhaḍnāth is worshipped twice a day. The arrangements at the monastery for charity are quite like those at Dhinodhar, but on a much reduced scale. A legend tells how Rāo Bharmiljī, with his army, was once entertained at this place, Udekāṇṭh, who later was made head of the monastery providing food for the host from one small dish.[6] Another

[1] *Bombay Gazetteer*, vol. V, p. 86.
[2] *Bombay Gazetteer*, vol. V, p. 85.
[3] *Bombay Gazetteer*, vol. V, pp. 87, 88.
[4] *Khakhar*, p. 12. [5] *IA*, vol. VII, p. 53.
[6] *Bombay Gazetteer*, vol. V, p. 88.

legend tells how the angry Kaṇṭhaḍnāth frustrated the plans of the Samma chiefs in their efforts to build a fortress (in A.D. 1300) on Kaṇṭhkot Hill. The ascetic was in possession of the hill and did not care to be dispossessed. As fast as the chiefs built the walls he threw them down, through the exercise of his powers of magic. He was pacified, eventually, and the fort was completed and named after him.[1]

The Kānphaṭas of Śivarāmāṇḍap, in BHŪJ, who are now independent of Dhinodhar, were established, in 1749, by Rāo Desaljī, who gave land to a Yogī of Dhinodhar. These monks were later replaced by Sevanāth Śrīnagar, whose line still continues. They are of the sect of Śāntināth[2] and worshippers of Śakti.

The monastery at DHINODHAR[3] is one of the most important centres of the Kānphaṭas in Western India. Difficult of access, it is situated at the base of a lofty hill, surrounded by jungle, on the edge of the Rān, twenty-seven miles north-west of Bhūj. Some of the shrines belonging to the establishment are found upon the top of the hill.

Dhinodhar means 'holder of patience' and refers to the ability of the hill to bear the weight of the sin and penance of Dharamnāth.

In approaching the place[4] from Āral, a branch of the monastery, the first five miles of the journey to Dhinodhar are, for the most part, over fairly level sand, covered sparsely with thorn and cactus. The last mile, leading to the summit of the hill, is very steep. The hill has an elevation of 1,268 feet, and part of the ascent is upon its almost perpendicular side. Here there is a flight of 638 stone steps. The ascent is unshaded.

---

[1] *Bombay Gazetteer*, vol. V, p. 88; *IA*, vol. VII, p. 53.

[2] *Bombay Gazetteer*, vol. V, p. 87.

[3] See *JRAS*, 1839, pp. 268–71; *IA*, 1878, pp. 47 ff; Khakhar *Report on the Architectural, and Archæological Remains in the Province of Kachh.*

[4] The author visited the pīr of Dhinodhar at Āral, March 29, 1924. He was received in audience and was seated on the gaddi beside the pīr. All his questions were courteously answered, and the Yogīs were most friendly. A guide was sent with the author to Dhinodhar, and instructions were given to provide whatever the visitor should require. With him were the Reverend Musa Karshan of Ranpur in Kāṭhiāwār, and Mr. Faqir Chand Lallu Bai of Bhūj.

The top of the hill presented (in 1924) quite a different appearance from that described by Khakhar (1879). There was then upon the hill a temple, about six feet high and five and three-fourths feet square, with a Musalmān dome, dedicated to Dharamnāth. The entrance was small and there was no door. The temple marked the spot where Dharamnāth performed his famous penance; and within it was found the stone, in the hollow of which he rested his head during the twelve years that he stood upon his head there. This stone was an object of worship and was covered with red lead and ghi. The temple contained also a marble statue of the saint, about three feet high, wearing the ear-rings of the sect. Besides, there were three small liṅgas and some brass and stone idols in the shrine. A light has been kept burning there since Dharamnāth's time. The temple faced east. Close by was a dhūnī, or Yogī's fire, which had been kept burning since the time of the saint.[1]

Since then the temple has been enlarged and a veranda has been built on the front. The roof is now bordered with a saw-toothed parapet. The main, large dome is over the temple proper. In front of this is a medium-sized dome, and in front of this, in a line across the veranda, are three small domes. The plinth of the temple with the veranda measures 13 ft. by 26½ ft. That of the veranda being 13 ft. square. The inside of the temple is 8 ft. square. In the centre of the floor is a square of white marble upon which is the caran of Dharamnāth. This square is bordered with black marble. At the left, in front of the caran, is an incense lamp. On the left of the marble square are five liṅgas, a Gāurī-Śankar image and the stone on which Dharamnāth rested his head. It is not covered with red lead and ghi. On the right of the caran are a bell, two drinking vessels of muslin pattern and a shell. Behind the caran are three fairly large conch shells. Over the caran in the ceiling, a curtain is stretched horizontally. Over the door of the temple and on the front pillars of the veranda large tridents are drawn in red lead.

To the left of the temple is a low building in which a

---

[1] Compare *Bombay Gazetteer*, vol. V, p. 86.

dhūnī is kept burning perpetually. This building, too, is decorated with tridents painted in red lead.

Between the temple and the shed which contains the dhūnī is a small platform, 3 ft. 10 ins. by 3 ft. 7 ins. upon which, in yellow stone, is the caran of Jotnāth.

In a line in front, and to the right of the temple, extend a series of small one-room temples, each square with a saw-tooth parapet on the top and surmounted with a domed roof with a cone-shaped ornament on the top. All these temples have large red tridents painted on them. In order, looking east, these temples are to Bāl Bhāiroṁ, Viṣṇu Bhāiroṁ, Kāl Bhāiroṁ, and Hiṅg Lāj Devī. Each contains a small slab set up at the back with the image of the appropriate god or goddess engraved upon it and painted red. Still further to the east stands a slightly larger temple to Śiva with a liṅga inside, painted red. This temple also has a domed roof.

Further to the east, a little in front of the temple of Dharamnāth, but at a slightly lower level, a slab of stone is set up and painted red. It is for Bhāiroṁ.

Directly in front of the temple of Dharamnāth, but at a lower level, is a dharamśāla, or rest house. This long, narrow building faces north. It is decorated with Vaiṣṇavite images of Kṛṣṇa, Rādha, the Gopīs and others. In the middle of the front face of the dharamśāla, and above the level of the doors, is a head of Jogeśvar, with the large ear-rings, painted red.

North-east of the dharamśāla is a cook house.

All of the structures are in good repair and are substantial. They are said to have been built about thirty years ago. The older temple was built in 1821.[1] The buildings on the top of the hill were in the charge of an Āughar. The officient was a native of Agra. He conducted worship at the temple twice a day, blowing a conch three times, and making simple offerings. Besides this, he attended to the dhūnī. For the greater part of the year he had to carry water for all purposes from Āral.

---

[1] *IA*, vol. VII, p. 51.

Just below the summit of the hill, and to the right, is a tank which is filled with water during the monsoon.

The descent to the monastery leads down through a very narrow and precipitous gorge, full of rocks of all sizes, the course of a mad mountain stream during the rains. In places, the rocky sides of the ravine are covered with white spots which give point to the story that the hill became leprous when a portion of it broke away under the weight of Dharamnāth's sins. The gorge separates the broken portion of the hill from that on which Dharamnāth finally performed his penance. This ravine and the white spots are pointed out as evidences of the truth of the legend concerning the saint.

An hour's descent leads to the level of the jungle. Then the monastery, which lies on the eastern side of the hill, comes into view. The path passes close to a temple of Hiṅg Lāj Devī, a place of pilgrimage for some who are not resolute enough to journey to her shrine on the Makrān coast.

At the monastery, which marks the place where Dharamnāth lighted his dhūnī, when he came down from the hill after he had performed his penance, fewer changes have been made than at the top of the hill. The grounds of the monastery are enclosed by a wall, in some places in disrepair. Part of the wall is loopholed after the fashion of old Indian forts. Most of the buildings within the wall are in splendid repair and give evidence of the prosperity of the establishment.

Besides dharamśālas and residential quarters, the chief places of interest are the temple, or shrine, of Dharamnāth, the samādhs and the kitchens.

The temple of Dharamnāth is now quite a pretentious building, on an elevated platform, with a surrounding wall and an elaborate gateway from which a stairway leads to the shrine. The entrance was built in 1899. The temple proper is rectangular in shape, with slightly sloping walls, having a domed roof and a saw-toothed parapet, and facing east. It contains a small, marble statue of the saint, about 15 ins. high, wearing the large ear-rings. There are a few small liṅgas, some brass idols, a trident, a bell and a lamp in the shrine. The platform is of white marble bordered with black. The walls and floors are tiled in squares of black and white marble with small yellow blocks at the angles of the black and white squares. In one corner of the shrine is a fan of peacock feathers. In a niche in the wall is a large lamp bowl, which is fed with ghi, in which, it is claimed, a wick has been kept burning since the time of Dharamnāth. To the left of the image is a horse, the mount of Rāwa Pīr, and beside it another. In front of the image is a five-bowled lamp fcr worship and a box. Drums and bells are provided in the temple.

There are sixteen samādhs, tombs of pīrs, in the enclosure. Some represent two, some four pīrs by as many yoni-liṅgas. These phallic symbols are painted red. The samādhs are rectangular in shape and have domed roofs.

Among the most interesting features of the monastery are the kitchens, for the place is noted for its practice of charity, and all who come to the monastery are fed. One of the kitchens contains a dhūnī which has been burning since the days of Dharamnāth. On each side of this fire are four huge caldrons resting in stands. They are about five feet from the ground. They are named Gaṅgā, Jumnā, Sarasvatī and Bhāgīrathī. They are very old and it is said that they were brought to Dhinodhar by Dharamnāth. They are now used only once a year, for the cooking of the food to be given in charity at the annual mela on Nāurātri, in October.[1] The caldrons are objects of worship. In the kitchen opposite to this are two very large copper caldrons which are used on alternate days for cooking food at all other times. Adjoining this kitchen is the store room. It contains an image of Rāwa Pīr mounted on a horse. This image, which is painted red, is an object of worship. The room contains three large mills for grinding grain.

The monastery, which has about sixty Yogīs and a few Āughars in residence,[2] is presided over by a pīr. The present

---

[1] A special feast is given on *Gokal Atham* in August, but it is not certain that these caldrons are used at that time.

[2] In 1838 twelve were reported in residence. Khakhar reported about fifty.

incumbent (1924) has a special disciple, a boy of about nine years, for whom he shows great affection.

Life at the monastery is for the most part regular and uneventful. The morning and evening worship; such study and teaching as may be, apparently not very much; and the daily giving in charity of food to all who come, make up the day.

The Yogīs are strict celibates. Some of them are young. One boy of about seventeen (1924), a Kānphaṭa, was very restless, and they were contemplating letting him leave the place.

The healthy appearance of the Yogīs, the good condition of the buildings and the general cleanliness of the place indicate a high state of prosperity. The monastery owns about twenty villages[1] and has an income of about one hundred thousand rupees a year, of which the Rāo of Kacch appropriates twenty-five per cent. Various members of the establishment spend fully eight months of the year in the villages looking after the revenues of the monastery.

There are branches of the monastery at Āral, at Maṭhal and at Baladhiya.[2]

Dharamnāthīs belong to the Satnāth sect of the Panjab and Nepāl.[3] Their founder was a disciple of Gorakhnāth.

The power of the Yogīs of this place was broken in the sixteenth century, when they lost Koteśwar and Ajāipal to the Atīts.

The fame of Dhinodhar rests on the story of the penance of Dharamnāth. The legend is as follows:[4] Dharamnāth came from Peshāwar to Kāṭhiāwār, and thence to Kacch, in search of a suitable place to perform penance. He had with him a friend, Śaranāth and a disciple, Garībnāth. He first lighted his dhūnī and set up his abode under a tree near the palace of a chief at Ryāṁ. This palace was about two miles north of Māṇḍavi, in Southern Kacch, a place called Paṭṭan.[5] He then sent Garībnāth out to beg. The people of the place

---

[1] Postans (1839) made a similar statement.

[2] *IA*, vol. VII, p. 51.

[3] See also *IA*, vol. VII, p. 50.

[4] See *JRAS*, 1839, pp. 268–71; *IA*, vol. VII, pp. 48, 49. The account as given to the author in 1924 was substantially as reported by earlier visitors.

[5] Postans, *JRAS*, 1839, p. 268.

were very hard-hearted, and no one, except an old woman of the carpenter caste, gave alms. Garībnāth did not report the short-comings of the people to his master, but sold wood in the town and bought grain. The old woman cooked for Dharamnāth. Thus twelve years were passed in penance. Then Dharamnāth discovered by accident how he had been treated by the people and how Garībnāth and the old woman had suffered for him. In hot anger he upset his alms-bowl and cursed the people, saying, 'Be buried all the Paṭṭan cities.' So all the cities in Kacch bearing this name were swallowed up, with their inhabitants. Only the old woman escaped.

On account of this rash deed Dharamnāth determined upon a second penance. So he sought a place that would bear the weight of his sins. He chose Dhinodhar, but a portion of the hill split off under his weight, and sides oft e fissure became leprous in spots. He finally decided that he could ascend Dhinodhar if he went up the hill with his back to it. In this way he reached the summit. He then stood on his head there for twelve years, resting on a conical ball of hard stone.[1] Garībnāth and the woman, Cāran Deval, served him. This penance so shook the seat of Indra that a council of the gods, Nāthas and Siddhas was held to determine what should be done. It was decided that they should go and ask Dharamnāth to bring his penance to an end. He told them that, when he stood upright, which ever way he should look first all things would be consumed by fire—cities and towns would become ruins and would be abandoned and cultivated lands would become barren and desolate. Garībnāth, after consultation, asked Dharamnāth to look first toward the north-west. He did so and the sea dried up leaving only the present Rān.

The company, with Dharamnāth, then descended the hill. On the way down they decided to have *bhaṅg*. As no water was to be found, Pīr Pathāo struck his dagger into the hillside and a spring burst forth. At the foot of the hill, to the east, Dharamnāth lighted his dhūnī, and there a monastery was established. Dharamnāth then disappeared.

---

[1] Or, on a *pan* leaf. *JRAS*, 1839, p. 268.

There is a tradition which states that he was reborn from a blister on the hand of Cāran Deval. He was then known as Rāwal Pīr. Under this name he has a temple on the coast east of Māṇḍavī.

But it seems that Dhinodhar was a famous place when Dharamnāth took up his abode there. He came to Kacch from Peshāwar about 1382.[1] Still earlier it was known to Pīr Pathāo whose death is said to have taken place in 1209. The story is connected with the manner in which Pīr Pathāo gained possession of the cave at Pīr Arr, in Sind. This he achieved with the assistance of Gorakhnāth. A sādhu, Dayanāth, lived in this cave. The account of the amazing things that this man did in the presence of Gorakhnāth, who came to the help of Pīr Pathāo, contains elements that appeared later in the story of Dharamnāth. When Gorakhnāth came to Pīr Arr, in Sind, Dayanāth learned of it by supernatural sight. He became very angry and threw the hill into the sky and set it on fire by a breath. Then he departed to Dhinodhar Hill in Kacch. Pīr Pathāo went to Gorakhnāth and reproached him, saying, 'You are sitting here while Dayanāth has set the hill on fire and bolted.' The guru looked and saw that a fire was indeed burning between heaven and earth. But, as he was *looking*, the fire was extinguished and the hill dropped and cracked in two. Guru Gorakhnāth then perceived that Dayanāth was praying on Dhinodhar Hill, standing on his head on a betel-nut, and knew that after twelve months of austerity in this position, he could by breathing thrice blast all Sind. Thereupon Gorakhnāth extended his hand, although no one could observe this action, and seizing Dayanāth by the ear, brought him back to Pīr Arr. He then said to Dayanāth, 'Don't trouble the people. I promise you this blessing, that you and your successors shall never lack good horses and white clothes.' He then made him his disciple, split his ear, put an ivory ornament in it, and, placing a turban made of black thread on his head, sent him back to Dhinodhar.[2]

---

[1] *IA*, vol VII, p. 50.

[2] The whole legend is recorded in chap. nine.

Near DHAMAḌKĀ there is a well which is named after the famous Yogī.[1]

There are several places in Kāṭhiāwār which are associated with the name of Gorakhnāth.

Upon the sacred height at GIRMĀR there are many temples in ruins. The hill consists of five principal peaks, the highest of which, with an altitude of 3,666 feet, is associated with the name of Gorakhnāth.[2] Above the shrine of Ambā Mātā there is another, three feet square, dedicated to the great disciple of Matsyendranāth. It is said that Pārvatī, in search of Śiva, dwelt at Girnār, and that she continued to sing the praises of her Lord, until, at this spot, he finally showed himself to her.[3] In the Sind legends Girnār is represented as a noted place of resort and a favourite haunt of Gorakhnāth.

Nine miles east of Pātan and six miles west of Prāchikuṇḍ, is GORAKHMAḌHI, also named after the great saint. The place is situated on the Sārasvatī River and is one of the most important in the west. Here, in a cave, deep underground, are three images of Gorakhnāth and one of Matsyendranāth. Gorakhnāth (the guru of Rukmībāi, consort of Kṛṣṇa) is the deity of the monastery at this place. In 1884, there were about forty monks in residence.[4] All were celibates, except the Bāwā, or pīr, who is allowed to marry to keep up the succession. If he has no son, he may adopt from among his flock. He was called Nāthjī. Here all things are held in common. Some of the monks follow secular callings, some are land owners, and the head of the establishment possesses large estates. Great licence in food, drink and women is allowed. Food is distributed twice a day. Monks eat with sannyāsīs and provide the food out of the revenues of the monastery. Many sannyāsīs make the pilgrimage to this

---

[1] *Khakhar*, p. 4.

[2] *Bombay Gazetteer*, vol. VIII, p. 441; *Rās Mālā*, vol. I, pp. 7, 154. Tod's *Western India; JASBe*, vol. VII, p. 865. Lieut. M. Kittoe, article, 'Notes on a Journey to Girnar, etc.'

[3] *Archæological Survey*, 1879. *Kāṭhiāwār and Kacch*, pp. 155, 175.

[4] *Bombay Gazetteer*, vol. VIII, pp. 154–56, 446; *Khakhar*, p. 3.

place. Atīts, or Gosāins, are the officients at the Śiva and Devī temples.[1]

Traditionally, Gorakhnāth lived in the neighbourhood of Dwāraka in the Dvāpara Yuga and he is supposed to have lived somewhere in Kāṭhiāwār, 'three months' journey west of Gorakhpur in the Kali Yuga.'[2]

There are several places in Western India where Gorakhnāth is revered. On the top of TURANMAL Hill, a tableland long and narrow, with an elevation of from 3,300 to 4,000 feet, and having an area of about sixteen square miles, situated in the Sātpurā range of hills, in the Khandesh District of the Bombay Presidency, are a fine artificial lake and the remains of many temples locally ascribed to the saint, Gorakhnāth.[3]

About three-quarters of a mile south-east of SHĪRĀLĀ in the Sātāra District, is a grove called Gorakhnāth or more correctly Gorakṣanāth after the presiding deity. The grove consists chiefly of fine old tamarinds. The image of the presiding deity of the grove is a large stone, like a mill-stone, placed on the north side of a gigantic old tamarind of the species known as Gorakhamlī. The bark of this tree is scarred everywhere in every direction by natural lines and cracks. These are supposed to be characters written by the deity in an unknown tongue; and every Kānphaṭa devotee who comes to worship here gets his name written on the tree, whether he announces it or not. It is of interest to note that Gorakhnāth, the patron deity of the grove, is tending to rank as a manifestation of Śiva.[4]

There are hills north of AHMADĀBĀD, in the Deccan, called Gorakhnāth.[5]

In THĀNA, at Ganeśpuri, are several hot springs, in the bed of the river, one of which is called Gorakhmacchindar. The water is very hot.[6] And two old hill forts in Thāna are

---

[1] *Bombay Gazetteer*, vol. V, p. 87.

[2] *Martin*, vol. II, p. 484.

[3] *Bombay Gazetteer*, vol. XXIV, p. 66.

[4] *Bombay Gazetteer*, vol. XIX, p. 587; also *Religion and Folklore of Northern India* (1926), p. 403. *Imlī*, the sour tamarind.

[5] *Bombay Gazetteer*, vol. VII, p. 5.

[6] *Bombay Gazetteer*, vol. XIII, p. 16.

called Gorakhgad and Macchindragad.[1] In the neighbouring caves are signs of ancient residences.

There is at TRIMBAK,[2] eighteen miles from Nāsik, a monastery of the Bāirāg panth of the Kānphaṭas. This establishment is situated at the foot of the hills and possesses some fields and considerable grass land. The resident monk claimed that the land was granted to the monastery by 'the Peshwa.' The building itself is roomy but unsubstantially built. On the large, stone platform, which faces the monastery, is a huge, three-sectioned stone, painted red and representing Bhāiroṁ. 'Eyes' of silver are inset in the figure. The place is decorated with trisules and flags. Red paint is everywhere. On three sides of the platform are samādhs one of which is said to have contained the body of Aurangzeb, the last great Moghul.[3] At the time of the author's visit,[4] the establishment contained three or four Āughars, one Kānphaṭa, Narbadnāth, and a wandering Rāwal. One of the Āughars was a woman. High upon the hillside, in a cave, close to the source of the Godāvarī, is a stone image of Gorakhnāth, about fifteen inches high.[5]

Rose says that the chief seat of the Dharamnāthīs is on the Godāvarī.[6] Morris (1876) said that the source of the Godāvarī was at Trimbak, on a hill approached by 690 stone steps flanked by a low stone wall. 'At the top is a stone platform, built at the foot of the rock out of which, drop by drop, issues the water of the stream, and an image under a canopy has been so placed that the water trickles through its mouth into a reservoir.' This is the source of the Ganges as well,[7] the channel being underground. (But 'Ganges' is a name applied to many sacred streams.)

Professor A. V. Williams Jackson describes[8] a visit to the cave of Bhartṛhari at old UJJĀIN. In the inner cave or hall

---

[1] *Bombay Gazetteer*, vol. XIV, p. 101.

[2] 'Three-eyed.' See *Imperial Gazetteer*, 1908, vol. XXIV, p. 49.

[3] See p. 70. [4] December 21, 1924.

[5] *Bombay Presidency Gazetteer, Nāsik*, 1883, vol. XVI, p. 654.

[6] *RTCP*, vol. II, p. 396.

[7] Henry Morris, *A Descriptive and Historical Account of the Godavery District*, pp. 2, 6.

[8] *JAOS*, vol. XXIII, pp. 313 ff.

is to be found a figure, or picture, of Gorakhnāth with Gopicand on his left. Nearby, in the underground vault, is the caran of Matsyendranāth. An opening in the roof of the cavern is said to lead ultimately to Benares.

At Pāe Dhūnī, a very old religious centre in the city of BOMBAY, there is a cramped establishment of the Kānphaṭa Yogīs. It is used by all twelve of the panths and is one of the four monasteries under the Maṭha at Nāsik. The mahant, in 1924, was Maharāj Bhithutī Nāth of the Bāirāg division of the order. The mahants, here, are chosen at the Kumbh Mela and for twelve years. At Pāe Dhūnī there is a caran (*pāe*), a dhūnī, and a temple of Bhāiroṁ, all under the control of the Kānphaṭa Yogīs.

The famous temple of EKLIṄGAJĪ, in Rājputāna, bears important relations both to Bappa and to the Kānphaṭa Yogīs.[1] It is situated twelve[2] or fourteen[3] miles north of Udāipur, in a narrow defile of the mountains. Across the mouth of the gorge, to the north of the temple, is a gateway with a crowning wall extending along the heights on either side. From the gateway to the temple, the walls of the gorge on both sides are perpendicular. To the south, and above the temple is a lake. The entrance to the temple, on the south, is a massive portal, built at the western extremity of the great dam which confines the waters of the lake. The shrine is sacred to Mahādeo (Śiva), the tutelary divinity of the Rājpūts.[4] Śiva is worshipped here as Ekliṅgajī and as Īśvar Chāumukhī (the Four-faced Lord). The image of Īśvar Chāumukhī is of black marble.[5] The temple itself is of white marble, large, well-proportioned, open-vaulted, supported by columns and surmounted with a pyramidal pinacle, or *śekhra*.[6] Outside of the temple and immediately in front of the four-faced image, is a cast bronze bull of natural size, well executed. Within the quadrangle are miniature shrines containing some of the minor deities. The high priest of the temple is a Gosāin, celibate. The office is continued by

---

[1] *BHCS*, p. 403. [2] *Tod*, vol. II, p. 299.
[3] *JAS By*, vol. XXII, p. 151.
[4] *Tod.*, vol. I, p. xxxvi; vol. II, p. 598.
[5] *Imperial Gazetteer*, vol. XXIV, p. 104.
[6] *Tod*, vol. II, p. 600.

adopting disciples.[1] The Gosāins wear a crescent symbol of Śiva on their forehead, braid their hair and bind it about the head, put ashes on their bodies and wear garments coloured with ochre. They live in monasteries, and are addicted to drugs and liquors.[2] They can muster many Kānphaṭa Yogīs. Brāhmans, Rājpūts and even Gūjars may belong to the order. Some of the Gosāins follow secular employments and are wealthy and some are soldiers. They bury their dead in a sitting posture and erect a conically-formed tumuli over them. The Rājas of Mewār, Udāipur, are diwāns, or vice-regents of Śiva, and, when visiting the temple, supersede the high priest in his duties and perform the ceremonies.[3] The Yogī at Nāsik said that the priests of the temple are now Liṅgāyats.

Two interesting shrines of the Kānphaṭas in Bengal are at MAHANAD in the Hoogly District and at the Cantonment of DUM DUM near Calcutta.[4] The latter place is called Gorakh Bansuri, or Gorakhbansi. The establishment at this place, though small, is of considerable interest. The buildings are not large. The grounds contain many samādhs. In the principal temple there is a large image of Gorakhnāth, wearing yellow robes, and having the split ears and the ear-rings of his sect, greatly exaggerated. In the centre of the main site of the establishment is a large cement platform set with mosaics, in the south-east corner of which is a large red samādh. North of the platform is the temple of Gorakhnāth. It is in shape like the ordinary temples of Bengal, with the characteristically arched dome. On the opposite side of the platform is a temple of Mahādeo. To the west is the small monastery with the quarters of the pīr. North-west of the platform is the dhūnī, under a shed. To the east of the temple of Gorakhnāth is a small platform for Bhāiroṁ, with a group of trisules painted red. East of the platform, and at the north is a small shrine to Kālī; and beyond this is the 'place' of Manasā,[5] over which is a tall palm. To this

[1] Tod, vol. II, p. 601. [2] *Tod*, vol. II, p. 601.

[3] *Tod*, vol. I, p. xxxvi; *Imperial Gazetteer*, vol. XXIV, p. 104.

[4] *BHCS*, p. 403.

[5] Manasā, sister of a Vāsuki (Bāsak), the King of Serpents, is the Queen of Snakes and protects her devotees from reptiles. See W. J. Wilkins, *Hindu Mythology*, p. 395.

palm are attached small bits of rag in which pebbles are tied. These register vows. After the completion of the vow, the pebbles are offered to Gorakhnāth. A flight of steps leads down to a tank at the east. The samādhs lie in the cemetery at some distance to the south-west. The establishment has but little endowment, and there are but three or four Yogīs and a varying small number of Āughars in residence. The mahant had travelled but little, and was not well informed. He was of the Kaplāni sect and his name was Lachmannāth. There was then at the place[1] a Yogī of the Kapalmuni panth, Śaṅkarnāth by name, from Gaṅgā Sāgar.

In the city of PURĪ (Jagannāth Purī) is a gaddi, or seat, of the Satnāth sect of the Kānphaṭas.[2] The establishment shows some signs of age. The grounds are fairly large, but the buildings are small and the temple has a thatched roof. In the front of the latter is a pillar surmounted by an image of Garuḍa. Another temple, also with a thatched roof, contains an image of Bhāiroṁ with three heads and one leg. There is a shrine also to Alaknāth. There are a few samādhs, one with a long wooden liṅga over it. The mahant wore a patchwork coat and cap, which he said were distinctive of the Satnāth sect. He carried a 'club,' made of straw and covered with cloth, called sudarṣan, and had wristlets and armlets of copper from Kedārnāth and of iron from Badrināth. His ear-rings were of copper and were cylindrical. His name was Nardhārināth.

---

[1] August, 1924.

[2] The author visited the place in November, 1924.

CHAPTER SEVEN

RELIGION AND SUPERSTITION

NOT only do Gorakhnāthīs recognize and worship the greater and lesser gods of the Hindu Pantheon; but also they follow the popular forms of Hindu belief, having concern for saints and other spirit powers, especially those that are evil; practising magic, exorcism, witchcraft and some primitive medicine; giving attention to lucky and unlucky days[1]; and following the superstitions of the populace.

Some Yogīs do not eat fish because Matsyendranāth was born from a fish; while others do not observe the taboo.[2]

Some hold the red dāl (*māsūr*) taboo because it resembles drops of blood. Carrots and turnips are eschewed for prudish reasons.[3]

An interesting device for detecting good and bad omens has to do with breathing. 'To have both nostrils free and to be breathing through them at the same time is not good, and one should not begin any business in this condition. If one is breathing only through the right nostril, the left being closed, the condition is propitious for the following actions: to eat and drink, for digestion will be rapid; to fight; to bathe; to study and read; to ride on a horse; to work at one's livelihood. A sick man should take medicine while he is breathing only through his right nostril. To be breathing through the left nostril is propitious for the following undertakings: to lay the foundations of a house, and to take up residence in a new house; to put on new

---

[1] *Bombay Gazetteer*, vol. XXI, p. 185.

[2] *Matsya* means 'fish.' The saint's other name, *Mīna*, also means fish.'

[3] *NINQ*, vol. I, para. 117.

clothes; to sow seed; to do service or to found a village; to make any purchase. The Yogīs practice the art of breathing in this manner by stopping up the right and left nostril alternately with cotton wool and breathing through the other. If a man comes to a Brāhman to ask him whether some business or undertaking will succeed, the Brāhman breathes through his nostrils on to his hand; if the breath comes through the right nostril, the omen is favourable and the answer is 'yes'; if through the left nostril, the omen is unfavourable and the answer is 'no'.[1]

'There are many points in connection with regulation of breath which we nowadays class among superstitions, since we have lost the rationale. Thus it is said that one's undertakings will all prove successful if he commences them when he respires through his right nostril. Similarly, if you start from your home to visit a friend, and wish to know whether you will find him or not at home, examine your breath; if it flows through the right nostril, you will see him, otherwise not. There are others who could tell the hour of the day from the motion of their breath. It is said, that in every healthy person the breath (technically known as *sura*) changes from one nostril to the other at well-established regular intervals, and thus from its being right- or left-sided, those practised in it can approximately say the hour of the day.'[2]

Rose quotes from the '*Hāuz-ul-Hayāt* (Well of Knowledge),[3] which says that, if a man closes his eyes, ears and nostrils, he cannot take cold; that the right nostril is called the sun, and the left the moon; that from the former he breathes heat, and from the latter cold air.'[3] Here is undoubtedly an evidence of the influence of Yoga doctrine on Islam.

'It is an established custom amongst the Yogīs that, when malady overpowers them, they bury themselves alive. They are wont also, with open eyes, to force their looks towards

---

[1] E. V. Russell and Hira Lal, *The Tribes and Castes of the Central Provinces of India*, vol. III, p. 247. Quoted by permision of the Macmillan Company, Publishers.

[2] Rai Bahadur Sris Chandra Basu, *The Sacred Books of the Hindus*, vol. XV, Pt. 4, p. 44 f.

[3] Rose, *The Darvishes*, p. 382.

the middle of their eyebrows, until so looking they perceive the figure of a man; if this should appear without hands, feet or any member, for each case they have determined that the boundaries of their existence would be within so many years, months or days. When they see the figure without a head, they know that there certainly remains very little of their life; on that account, having seen the prognostic, they bury themselves.'[1]

For the horrible rite of divination by the use of a full-time fœtus see below, chapter eight.

In the cure of disease Yogīs make use of exorcism. In Almora, for instance, the drum, dancing and medicines are not used in the process; but it is performed in the name of Bhāiroṁ or of Gorakhnāth. The *cimṭa* (firetongs), which are of iron; branches of the nīm tree and of the *jatela* tree; and the hān morcal, or fan of peacock feathers,[2] are used, along with spells, to drive out disease or evil spirits. The article employed is moved over the body of the afflicted person so as to 'sweep' out the disease, or the spirit causing the trouble. The 'sweeping' is done from the head toward the feet. The practice is applied to snake-bite as well as to other afflictions. Morning and evening are auspicious times for the practice of exorcism.

Kānphaṭas have a considerable reputation in the practice of medicine. Their method is in part that of exorcism and in part the use of magic, of charms and of drugs.

A certain Yogī at Almora claimed (1924) that he was widely employed to heal the sick, and that he had wrought cures where doctors, even Western doctors, had failed. He cited in particular a case where he claimed that he had cured a paralytic woman. He did not discuss his method.

Various substances are applied or administered for medicinal effect. Ashes, with a spell pronounced over them, are used as a ṭīkā, made with the thumb on the forehead, to effect the cure of illness or barrenness, or to protect from the evil eye. In the legends are related many instances of the use of ashes for magical effects.[3] Powdered rhinoceros skin is

---

[1] *Dabistan* vol. II, pp. 138, 9.

[2] *SHTC*, p. 262. [3] See chap. nine.

dusted into wounds as a healing substance. The use of ashes from the dhūnī is described in the study of the legends about Goraknāth. Yogīs at Gorakhpur wash a large nummulite, obtained in Sind, in water and administer the solution to women to insure easy delivery. The Yogīs at Gorakhpur have long had a reputation for pronouncing spells which are specially efficacious in restoring children to health.[1]

Yogīs make and sell charms of various kinds; some are given to children as a protection against the evil eye. As the descriptions, especially in chapter one show, Kānphaṭas make a considerable use of amulets themselves. Many of these are of the usual form, box-shaped or cylindrical, made of copper or some other metal, often of silver, and worn on the arm or hung from the neck. In the receptacle are placed a variety of objects.

The ear-ring carries with it special protection and vouchsafes success in all undertakings.[2] And the thread (kaṅgna), worn about the wrist, or on the upper arm, serves a protective purpose. Ornaments hung from the neck and worn on the fingers may perform a similar office. A silver tooth-pick attached to the sacred thread serves to ward off the evil eye.

In some parts of the Konkan the *swastika* is used as a symbol of Śiva.[3]

Quite in keeping with the claims to supernatural power, which skill the Yoga is supposed to confer, is the popular belief that Yogīs work in magic. And the practice is carried on.

In Gujarāt drought was attributed to Indra and a sorcerer was called in who made offerings to *Mātājī* (the Mother Goddess), in potsherds representing human skulls out of which the Yoginīs (female demons), her attendants, delight to eat. The offerings were carried outside the city and set down beyond the east gate, in a circle already prepared, and the food was then given to outcastes and to dogs.[4]

In various parts of the country Yogīs have a reputation

---

[1] Buchanan reported this many years ago. *Martin*, vol. II, p. 484.
[2] *E.g.*, so they say at Śrīnagar. See section on Ear-rings.
[3] Enthoven, *Follkore of Bombay*, p. 45.
[4] *Rās Māla*, vol. II, p. 321 (Rawlinson's Edition).

for being able to control hailstorms and rain. In Siālkot the Yogī who is able to check a hailstorm or to divert it into waste land is called *rathbanā*.[1] These are well known at Ṭilla. In the Central Provinces he is called *gārpagāri*.

Wool being a protective, the Yogī uses it for his sacred thread, for kaṅgnas, and often in his head covering. When Gorakhnāth wished to draw Puran from the well in Siālkot, he sought a thread spun by an unmarried virgin.[2]

Instances of the practice of the black art are reported. Near Patānkot, *zaṛi būti*, a herb, is mixed with the ashes of an unmarried Hindu and given to an enemy in order to bewitch him. The effect of this potion can be overcome only by the incantations of another Yogī.[3] For the phase of the practice of black magic covering the control of spirits through ceremonies over a corpse see below under 'Vāmacāra.' Left-hand Śāktas, with the intention of killing an enemy, make an image of flour and clay, stick razors into the breast, navel and throat; and pegs into its eyes, hands and feet. A fire sacrifice is made with meat; and an image of Bhāirava or of Durgā holding a trident is placed so that the weapon pierces the breast of the image, and death is invoked on the person whose destruction is intended.[4]

The subject of the possession and of the exercise of supernatural powers for which Yogīs are famous all over the world, will be considered in a following chapter.

The use of blood is evidenced on every hand, in red ochre smeared on images and symbols, in the tīkā, and in actual offerings. A survival of blood used magically, reduced to blood drawn from the tongue or little finger of the worshipper,

---

[1] *RTCP*, vol. II, p. 398. See *Census Report, Berār*, 1881, p. 58.

[2] *Temple*, vol. II, p. 432.

'The Jogīs flew thence and went straight to the land of Kārū.
Seeing the virgins spinning they demanded a thread.
Spake a beldame of a hundred years: "I tell you truth,
The spinning wheel was made in the Golden Age; the skein and ropes in the Silver Age;
The thread was drawn in the Third Age and went up into heaven."
If ye be the disciples of a saint, bring down the thread.'

[3] *RTCP*, vol. I, quoting *NINQ*, vol. I, para. 117.

[4] *CTC*, vol. I, p. 137.

is suggested in the case where Gorakhnāth drew *water* from his finger when he restored Mahitā and Sīlā Dāī to life.[1]

It was believed that Śāktas formerly ate portions of the flesh and drank the blood of the victims sacrificed at their secret orgies.[2] Undoubtedly there is involved here the idea of magic. The practices described under Kāmākhyā, below suggest customs which have passed there and in Orissa by less than a century.[3]

Bhattacharya says that Kāmārs, blacksmiths, are Śakti worshippers and that they are usually employed in slaughtering animals used in sacrifice to the bloodthirsty gods and goddesses that receive the adoration of Śāktas.[4]

In connection with the sacrifice of the rhinoceros, most Gurkhas offer libations of blood after entering its disembowelled body. On ordinary 'Śrādh' days the libation of water and milk is poured from a cup carved from its horn. Its urine is considered antiseptic, and is hung in a vessel at the principal door as a charm against ghosts, evil spirits and disease.[5]

Many objects are held sacred, or are regarded almost as fetishes, because of their associations, or through the sanctity of the substances from which they are made, or to which they are related. Ear-rings, made of earth[6] (and of other substances); the four ancient caldrons at Dhinodhar; and numerous dhūnīs, particularly those at Pāi Dhūnī, Gorakhpur and Dhinodhar may serve as examples.

The Ganges, especially, and other rivers such as the Godāvarī are held sacred by them, as by all Hindus. At Deoprayāg, in the Himālayas, where the Bhāgīrathī and the Alaknanda join to form the Ganges, the former, the swifter stream, is said to be sixteen annas pure and the other but fifteen annas. This is an ancient important site.

At the Śivarāmāṇḍap temple the statue of a bronze horseman, Nakaland (the coming incarnation of Viṣṇu), is worshipped; and at Dhinodhar the mount of Rāwa Pīr.[7]

---

[1] *Temp.*, vol. I, p. 362. [2] *Modern India and the Indians*, p. 64.
[3] See *Modern India and the Indians*, p. 65. [4] *HCS*, p. 243.
[5] Landon, *Nepāl*, vol. I, p. 292, quoting H. H. General Kaiser Sham Sher Jang Bahādar.
[6] So reported at Ṭilla. [7] *Bombay Gazetteer*, vol. V, p. 87.

An interesting incident in tree-worship is reported in the north-west. On the fifteenth and eleventh of Phāgun, Kānphaṭas, like villagers of the Panjab, worship the *āṅolā* tree, or *phyllanthus emblica.* This tree is the emblic myrobolus, a representation of the fruit of which is used for the finial of Buddhist temples. Its worship is now connected with that of Śiva. Brāhmans will not take the offerings. The people circumambulate the tree from left to right, pour libations, eat the leaves and make offerings, which are taken by Kānphaṭa Yogīs.[1]

Some Nāthas worship the pāduka of Gorakhnāth and of Matsyendranāth on the Śivrātri. Their carans are regularly worshipped.

Many animals are held sacred, or are in some way given special attention by Goraknāthīs. Like all Hindus, they worship the cow. There are special taboos against fish.[2] Of special interest to the Yogīs are the rhinoceros, the black buck, dogs and snakes.

The rhinoceros receives considerable attention. The rulers of Nepāl and others who come to look at those held in captivity for example at Calcutta, always worship them. In their worship of the sun, Yogīs wear a ring of rhinoceros horn on the second finger of the right hand; and in other forms of worship this same practice obtains. Some who do not wear the cuṭiya, use a ring of rhinoceros horn when making an oblation of water. Ear-rings of rhinoceros horn are very much prized. One explanation why men hold the rhinoceros sacred is that the animal bows its head slowly like an elephant; and the latter animal is sacred to Ganeśa, son of Śiva. Still another reason is that Śiva ordered rings of rhinoceros horn to be worn. The body and legs of the rhinoceros are offered to Gorakhnāth. It is further said that the Pāṇḍavas once killed a rhinoceros and used its skin as a vessel in which to offer water to the sun. Hence the animal is

---

[1] *RTCP*, vol. I, p. 238. The āṅolā (*sk. āmalaka*) is an object of worship as the *Birham birich* (Brahm tree): 'He who in October eats beneath the āṅolā tree to Heaven will surely go with all his family.' Quoted from Fallon, *Hindustani-English Dictionary*, p. 168.

[2] See above, p. 125.

regarded as sacred.[1] Moreover, Rām Candra had a shield of rhinoceros hide. Besides, the animal is closely associated with mud, and so rings of the horn of the animal are buried with the body of a Yogī, although rings of metal or of precious stones are not.[2] Kirkpatrick reported the forests on the southern slopes of Nepāl to be greatly infested with rhinoceroses.[3]

The black buck is revered, and its horn and skin are used by Yogīs. A story which explains this fact is as follows: King Bhartṛhari, while out hunting, came upon a herd of seventy hinds and one stag. He was unable to kill the stag; and, finally, one of the hinds asked him to kill her. But he said that as a man of the warrior caste he could not do so. She then asked the stag to receive the king's arrow. As the stag fell, he said, 'Give my feet to the thief, that he may escape with his life; my horns to the Yogī, that he may use them as his whistle (*nāḍ*); my skin to the ascetic, that he may worship upon it; my eyes to a fair woman, that she may be called *mirga nāinī* (having eyes like a deer); and eat my flesh thyself.' It is said that Bhartṛhari soon afterwards met Gorakhnāth who accused him of having killed one of his disciples. Bhartṛhari replied that if he had, then Gorakhnāth could restore him to life. Thereupon Gorakhnāth threw some earth upon the stag, thereby restoring him to life.[4]

Reference is made[5] to legends in which the name and the deeds of Goraknāth are associated with serpents, especially the rain or water-controlling serpents (nāga) of Nepāl. Notice is taken, also of the story of the great war for the extermination of serpents (nāga) under the leadership of Janmegi. In the story of Gūgā, serpents and Gorakhnāth

---

[1] This story was told at Śrī Nagar, in the Himalayas. See above.

[2] The rhinoceros was declared to be sacred by Aśoka, in one of his Pillar Edicts. See Radhakumud Modkeji, *Aśoka*, p. 181. In *Manu* (3: 271, 272) the rhinoceros is one of the animals whose meat satisfies the manes for an endless time when offered at the Śrāddha. The story referred to above confirms this. It is hermits' food universally On the Indian rhinoceros see *EB*, 13th ed., vol. II, p. 771; vol. XVI, p. 976; vol. XXIII, p. 243. The horn is a mass of hairs cemented together by cells. See also *JAOS*, vol. LI (1931), pp. 276 ff.

[3] *An Account of the Kingdom of Nepāl* (1793) p. 19.

[4] *RTCP*, vol. II, pp. 403, 404.

[5] See chap. nine.

both play an important part.[1] Yogīs celebrate the Nāgpañcamī festival. Images and pictures of serpents are found about their shrines and monasteries. The Sepalas[2] are snake-charmers. Besides these, there are other Kānphaṭas who exhibit snakes at melas; and there is a group or tribe, called Kor Mantar, who are Kānphaṭas, but who live in the jungles and are not often seen, who eat snakes.[2] Furthermore, there is the relation between Śiva and serpents, which lends some significance to the fact that these Yogīs trace their line of teachers back to the great god of destruction. Śiva is represented with a cobra, or other snakes, in his hand, about his neck or twisted in his hair. But here the significance is not so much of the worship of the serpent, as that of terror, or fear, aroused because of Śiva's sinister character, the serpent serving as a weapon.[3] Associated with the liṅga, the significance of the snake may be partly that of worship. In the wall of the steep stairway leading down to the Nāg Kuaṁ, or Serpent-Well, in Benares, is a sculptured three-headed serpent, and on the floor a serpent is represented crawling towards the liṅga. Both Nāg and the well are worshipped.[4] The only time during the year that the well is visited for religious purposes is on the Nāgpañcamī,[5] when

---

[1] *IA*, vol. II, p. 124. See chapter dealing with legends. It is of interest to note that the Great Śālavāhana was a Nāga. *Tod*, vol. I, p. 82. See the legends about Puran Bhagat.

[2] Reported at Ṭilla.

[3] See *Tree and Serpent Worship*, p. 69. Compare *CR*, 1897, pp. 50 ff.

[4] *The Sacred City of the Hindus*, p. 89.

[5] *The Sacred City of the Hindus*, p. 220. This well, which bears marks of considerable antiquity, is situated in the north-western part of the city, and is dedicated to the Nāgarāja, Ananta or Śeṣa, who is believed to have incarnated himself in Patañjali, the famous grammarian and author of the *Mahābhāsha*. On that account the grammarians of the city gather on the spot to discuss grammar on the fifth of the bright half of the month Śrāvan. This is the date of the Nāgapañcanī or Festival of the Nāgas. On this occasion common folk, too, repair to the ancient well and make their offerings, the average attendance being estimated at 4,000 persons.

Four flights of steps, numbering altogether forty steps, lead down to a large circular well which is considerably below the level of the street. There is a stone slab with a Nāgarī inscription

women visit the well on one day and men on the next. Worshippers bathe in the well. Respectable people do not tarry there. The well is recognized as a place of pilgrimage, Karkoṭak Nāg Tīrth.[1] In Benares Śiva is worshipped as Nāgeśwar, Lord of Serpents; and in the United Provinces and in the Himālayas as Rikheśvar, Lord of Serpents (Nāgas).[2]

Snakes are the servants of Rāja Bāsuk, with whom Gūgā had dealings. One legend makes Gūgā's bride the daughter of Bāśaknāg. The Rāja has a temple at Priyāg (Prayāg) which is a place of pilgrimage, especially at the time of the Nāgpañcamī.[3] A saying connected with Gūgā may be of interest. 'It is a good thing for a Hindu to listen to the tale of Gūggā at night during the Dīwālī festival as a means of preventing snakes entering houses.'[4]

Serpents are associated with Bhāiroṁ. Images of Devī and Nāga are often found side by side.[5]

Nāgas are beneficently inclined and are connected with water and the giving of rain, or when angry with sending hail.

'The same idea seems to underlie the following legend which is current in Nepāl. In the days of King Guṇakām, so the story goes, the country of Nepāl was visited by a terrible famine which lasted for seven years. Since all prayers were vain, the king had recourse to the great magician, Śāntikāra. This master, while using the proper incantations, drew a magical eight-petalled lotus-flower, which he filled with gold and powdered pearls. Then he made therein the effigies of the nine great Nāgas, and by his spells induced them to occupy their proper places. Varuṇa, white of complexion, wearing a sevenfold, jewelled nāga-hood, and carrying a lotus and a jewel in his hands, took his position in the centre;

---

let into the wall. The *pūjārī* declares that the well gives access to Pātāla, or the nether world, the abode of snakes. A snake image is said to exist inside the well, below the water level. Besides, there are snake stones let into the well. See *Indian Serpent Lore*, pp. 267, 288.

[1] *Ibid.*, p. 220. Karkoṭak Nāg was the Serpent King of Nepāl who dwelt in the lake, Nāgavāsa. See also Landon, *Nepāl*, vol. I, p. 182. He is of the royal house of Kashmīr.

[2] *ERE*, article, 'Serpent Worship,' vol. XI, pp. 415, 418. But see above, p. 82.

[3] *IA*, vol. II, p. 124.

[4] *PNQ*, vol. IV, para. 178.

[5] *IA*, vol. II, p. 124.

Ananta, dark blue, in the east; Padmaka, with his five hoods and of the colour of a lotus-stalk, in the south; Takshaka saffron-coloured and nine-hooded, in the west; Vāsuki, greenish with seven serpent heads, in the north; Śaṅkhapāla, yellowish, in the south-west; Kulika, white coloured and provided with thirty hoods, in the north-west; Mahāpadma, gold-coloured, in the north-east. Only Karkoṭaka, who was portrayed in blue colour like a human being with a snake tail, remained absent, as he was ashamed of his deformity and would rather expose himself to the deadly influence of the spells than appear in person.

'On the advice of Śāntikāra, the king himself went to secure the help of the obstinate Nāga and, notwithstanding his remonstrances, forcibly dragged him along by the hair. When the nine great Nāgas had thus been brought together Śāntikāra worshipped them and besought them to reveal unto him a remedy against the drought. Then they told him that he should paint their images with the blood of Nāgas, and for the purpose they offered him their own blood. As soon as the wizard had followed their instructions the sky darkened. Clouds overcast the celestial vault, and heavy rain began to pour down. This is the rite known as Nāga-sādhanā which has been resorted to ever since when the country was threatened with famine. The remedy, M. Levi says, "has lost nothing of its credit and is practised in Nepāl up to the present day." '[1]

Vogel[2] says that worship is seldom devoted to live serpents, but usually to gods or saints who are considered able to give protection from snake bite.

Dogs, especially black dogs, are associated with Bhāiroṁ and are venerated.[3]

To Yogīs who haunt the jungles are attributed power over wild beasts and 'you may hear in any Indian village of Yogīs to whom the cruel beasts (e.g. tiger, leopard) are as lap-dogs;

---

[1] J. P. Vogel, *Indian Serpent-Lore of The Nagas in Hindu Legend and Art*, pp. 226, 27. See description of the festival of Matsyendranāth in Nepāl, below.

[2] *Indian Serpent-Lore*, p. 268.

[3] See Underhill, *The Hindu Religious Year*, p. 117. See also descriptions of Bhāiroṁ, below.

and stories where a rāja, out hunting, endangered by a mad wild elephant or a ferocious tiger is saved by the appearance at the critical moment of the Yogī, who orders the obedient beast away.'[1] It is believed that Yogīs live in the jungles surrounded by tigers and ride on them.

The spirits of Yogīs are worshipped at the samādhs. For example. the Āipanthīs of Rohtak offer, at noon, food on all samādhs and set a lamp of ghi at each one. The food is then distributed. Such worship takes place over the graves of Yogīs at all monasteries. While making offerings of food and water to their sainted dead, Yogīs make use of the pavitṛi.

Besides, Gorakhnāthīs worship nine Nāthas and eighty-four Siddhas. Nāthas are religious leaders, or gurus, or guides, who derive their names from Ādinātha, or Śiva. Śiva himself is called a Nātha. While the word nātha is a synonym for Hindu Yogī,[2] and while it is a sect name of the Kānphaṭas,[3] still, in this connection it refers to the nine great, or deified and immortal teachers of the sect, of whom Gorakhnāth is sometimes called the chief.[4] They now live far back in the holy Himālayas. Their names are: Gorakhnātha (the chief Nātha), Matsyendranātha, Carpaṭnātha, Mangalnātha, Ghugonātha, Gopinātha, Prāṇnātha, Sūratnātha and Cambanātha.[5] They are not related to the divisions of the order.[6] In another list nine Nāthas are named, each of whom is identified with a Hindu god. These are: 1. Āuṁgkār Ādinātha (Lord of Lords), Śiva; 2. Shelnātha (Lord of the Arrow Shaft), Kṛṣṇa or Rāma Candra; 3. Santoknātha (Lord of Gratīfication); 4. Acalacambhunātha (Lord of Wondrous Immortality), Hanumān or Lakṣman; 5. Gajbali Gajkāṇṭhnātha (Lord of the Elephant's Strength and Neck), Ganeśa Gajkarṇa (Elephant-Eared); 6. Prajnātha, or Ūdāinātha (Lord of the People), Pārvatī; 7. Māyārūpī Macchendranātha (The Wondrous Form), Guru of Gorakhnātha; 8. Gathepiṇḍe Ricayakari, or Naraṅṭhar, Śambhujāiti Guru Gorakhnātha; 9.

---

[1] *Man and Beast of India*, pp. 355 ff. See Hunter, *Statistical Account of Bengal*, vol. I, p. 119.

[2] *RTCP*, vol. II, p. 389.

[3] Compare *OMAS*, p. 185.

[4] *Temp.*, vol. I, p. 358, note.

[5] *OMAS*, p. 186. *BHCS*, p. 404.

[6] *Panjab Census, Report*, 1891, p. 115.

Gyānsarūpe, or Purakh Siddh Caurañjwenātha, or Puran Bhagat.[1] Still another list is given by Kitts[2]: Oṁkārināth, Viṣṇu; Saṁtokanāth, Viṣṇu; Gajboli, Gajāna, Hanumān; Acaleśvar, Gaṇpati; Udayanātha, Sūrya; Pārvatī Prem, Mahādeo; Santhanātha, Brahmā; Gyānijī Siddhacewaraṅgi, Jaggannāth; Māyārūpī, Matsya. The Nāthas are also the guardian spirits of the Himālayan peaks.

The Siddhas[3] are famous saints, of exceptional purity of life, who have attained to a semi-divine existence through the practice of Yoga. They are supposed to be living in the fastnesses of the Himālayas.[4] In the Nānak Śākhī an account is given of Nānak's visit to their retreat. There he finds, in the residence of Mahādeva, Gorakhnāth, Bhartṛhari and others in company with these perfect Yogīs.[5] At another time Nānak met, at Gorakhhatri, eighty-four Siddhas who performed miracles and wonders before him. One made a deer-skin fly in the air, another caused a stone to move about, a third gave forth fire and a fourth caused a wall to run about.[6] Later, he and Gorakhnātha talked together there.[7] Siddhas are referred to in Macauliffe.[8]

Besides the chief Siddhas there are others who are supposed to be still upon the earth.

It is a well-known belief that the Nāthas and the Siddhas follow Gorakhnāth in his wanderings, and that the path of this journey may be traced by the small trees bearing sugar candy which spring up wherever they go.[9]

There is, besides, a class of spirits, or beings, Siddhis, whom legends connect with Gorakhnāth. Generally they plague mankind. There are, however, celas who know the mind of their Siddhis and who can avert their anger, for a consideration.[10] Siddhis have special worshippers whose distinctive emblem is a silver siṅghi or cylindrical ornament,

---

1 *RTCP*, vol. II, p. 397. 2 *Census Berar, Report*, 1881, p. 59.
3 *RTCP*, vol. II, pp. 397, 398.
4 See *ERE*, vol. II, p. 94. A partial list of them is given in *Wi*, p. 214, note 2.
5 *Tr.*, p. xl. 6 *Tr.*, p. xlii.. 7 *Tr.*, pp. xlii, xliii, xliv.
8 *Mac.*, vol. I, p. 41.
9 *RTCP*, vol. II, p. 396.
10 *Census of the Panjab*, 1891, p. 115.

worn on a thread round the neck.[1] Villagers consider the Siddhis as demons who have received their power from Gorakhnāth. In the lower Himālayas of the Panjab, in Ambāla, and Hoshiyārpur, Siddhis are worshipped in the form of stones, under various names. There are several that are known by name: Ghāzidās has a considerable reputation near Una; and Cānu, said to have been a Camār (Camārs feast on goats and sing songs to him on certain occasions);[1] and Kāla Pīr worshipped in the low hills and throughout the eastern districts of the Panjab, and, more particularly as Kāla Mahār by the Sindhu Jāṭs as their forebear.[2] Sindus of Khot in Jīnd and Khātis and Lohārs worship him there. His samādh at Khot is in charge of an Āipanth Yogī.

Gorakṣa is sometimes considered as a name of Śiva, and Gorakhnāth is often looked upon as a manifestation of the dread god, and as such receives worship in some Śāivite temples. He is worshipped also in temples of his own. At Gorakhpur, where his gaddi is situated, his caran occupies the place of worship in the temple. His caran is an object of worship in Kāṭhiāwār also.[3] Images of Gorakhnāth are found in many places; for example, at Gorakhmandi,[4] in various places in the Himālayas, both in Garhwal and Kumaun, and at Trimbak:[5] and he is represented by a very large, realistic image in the shrine at Gorakh Bansuri. Furthermore, at some shrines of Gūgā his images, or shrines, are to be found, and also in some temples of Bhāiroṁ. Each year a stone liṅga is carried in procession from Dāṅg Cangra to Devī Pātan, and is worshipped on the way and for a period of four days at the latter place because it is supposed to contain the spirit of Gorakhnāth.[6] He is a household god among the Kānphaṭas of Belgaum.[7] The Gurkhas of the hills worship him in a special place in their houses, where lamps, flowers, sweetmeats and bel leaves make up the offerings;

---

[1] *OMAS*, p. 186, quoted from the *Panjab Census, Report*, 1891, p. 115. This is the siṅgnād.

[2] *RTCP*, vol. II, p. 397.

[3] *Bombay Gazetteer*, vol. VIII, p. 155.

[4] *Bombay Gazetteer*, vol. VIII, pp. 446, 447.

[5] See chap. six.

[6] For details of these references, see chap. five.

[7] *Bombay Gazetteer*, vol. XXI, p. 185.

and in the temples through pūjārīs of the sect. The morning and evening worship consists of the ringing of bells, the beating of drums, the circumambulation of the shrine and the offering of food which is then distributed in the form of prasād.

The worship of Dharamnāth is not so widespread as is that of his predecessor, his chief centre being at Dhinodhar, where his shrine is at the top of the hill. A temple containing his image is found in the compound of the monastery at the foot of the hill.[1] The service of worship is held twice a day. The image is washed and worshipped and flowers and leaves are offered. Incense and ghi are burned and a light (*artī*) is waved amidst the sounds of bells, gongs and drums, and the worshippers prostrate themselves before the image.

Other noted Yogīs of the sect receive reverent attention and gurus and mahants are recipients of offerings, the food placed before them being distributed as prasād.

The services of worship are in the hands of special officers, or pūjārīs. These persons are found at all the principal shrines and seats of the sect.

Besides this, Gorakhnāthīs serve as pūjārīs, or officiants, at various temples, especially to those of Bhāiroṁ and Śakti, and at some temples of Śiva.[2] In Benares they serve as priests of Kāl Bhāiroṁ,[3] and in the Himālayas, e.g. Almora, they are in possession of many temples of Bhāiroṁ, where they conduct worship. Some of these places of worship, as already stated, are in possession of women of the sect. All of the temples of Bhāiroṁ, except those where Khasiyas serve, are in their hands.[4] In the Panjab and in Northern India these Yogīs often act as priests for the village gods.[5] In the Himālayas they serve as priests of the lower Śakti worship and of the village gods.[6] They also act as pūjārīs at some shrines of Hulikā and of Sītalā Mātā. At Kurukṣetra, in the south-west of Rām Rāī, there is a temple of Kapilā Yakṣa,

[1] Compare *Bombay Gazetteer*, vol. V, p. 87.
[2] *Wi*, p. 217. [3] *SHTC*, p. 262; *Wi*, p. 217.
[4] Atkinson, *Himalayan Gazetteer*, vol. II, p. 865.
[5] *ERE*, vol. XII, p. 835; *Martin*, vol. III, p. 336; *CTC*, vol. III, p. 1.
[6] *CTC*, vol. III, p. 159.

the door-keeper of which was a Kānphaṭa Yogī.[1] Gorakhnāthīs are also in charge of the temples and shrines at the centres of their organization, temples of Śiva, Bhāiroṁ, Devī and others. Buchanan reported at Gorakhpur Kānphaṭas who were serving Śudras in their worship of Śiva.[2] At Dhinodhar the pīr takes charge of the annual sacrifice at the top of the hill on the Nāurātri (Śivrātri).

The ritual of worship is that of the ordinary type. An example may suffice. At Devī Pātan, at the noon-day offering to Bhāiroṁ, the pūjārī, taking in his hand a small dish heaped with cooked rice, walks around the shrine, or platform, his right hand towards it, pouring water as he goes. He next places the dish of rice before the platform, and then throws the food out for the dogs. At the same place the evening worship is begun by the beating of the kettle drums and the ringing of the temple bells. After this has gone on for about half an hour, the temple doors are opened, and the offerings to the Devī are made in the usual way.

The offerings used in worship in temples and at samādhs are those commonly given to Śiva (Mahādeo) such as flowers, bilva leaves, dhatura, water, uncooked rice, sweets and camphor. Cocoanuts, cooked food, leaves of thick bread (roṭ) and incense are also presented to the gods and saints. Offerings of food are consumed by the worshippers. Before mahants and the chief gurus food and sweets are offered and consumed as prasād. In procession at the annual mela at Tulsipur all sorts of things, including food, sweets, and chickens are presented before the pīr and carried away as holy, or left in his path. The Triśul, usually of iron, sometimes of bamboo, nearly always painted red, is commonly offered to Bhāiroṁ. At the right of the approach to the door of the shrine at Gorakhpur, there is a very large collection of such weapons, and the space below the platform is said to be filled up with them.

The blood sacrifice is common. Animal sacrifices include, in Nepāl, buffaloes and goats, and an occasional rhinoceros. In many places, as in Nepāl and at Devī Pātan, slaughter is

---

[1] *IA*, 1894, p. 300, *Archæological Survey of India*, vol. XIV, p. 86.
[2] *Martin*, vol. II, pp. 484, 485.

carried on on a large scale.[1] At Devī Pātan the sacrifice of suckling pigs is made close to the temple. At Dhinodhar two buffaloes, one of which is given by the Rāo of Kacch and the other by the Yogīs, are sacrificed to Bhāiroṁ on the Nāurātri of Dasehra. At Gorakhpur, at the same festival, even Hinduised Musalmāns sacrifice animals at the shrine.[2] On the question of human sacrifice see the description of Kāmākhyā. Gorakhnāth and Bhīmsen are said to have substituted the sacrifice of buffaloes for that of human beings.[3]

An interesting ceremony is that in which a drop of blood from the little finger or from the tip of the tongue is offered to Bhāiroṁ. This is done by one who does not eat flesh, or who does not care to offer animal sacrifice. Again, it is said that if no goat is provided for the worship of Bhāiroṁ at Kālrātri, the pūjārī must offer some of his own blood, or he must offer what Bhāiroṁ requests, speaking through a worshipper who drinks the blood.

In former times, at Dhinodhar, when trouble threatened. Yogīs used to commit *trāga*, sacrificing one of their own number, so that the guilt of his blood might fall upon the oppressor's head.[4]

In the left hand worship of Śakti the sacrifice takes the form of the five tattvas, or 'realities'—wine, flesh, fish, parched grain and sexual intercourse.[5]

Some attention should be given to the religious festivals of the Hindus with special reference to Yogīs.

Besides the melas and festivals connected with special shrines, such as that at Devī Pātan, and described above, and the great melas at the sacred places of Hindustan, the Kānphaṭas celebrate the sacred seasons belonging to the worship of Śiva. Among these is the Nāurātri of Dasehra. This is the celebration of the nine nights (and ten days) of the light half of the lunar month Aśvina (the time of the

---

[1] See account in chap. five.

[2] Alexander, *Statistical Description and Historical Account of the North-Western Provinces of India, Gorakhpur*, p. 365.

[3] *Martin*, vol. III, p. 38. Or the eating of buffaloes in the place of human sacrifice.

[4] *Bombay Gazetteer*, vol. V, p. 87.

[5] See next chapter, under the description of Śakti.

autumnal equinox). At Dhinodhar the pīr takes charge of the annual sacrifice which is performed on the top of the hill. This is the only time during the year when he makes the ascent. During this festival a special offering in charity is made at the monastery, the food being cooked in the four famous caldrons that date from the time of Dharamnāth.[1] This is also an important occasion at Kāmākhyā and at Gorakhpur. The great festival at Ṭilla takes place at this time, when throngs of men, women and children make the difficult ascent and are supplied with accommodation, food and coverings while there.[2] For here, as at other places, the Yogīs pride themselves on their liberality.

Gorakhnāthīs recognize also the feasts of Śivrātri.[3] The thirteenth of the light half of each lunar month is sacred to Śiva, and he is worshipped at sunset, a fast being kept until the stars appear. However, it is the dark thirteenth of each month that is called Śivrātri and that is devoted to the worship of Śiva the terrible. The Śivrātri of Māgh (some say Phālguṇa), Mahāśivrātri, is the chief day of the year for his worship. A very famous legend explains why this is so, why worship at this time is of absolute value.[4] A hunter, a man of bad character, going out to hunt one day, which happened to be *Māgha kṛṣṇa* thirteenth (the thirteenth of the dark half of the month of Māgh), passed a Śiva temple, and saw a number of people worshipping the liṅga, singing, calling out 'Śiva, Śiva,' etc. Mockingly the hunter imitated their cries, and without his knowledge or desire, the very utterance of the god's name on that holy day removed some of his sins. He killed nothing that day, and had to keep an involuntary fast. As night came on, through fear of wild beasts, he climbed into a tree, which happened to be a

---

[1] See p. 115; and *IA*, vol. VII, p. 51.

[2] Rose, *RTCP*, vol. I, p. 289, says that the fair is not attended by many now, on account of the difficulties of the road, but that Yogīs make an effort to visit the cave at Ṭilla.

[3] See Murdock, *Hindu and Muhammadan Festivals*; Wilson, *Religion of the Hindus*, vol. II, pp. 201 ff, 395; Underhill, *The Hindu Religious Year*, pp. 93 ff; as well as the works of Monier-Williams, Mukerji and others.

[4] Told by Underhill, *Hindu Religious Year*, p. 93, from the *Skanda Purāṇa* and *Śiva Purāṇa*. The story has been reported many times.

bel tree (the wood-apple, sacred to Śiva), but was unable to sleep, owing to the cold, thus keeping an involuntary vigil. Not only so, but, shivering and shaking, he dislodged a number of bel leaves, which fell, together with moisture, from the tree on a stone Śiva liṅga beneath, thereby offering, involuntarily, bel leaves and cool water to the god. The cumulative merit of all these involuntary acts not only released him from past sins, but caused his reception into Śiva's abode of Kāilāsa.

According to this tradition, the celebration marks the day when Śiva first manifested himself, as a marvellous and interminable liṅga, to Brahmā and Viṣṇu.[1]

The establishment of the festival is attributed to Śiva himself. The worship of Śivrātri is open to all classes, even to Caṇḍālas and women, the use of mantras, except *Oṁ*, being permitted to them.

The fast for the Śivrātri lasts for twenty-four hours. The worshipper abstains from food and drink during the day. At every third hour during the night the liṅga must be worshipped with offerings of flowers, dhatura, ketiki (*Sk. Ketaka*, *Paṇḍanus odoratissimus*, used only at this time), and bel leaves. It must be bathed in succession with milk, curds, ghi and honey; and with water from the Ganges; or water from some other running stream is poured over it. Gesticulations are prescribed and prayers are addressed to various subordinate divinities connected with Śiva.[2] On the morning of the fourteenth the worshipper must bathe, and after anointing himself with sesamum oil, worship the liṅga with mantras, with the recitation of the 1,008 names of Śiva, offering 1,000 or 108 bel leaves. At the conclusion of worship the priest recites the story related on the preceding page.

In addition, Kānphaṭas stay awake all night, singing songs in honour of Gorakhnāth,[3] and worship the feet both of Gorakhnāth and Matsyendranāth.[4]

On this night a flag is said to ascend the face of the cliff at Ṭilla, from the bottom to the top, by the help of an unseen hand.[5]

---

[1] *Īśāna Saṁhitā*. [2] For details see *Wi*, vol. II, pp. 213 ff.
[3] *RTCCP*, vol. III, p. 252. [4] *Census Report, Berār*, 1881, p. 60.
[5] *Census Report, Panjab*, 1891, p. 117.

The worship of Śakti is involved in this festival.

Vāmacārīs keep, besides the Mahārātri, the night of Kālarātri (of *Kriṣṇajanmāṣṭamī*), the Mahārātri, or Kālīśaturdaśī, of the fourteenth of the second half of Aśvina, and the Dāruṇīrātri kept on the day before the Holi festival (the fifteenth day of the first half of Phālguṇa). Moreover, nine nights in each of the months, Aśvina, Cāitra, Pāuṣa and Āṣādha are observed as holy. Ceremonies performed on any of these nights must of necessity confer superhuman power on the worshipper.

The observances of Śivrātri expiate all sin, secure the attainment of all desires during life, and union with Śiva, or final release, after death. The liberal Akbar was initiated into the secrets of the Yogīs, and on the Śivrātri ate and drank with them, expecting to prolong his life fourfold thereby. He wore his hair in their fashion, and anticipated the liberation of his soul by the fontanelle, as they teach.[1]

The festival of Śivrātri is a comparatively modern celebration.[2]

Kāl Bhāiroṁ is worshipped, as a manifestation of Śiva, on the dark eighth of the lunar month, particularly on that of Kārttikā, which is considered his birthday. At his temple at Bhudargad, a mela is held on the first ten days of the dark half of Māgha. At Devgad he has a temple where, it is believed, all sickness due to evil spirits may be cured. Fairs are held there on the Mahāśivrātri and on the eleventh to the fifteenth of the light half of Kārttikā.

At a temple of Bhāiravanāth at Sonāri a fair is held from the eighth to the fifteenth of Cāitra.

At Kāṭhmāṇḍu in Nepāl there is a procession at this time.[3]

Connected with the name of Matsyendranāth[4] is the annual festival, the most popular of all festivals, at the capital

---

[1] *Wi*, vol. II, p. 395.

[2] See Underhill, *The Hindu Religious Year*, pp. 96, 117, 131, 151, 164, 174 for further references.

[3] See chap. 'Legends'; and Levi, *Le Nepāl*. vol. II, pp. 44 ff.

[4] See Landon, *Nepāl*, for description and some good pictures. See also for these festivals, Kirkpatrick, *Kingdom of Nepāl*, pp. 192, 194, 195.

of Nepāl. This ceremony brings in the rains of the spring. Matsyendranāth came into Nepāl to release the Nāgas whose confinement by Gorakhnāth had brought on a twelve years' drought. It is believed that without Matsyendra's influence the heavens would still withhold the rains. This procession of Matsyendranāth marks the solemn opening of the religious year. It has become the annual fête of the land. The object of veneration at this festival is a small image of Matsyendranāth, an idol about three feet high, painted red. It is evidently very old. During the whole period of the celebration a company of soldiers, under the command of a *sardār*, accompanies the idol.

On the first day of Vāiśākhavadi,[1] the Nikhus of Pātan take the idol from the temple and carry it in procession to the south of the town, to the exact spot where, under a tree, Narendra Deva and his company halted on their return from Kāpōtal with the pot in which Matsyendranāth, in the form of a bee, was confined. There the idol is placed upon a stone platform, undressed, and bathed, except the head which they are not permitted to touch. This is the 'Bath of Matsyendranāth.' The sword of the king, equivalent to the sceptre of Nepāl, is then presented to the god; and the idol is brought back to its temple, painted and dressed.

On the eighth day the idol is exposed to the sun. The Nikhus, who are Śāivites, then make the idol over to the *Banras*.[2]

On the twelfth and thirteenth the Banras perform the ten ceremonies, beginning with the conception of Matsyendranāth, introducing the god as an infant to be born in the regular ranks of society.

On the first of Vāiśākhiśudi the procession of the cars begins. Two cars are provided; one, very large, in the eastern outskirts of Pātan, near the Cāitaya of Aśoka,[3] the other, a smaller car, in Pātan itself, in the court of the temple of Matsyendranāth. The larger car carries, on a platform of

[1] The dark half of Vāiśākha, an auspicious month corresponding to April–May.

[2] Monks of Nepalese Buddhism, who are not celibate.

[3] Landon, *Nepāl*, vol. I, p. 209, note 2. At the northern stupa of Aśoka, the wheels of the car are kept.

wood, a chapel, square, plated with gilt, which has around it a footpath permitting circumambulation. The roof of the chapel supports a pyramid of lattice work interlaced with ribbons. On the top of the pyramid, twenty or twenty-five metres high, is set a gilded image of Vajrasattva, which is crowned with a bouquet of leaves. Landon says that the superstructure of the car is raised to some sixty feet, being renewed annually; that this 'sky-piercing car' is about twenty-five feet broad and that in old days no house in Pātan was allowed to be taller than the spire of the car of Macchendranāth.[1] The four wheels of the car have for ornaments eyes of Bhāirava. Fastened to the axles is a long, light pole which is bent back to the front, and which bears on its extreme end a head of Bhāirava. The second car is not a reproduction of the other, but a distinctive one on which is placed the small red image. It is drawn by the crowd. The route is divided into three stages at each of which there takes place a regular programme of sacrifices and offerings. The most important stage is the last, at the fountain of gold, the grove of Narendra. All the Newār population of Pātan takes part in the fête, and the king, followed by the prime minister and the nobles, all mounted on elephants, joins the procession. The cars are turned to the right of the grove, and are kept there for two nights. At another station, a short distance away, the cars are halted for from ten to twenty days, waiting for a propitious time for the *Gūdṛī Yātrā*. When the astrologers have discovered a favourable day, the procession moves on and the cars are drawn to the parade grounds at the north-east of the village. There they remain for three nights awaiting the great day of the festival, the day when the idol is undressed before the people. All are eager to take part in this ceremony. The Banras in full dress, clothed in red robes, their heads freshly shaved, lean the small car against the larger one. They take from its sacred niche the holy image and remove, piece by piece, its tinsel-spangled garments. It is the shirt which all wish to see, and the priests show it solemnly to the crowd. The people bow, worship and prostrate themselves before it.

[1] Landon, *Nepāl*, vol. I, p. 210.

After this ceremony, the image is free to leave Pātan. The undressed idol is transferred, under a shower of flowers and offerings, to a sort of holy ark, which the Banras carry on their shoulders. As the procession passes Bāgmati, flowers are strewn in the way and fireworks are set off. Bāgmati is the old Amarāpura, the place where one of the bearers of the pot, which contained Matsyendranāth, barked like a dog, when the company was returning from Kāpōtal.

The image is kept for about six months at Bāgmati. It is then returned to Pātan.

On every twelfth year Matsyendra refuses to travel in the usual manner. Consequently, at Bāgmati, a car is made, on which it is possible both to carry and bring back the god. In this instance the procession goes right across the uneven fields, through furrows, streams and gullies, avoiding the roads.

One of the most recent descriptions of this festival, reported by eye-witnesses, is as follows:

'The Machendrajātra is divided into three portions. Firstly, the bathing of the image of the god near Narendra Deva's tree in Pātan; secondly, the parading of the image in a car through the streets of Pātan; and thirdly, the unrobing of the image and exhibition of his shirt to the people. The image is taken out of the temple of Macchendra at Pātan and, in the presence of a large crowd, is bathed and carefully washed on the stone platform beneath the sacred tree. After this, he is carried back with much pomp to the temple, and there painted and got ready for his appearance at the principal ceremony. Seventeen days after the bathing ceremony, the image is dragged through the main streets, and on this occasion there are two cars, each consisting of a square chamber, covered with copper-gilt plates in the case of the larger and with thatch in the case of the smaller. These are placed on rough wagons, some six or seven feet high, and in the larger one is placed the image of the god. The cars are dragged, by means of ropes, by about one hundred and fifty men, and the whole circuit of about a mile and a quarter is performed in three stages, at the end of which a halt is made at some previously appointed spot, where sacrifices are performed and great feasting takes place. The third stage includes the circuit of Narendra Deva's tree, and at this place the cars stand for two whole nights. After this they proceed to an open space near the city, called Puriya Tāl, where they remain for another ten to twenty days, awaiting the auspicious day for them to be dragged to the parade grounds for the disrobing of the image. On the day of the disrobing about six Banras, dressed in red and with shaven heads, bring the small car to the side of the large one. The Banras then proceed to undress the image as he sits in his car, taking off his clothes piece by piece until they come to the shirt. This is then held aloft for all to see and worship, after which this also is packed away in a box. The Banras now take the unclothed image out of its shrine and place it in the smaller car which is now borne in triumph to Bhungmatti, a spot near Pātan where Narendra Deva halted during his return from pilgrimage, where it remains for six months.'[1]

The religious year which opens with the procession of Matsyendranāth, of Pātan, closes with the festival of Little Matsyendra at Kāṭhamāṇḍu. This second is quite different from the former festival. The image of Little Matsydendra is not red, but white. It does not represent Padmapāṇi, but Samantabhadra.[2] The origin of the fête goes back to the fifteenth century, and is explained as follows. Some potters, while digging for potter's clay, exhumed a statue which dated from the reign of Guṇakāmadeva, and which was none other than Sāmu Matsyendra. The king had the image repaired and built for it a temple. In the seventeenth century Partāpa Mālla established in honour of this god a car festival, which continues down to today. Barring accidents, it lasts four days, from the eighth to the eleventh of Cāitraśudi. Only Newārs celebrate this festival. But the ninth is a day of general celebration, because on that day the Gurkhas observe a Hindu festival in honour of Rāma.[3]

The festival of the Nāgpañcamī, on the fifth lunar day of

---

[1] *The Gurkhas*, pp. 174–5.

[2] For a full account of these festivals see Levi, *Le Nepāl*, vol. II, pp. 44 ff.; 59 f. and Landon, *Nepāl*, vol. I, pp. 212 ff.

[3] The festival of *Rāma navamī*. But, ordinarily, at least in Tibet, Avalokiteśvara is painted white. What is the relationship? See Frankle, *Antiquities of India and Tibet*, vol. I, p. 94.

the light half of Śrāvaṇa, in the rainy season, is observed by Kānphaṭas. The black cobra is venerated, and the Yogīs engage in conversation about snakes and exhibit them, some even carrying them about.[1] Figures of serpents and birds are painted on the walls of houses. Seven days before the festival a mixture of wheat, grām and pulse is steeped in water; and on the morning of the Nāgpañcamī, a wisp of grass is tied up in the form of a snake, dipped in the liquor, and placed with honey and sweetmeats before pictures of serpents. A fast is kept from noon on the fourth of Śrāvaṇa, and the worshipper bathes at dawn on the fifth. Either an earthen image of a cobra, or a picture, must be worshipped. Saucers of milk are placed near known or suspected snake-holes as offerings. People abstain from digging, plowing, or otherwise disturbing the earth, whereby snakes might be injured. Women abstain from grinding, pounding rice, even from slicing vegetables. On the fifth, feasts are held and presents are made.

The pageant of Gūgā known as the Chaṛī Mela, is celebrated at this time.[2] The *chaṛī* is sometimes carried by Yogīs, who sing songs in his honour and beg.

At Śirālā, a centre of snake worship, where there is a temple of Gorakhnāth,[3] a fair is held on Nāgpañcamī, when snakes are caught and worshipped, afterwards being set free.

Where there is a special shrine (*sthān*) for serpents, as at Devī Pātan, it is utilized for this occasion.

Reference has already been made to the mela at the Serpent Well in Benares, during this festival.

---

[1] *E.g.* in Almora. Devī Pātan reported this also.

[2] See *The Chamārs*, p. 151 f. In some places Musalmān Yogīs carry Gūgā's *Chaṛī*. *IA*, vol. XXVI, p. 84.

[3] Underhill, *The Hindu Religious Year*, p. 174. See also above, under 'Serpent-worship.'

CHAPTER EIGHT

THE PANTHEON

Yogīs are essentially Śāivites. The range of their interests and of their historical connections includes, however, other elements. In the first place, Viṣṇu is not without attention. The images on the face of the *Dharamśāla* on the top of Dhinodhar serve as an illustration. Hanumān and Rām Chandra have their shrines at certain monasteries, such as that at Ṭilla, and both, together with aspects of Vāiṣṇavism, and even Viṣṇu himself, are assimilated to certain divisions of the Gorakhnāthīs and are constantly noted in the legends.[1] The image of Garuḍa is found in the establishment at Purī. Hanumān is represented in certain forms of the ṭikā. The rudrākṣa of ten faces symbolizes the ten *avatāras* of Viṣṇu. Many of the Vaiṣṇavite Bhaktas of Western India trace their doctrines through Gorakhnāth. At Gorakhpur the decorations on the *samādhs* and shrines contain many Vaiṣṇavite symbols and images. According to the *Śiva Saṁhitā* the chanting of the name of Viṣṇu is necessary in Yoga practices when the attention is directed to the cakras.[2]

Buddhist elements and contacts are numerous. Not only is the Tāntra-Yoga system, which the Yogīs follow, a mixture of late Buddhism with Brahmanistic elements, but also the history of the Kānphaṭas shows many Buddhist marks. In Bengal, Matsyendranāth, Gorakhnāth, Hāḍi and others are claimed as Buddhist saints. According to Bengal traditions Gorakhnāth was originally a Buddhist by the name of

---

[1] See chapters on 'Sacred Places'; and also tables of the divisions of the Goraknāthīs in the appendix to chapter four, and their *Paramparās* in Abbott's books.

[2] 3. 35.

Ramaṇavajra belonging to the Vajrayāna.[1] He became a convert to Śāivism, took the new name, and became the great protagonist of the latter cult. These men were related also to the Dharma movement. One of the Yogī castes of Bengal is still known as the Dharmagiri Yogī. Śākya, one of the godlings of the death ceremonies, mentioned on page forty-two, points in the same direction. In Nepāl, Matsyendranāth is identified with Avalokiteśvara, and his annual festival there swings around an ancient Buddhist image (Levi). A book in tenth-century character Bengali is attributed to him. It is not a Buddhist work. Furthermore, the struggle between movements, indicated at the beginning of Chapter Four may point to this period. Śaṅkara was a great protagonist of Śāivism in the east. The struggle which he inaugurated was continued for centuries before Buddhism was overcome, yet elements of it persist and continue in modern forms of Tāntric Hinduism. Ramifications of the sect of the Kān-phaṭas in the north-west and beyond the borders of India, point to Buddhist influences.

Jāin contacts are not wanting; and the sons of Matsyendra-nāth, Nīmnāth and Pārasnāthpūj are both Jāin saints. A Jāin temple near Pāe Dhūnī in Bombay city shelters an idol of Ghorajīnāth, bedecked with gems.

The Islamic contacts with the organization are evidenced in the modern possession of such shrines as that at Hiṅg

---

[1] Consult *Sen*, p. 28; *Or.*, especially the Introduction; Tāranāth; *The Art of the Pal Empire*, by French, which illustrates this period, especially Vajrayāna. The stages of Buddhist development in Bengal from about the seventh century of our era were: Mantra-yāna, which substituted invocations for Dhāraṇīs, in the use of short words and letters in invoking the spirits of the Buddha and the Bodhisāts; Vajrayāna, in which was a mixture of mystical philosophy and sensuality with the worship of Nirātma Devī, the Formless Void into whose embrace the devotee, bent on *bodhi* lept, there enjoying something like the pleasures of the senses, and finally disappearing; and Kālacakrayāna, through which deliverance from the wheel of destruction was achieved. These Buddhist elements were absorbed into the Nāthamārga. This form of religion arose outside of Buddhism. Matsyendranātha was a Nātha. Tradition shows him carrying his sectarianism into Nepāl, and Gorakhnāth as his disciple. Of the Great Nāthas, Gorakhnāth was the only heretic (from Buddhism).

Lāj by Muslims and in the worship conducted at the tomb of the Muslim at Devī Pātan. Here, at four o'clock in the morning, and at six in the evening, milk, rice, incense and a lamp are placed. There are groups of Musalmān Yogīs. These notices are merely suggestive, not exhaustive.

The chief concern of the Yogīs is, however, with Śiva and the Śāivite faith. In the symbols everywhere in evidence at their sacred places, in the legends and in ceremony, Śiva and his consort are always to the front. The festivals at numerous establishments of the Kānphaṭas are peculiarly Śāivite. And at Dhinodar, to cite one example, the head of the monastery repeats a hymn in Śiva's honor on the second of every month.[1] Or, it might be said that his Śakti is paramount.

In this account of Śiva, attention is confined to such aspects of his history, character, and activities as are pertinent to the beliefs and practices of the Yogīs.

While the beneficent aspects of his character are persistently emphasized, his name being the expression of his auspicious character, and while he is an object of devotion by his followers, still, Śiva's other and sinister aspects, in which he appears as extremely irascible in temper and as easily aroused to deeds of violence, are conspicuous; and his fierce, wild character is never lost sight of. It is Śiva the destroyer, the terrible, at the same time reproducer, or recreator, who is constantly worshipped. These characteristics are brought to the fore in the great part that Bhāiroṁ (Bhāirava) plays in the worship of the Kānphaṭas and in the place that the yoni-liṅga and the adoration of Śakti occupy in their cult. Moreover, Śiva is the ascetic *par excellence*, the chief of the Yogīs, Yogeśvar. Indeed, it is Śiva who revealed to Pārvatī the secret doctrine of the Yoga, and it was because a certain Matsyendranāth, in the form of a fish, overheard Śiva as he expounded the teaching, that the Gorakhnāthīs are now in possession of this secret of Śiva. (Pārvatī went to sleep while Śiva was expounding the doctrine.) And it is he who has taught by example that the attainment of bliss is by voluntary torture of the flesh, by the subjugation of the turbulent passions, and by undisturbed meditation. In the cult both meditation and physical

---

[1] *Bombay Gazetteer*, vol. V, p. 87.

discipline are emphasized, while even licence of every kind is made to serve in the attainment of *samādhi*. Their Haṭha Yoga includes the use of *dhāuti* and certain secret practices as well as the practice of the *śrīcakra* and other *vāmacāra* rites, and of the use of drugs, all aiming at *rapport* with the mystic, superhuman, creative forces of the universe. Thus, both Śiva and his consort are inseparably involved in the cult and its traditions.

Śiva, Mahādeva, as the great ascetic, appears quite naked, with one face, with matted hair, ash-besmeared, sitting in profound meditation under a banyan tree, or under a canopy formed of hooded serpents, or in a remote mountain retreat, passionless, motionless, immovable, rooted to the spot for millions of years.[1] In the *Purāṇas* he is depicted as a mendicant dressed in a tiger's skin, with matted locks and with snakes serving as ribbons and apron strings. He carries a trident. His half-shut eyes are watery, and his garb and demeanour suggest a person under the influence of wine and narcotics.[2] Dakṣa's description of Śiva is as follows.[3] He roams about in dreadful cemeteries, attended by hosts of goblins and spirits, like a mad man, naked, with dishevelled hair, laughing, weeping, bathed in the ashes of funeral piles, wearing a garland of skulls and ornaments of human bones, insane, beloved of the insane, the lord of beings whose nature is essentially darkness. In another passage he is described as bearing the liṅga desired by devotees, ashes, a staff, a tuft of hair, an antelope's skin and a digit of the moon, his body shining like an evening cloud. He has great powers of concentration, and once, when disturbed, by the fire of his third eye he burned Kāma to ashes.[4] He is called Bōlānāth, Lord of Forgetfulness, and as such wanders about in abstraction, drowsy with drugs, or sinks in meditation.' 'Bom, Bom,' is a cry meaning 'forgetfulness.'[5]

---

[1] See *Brahmanism and Hinduism*, chap. four.

[2] *BCHS*, p. 367.

[3] Quoted from the *Mahābhārata* by Atkinson in *The Himalayan Districts*, vol. II, p. 722.

[4] Here belongs the whole history of the site, Kāmrūp, and the goddess Kāmākyā. See below, pp. 166 ff.

[5] *Bengali Religious Lyrics*, Śākta, pp. 16, 42.

In like character he appears in the *Great Epic*.[1] There we have the typical Yogī, intent on the attainment of ecstatic and magical powers through self-torture and self-induced vacuity, apathy and trance, accompanied by intervals of morbid nervous and cerebral exaltation.[2] Another description of Śiva will intensify the picture. 'He wears an ornament of serpents made of leather; has a third eye painted with soap-stone on his forehead; holds a trident in his fist; carries a cunningly designed lute; has a mass of braids piled like a diadem on his head; puts on a black cloth like an elephant's skin; daubs his body with ashes; and has a garland of skulls hanging about his neck.[3] With this description are associated awful rites of black magic. Barth says: 'From the outset, and more than any other Hindu religion, Śāivism has pandered to ascetic fanaticism. No other has exhibited so many horrible and revolting observances, or has worn with so much ostentation the badge, often singular enough, of devotion.'[4] These descriptions lend significance to the study of the Śāivite cults that preceded that of the Kānphaṭas and of which these later Yogīs are the descendents.

In besmearing his body with ashes, Śiva relates himself to goblins and all the horrors of the cemetery. And in this practice the later ghastly and ghoulish aspects of asceticism come into view. Such sects as the Kāpākika[5] which were the precursors of the Gorakhnāthīs, and the Aghorīs made much use of some of these elements.

With Śiva is associated the bull, and the phallic element in his worship is always present. The samādhs of the Yogīs are surmounted by the yoni-liṅga; these emblems are symbolized in the siṅgnād and the pāvitrī of their sacred thread; the brand mark which Yogīs receive at Koteśvar is a representation of these same figures; and, of course, every temple of their sect contains these symbols. The worship of the liṅga

---

[1] *E.g.*, 12, 328; 8, 23.

[2] Compare Gough, *Philosophy of the Upanishads*, pp. 18, 19.

[3] Hemavijaya's *Kathāratnākāra*, Story 133, rendered by Bloomfield, *JAOS*, vol. XLIV, p. 209.

[4] *Religions of India*, p. 214.

[5] See chap. ten.

is very old in India,[1] and it is probable that it owes its origin to aboriginal sources. It is possible that this worship, like that of Śiva himself, in some of his aspects, found its way into Brāhmanic culture slowly at first. At any rate, early references to phallic worship are few. There are two in the *Ṛig Veda* (7, 21, 5; 10, 99, 3), if such be the meaning of *śiśna*. The term is one of reproach and descriptive of non-Aryans. In later times, Sāyaṇa remarked that those who sported with the *śiśna* were unchaste. The *Rāmāyaṇa* does not know the liṅga[2] but in the *Didactic Epic* it, like Śiva himself, is fairly well-known.[3]

'Śiva' is not the name of a god either in the *Ṛig-* or in the *Atharva-Veda*, but the word, which means 'auspicious,'[4] is used to describe Rudra. As a god, Śiva does not appear before 200 B.C.

Rudra, of the Vedic pantheon, is quite un-Aryan in his character, but he exhibits some characteristics which are of interest in this study, both from the point of view of the physician, of one manipulating the storms, and of his horrible and terrible acts. In the *Ṛig Veda*[5] he is intelligent; bountiful; a healer of cattle, kine, men and children; a dispenser of healing remedies; a granter of prosperity. He is ruddy in colour. Withal, he is strong, impetuous and crooked, and he injures vengefully; he is described as having braided hair and as the unshorn ascetic; he is fierce, purifying, rain-dispensing;[6] he is the father of the storm gods (Maruts),[7] the wielder of the thunderbolt, the bow and arrow; he is renowned as youthful, mounted on his chariot, and like a wild beast, destructive, fierce, a terrible and manslaying god; he is the roaring god of

[1] *Iconography, Indian*, vol. II, pt. 1, p. 55; Muir, *Sanskrit Texts*, vol. IV, p. 345. The earliest known representations of the liṅga are of the first century: (1) from Bhīṭā, now in the Lucknow museum; (2) at Gudimallam in North Arcot. See *ERE*, vol. XI, p. 92. See also *Marshall*, vol. I, pp. 58 ff. There seems to have been a counterpart of Śiva in the ancient Indus civilization.

[2] *ORLI*, p. 48.

[3] *E.g.*, 8, 33: 45; 7, 200–1, 93–96, 202, 203; 13, 14: 233 ff.

[4] *Rig Veda*, 1, 64: 8.

[5] 1, 143: 1-11. Compare 1, 114.

[6] 1, 64: 2.

[7] 1, 85: 1, etc.

the monsoon, of the lightning in its destructive function.[1] In the *Satarudriya*[2] the god's one hundred aspects are set forth. The older characteristics, already enumerated, are repeated and his terrible, cruel, fierce nature is emphasized. He is blue-necked. A sinister phase of his character is brought out in that he is a patron of robbers, rogues, pilferers and murderers, and the guardian of roads. Withal he is auspicious (*śiva*).[3] If in the *Ṛig Veda* he is malevolent, in the later Vedas he is more fierce and terrible.[4] It is in the *Yajur Veda* that Rudra is first called Īśvara and Mahādeva, and that he begins to appear as Śaṅkara and Śiva as well. In the *Atharva Veda* and in the *Brāhamaṇas* Rudra is called the Lord of Animals, Paśupati.[5] In the *Atharva Veda* his wide-mouthed, howling dogs, who swallow their prey unchewed, are mentioned.[6] He gives consumption and poison and is the destructive lightning.[7] In the *Upaniṣads* he takes on the characters of creator and sage and is described pantheistically.[8] In the *Atharva Śīras* Rudra is set forth in similar fashion; is identified with Gāurī, Umā, Viṣṇu, Brahmā, and Maheśvara, and is spoken of as immortal, imperishable, the creator, sustainer and destroyer.

His epithet, Paśupati, brings to view his character as sparing cattle, as significant of his beneficent aspects.[9] As the Lord of the open fields, he is Lord of the cattle which roam in them. Also he was the god that held sway over regions away from home, over fields, wildernesses, cemeteries, mountains, old trees and rivers. Whenever a man came to anything which inspired awe and terror, Rudra was the god thought of and prayed to to protect. . . . In Rudra-Śāivism the sentiment of fear is at the bottom, however concealed it may have become in certain developments of it, and this sentiment it is that

---

[1] The references are (besides those quoted): 1, 122: 1; 2, 33: 1-15; 3, 2: 5; 4, 3: 1; 5, 41: 2; 5, 42: 11; 5, 59: 8; 5, 60: 5; 5, 28: 7; 6, 66: 3; 6, 74: 1 ff; 7, 10: 4; 7, 35: 6; 7, 40: 5; 7, 46: 1, 2; 7, 56: 1; 7, 58: 5; 8, 13: 20; 8, 20: 17; 8, 29: 5; 8, 61: 3; 10, 64: 8; 10, 66: 3; 10, 92: 5; 10, 93: 7; 10, 125: 6; 10, 126: 5; 10, 126: 1; 10, 169: 1.

[2] *Vājasaneyi saṁhitā*, 16, 1-66.

[3] *E.g.*, verses 2, 3, 41.

[4] See references in Macdonell's *Vedic Mythology*.

[5] A root Śāivite sect of the Yogīs are the Pāśupaṭas.

[6] 11, 2. [7] 11, 2: 26. [8] *Śvet. Up.*, 3, 1 ff.

[9] *Vaiṣṇavism, Śaivism*, etc., p. 102.

has worked itself out in the formation of the various Rudra-Śāiva systems of later times.[1]

In the *Rāmāyaṇa*, Rudra is called Mahādeva and Śiva, as in the *Didactic Epic*. He curses Kāma;[2] receives Umā from Himāvat;[3] his cunnubial life with her is described;[4] and he catches Gaṅgā as she falls from heaven.[5]

With the *Didactic Epic* Rudra has become Mahādeva, or Śiva; and Śiva meets with growing recognition as the equal of Brahmā and Viṣṇu, is worshipped by Kṛiṣṇa[6] and even transcends the gods.[7] One of his female devotees thus describes him (Mahādeva, Śiva;[8])

> He assumes many forms of gods (as Brahmā, Viṣṇu, Indra, Rudra) and of men, of goblins, demons, barbarians, tame and wild beasts, birds, reptiles, fishes, with many varieties of human disguises etc. He is the soul of all the worlds, all-pervading, residing in the heart of all creatures, knowing all desires. He carries a discus, a trident, a club, a sword, and an axe. He has a girdle of serpents, ear-rings of serpents, a sacrificial cord of serpents, an outer garment of serpents' skins. He laughs, sings, dances charmingly, and plays various musical instruments. He leaps, gapes, weeps, makes others weep; speaks like a mad man or a drunkard, as well as in sweet tones. He laughs terrifically. He is both visible and invisible, on the altar, on the sacrificial post, in the fire, a boy, an old man, a youth. He dallies with the daughters and the wives of the Ṛiṣis, with erect hair, obscene appearance,[9] naked, with excited look. He is one-faced, two-faced, three-faced, many-faced.

All through the *Anuśāsanaparva*, Mahādeva is exalted and his old character as the terrible is emphasized. Even the gods, at the sound of the twang of his bow, are afraid.

Again Rudra (Śiva) burns up the three cities (Tripura) of the Asuras,[10] in the heaven of gold, in the atmosphere of silver on the earth of black iron. These he destroyed with a single arrow with one half of the strength of the gods.[11] He eats

---

[1] *Vaiṣṇavism, Śaivism*, etc., p. 106.

[2] I, 12: 10 ff. [3] I, 36: 20. [4] I, 37: 5 ff. [5] I. 43: 48.

[6] *Vanaparva*, 1, 513-1,656; *Droṇaparva*, 2,838 ff; 2,862 ff.

[7] *Anuśāsanaparva*, 588 ff; 839 ff.

[8] *Anuśāsanaparva*, verses 731 ff., 742 f., 745, 746, 748, 749, 751, 742. Quoted from Muir, *Sanskrit Texts*, vol. IV, p. 160.

[9] *Ingenti membro virili proeditus.*

[10] *Karṇaparva*, 1,402 ff. Compare the story of Dharamnāth and the destruction of cities in Kacch.

[11] *Karṇaparva*, 1,433 ff.

flesh, blood, marrow, and is fiery and fierce. He frequents cemeteries, performs awful rites there, and is very terrible. Kings offer human sacrifice to him[1] and make such offerings as are now made in his temples. He is the chief of Bhūtas (Demons) and he is served by Bhūtas, and Pisācas, and is called Bhāirava.

Śiva is, then, the terrible Rudra, whose qualities are thus preserved.

Still, there is evidence that Śiva had not fully attained to equality with the other gods when the *Epics* were being rewritten.[2] He evidently gained his position of equality partly by bullying the gods. One of the most famous stories about him is concerned with the sacrifice of Dakṣa.[3] To this sacrifice Śiva was the only one of the gods not invited. In the same epic he is represented as having a contest with Kṛiṣṇa[4] after which no difference is discernible between Viṣṇu and him.[5] Kṛiṣṇa acknowledges his greatness and receives eight boons from both[6] Mahādeva and Umā.

In the *Liṅga Purāṇa* is found the description of the famous appearance of the liṅga whose extremities neither Viṣṇu nor Brahmā was able to reach.

Śiva evidently owes his origin, in part at least, to the north, to the mountains.[7]

One or two other acts attributed to Śiva need to be recorded. His third eye is of great significance. The story of the burning of Kāma has been mentioned. When Umā put her hand over his eyes, the whole world became dark and lifeless. Suddenly the gloom is dispelled by a great flame which burst from Mahādeva's forehead, in which a third eye, luminous as the sun, was formed. By the fire of this eye the mountain was scorched and everything upon it consumed. But, when Umā stood in a submissive attitude before him he restored the Himālaya to its former condition.[8]

---

1 *Sabhāparva*, 626. See *Sabhāparva*, 653, 861 ff.
2 *Rāmāyaṇa*, V, 89: 6 ff.
3 *Śāntiparva*, 13,265, 10,226–58, 10,275 ff.; *Rāmāyaṇa*, I, 66, 7, ff.
4 *Harivaṁśa*, 10,648.
5 *Harivaṁśa*, 10,660 ff.
6 *Anuśāsanaparva*, 1,023 ff.
7 See Gough, *Philosophy of the Upanishads*, p. 18.
8 *Anuśāsanaparva*, 6,355 ff.

The *Epics* show Śiva also as the sage, the philosopher.

Śiva is often depicted wearing the ear-rings of the Kānphaṭas[1].

Thus the descriptions of Śiva (and Rudra) exhibit, both as to form and practice, certain beliefs of the Yogīs.

Śiva now dwells on Kāilāsa,[2] beyond the Himālayas. There he has in his company Pārvatī and a considerable following, including the Gaṇas, the Nāthas and the Siddhas. This is his abode.

References in other chapters show that Śiva is variously worshipped under such names as Paśupati and Śambhunāth, whose votaries in Nepāl offer sacrifices of blood. Yogīs in their worship give special attention however, to Bhāirava, or Bhāiroṁ, and to Śakti, and this worship is often both intemperate and licentious. It is to Bhāirava, as the embodiment, in human form, of the most terrible aspect of Śiva,[3] that the Kānphaṭas, as did the sects that preceded them, give special reverence. Bhāiroṁ is worshipped both by Yogīs and by Śāktas.[4] He has from eight to twelve forms, but he is best known as Kāl Bhāiroṁ.[5] Particularly, in North India he is represented with a dog; in middle India as a snake-girdled drummer or by a red stone. He is often pictured with eight arms, with a garland of skulls, with ear-rings and armlets of

---

[1] See *e.g.*, the carved liṅga at the temple of Paraśurāmeśvara in North Arcot. See chap. eleven. See also *Wi*, p. 212, note 1, where it is stated that images depict Śiva with the great rings.

[2] See *Vanaparva*, 15,801.

[3] In his terrible form he is said to have frightened even Akbar, as he appeared before that great Moghul.

[4] A group of ascetics allied to the Jogīs, who are special devotees of Bhāiroṁ, besmear themselves with vermilion and oil, go about the bazaars begging and singing his praises, striking themselves with whips. Crooke, *Popular Religion and Folklore*, p. 97.

[5] The *Census Report of the North-Western Provinces & Oudh*, 1891, p. 207, gives the following names: Kāl Bhāiron, Bhūt Bhāiron, Nand Bhāiron (Nand = happiness), Suth Bhāiron, Batuk Bhāiron. (Tradition says that Batukanāth, a Kāpālika, was a follower of Śaṅkara). Dawson, *Classical Dictionary of Hindu Mythology*, etc., p. 45, gives the eight names as follows: Asitāṅga (black-limbed), Sanhāra (destruction), Ruru (a dog), Kāla (black), Krodha (anger), Tāmra cūḍā (red-crested), Candra cūḍā (moon-crested), Mahā (great). He is also known as Kapāla, Rudra, Bhīshaṇa. Un-matta, Kupati, Bāl Bhāiron (Bāl = child) and Laṭh Bhāiron (Laṭh = club).

snakes, with a serpent coiled around his head, in his hands a sword and a bowl of blood. As worshipped by Kunbi cultivators of the Deccan, he is represented as a man standing, in one hand a trident, in the other a drum shaped like an hour-glass, while he is encircled by a serpent. He lives in an unhewn stone smeared with oil and vermilion.[1] His name, Bhūt Bhāiroṁ, Lord-of-Malignant Ghosts, intensifies his aspect of terror. He is identified with Kapālin, who creates and destroys. His sign of authority is the trident. Again, Bhāiroṁ carries a club and a black bottle and is accompanied by a black dog, or rides on a dog. When he uses a dog as a vehicle he is called Śvāśva ('He whom the dog serves as a horse'). He plays a considerable part in legend as a great eater. Śiva is approached through him, and he commands the demon hosts as the lieutenant of Śiva. He is the guardian, or door-keeper, of Śiva's temple, particularly as Kāl (black) Bhāiroṁ. In Benares he is the guardian of all the temples of Śiva, and is known as the Kotwāl (police officer) of that city. In the hills of Kumaun and Garhwāl the popular worship of Bhāiroṁ is in the hands of the Yogīs[2] and the principal place of worship is at Kedār.[3] In Gorakhpur his station is marked by massed triśules about a red masonry mound in front of the veranda and to the left of the main door of the shrine of Gorakhnāth. In the monastery at Purī, Bhāiroṁ is represented with three heads and one leg and his image is protected by a roof of straw. Images of Bhāiroṁ are to be found at the establishments at the Takṣila Gate, Lahore, and at Amritsar. In Trimbak he is represented by huge stones painted red and having eyes of silver. In many places triśules of bamboo or of iron, large and painted red, mark his station and huge pictures of triśules, painted red are often in evidence.

In the Panjab he is identified (but this has been questioned) with the godling of the homestead. He receives offerings of grain, and animals are sacrificed to him. Liquor is poured out to him. He wards off disease and death and protects both

[1] Crooke, in *ERE*, vol. V, p. 10. See p. 121, above.

[2] Atkinson, *The Himalayan Districts*, vol. II, p. 808.

[3] Atkinson, *The Himalayan Districts*, vol. II, p. 770. This is the famous Kedār in Garhwāl.

men and cattle. Some worship him for the gift of children.[1] Since it is believed that Mother Earth is his consort, he symbolizes fertility. Young girls of the Dhīmār, or water-carrier caste, used to be married to him at Basdāda in Rewāri. They always died soon afterwards, so the practice was discontinued. The Mallāh boatmen of Agra used to marry their daughters to him. This was because the god once saved a sinking boat. Afterwards the family used to marry one of their girls to him and leave her at his shrine where she survived less than a year; so now a doll made of dough is formally wedded to him.[2]

In the Panjab every important town has a shrine of Bhāiroṁ. He is worshipped on Sundays and Tuesdays with offerings of *urd* cakes, flesh, milk, spirits, flowers and sweet-meats (*laḍḍu*) and the offerings are consumed by the worshippers.[3] At Devī Pātan the noonday offering is a saucer heaped with cooked rice, which is placed before Bhāiroṁ's platform, after water has been poured all around it. The rice is then thrown to dogs. In Benares images of dogs, made of sugar candy, are offered to him. Those who die at his chief temple at Benares believe that they undergo expiatory punishment known as *Bhāiravī-yātanā*, and then proceed immediately to final bliss. These persons are known as *Rudrapiśāca* (Rudra's spirits). Other men, on dying, fall into Yama's hands and have to return to the earth in successive births. He has many worshippers in Benares and in the adjoining districts. Hopkin's rather final statement is that his adherents are ignorant peasants and dissolute beggars.[4] Sārangihār Yogīs beg in the name of Bhāirava.

This god seems to be of Dravidian, or aboriginal, origin,[5] and to have been inherited from the Kāpālikas and others of the same sectarian strain. In the famous *Prabodhacandrodaya*, a Kāpālika controls Bhāirava.[6]

---

[1] Briggs, *The Chamars*, p. 156.
[2] *Popular Religion and Folklore*, p. 246.
[3] *CTC*, vol. III, pp. 157, 158.
[4] Hopkins, in *ERE*, vol. II, pp. 538, 539.
[5] Crooke in *ERE*, vol. I, p. 10.
[6] Crooke, *Popular Religion and Folklore of Northern India* (ed. 1926) contains much material on Bhāiroṁ, which has been freely used.

As worshippers of the consorts of Śiva, Yogīs are Śāktas. A study of the sacred places of the Kānphaṭas and of their traditions makes plain this aspect of their cult.

Śakti means 'force' and, consequently, the divine power or mysterious force of creation is personified in the Goddess. This creative energy is personified also in goddesses and nymphs of every order and in every woman, as well as in the females of every beast. All females are of the same source and order.

Śākta worship is always related to the adoration of the phallus, which is in every instance associated with the vulva in symbol.[1]

It is said that since children bear neither the marks of Brahmā (the lotus) nor of Viṣṇu (the discus) nor of Indra (the thunderbolt), but are marked either with the male or the female organs, therefore offspring is derived from Mahādeva. So all are marked either with the organ of Devī (Umā) or that of Mahādeva.[2]

Turning then to the worship of Śakti, it is to be noted that Devī, in her more general character, is Ambā, the mother-goddess, the great power of nature and mother of the universe (Jaganmātā, Jagadambā), mighty, mysterious force. Śakti has two functions, (1) to direct and control the working of the natural appetites and passions, whether for the support of the body by eating or drinking, or for the propagation of living organisms through sexual cohabitation, and (2) to direct and control the acquisition of supernatural faculties (*siddhi*) whether for man's own individual exaltation, or for the annihilation of his opponents.[3]

Back of this conception of Śakti lies the emergence of self-consciousness in the One Being. In this Universal Reality there appears a double nature as soon as self-consciousness is born, a nature partly male, partly female. As the word (Ardhanārī) indicates, the female aspect of the duality is the more significant. In this duality the female aspect is

---

[1] See Sir John Marshall on Śāktism in the ancient Indus civilization. *Marshall*, vol. I, pp. 52 ff. See above, pp. 154, 155.

[2] *Anuśāsanaparva*, 822 ff.

[3] *Brahmanism and Hinduism*, pp. 185, 186.

looked upon as the active energy or substance through which creation takes place. It is in this aspect of Reality that the goddess becomes the object of devotion. This idea is very old. In the *Ṛig Veda* (10, 129: 4) the statement is made:

> Desire entered the One in the beginning:
> It was the earliest seed, of thought the product.
> The sages searching in their hearts with wisdom,
> Found out the bond of being in non-being.
>
> * * * *
>
> Creative force was there, and fertile power:
> Below was energy, above was impulse.[1]

The notion that the universe proceeds from the female principle brought into union with the male is developed in the description of the parenthood of Dyaus-Pṛithivī.[2] The *Ṛig Veda* has also its female deities, such as Āditi, mother of gods, and Uśas. Early the idea appears that the one being, unhappy alone, divided itself, becoming male and female, and that through these, human beings and other forms of life arose.[3] The idea appears also in *Manu*[4] and in the *Purāṇas*.[5] These two, male and female, are identified with the *puruṣa* and *prākṛitī* of the Sāṁkhya system. The goddess is *mūla-prakṛitī* and *māyā*, mother of gods and men.[6] In mediæval Indian sculpture, Śiva is represented as *ardhanārī*, a form in which his left side is female and his right male.[7] A present-day representation of this view is the yoni-liṅga symbol.

In the *Tantras* the association of male and female functions is carried out in great detail. The pairs as aspects of the one appear in less and less subtle form as the evolution of the world proceeds. In each level there is both their potential and their actual activity. And the Śakti as the formative, creative principle is the receptacle of the seed (*bindu*) of Śiva. So also in all the cakras appears this duality. Through Śiva and Śakti a bindu (drop) is formed which develops into a female

---

[1] Macdonell, *Hymns from the Rig Veda*, p. 19.

[2] *Rig Veda*, 10, 110: 9; 3, 3: 11; 1, 155: 3.

[3] *Śat. Bṛh.*, 14, 4, 2, 4, *etc.*; *Bṛh. Up.*, 1, 4, 3, etc.; *Chānd. Up.*, 6, 2: 3. [4] 1, 5, *etc.*; 1, 32.

[5] *E.g.*, *Viṣṇu Purāṇa*, 1, 7 : 6 ff.

[6] See *Prakṛiti Kaṇḍa* of the *Brahma Vāivratha Purāṇa*.

[7] See for example, the caves of Elephanta, eighth century A.D.

element, Nāda (sound), containing in itself the names of all things to be created. With Bindu and Nāda are associated male and female elements so that a substance *Kāma-Kāla* is formed from which creation ensues. This is their manifestation.

The Śākta system is more closely associated with Śiva, in practice and interest, than with either Brahmā or Viṣṇu. The emphasis on Śakti is strongest in the *Tantras*[1] where force is personified as a female deity and where the wives of Śiva receive undue attention to the neglect of Śiva himself. Today Śāktism is essentially a branch of Śāivism.[2] And this form of Hinduism looks to the consort of Śiva for its exemplification. Devī is often confused with his consort, and the word 'Devī' must be viewed both as the name of the divine goddess and as that of the wife (as Umā, Pārvatī, etc.), of the dread god.

In Śakti all of the characteristics of Śiva are intensified. Since he has his two colours, so she has her white half and her black half. And each of these aspects has its personification. In her milder character she is known as Umā, Gāurī, Pārvatī, Jaganmātā, Bhavānī. In her fiercer character she is Durgā, Kālī, Śyāmā, Cāṇḍī, Bhāiravī, Kālikā.[3] Other names are employed, *e.g.*, Mahābhavānī is prominent in creation, Mahābhāiravī in destruction.

Umā is the gracious consort of Śiva. She is known as early as the *Kena Upaniṣad*[4] and the *Taittirīya Āraṇyaka.*[5] She is often known as the daughter of Dakṣa[6] and again as the daughter of Himāvat (the Himālayas). As the active power, or energy, of Śiva, she assumed a body in order that she might

---

[1] The *Tantras*, which are viewed as the direct revelation of Śiva to Pārvatī, are later than the better known elements of the religious literature of India. They deal with esoteric and erotic elements of Śākta worship, opening their *way* to all persons regardless of caste and sect. These works are concerned with Yoga and with the coiled or sleeping goddess (Kuṇḍalinī). They are spoken of as the Fifth Veda. See chap. thirteen.

[2] *Brahmanism and Hinduism*, p. 181.

[3] Dawson, *Classical Dictionary*, etc., p. 87.

[4] 3: 12. As early as fourth century B.C.

[5] 10: 1, 150.

[6] *E.g.*, *Rāmāyaṇa* 1: 66, 7 ff.; *Sāntiparva*, 10,226–58; *Bhagavata Purāṇa*, 4: Sections 2-7.

be united with him in due form. In the account of the sacrifice of Dakṣa it is related how Umā died of mortification because Śiva, her consort, was not only not invited, but was ridiculed. As having died then, she is called Sati.[1] She was reborn in the family of Himāvat, and is thus called Pārvatī (Daughter-of-the-Mountain).[2] Śiva and Pārvatī are described as living together on Kailāsa, and as either making love to each other or as engaged in deep philosophical discourse.

Pārvatī was of very dark complexion, and on this account a quarrel arose between herself and Śiva. But she took to severe penance the result of which was that she was changed to a light, golden colour, whence her name Gāurī ('white').[3] The conventionalized pattern on Indian prints is of the foot of Gāurī.[4]

She is sometimes identified with Ambā.

Turning now to the more formidable aspects of Śakti, there are several names to consider.

Durgā, 'the Unapproachable,' is Śiva's consort in the aspect of warrior. Her name is derived from that of the demon whom she slew. She is sometimes identified with

[1] Compare *Bhagavad Purāṇa* 4: Sections 2–7. Mention has been made of the dismemberment of his body by Viṣṇu. The little book *Sati* by D. C. Sen tells the same story.

[2] Thus also in the *Bhagavata* and *Viṣṇu Purāṇas*. Umā is known to the *Rāmāyaṇa*; *e.g.*, 1, 36. In the *Harivaṁśa* she is one of the daughters of Mena and the wife of the austere Mahādeva. Also in the *Anuśāsana*, 997 ff., Umā (and in verses 837–41 Pārvatī) is known. These references are to but a few of the passages that might be cited.

[3] Mentioned in the *Atharva Śīras* (age of the *Didactic Epic*).

[4] Underhill, *The Hindu Religious Year*, p. 51.

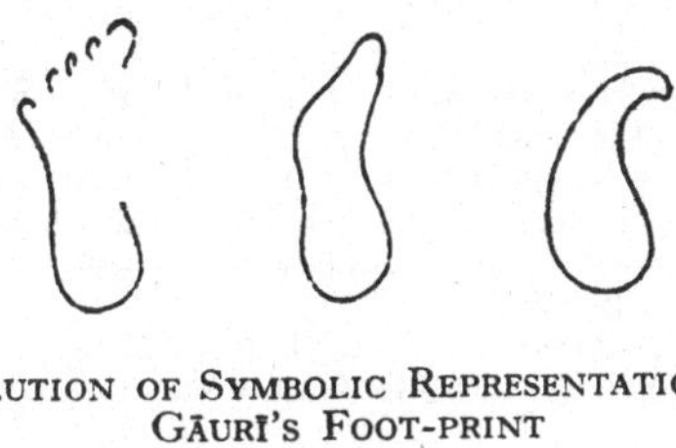

EVOLUTION OF SYMBOLIC REPRESENTATION OF GĀURĪ'S FOOT-PRINT

Pārvatī. One of Durgā's chief forms is that of the four-armed Kālī, who thirsts for blood, preferably that of human beings, although in these days, she has to be satisfied with that of animals. She is most terrible of aspect, garlanded with heads of demons, gorged in blood, with skulls about her blood-besmeared throat, having dead bodies for ear-rings, carrying two dead bodies in her hands, and inhabitant of burning grounds (for the dead). Kālī is the most terrible aspect of Durgā and Śakti, excepting perhaps that of Bhāiravī. In the *Bhiśmaparva* she is Kāpālī. By the Kāpālikas and the Kālāmukhas her fierce spirit was appeased both by animal and by human sacrifices. Durgā represents the destructive forces of the world.

There are other forms of Śakti, essentially of her darker aspect, to which reference has been made. Of these the first to be mentioned is Kāmākhyā, a local name for Durgā, chiefly because her shrine in Assam seems to have been the headquarters of the Tāntric worship, the place of its origin and that from which it spread into Nepāl and Tibet.[1] She is especially connected with the Vajrāyana. It is said that the Assamese shrine was the headquarters of the Vāiṣṇava sect of the *Mahāpuruṣias*.[2]

The following account of Kāmākhyā and her shrine is essentially that given by Eliot,[3] but with some additional notes. The chief sanctuary of Śāktism is at Kāmākhyā (or Kāmākṣā) on a hill which stands on the banks of the Brāhmapūtra, about two miles below Gāuhāti, in the Kāmarūp District of Assam. The place is mentioned in the *Padma Purāṇa*. The Kāmarūpa kingdom was of some antiquity,[4] being mentioned in the *Mahābhārata*. Copper plates of these

[1] *ERE*, vol. II, pp. 479-501; *Wi*, p. 29; Gait, *History of Assam*, p. 57.

[2] Eliot, *Hinduism and Brahmanism*, vol. II, pp. 280, 289. See also *Imperial Gazetteer* (1886), vol. VII, p. 349, and Gait, *History of Assam*. Mahāpuruṣias are a Vāiṣṇavite sect of Upper Assam; disciples of Sankaradeva (b. 1449), not of the Cāitanya, Rādhā-Kṛiṣṇa type, but of that of the *Bhagavad Gītā*. See *Social History of Kāmarūpa* by N. N. Vasu, vol. II, pp. 115 ff.

[3] *Hinduism and Brahmanism*, vol. II, pp. 286 ff.

[4] Hiuen Tsiang visited King Bhāskara Varman in the first half of the seventh century. See Gait, *History of Assam*, p. 30.

kings, dated in the ninth, tenth, eleventh and twelth centuries are known. The hill on which the shrine stands, also known as Kāmagiri and as Nīlācal, marks the spot where the organs of generation of Sati fell when her body was dismembered by Viṣṇu. It is, therefore, one of the famous pīṭhas. Besides, this is supposed to be in the country where Kāma, who had been reduced to ashes by the fierce glance of Śiva, recovered his natural form (Kāmarūpa).[1] The temples at this place have been rebuilt several times; and, in the eighteenth century, were munificently endowed by an Ahom king, and placed under the management of a Brāhman from Nadia in Bengal, with reversion to his descendants who bear the title of Pārbatiya Gosāins. Considerable estates are still assigned to their upkeep. There are ten shrines on the hill, dedicated to various forms of the Śakti. The situation is magnificent, commanding an extensive prospect over the Brāhmapūtra and the plains on either bank, but none of the buildings are of much architectural merit. The largest and best is that dedicated to Kāmākhyā herself, the goddess of sexual desire. It is of the style usual in Northern India, an unlighted shrine surmounted by a dome, and approached by a rather ample vestibule, which is also imperfectly lighted. An inscription has been preserved recording the restoration of the temple about 1550, but only the present basement dates from that time, most of the structure being recent. Europeans may not enter the shrine, but an image of the goddess may be seen from the side door. In the depths of the shrine is said to be a cleft in the rock, adored as the *yoni* of Śakti. In front of the temple are two posts to which each day at noon a goat is tied, and decapitated. Below the principal shrine is a temple of Bhāiravī. The spot attracts a considerable number of pilgrims from Bengal, and a wealthy devotee once built a villa on the hill and paid visits to it for the purpose of taking part in the rites. The most esteemed scriptures of the sect are *Yoni Tantra*, *Mahānirvāṇa Tantra*, and the *Kālika Purāṇa*. Kāmākhyā is worshipped both by love and by sacrifice. The rites of the five M's[2] are frequently performed here. The horrible side of worship is attested by the fact that Aghorīs

[1] Gait, *History of Assam*, pp. 11, 12.

[2] See pp. 172 ff.

are often found in the temple. Furthermore, Kāmākhyā requires sacrifices of blood. Human sacrifices were offered to her down to quite recent times. In 1832 Government put a stop to the practice.[1] It is not denied that such sacrifices would be offered there now if the law allowed. She requires the sacrifice of a man without blemish.[2] At the dedication of the temple in 1565 the heads of 140 men were offered to her on salvers made of copper.[3] There used to be a class of persons called Bhogīs[4] who were voluntary victims to the goddess. From the time that they announced that the goddess had called them they were treated as privileged characters and could do whatever they desired. Every woman was at their command. But they were put to death and offered at the annual festival. The *Kālika Purāṇa* devotes a chapter to rules covering the performance of the human sacrifice.[5] It

---

[1] C. J. Lyall, *Jr. Soc. of Arts*, vol. LI, pp. 612–31.

[2] *ERE*, vol. II, p. 134.

[3] Gait, *History of Assam*, second edition, p. 58.

[4] Bhogīs were dedicated to Āī, a goddess at Kāmarūpa. Gait, *History of Assam*, p. 58. Cf *Āī panthī*.

[5] The following account is from *Asiatic Researches*, vol. V, pp. 371 ff. and is based upon the *Rudhirādhyāya* ('The Sanguinary Chapter') there translated.

Śiva says that the proper sacrifices include cattle, the rhinoceros, men, and blood drawn from the offerer's own body. The second has nine months value, while that of the third satisfies the goddess for a thousand years. The flesh of the rhinoceros pleases her for five hundred years, while the sacrifice of three men satisfies her for 100,000 years. The goddess is Kāmākhyā, Cāṇḍeka or Bhāiravī. The head of the human victim goes to the second. Human blood should be offered in an earthen or in a metallic vessel. Females, except human, are not to be offered. For human sacrifice the consent of the prince is necessary. Human heads and blood should be presented on the right side with eyes averted. On the day preceding the sacrifice, the preparations include the use of *mantras*, and the touching of the head with the sacrificial axe. In the sacrifice the head of the victim should fall just right—there are good and bad omens connected with the facial expressions and sounds which arise.

If the face smile, the indication is prosperity and long life. If it speak, whatever it says will come to pass, should the sound be 'hoont,' the prince will die. Should phlegm issue from the mouth, the sacrificer will die. Should the name of a deity be uttered, the sacrificer will obtain wealth. At the time of presenting the blood, should the victim void fæces or urine, or turn about, certain death awaits the sacrificer. The sacrificer must take some of the blood between his

states that they should not be performed by the first three castes, which is perhaps a way of saying that though they may be performed by non-Āryans under Brāhmanic auspices, they form no part of the Āryan religion. But they are recommended to princes and ministers and should not be performed without the consent of princes. The ritual bears little resemblance to Vedic sacrifices, and the essence of the ceremony is the presentation to the goddess of the victim's severed head in a vessel of gold, silver, copper, brass or wood, but not of iron. The axe with which the decapitation is to be performed is solemnly consecrated to Kālī and the victim is worshipped before immolation. The sacrificer thinks of Brahmā and the other gods as being present in the victim's body and then prays to him directly as being all the gods in one. 'When this has been done,' says Śiva, who is represented as himself revealing these rules, 'the victim is even as myself.' This identification of the human victim with the god has many analogies elsewhere, particularly amongst the Khonds. Added to these horrible and abominable acts of the Vāmacāra rites and the bloody sacrifice is the reported practice of divination by the examination of a child cut out of a pregnant woman at full time.[1]

Other forms of the Śakti need less description here. The temple and the worship of Hiṅg Lāj Devī has been referred to already.

Āśāpūrā Devī, or Mātā, has been mentioned in connection with the white beads which pilgrims visiting Hiṅg Lāj wear. She is the fulfiller of desire and is widely known. Images of her are found in the temple at Hiṅg Lāj, at Chāul, in the Kolāba District of Bombay, and at Madh, about fifty miles north-west of Bhūj, and she has a temple at Koteśvar. She is the household goddess of the Rao of Kacch, and the image in the temple there is a rock, about six feet high and six feet broad at the base, painted red. She grants children.

---

thumb and third finger and discharge it towards the south-west, on the ground. The human victim must be twenty-five years old. In some cases an image may be substituted. And there may be magic substitution of a human enemy. The sacrificer's own blood must be drawn above the navel. A burning wick on the flesh may be used as sacrifice. . . .

[1] *History of Assam*, p. 58.

There was a sect known as Āśāpūrīs, the sect of Mekhapanthīs.

The worship of a young girl is exemplified in Bālasundarī, Tipurāsundarī, Tipurākumārī. She is one of the Mahāvidyas.[1] The worship of a girl of sixteen is common in Malabār. In the Himālayas she is worshipped for the protection of children as well as to obtain them. In Almora a Yogī took the author to see the temple of this goddess. Tipurā Devī has a shrine on the top of Dunagiri, near Dwārahāt, which is under the care of Gīrī Jogīs, as is the temple of Kedār (in Dwārahāt). An old woman of the Gīrī Jogīs resided (1924) at the latter place, and the shrine at the top of the hill is in charge of a member of the same family. No flesh is offered there. As is sometimes done in prayer before the gods in India, barren women stand the whole night before Tipurā, holding the right hand clasped over the left and a one-wicked lamp in the right hand. The lamp is kept burning all through the night. The goddess will remove their reproach.

After a bath in the morning, persons in Almora offer flowers before the goddess as a protection against false accusation. The Yogī attempts to identify the self with Tipurāsundarī by thinking of himself as a woman.[2] Tipurāsundarī is the goddess in view in the sensual worship of Śakti.

Bhāiravīs and Nāyakas are represented in Vāmacāra rites, where the men impersonate Bhāirava. The Nāyakas, eight in number, are mistresses, not necessarily mothers. With them is connected no other idea than that of illegitimate sexual love.[3] In the *Chandrodaya*,[4] Mātā Bhāiravī is described as follows:

> Her aspect is horrible, her ear-rings are human skulls; thunderbolts are shot from her eyes; her fingers are deformed by hair which is the colour of pale yellow flame; and she rolls her tongue between her tusks, being like the moon in her phases.

---

[1] These are ten in number and are the sources of the goddess's highest knowledge, i.e., knowledge which confers preternatural powers.

[2] See *Vaisnavism, Śaivism*, etc., p. 146.

[3] They are Balinī, Kāmeśvarī, Vimalā, Aruṇā, Medinī, Jayinī, Sarveśvarī, Kāuleśī. See Monier-Williams, *Brahmanism and Hinduism*, p. 188. To this list should be added Lalatī.

[4] Taylor's translation, p. 47.

The Mātrīs are also recognized. At Dhinodhar, Mātā (Ambā) has her song of praise (*stotra*) sung on the seventh of each month.[1] Khakhar reported that 'they (i.e., at Dhinodhar) worship Śiva, following the ritual of Mātā.'[2]

Yoginīs, sometimes eight in number, are fairies or sorceresses created by and attending on Durgā. At other times they are looked upon as mere forms of Durgā, sixty to eighty-five in number, and capable of increase to the number of 10,000,000. They are terrific in form, malignant in disposition, possessing magical powers. Like the Ḍākiṇīs, who are fiends of most repulsive habits, and who are impish servants of Kālī, the Yoginīs are perpetrators of all mischief. Both the Sākinīs and Ḍākiṇīs play a considerable part in the symbolic representations of the cakras of the Haṭha Yoga.

Descriptions of Kuṇḍalinī will be found in the chapters expounding the *Gorakṣaśataka*. She is the coiled, or sleeping, goddess whose awakening is the object of the Haṭha Yoga as practised by the Kānphaṭas.

Of the remaining goddesses, Bimbā or Mumbā, specially worshipped in Bombay and in the vicinity of that city, should be mentioned. She may be Vimalā of the Nāyakas (?)

The worship of the Yogīs includes both aspects of Śakti ritual, that of the right-hand path which follows the *Purāṇas* and does not display undue preference for the erotic elements,[3] and that of the left-hand path (Vāmacāra), which follows the *Tantras*. The right-hand worship does not contemplate impure practice, although bloody sacrifices and the cruel beating of animals to death with the fists is not considered '*impure*.' Many rites connected with the Durgāpūja border on Vāmacāra. Left-hand worship is not in good repute and is not readily acknowledged by worshippers. All forms of the Vāmacāra (left-hand practice) require the use of all or some of the five makāras. The predecessors of the Yogīs, the Pāśupatas, the Kālāmukhas and the Kāpālikas were Vāmacāras.[4] The Durgāpūja and the Cakrāpūja are among the chief elements of the worship. Bloody, horrible and erotic elements are to the front.

---

[1] *Bombay Gazetteer*, vol. VII, p. 51. [2] p. 10.
[3] See *BHCS*, pp. 409 ff. [4] *Śakti and Śākta*, p. 89.

Kānphaṭas, who worship both the liṅga and the yoni, hold that restraint of the passions is unnecessary for the attainment of samādhi. They worship the female herself as the entire manifestation of the male.[1] Consequently much attention is given to Vāmacāra rites, rituals of the left side, or female side, of the undivided Supreme. These rites centre around the cakra and are the cakrapūja, the worship of the holy circle. Mystic ends are sought through concentration of the mind on Devī as sitting in the lap of Śiva in the Lotus Garden; by the worship of a picture of the female organ drawn in the centre of a figure representing nine such, the Śrīcakra of ten; or by the worship of a living, beautiful woman; or in secret forms of intercourse where there are no distinctions of caste, in the *Bhāiravīcakṛa*.[2]

This worship is much more widespread than might be inferred from the practice of the Yogīs. While left-hand rites are carried out in secret, Bengal and the Himālayan region are greatly affected by them and their influence is felt much farther afield. From at least the third or fourth century A.D., these horrible and obscene rites have been practised. In the hills the Yogīs follow the Tāntrika ritual which is distinguished for its licentiousness. They eat flesh, drink wine and indulge in the orgies of the left-hand sect. The practices are more widespread in Garhwāl than in Kumaun.[3] Knowledge of the practice is admitted by Yogīs, in the plains as well as in the mountains. In this form of Hinduism is offered to women the so-called homage of sexual love and carnal passion and by yielding free course to all the grosser appetities, wholly regardless of social rules and restrictions, the worshippers of the female form (Śakti) in nature seek to gratify the goddess representing that power, and through her aid to acquire supernatural faculties and even ultimately union with the Supreme Being.[4] For the initiate the union of male and female in worship is that of the bi-sexual form

---

[1] *CTC*, vol. III, p. 159. [2] Compare the posture of *Yab-yum*, below.

[2] See *Vaiṣṇavism, Śaivism*, etc., p. 146 f, where the matter is more fully stated. The *Bhāiravī*-and the *Tattva-cakras* are described in *The Serpent Power*, pp. 175 ff., 181 ff.

[3] Aitkinson, *The Himalayan Districts*, vol. II, p. 865.

[4] *Brahmanism and Hinduism*, p. 190.

of Īśvara. 'In that aspect Śiva and Śakti unite and, as ardhanārīśvara live in the enjoyment of perfect joy in the body of the kulasādhaka.'[1]

Of this worship the cakrapūjā is an essential element, and its description is necessary. At their chief ceremony a circle is formed, composed of men and women, without respect of caste or relationship. Five M's (makāras) are required—wine (*madya*), flesh (*māṁsa*), fish (*matsya*), parched or fried grain (*mudrā*) and sexual union (*māithuna*).[2] The object of the worshippers is not merely to break through the restraints of caste and to give themselves up to licentious practices, but, as just stated, to acquire magical and mystical powers and the sense of unison with the Supreme through the thrill supposed to accrue from this sort of utter abandonment of self.

Ward's account of this ceremony is as follows.[3]

> The person who wishes to perform this ceremony must first, in the night, choose a woman as the object of worship. If the person be a *Dakṣinacārī* (right-hand practice), he must take his own wife; and if a *Vāmacārī*, the daughter of a dancer, a *kupalee*, a washerman, a barber, a chudalu or of a Musulman or a prostitute; and place her on a seat or mat; and then bring boiled fish, fried peas, rice, spirituous liquors, sweetmeats, flowers and other offerings; which, as well as the female, must be purified by the repeating of incantations. To this succeeds the worship of the guardian deity; and, after this, that of the female, who sits naked. . . . As the object of the worship is a living person, she partakes of the offerings, even of the spirituous liquors; and of the flesh, though it be that of the cow. The refuse is eaten by the persons present, however different their castes; nor must anyone refuse to partake of the offerings. The spirituous liquors must be drunk by measure; and the company while eating must put food into each others mouths. The priest then—in the presence of all—behaves toward the female in a manner which decency forbids to be mentioned; after which the persons present repeat many times the name of some god, performing actions utterly abominable; and here this most diabolical business closes.

Wilson gives in a footnote on pages 258 and 259 of his *Religious Sects of the Hindus*, a translation from a section of the

---

[1] *Principles of Tantra*, vol. I, pp. 51–52.

[2] 'Wine, flesh, fish, *mudrā* and *māithuna*, are the five-fold *Makāra*, which takes away all sin.' *Madyam māṁsañca matsyañca mudrā māithunamevaca makārapañcakañcāiva mahāpātakanāśanam.* (Quoted and translated, *Wi.*, p. 256, n. 1.)

[3] *View of the History, Literature and Religion of the Hindus*, vol. I, pp. 247, 248.

Rudra Yamala, which corresponds to Ward's description. And Aitkinson[1] remarks that the descriptions given by Ward and Wilson fairly represent the practices in the mountains. And he adds that each step in the service is accompanied by its appropriate mantra in imitation of those used in the five-fold offerings of the regular sacrifice. In the great service of the Śrīcakra the worshippers, male and female, are placed in a circle around the officiating priest as representatives of the Bhāiravas and Bhāiravīs. The priest then brings in the naked woman to whom offerings are made as the living representative of Śakti, and the ceremony ends in orgies which may be better imagined than described. It is not therefore astonishing that temple priests are, as a rule, a degraded, impure class, cloaking debauchery and the indulgence in wine, women and flesh under the name of religion. In some instances the breast-clothes of the women are drawn as lots to determine how the participants shall pair. This is known as *coli-mārg* (*coli* = breast cloth). To these practices all classes are admitted and they are practised mostly in a mixed society. Garhwāl is more frequented by pilgrims and wandering religious mendicants, and this is given as a reason for the more frequent public exhibition of their ceremonies there. In Kumaun the custom exists, but it is generally observed in secret, and none but the initiated are admitted even to the public ceremonies. For the private ceremony the worshipper may take a dancing girl, a prostitute, a female devotee, a washerwoman or a barber's wife, and seating her before him, go through the various rites and partake with her of the five-fold makāra.[2]

Ward stated that the practices of the left-hand were then on the increase.[3] The practices are clearly in vogue still, as reported above from the author's more recent inquiries.

The system of the Śāktas inculcates an exclusive adoration of Śiva's wife as the source of every kind of supernatural faculty and mystic craft. When the object of the ceremony

---

[1] *The Himalayan Districts, etc.*, vol. II, p. 866.

[2] Sovereign mistress of *Kula*, he who knows *Kula*, the five *Kulatattvas*, and *Kula* worship is liberated while yet living. (*Tantra of the Great Liberation*, VII, 111.)

[3] *View of History*, etc., (1817) vol. I, p. 248.,

is to get control of impure spirits, a dead body is necessary. The adept who, alone, at midnight, in a cemetery, or a place where bodies are burnt or buried, seats himself upon a corpse, makes the usual offerings, without fear,[1] makes the Bhūtas, the Yoginīs and other male and female goblins his slaves.[2] This is the *Sava Sadhan*.

The relation of the Śakti worship to the Haṭha Yoga is very intimate. Magical powers may be acquired through discipline of Yoga or by the worship of Śakti, or by the use of Yoga to control Śakti.

But there are means besides those already described by which the goddess may be propitiated, and which form part of the cult of the Yogīs. These are the use of *mantras*, *bījas*, *yantras*, *kavachas*, *nyāsas* and *mudrās*.

Mantras, although they be texts taken from the *Ṛig-*, *Yajur-* or *Atharva-Vedas*, are really spells or charms which, if properly uttered and repeated, possess in themselves mystical powers for good or ill. The *gāyatrī*, as well as its metre, is employed by Yogīs. They also make use of syllables and single sounds. Mantras find their place in initiation ceremonies, and in the practice of Yoga.

Bījas are letters[3] or syllables invented to denote the root (*mūla*) or essential part of mantras, or the name of some deity to whom they may be addressed, or some part of the body over which the deity presides. Bījas are essentially mantras. Thus, the fifty letters of the alphabet are distributed over the petals of the lotuses or cakras of the body. The fifty letters are thought of as young maidens.[4] The syllable *OṀ AUṀ*, (*praṇava*, *omkāra*) may serve to illustrate the use of bīja (and mantra) by Yogīs.

The origin of the syllable is unknown, but it is probably in some way connected with the intonation of the sacrificial

---

[1] The belief is that those who undertake but fail to go through the performance to the end become insane from that moment. Consequently, from this fear as well as from that arising for the demon haunted cemetery, the ceremony is most dreadful. See *BHCS*, p. 412.

[2] *Wi.*, p. 257.

[3] Letters possess supernatural qualities and attributes as representing eternal sound.

[4] Macdonald, *CR*, vol. CXV, p. 58.

mantras.[1] It is alluded to as early as the *Taittirīya Saṁhitā*. Its asservative use appears in the *Brāhmaṇas;* it is also connected with the sacrifice. Its use as a mystical symbol embodying the essence of the *Vedas* and of the Universe is known as early as the *Brāhmaṇas*, where it is assimilated to the three *Vedas*, to the words *Bhūḥ*, *Bhuvaḥ* and *Swar*, to *Agni*, *Vāyu* and *Āditya*, and to earth, atmosphere and air. The use of the syllable develops steadily. In the *Upaniṣads*, meditation upon it takes the place of the study of the *Vedas*, and it becomes a symbol of the Brahma. In later *Brāhmaṇas* its use is developed and its magical values stressed. It becomes the means by which the seeker for Brahma can attain union with the Brahma; consequently for this purpose, little value is set upon knowledge of the scriptures, but the study of the syllable takes the place of study of the *Vedas*. In ritual use it stands between human and divine utterance. In the *Sūtras* ascetics use *OṀ* as an object of meditation, as the root of the tree of the *Veda* and its essence, and by this means become united with the Brahma. In the Yoga praxis it has purificatory powers. In forms of Yoga it is brought into connection with Īśvara and under the name praṇava is said to express him. Reflection upon *OṀ* removes obstacles and is an aid to right knowledge. Popularly, it is assimilated to various triads including that of Brahmā-Viṣṇu-Śiva.[2] For instance, it is enjoined upon Yogīs to repeat *OṀ*; that, taking a suitable posture (*āsana*), they should repeat *OṀ* 20,736,000 times in silence and meditate upon it daily after deep inspirations;[3] and that they should repeat it audibly, also, 12,000 times. According to the *Śiva Samhitā*, the *bīja mantra* as a whole is *oṁ-āiṁ-klīṁ-strīṁ*.

Yantras are mystic diagrams, often combinations of triangular figures, supposed to possess occult power. Each goddess worshipped by the Śāktas has a yantra, sometimes placed in the centre of a lotus diagram. They are regarded as effective

[1] For an explanation of the origin of some of the mantras, see Bhattacharyya, *Sādhanamālā*, Introduction, p. 72 f.

[2] This statement is based upon Keith's article in *ERE*, vol. IX, pp. 490 ff. See Bloomfield in *JAOS*, vol. XIV, p. cl.

[3] *RTCCP*, vol. XXXI, p. 246. See discussions under Breathing, below.

as mantras, and in combination with them are most powerful. These also are found in the drawings of the cakras. Yogīs have mystic diagrams, representing the four elephants supporting the four corners of the earth, printed and painted on calico.[1]

The triangle standing on its apex represents the yoni; and two triangles superimposed, as in the seal of David, symbolize the yoni-liṅga. In some of the cakras (see Chapter Fifteen) both the single and the double triangles are used as just described. Sir John Woodroffe, in his article on the 'Indian Magna Mater,' publishes a drawing in colours of the Śrī Yantra, showing four male imposed upon five female triangles. The four represent evolved or limited aspects of conscious power; the five denote the five vital functions, the five senses of knowledge, the five senses of action, the five subtle and the five gross forms of matter. The superimposition of the four upon the five shows the union of Śiva and Śakti. The triangles untied make a figure with eight lotus petals. These are surrounded by a lotus of sixteen petals and in turn by a field of yellow and a 'fence' with four 'gates.' By the intersections of the triangles nine circles (cakra) are described: a central point bindu-cakra of bliss; a white inverted triangle; eight red triangles; ten blue triangles; ten red triangles; fourteen blue triangles; eight red triangles; sixteen blue triangles; and the yellow surround. Each cakra has its own name, and in each are a number of lesser deities presiding over forms of mind, life and body and their special functions. The worshipper of the Yantra seeks union with the Mother of the Universe in her several forms, as mind and matter, and their *devatas*, as a step to Yoga union with her as she is in herself, the Universe. Thus, the world is lifted to the divine plane in the consciousness of the worshipper himself; and the Yantra is transformed in his consciousness from a material object of lines into a mental state of union with the Universe, its divinities and Supreme Deity. There follows auto-realization as Mindless-Consciousness. Thus the *Śrī Yantra* is the Universe and its Causal Powers of various aspects; and the worshipper realizes himself as a *Śrī Yantra*.[2]

---

[1] *Man and Beast in India*, p. 215.
[2] *Indian Acts and Letters*, vol. II (1926).

Kavacas are amulets used as protection against evil influences or to obtain some desired end. They consist of stone, a piece of paper or metal leaf, with mantra and yantra upon them. They are worn around the neck, breast, arms or loins. Their special use is in time of pestilence or epidemics. A further use is to propitiate a goddess or to induce certain bodily conditions favourable to production of male offspring.[1]

Nyāsa is the assignment mentally of various parts of the body to the protection of tutelary presiding deities, with the imposition of the hands, or fingers, and the repetition of texts and mystical words and the use of symbols.[2]

Mudrās are the interwinings of the fingers with occult meaning, and certain postures or contortions of the body or of parts of it.

All of these elements of the Śākta system are found in the doctrines and practices of the Yogīs, and are described or implied in their manuals.[3]

---

[1] See also under 'Charms.'

[2] In the illustrations in *The Serpent Power* may be found the graphic representation of the four devices described above. While these elements in the system of the Yogīs might have been discussed among the topics in the preceding chapter, it seemed best to append them to the account of the gods with whose manipulation they are associated. See also other works of the author of *The Serpent Power*.

[3] See chapters on the Haṭha Yoga below, *e.g.*, the exposition of the *Gorakṣaśataka*.

CHAPTER NINE

LEGEND

FROM medieval times onward, Gorakhnāth (Gorakṣa Nātha) is the well-known wonder-worker and master Yogī of northern and western India; and he, and members of his order, are celebrated in legend and song in countless villages. From Nepāl to Rājputāna, from the Panjab to Bengal, from Sind to the Deccan, tradition and folklore are full of allusions to Gorakhnāth and recount his wonderful deeds. He is the famous saint and worker of miracles; the founder[1] and outstanding teacher of the Śāivite sect of ascetics, practicers of the Haṭha Yoga, who are vulgarly called Kānphaṭas; the great teacher of the Śāivite faith, the Brāhmanical opponent of the Vāiṣṇava reformers of northern India of the school of Rāmānanda;[2] the patron saint and tutelary of the state of Gorakṣa,[3] whose royal house now rules in Nepāl;[4] and, finally,

[1] *BHCS*, p. 403.

[2] *Gr. ERE*, vol. VI, p. 329. 'He appears to have been the Brāhmanical opponent of the free-thinking reformers of mediæval India, headed by Rāmānanda, Kabīr and others who flourished in the fourteenth and fifteenth centuries.' *Temp.*, vol. I, pp. 127 ff. This opinion is based upon the view that Gorakhnāth was a contemporary of Kabīr. But Gorakhnāth belongs to an earlier time. See chap. eleven.

[3] *Gr. ERE*, vol. VI, p. 329; Buchanan in Martin, *The History, Antiquities, Topography and Statistics of Eastern India*, vol. III, pp. 387, 535; Kirkpatrick, *Kingdom of Nepāl*, p. 192.

[4] Levi, *Le Nepāl*, vol. I, p. 352. Vincent Smith, *Catalogue of the Coins in the Indian Museum, Calcutta, including the Cabinet of the Asiatic Society of Bengal*, vol. I, pp. 289–93, records the following: A silver coin of Pṛthvi Nārāyaṇa (A.D. 1768–74); date on obverse 1691 Śāka; reverse, central circle enclosing legend, *Śrī Śrī Bhavānī;* marginal legend, each character in an ornament, *Śrī Śrī Śrī Gorakhnāth.* A silver coin of Pratāpa Siṁha (A.D. 1794–97); obverse, date Śāka 1697 = A.D. 1775); reverse, central circle enclosing legend *Śrī Śrī Guheśvarī*; marginal legend, *Śrī Śrī Śrī Gorakhnātha.* Four silver coins of Rāna

the rival, and eventually victor over Matsyendranāth, the ancient Buddhist[1] protector of Nepāl.

Bahādar (A.D. 1777–99); coins of 1787 and 1790 = Śāka 1709 and 1712; reverse central circle enclosing dagger with wreath, and the legend *Śrī Bhavānī*; marginal legend in ornaments *Śrī Śrī Gorakhnātha*. One gold and two silver coins of Gīrvān, Yuddha Vikrama (A.D. 1799–1816); obverse date, 1724 Śāka = A.D. 1802, 1730 Śāka = A.D. 1808, 1737 Śāka = A.D. 1815; reverse, central circle enclosing sword or dagger with wreath and the legend *Śri Śrī Śrī Bhavānī*; marginal legend in ornaments, *Śrī Śrī Śrī Gorakhnātha*. Four silver coins of Rājendra Vikrama (A.D. 1816–47); dates on obverse 1738, 1742, 1745 and 1746, Śāka = A.D. 1816, 1820, 1823 and 1824; reverse, central circle enclosing dagger with wreath and the legend *Śrī Bhavānī*; marginal legend in ornaments *Śrī Śrī Śrī Gorakhnātha*. Two gold coins, of Surendra Vikrama A.D. 1847; date on obverse, 1794 Śāka = A.D. 1842; reverse central circle enclosing legend *Śrī Śrī Śrī Bhavānī*; marginal legend in ornaments *Śrī Gorakhnātha*. And six silver coins; obverse dates Śāka 1771, 1773, 1775, 1780, 1780 and 1794 = A.D. 1849, 1851, 1853, 1858, 1858, and 1872; reverse *Śrī Śrī Śrī Bhavānī* and as on others *Śrī Śrī Śrī Gorakhnātha*. One silver coin of Pṛthvī Vīra Vikrama; obverse, date 1806 Śāka = A.D. 1884; reverse, central circle enclosing dagger with wreath and legend, *Śrī Bhavānī*, and marginal legend in ornaments, *Śrī Śrī Śrī Gorakhnātha*.

The following coins are described in *The Supplementary Catalogue of the Coins in the Indian Museum, Calcutta, Non-Muhammadan Series*, by Pandit B. B. Bidyabinod, pp. 75–78: a silver coin of about 1771, of Pṛthvī Nārāyaṇa, of the Gorakhati Dynasty (A.D. 1768–74); reverse marginal legend *Śrī Śrī Gorakhnātha*. A silver coin of Pratāpa Siṁha (A.D. 1774–77); reverse outer legend *Śrī Śrī Śrī Gorakhnātha*. A silver coin of Rāna Bahādur (A.D. 1777–99); reverse marginal legend in compartments *Śrī Śrī Śrī Gorashanātha*. Five silver coins of Gīrvān Yuddha Vikrama, (A.D. 1799–1816); reverse marginal legend in compartments *Śrī Śrī Śrī Gorashanātha*, dates 1802, 1811, 1811, 1812, 1809. Six silver coins of Rājendra Vikrama (A.D. 1816–47); reverse marginal legend in compartments *Śrī Śrī Śrī Goraṣhanātha*, dates 1816, 1819, 1820, 1828, 1846, 1826.

The writer has seen recent coins (Samvat 1974) of Śrī Śrī Tribhavānī Bīr Vikram Sahadeva Bahādur which have on the reverse the legend *Śrī Śrī Śrī Gorakhnāthji* enclosing the legend *Śrī Bhavānī*. The armorial bearings of the kings of Nepāl include the *pāduka* (footprints) of *Śrī-108-Gorakhnāth*, the guardian deity of Gorakha whence the kings came. Gorakhnāth's name is preceded by six *Śrī's*, those of kings and others by fewer. See Landon's *Nepal*, vol. I, p. 233 and note 1. Kirkpatrick, *Kingdom of Nepāl*, p. 218 mentions a coin bearing on one side '*Śrī Śrī Śrī Goorkhnāth, Śrī Bharvānī*.'

[1] See below. Matsyendranāth is identified with Avalokiteśvara

It is claimed that his followers, who were originally Buddhists, became Śāivites, on the fall of the Sena dynasty in Nepāl, towards the end of the twelfth century,[1] for the purpose of gaining political power by pleasing their heretical rulers.[2] On the other hand, it is said that he brought about the overthrow of the Newārs by the Gorkhas; and that he gave them the land, having proved his power by a twelve years' period of meditation during which no rain fell.[3] It was then that Matsyendra (Macchendar) was called from Saṅgaldip (Ceylon) to break Gorakṣa's long mental concentration.

In Buddhist Tibetan tradition, he is described as a magician.[4]

A bit of record strangely states that he was the foster-father and the teacher of Muhammad;[5] and another fragment reports him as having taught Gūgā the Muslim creed.[6] In Sind he is known as Dātar Jāmil Shāh.

Gorakhnāth has long since been deified, and, in popular religion, is considered a representative, even an embodiment, of Śiva.[7] His name is also given to Śiva. He is the creator.[8] In the dice-throwing ordeal in the Rasālū legend he is petitioned as a god.[9] In the story of Hīr and Rāñjha he is worshipped with a platter of milk and rice.[10] And he is invoked elsewhere as a god.[11]

According to some, his name implies his origin; because the formless creator from the sweat of his own breast created

---

in Nepāl. One tradition shows him entering the country from Assam, another from Ceylon. But both of these traditions could indicate non-Buddhist origins. Still, Buddhist Tāntrism is older than the Hindu form and hails from eastern India.

[1] *Gr. ERE*, vol. VI, p. 329.
[2] Tessitori, *ERE*, vol. XII, p. 834.
[3] Told to the author at Gorakhpur, 14 November, 1924.
[4] Levi, *Le Nepāl*, vol. I, p. 355.
[5] *Dabistan*, vol. II, p. 129. He is called Bābā Rin Hājī.
[6] *Temp*, vol. III, p. 299.
[7] *Dabistan*, vol. II, p. 128; *Gr. ERE*, vol. VI, p. 329; also *BHCS*, p. 403; *Panjab Census Report*, 1891, p. 114.
[8] *Mac*,. vol. I, pp. 173, 174.
[9] *Temp*, vol. I, pp. 245, 314.
[10] *Temp*, vol. II, p. 508.
[11] *E.g.*, *Temp*, vol. I, pp. 314, 425 ff.

Gorakhnāth. In 'Ghor-nāth,' 'ghor' means 'filth.'[1] More definitely, his name Gorakhṣanātha may mean 'Lord of Cattle'[2] or 'Lord of Gorakṣa,' thus suggesting Śiva on the one hand and Nepāl on the other.[3] Oldfield[4] says that the country of Gorakṣa derives its name from Gorakhnāth, an eminent saint who resided in a cave which still exists in the hill on which the city of Gorkha is built. According to another tradition, Gorakhnāth found an old shrine of Gorkha, an ancient deity, made the place famous, took the name of the diety of the shrine and gave the name to the city of Gorakhpur. (This must really refer to Gorkha in Nepāl.)

The reference to Gorakhnāth, already made, as having been created from the sweat of the creator's breast, may be linked with other statements. In the Panjab a legend is current to the effect that Gorakhnāth was born of dung and was found by Matsyendranāth who made him a disciple.[5] From Nepāl[6] comes the story that Śiva after he had recited the Yoga doctrine to Pārvatī, standing on the sea shore,[7] while Matsyendra (in the form of a fish) was listening, gave something to a woman to eat, with a promise that she would obtain a son. The woman did not eat the substance, but cast it upon a dung-hill. Twelve years later, Matsyendra passed by the same spot and asked to see the child. He heard what the woman had done and asked her to search in the dung heap. She there discovered a boy of twelve years. That boy was named Gorakhnāth. Matsyendranāth became his spiritual master and he served as a dutiful disciple.

There are variants of these stories. In the *Tah-qīqāt-i-Chishti*, it is related that a devotee of Śiva, desiring offspring,

---

[1] See *RTCP*, vol. II, p. 390. But ghor may mean 'intense,' 'terrific,' 'fearful', and refer to his austerities.

[2] Compare Paśupati, a name of Śiva.

[3] *Gr. ERE*, vol. VI, p. 328.

[4] *Sketches from Nepāl*, vol. II, p. 189.

[5] *RTCP*, vol. II, p. 390.

[6] Levi, *Le Nepāl*, vol. I, pp. 351, 352.

[7] It may be of interest to note that at Dah Pārbatiya, in Assam, in a window in an old brick temple of Śiva, there is a male, four-armed figure, holding in one left hand a *damru*, the peculiar small drum of Śiva. Below the window there is a representation of the waves of the sea. The Śiva is of the form Lakulīsa. The work is probably of the fifth or sixth century. *Archæological Survey of India*, 1924–5, p. 99.

received, at Pārvatī's intercession, ashes from Śiva's dhūnī. The devotee's wife was to swallow them. She did not, but threw them upon a dung-hill. Eventually a child was found there who was taken to Śiva, and, by him, named Gorakhnāth.

Another version of this legend relates that, when Gorakhnāth was seeking a teacher, he offered a loaf of bread on a pipal leaf at the seashore. A fish swallowed the offering and, twelve years later, gave a child in return. Śiva named this child Matsyendra, and he afterwards became Gorakhnāth's guru, or spiritual teacher.

Another story has it that Gorakhnāth was a son of Śiva by a cow.[1]

The estimation in which the people hold the deeds and powers of Gorakhnāth may be formed from a study of the more famous of the innumerable traditions and legends describing him and his disciples.[2]

Many of the legends, some of which have been recorded by Temple, *Legends of the Punjab*; by Synnerton, *Romantic Tales of the Punjab*; by Grierson, *The Story of Manikchandra* and in *The Adi Granth*, are sung even today by Goraknāthīs, and by other wandering singers as well, through the villages of the land. Amongst the most famous of them are those of Zahra, or Gūgā Pīr, Puran Bhagat and his brother Rāja Rasālū, Gopicand, Hīr and Rāñjha and Rānī Piṅglā.

Gūgā, or Zahra Pīr[3] was a Rājput who finally became a Musalmān. His birth and the wonderful deeds which he was able to perform were dependent upon the good offices of the saint, Gorakhnāth, who gave him his name and whose

---

[1] *RTCP*, vol. II, p. 391. And Gorakhnāth fathered Matsyendra by a fish. These are etymological explanations.

[2] Compare *Temp*, vol. II, p. 21.

[3] Briggs, *Chamārs*, pp. 151, 152, 170, 171; *Temp.*, Nos. 6, 52; *Indian Antiquary*, 1895, p. 47; 1897, p. 84; *OCCS*, p. 67; *S.P.G. Quarterly*, 1910; *Indian Witness*, Feb. 21, 1911. *PNQ*, vol. I, para 3; Crooke, *Popular Religion and Folklore of Northern India*, vol. I, pp. 211, 213; *Archælogical Survey of India*, 1878–79, vol. XIV; *JASBe*, vol. XVI, pt. 1, pp. 139 ff.; Elliot, *Memoirs on the History, Folklore and Distribution of the Races of the North-Western Provinces of India*, vol. I, p. 255; *Tod* (Crooke), vol. II, pp. 843, 1,027; vol. III, p. 1,450. See Rose, *RTCP*, vol. I, pp. 171–92 for comprehensive review of the materials on Gūgā.

disciple he finally became.[1] He is now worshipped as a snake godling, as one who has power over snakes and saves his followers from snake-bite. He grants boons, especially to barren women. Gūgā finally disappeared, together with his horse, in the bowels of the earth. He is especially revered by low castes, among whom sweepers and leather workers are prominent. In many places in the Panjab there are shrines connected with his worship, and these are often adjacent to shrines of Gorakhnāth.

Among the most famous heroes of the Panjab are Puran Bhagat and his half-brother Rasālū.[2] Puran, the elder, was betrayed by his father's younger queen, and was cast into a dry well to die. He suffered also the loss of his hands and feet. After twelve years he was rescued and healed by Gorakhnāth. Through powers which he obtained by austerities, Puran was able to grant his former betrayer, Queen Lunan, a boon and she bore a son named Rasālū. The exploits of this latter prince form a large body of legends. Rasālū's was a checkered life, full of love, adventure and intrigue. Puran became a Yogī, a follower of Gorakhnāth.[3] Rasālū finally became a Gorakhnāthī, and an ardent disciple of the great Yogī. Even Rasālū's parrot considered Gorakhnāth as his *guru* (teacher)![4]

A current legend concerning Puran Bhagat is as follows: A Khatrānī woman, when bathing in the Āik river, was wooed by a serpent called Bāsak Nāg. She conceived and bore a son who was named Sulivān. He rose to be a man of great power and wealth, and, through the assistance of the serpent, was made a king. His fame became so great that even Vikramāditya visited him at Siālkot. Sulivān refused to go to meet his royal visitor and a severe battle was fought in consequence, in which Vikramāditya lost his life. Rāja Sulivān had two sons, Puran and Rasālū. Puran became a

[1] *Temp.*, vol. III, p. 296.

[2] Puran Bhagat, *Swynn*, pp. 230 ff., 51 ff.; *Temp.*, No. 34, and in others also; Rāja Rasālū, *Swynn*, pp. 51–151; *Temp.*, vol. I, pp. 1 ff.; 243 ff.

[3] Puran Bhagat is called also Gyān Sarūpa, Purakhsiddh, Chāurañjwenāth and Chāuraṅginath. *RTCP*, vol. I, p. 125. Details of the stories of Puran Bhagat vary greatly. *Temp.*, vol. II, pp. 375, 403; Steele, *Tales of the Panjāb*, p. 235.

[4] *Temp.*, vol. I, p. 242.

faqīr. Rāja Sulivān had two queens, the older of whom was the mother of Puran. The other queen, who was much younger, was barren. When Puran became a man, this younger queen made improper proposals to him. He refused to yield to her and she, consequently, brought false charges against him. These the king confirmed. Puran was then put to death, his hands and feet being cut off, and his body was thrown into a well in Kārol, a village five miles from Siālkot. (The village is at present called Puranwāla.) After some days a Yogī, who came for water, found the body in the well. Having learned, upon inquiry, the story of Puran's temptation and death, he pronounced a charm (*mantra*) over the body and Puran was brought back to life, and his hands and feet restored. Puran became a Kānphaṭa Yogī. This well is still known as Puran's well.[1]

Several stories of Gopicand are available; among them one from the Panjab,[2] one from Bengal,[3] and another from Sind.[4] The second is told under the title 'The Song of Manikcandra,' although Manikcandra's son, Gopicand, is the hero of the song. The stories recite the struggle and the difficulties that lay between Gopicand and his attainment of sainthood, or, in other words, tell of his renunciation of his throne and his choice of the life of a Yogī.

Hīr and Rāñjha are the chief characters of a romantic story famous in the Panjab.[5] Rāñjha, an indulged son, had to leave home after his father's death. He finally met Hīr and hired himself out as a herdsman to her father. A long love intrigue led to scandal. Hīr was finally married to another man. Rāñjha then became a faqīr, joining the band of Gorakhnāthī Yogīs at Ṭilla.[6]

---

[1] The Hindu version of this account was read by L. Gaṅgā Rām, B.A., LL.B., to Alfred M. Daula in 1925. The statement was sent to the author by Dr. H. D. Griswold, from Lahore. See also *Sialkot Gazetteer*, 1921, p. 14.

[2] *Temp.*, vol. II, No. 18.

[3] *JASBe*, (1887) vol. XLVII, pt. 1., pp. 135 ff.

[4] Supplied by Mr. G. E. L. Carter, Collector of Bandra, through Dr. J. J. Modi. There is reference to this famous story in Buchanan, vol. III, p. 407 f.

[5] *IA*, 1921, Supplement; *Swynn.*, No. 1; *Temp.*, vol. II, No. 38 *OMAS*, pp. 266, 268.

[6] *Temp.*, vol. II, p. 546.

Rāñjha discovered the residence of Hīr and took up his abode on the river bank opposite her. He used to visit her taking with him savoury dishes of flesh food. On one occasion, unable to secure game, he prepared a portion of his own flesh. But Hīr was suspicious of the food and the expression of her doubts led to his confession. Thereupon she resolved to meet him at his place of abode. She used to cross the river on a float of earthen pots. Her female attendants, discovering this, substituted, one night, pots of unbaked clay. As Hīr reached mid-stream, the pots dissolved and she sank in the river. But Rāñjha heard her cry and swam out to her. They disappeared together.

The following descriptions of Gorakhnāth and of Yogīs of his order, based upon these and other familiar tales, exhibit a popular view of the Kānphaṭas. The references are suggestive, not exhaustive.

By reason of his perfection in ascetic practices, or Yoga, Gorakhnāth was supposed to have attained to superhuman powers. So great were these that he was even called a greater than Śiva.[1] In speaking of Goraknāth, his disciples say to Puran:

> He is beloved of God and his worship has been accepted by the Almighty. You can ask what you please of him.[2]

In the legend of Manikcand, Gorakhnāth is described as a *vidyādhāra* ('carrying occult knowledge')[3] a kind of supernatural being dwelling in the Himālayas, attending upon Śiva and possessing magical powers. He is not only superhumanly wise, but also very powerful.[4] In a contest with Rāñjha over the stolen conch Gorakhnāth calls himself a great magician, and boasts of power exceeding that of the seventy saints combined.[5]

Gorakhnāth exercised great powers over nature.[6] He gave Mayanā (Gopicand legend) a boon that she would not sink in water.[7] He turned the water of a well into gold and then into crystal.[8] In Mewār they still treasure a sword of the

---

[1] *JASBe*, vol. XLVII, pt. 1, p. 139. [2] *Swynn.*, p. 33.
[3] *JASBe*, vol. XLVII, p. 208. [4] *E.g. Temp.*, vol. II, No. 18, the *Legend of Gopicand*; *Temp.*, vol. II, p. 243.
[5] *Temp.*, vol. II, p. 551. [6] See also, below.
[7] *JASBe*, vol. XLVII, p. 210. [8] *RTCP*, vol. II, 394 note.

hero, Bappa, which is said to have been presented to him by Gorakhnāth, who pronounced over it an incarnation, thereby making it possible for Bappa to sever rocks with it.[1] When Gorakhnāth and his company came into the royal garden at Siālkot (where Puran Bhagat was imprisoned in the well) everything became green,[2] and the lakes were filled with water.[3] And at another time when he came into a dried-up garden, he scattered ashes on it, and it began to bloom.[4] His having caused a twelve years drought in Nepāl[5] has become famous. Again, he caused the very walls and all the instruments of a certain place to chant: 'Awake, Macchendra, Gorakhnāth has come.'[6] At Śīrālā in the Sātāra District in the Bombay Presidency there is a gigantic tamarind tree whose origin was a stick which Gorakhnāth stuck in the ground.[7] In Kāngra the Kumhārs (potters) say that their wheel sprang from the earning of the saint Gorakhnāth, which he gave them.[8]

Once he took the form of a fly[9] in order to avoid guards on the border of a certain king's country; at another time he changed himself into iron, and again into a frog.[10] He transformed certain of his disciples so that half of their bodies became gold and the other half iron.[11] He turned himself into a leper before Vāchal.[12] The disciples who were sent by Gorakhnāth to Kārū[13] to get the thread with which to draw Puran from the well, were turned by magic into bullocks. This was reported to him and he took ashes from his bag, charmed them and tossed them into the air. Thereupon the

---

[1] Crooke, *Things Indian*, p. 25.

[2] Steele, *Tales of the Panjab*, p. 235.

[3] *Temp.*, vol. II, p. 376. [4] *RTCP*, vol. I, pp. 179–80.

[5] Wright, *History of Nepāl*, pp. 140–4; Levi, *Le Nepāl*, vol. I, p. 348. [6] *RTCP*, vol. II, p. 394.

[7] *The Hindu Religious Year*, p. 174.

[8] *NINQ*, vol. III, p. 54. Quoted by Crooke, *Religion and Folklore of Northern India* (ed. 1926), p. 331. [9] *RTCP*, vol. II, p. 394.

[10] *Dabistan*, vol. II, pp. 139 ff.

[11] *IA*, 1906, p. 21.

[12] Cunningham, *Archæological Survey of India*, Reports, vol. XIV, p. 81.

[13] *Temp.*, vol. I, p. 180, suggests that Kārū may be Kāmārūp. Chariyāl (Sariyál) wife of Gūgā was the daughter of Sañja of Kāmārūp in Assam. She is still worshipped at a shrine near Gauhāti.

bullocks came to him and he patted them and changed them back into men. In return, being angry, he dried up all the wells, bringing their water into the one near himself. When the women came, all together, at his request to draw water, he took charmed ashes and, in the name of Matsyendranāth, turned the women into asses.

> Long ears, small hoofs (had they, and) grazed on the dung heaps.[1]

When their husbands came and appealed to him, he restored them to their human form. Reference has already been made to his having Puran's hands and feet restored after he had taken him from the well.[2]

Gorakhnāth left his body asleep on his mat, and descended to the under-world of the god of snakes and there obtained the magic incense for Bāchal.[3]

There are in the legends interesting accounts of his restoring people to life. In the *Bhartṛharinirveda* of Harihara (Act. II) Bhaṛthari made test of his queen, by sending a false report of his death. She became *sati* and the king was distracted. He received news that Gorakhnāth had power to relieve sorrow. The great Yogī came to visit him, and, seeing the situation, broke his bowl and wept over it, treating it with the same despair and sorrow that the king expressed over the body of the dead queen. Bhartṛihari offered the Yogī a better bowl, and Gorakhnāth promised to restore the queen to life. When she stood before him alive, the king refused to embrace her, since, in his despair, he had renounced the world, and he resolved to remain faithful to his vow.[4] A second version of the story contains other details. It is as follows. The last Chandravati Rāja of the Parmārs was Hūn. One day, while he was out hunting, he saw a Pārdhi, while hunting, killed by a cobra. The wife of the hunter, finding him, placed his body on the funeral pyre, and, after feeding the fire with portions of her flesh, became

---

[1] *Temp.*, vol. II, p. 438.

[2] Also see Steele, *Tales of the Panjāb*, p. 235.

[3] Cunningham, *Archæological Survey of India*, Reports, vol. XIV, p. 82.

[4] *JAOS*, vol. XXV, pp. 197–230. L. D. Gray, *The Bhartṛharinirveda of Harihara.*

sati. Impressed with this sight, Hūn decided to test his queen, the Rānī Priṅglā. So he related to her the whole occurrence. She, the daughter of Somachandra, replied that even on *news* of the death of her consort, she would become sati. Later, Hūn, on an expedition sent word of his own death. Although her *Āsso Pāl*,[1] plant revealed to her that the king was alive, she decided to prove her faithfulness by dying and being burned. Hūn, anxious about his message, hastened home, arriving in time to see the funeral fire. He wandered around the pyre for days refusing to be comforted. Gorakhnāth, happening at the place, asked the king why such mourning and received the reply that it was because of love for Rānī Piṅglā. Thereupon Gorakhnāth dropped his begging bowl and, as it broke, began to weep in imitation of Hūn. The king reminded the Yogī that his loss was not irreparable as was the loss of the queen. Then Gorakhnāth said that he could restore the Rānī to life. He sprinkled water over the ashes of the funeral pyre and twenty-five queens exactly like[2] Piṅglā appeared. When he sprinkled water over them a second time, only Piṅglā remained. But, since Hūn had already decided to become a Yogī, he refused to receive her. More water was sprinkled and the queen, casting a reproachful look at Hūn, disappeared. The king then became a Yogī.[3]

It is reported that Gorakhnāth destroyed the two sons of Matsyendranāth, in the presence of a Bania and afterwards restored them to life.[4]

In one of the Rasālū legends, that hero is described as trying to seduce the wife of his prime minister, Mahitā. In the end there was great trouble. The minister refused to believe his wife, Sīlā Dāī, innocent, turned ascetic and finally died. Then Sīlā Dāī became sati. Rasālū burned himself on

---

[1] Datatreya, her guru, had given her a seed, which, as a plant, would tell her whether her husband were dead or alive.

[2] Another version states that when King Bhartṛhari declared that there never could be another queen such as Rānī Piṅglā had been, Gorakhnāth showed him a hundred like her. *RTCP*, vol. II, p. 404.

[3] Major J. W. Watson, article, 'The Story of Rānī Piṅglā,' *IA*, 1873, p. 215 f.

[4] *RTCP*, vol. II, p. 395 note. The story has already been narrated.

the pyre with both of them.[1] Through the curiosity of Pārvatī, Śiva was led to go into the garden, where they had been cremated, to see what had happened. And then Gorakhnāth asked for the restoration of all three. Śiva sprinkled the pyre with water drawn from his finger and they were restored to life.[2] Then Sīlā Dāī and Mahitā were again married, Gorakhnāth starting the marriage procession.

Gopicand's sister was restored to life by the saint Gorakhnāth.[3]

In another legend it is said that Gorakhnāth killed the two sons of Macchendra, hung their skins on a tree, and then, after his inquiry about them, restored them to life.[4]

By casting some earth on his body, Gorakhnāth restored to life a disciple, who in the form of a stag, had been shot by Bhartṛhari.[5]

Mayanā, Manikcand's widow, though with child, was forced to perform sati but was miraculously preserved through the intervention of Gorakhnāth.[6]

On the other hand, the great Yogī is represented as creating persons. In the contest with Jālandharnāth (Gopicand legend) Gorakhnāth turned horse dung into locusts, or dung and a blanket, or a bundle of grass, and then into a human body and infused it with life. This man, who claimed Gopicand, was burned to ashes seven times and to be restored by Gorakhnāth.[7]

Moreover, like many other great ascetics he was able to grant children to barren women. Vāchal (Gūgā legend) received a son, Gūgā by name,[8] and Kāchal (Gūgā legend) two sons by favour of Gorakhnāth,[9] and Mayanā, widow of Manikcand, as a boon, obtained a son eighteen months after her husband's death,[10] the explanation being that he was given as a seven months' old foetus and his prolonged confinement in his mother's womb was due to his exceeding glory.

---

[1] *Temp.*, vol. I, p. 361. [2] *Temp.*, vol. I, p. 362, 'The water of life.'

[3] *JASBe*, vol. LV, p. 38.

[4] *RTCP*, vol. II, p. 394. This has been related above.

[5] *RTCP*, vol. II, p. 404. [6] *JASBe*, vol. XLVII, pp. 143, 210.

[7] *RTCP*, vol. II, p. 395. [8] *Temp.*, vol. I, pp. 142, 139.

[9] Kānipāo, a senior disciple, advised Vāchel to go to Gorakhnāth; *RTCP*, vol. I, p. 177.

[10] *JASBe*, vol. XLVII, pp. 142, 208.

Instances may be given to show Gorakhnāth as a great healer. In his youth he was forced to resort to magic to restore his own hands and feet which his stepmother had barbarously cut off.[1] He restored hands and feet to Puran Bhagat after the latter had lived helplessly in the dry well for tweve years.[2] This he did by the sprinkling of water and prayer.[3] He also restored Puran's sight, by going to Indra and obtaining help.[4]

Another evidence of Gorakhnāth's magic powers was in his insight. He was able to discern at a glance that Puran Bhagat was innocent.[5] Fairies (*pari*) visited Puran in the well and were sent by him to Gorakhnāth with news, and then the Yogī took steps to save 'my Puran.' Still, Gorakhnāth's powers of discernment were sometimes limited. In the *Dabistan* is the record of a contest of power between Gorakhnāth and a sannyāsī, Datateri, in which Gorakhnāth disappeared in the water in the shape of a frog. But the sannyāsī was able to find him and bring him forth. Then Datateri concealed himself in the water and Gorakhnāth in spite of all his searching could not discover him, for he had become water, 'and water cannot be distinguished from water.'[6]

Again Gorakhnāth exercised such power that King Jewar, intending to slay Vāchal with his sword, was unable to draw it from its scabbard.[7]

An interesting aspect of the exercise of power is through the use of the Yogī's name. Thus Chariyāl (Gūgā legend) was healed of snake bite.[8] And Gūgā, using the name, played on his flute and the sleeping king of snakes was awakened, and all his hosts with him. Then Tātīg Nāg went to find out who was playing. Gūgā told him that it was he,

---

[1] Steele, *Tales of the Panjab*, p. 235. Tāranāth in his *History of Buddhism in India*, p. 323, refers to this incident.

[2] Steele, *Tales of the Panjab*, p. 235.

[3] *Swynn.*, pp. 51, 230; *Temp.*,vol. I, pp. 2, 430 ff.

[4] *Temp.*, vol. II, No. 34.

[5] *Temp.*, vol. II, p. 429.

[6] *Diabistan*, vol. II, p. 140.

[7] *Temp.*, No. 6.

[8] *Temp.*, No. 6.

the son of Rāja Jewar, and then summoned the snakes to help him to win a bride from Assam (Kāmarūp).[1] And Gūgā, along with Tātīg Nāg, was conveyed to that country, miraculously, through Gorakhnāth's powers.[2] And, attacked by his half-brothers in the forest, Gūgā was able to defend himself against their murderous assault.[3]

Moreover, Gorakhnāth was able to exercise power over long distances. Thus he helped Gūgā to win at dice, and Rasālū likewise.[4] Appealed to by Gūgā from his mother's womb, Goraknāth so ordered events that Gūgā was born in his mother's father's palace.[5]

In like manner Gorakhnāth exercised such great power on behalf of his disciples that he proved himself superior to other Yogīs. In the *Tuhfāt-ul-Karam*[6] it is recorded how Gopicand (Pīr Pathāo)[7] of Pir Arr, in Sind, gained possession of the cave in the hill there, which was held by Dayanāth. Gopicand brought Gorakhnāth from Girnār to help him. Dayanāth was a man of superior powers. He had a stable-basket which used of itself to clean the stables and keep alight sufficient fires for the 125,000 faqīrs who used to live on this hill. He also had a bullock which used to fetch water from the river filling his *pakhal* (water bag) himself. His beggar's bowl used to collect and bring alms from Samahi, by itself, and from it the 125,000 faqīrs maintained themselves. He had a rag-rope and a cudgel, and if he wanted anyone bound and beaten, he said to the rope, 'Bind that man,' and to the cudgel, 'Beat him.' As soon as he would say these words the rope would bind the man and the stick would beat him. But when Gorakhnāth came into the neighbourhood, all these wonders ceased. Then Dayanāth knew that it was because of the greater power of Gorakhnāth. Thereupon he (Dayanāth)

---

1 *Temp.*, vol. I, pp. 178, 179, 180.

2 *Temp.*, vol. I. p. 192.

3 *Temp.*, No. 6.

4 *Temp.*, vol. I, p. 243.

5 *Temp.*, No. 6. Otherwise his mother would have been in disgrace.

6 Reported by Mr. G. E. L. Carter, I.C.S.

7 On the road beyond Karāchī is an old building in ruins, called 'Peer Putta' by Muslims and 'Gopee Chand Rāja' by Hindus.—Hart, *Journey*, p. 136.

got angry and threw the hill into the sky, and, setting it on fire by a breath, departed to Dhinodhar hill in Kacch. Pīr Pathāo went to Guru Gorakhnāth and reproached him, saying,

> You are sitting here while Dayanāth has set the hill on fire and cleared.

The guru looked and saw that a fire was indeed burning between heaven and earth. Even while he (Gorakhnāth) looked, through the power of his glance the fire was extinguished and the hill dropped and cracked in two. Gorakhnāth then perceived that Dayanāth was praying at Dhinodhar hill, standing on his head on a betel-nut, and knew that after twelve months' prayer[1] in this position he could by breathing thrice blast all Sind. Thereupon he extended his hand (to Kacch), though no one else could observe this action, and, seizing Dayanāth by the ear, brought him back to Sind. The guru said to Dayanāth,

> Don't trouble the people. I promise you this blessing, that you and your successors shall never lack good horses and white clothes.

He then made Dayanāth his disciple, cutting his ears and putting ornaments in them; and placing a black thread-turban[2] on his head, sent him back to Dhinodhar. Then Gorakhnāth and Pīr Pathāo came to this hill with their *murīds* (disciples). As soon as they reached it, it began to tremble, whereupon Gorakhnāth commanded:

> Drive a tent-peg and if that goes into the ground it will show that we can stay here; otherwise it must be that the hill is not intended for us and we must go away.

The peg was driven into the ground (although the place consists of solid rock) and Pīr Pathāo took possession of the cave in the hill.

Another incident showing Gorakhnāth's power is that in which he sent an invisible army to the help of Gūgā against Prithavī Rāj.[3]

In the Panjab legend of Śāntināth, Goraknāth overcomes

[1] Dayanāth and the number 12 remind us of Dharmnāth and that twelve years' penance. But this number runs through many legends.

[2] Note the turban of sheeps-wool thread worn by the mahant of Kāma.

[3] *RTCP*, vol. I, p. 181.

Jālandharanāth of whom Gopicand was afraid. The story relates that at this time there was a great gathering of faqīrs in Gopicand's city (which was in Bengal) to which came Gorakhnāth. To avoid this crowd Jālandharanāth retired to the bottom of a well and covered himself with horse dung. All efforts at removing this were unavailing because the dung removed by day replaced itself by night. Finally Menavantī, Gopicand's mother, asked that Jālandharanāth be brought forth from the well; but Macchendranāth pointed out how dangerous this would be for Gopicand,[1] since Jālandharanāth would kill him with the mere sound of his voice. However, Macchendranāth said,

> Let three images (*mūrti*) be made, one of iron, one of silver and one of gold, and I will so arrange that the strength of Jālandharanāth's wrath will be averted.

The images were made and Gopicand was ordered to approach the well and summon Jālandharanāth. At the sound of his voice, Jālandharanāth cursed him and bade him die, but only the iron image was destroyed. Again Gopicand called to Jālandharanāth and this time the silver image was destroyed. On the third summons the gold image was shattered. When Gopicand called the fourth time Jālandharanāth, realizing that there was a greater Yogī than himself present outside, came up out of the well.

It is said that when Bhīmsen, one of the heroes of the *Mahābhārata*,[2] lay benumbed with cold on the snow-covered Himālayas, Gorakhnāth revived him and made him king over the country stretching from the sources of the Ganges to Bhūtān.[3] A similar[4] tradition has it that, during Yudhisthara's journey through the Himālayas to heaven, his brethren fell behind and perished one by one. Only Bhimsen survived. He was saved by Gorakhnāth and made king of Nepāl.[5]

---

[1] See also *Temple*, vol. II, p. 23. The story of this contest with Jālandharanāth is told in legend no. 18.

[2] Martin, *The History, Antiquities, Topography and Statistics of Eastern India*, vol. III, pp. 38, 39, suggests that this was not a Pāṇḍava but a contemporary of Prithvī Rāj, one of Belkoth near the Kosi, a powerful chief.

[3] Cooke, *Popular Religion and Folk-Lore of Northern India*, vol. I, p. 91.

[4] *Gr., ERE.*, vol. VI, p. 329.

[5] *JASBe.*, 1878, p. 138.

An interesting aspect of his power over nature is found in legends which relate Gorakhnāth with serpent powers and functions. The whole cycle of Gūgā legends illustrates the first; and the various stories told about his control of the serpents in Nepāl, and the consequent failing of the rains, illustrate the second.

Gūgā received his power over serpents, through discipleship, from Gorakhnāth, and he learned the art of charming snakes likewise from his great guru.[1] Gūgā restored to life the bullocks that had been bitten by serpents while they were conveying his mother, Bāchal (Vācal), to her royal lord's (his father's) court.[2] Gūgā, in the name of Gorakhnāth, in the forest, played on his flute, and the serpents danced about him, although Bāsuk, their king, became angry. Then Tātīg Nāg (*nāg* = serpent) in the form of a Brāhman, was sent to Assam. The snake asked Gorakhnāth's aid and succeeded in securing Rāja Sañja's daughter, Chariyāl, for Gūgā. She was bitten by a snake and healed through the power of the name of the Gorakhnāth.[3] Rāñjha, another disciple, under pretence of curing snake bite, obtained access to Hīr.[4] In the story of Nirmal Dāī, the Nāga princess who was married to Parāg (Parikṣit) and on whose account the war of extermination of serpents was carried on, Nāg Tātīg finally slew Parāg.[5] When Parāg's posthumous son, Janmegi, attained the age of twelve he began to reign; and, finding out the cause of his father's death, sought the life of Tātīg. Tātīg in going to kill Parāg besought the aid of Macchendranāth (Matsyendranāth) and 'remembered Gorakhnāth.' In seeking to escape Janmegi, Tātīg appealed for help in turn to ascetics, to Śiva, to Macchendranāth and to Gorakhnāth in vain; but he finally escaped by meditation on Kṛiṣṇa.[6]

The Nepalese legend in its various developments is of considerable interest. Here another example of Gorakhnāth's

---

[1] *IA*, 1882, p. 35.
[2] *Temp.*, vol. I, p. 154.
[3] *Temp.*, no. 6.
[4] *Temp.*, vol. II, pp. 560–63.
[5] *Temp.*, vol. I, pp. 499–500. See *JRAS*, 1899, p. 313; 1891, p. 378. This is a famous story; its historical significance is not clear.
[6] *Temp.*, vol. I, p. 528.

power over nature is found, in his causing a twelve-years' drought in Nepāl. The story goes[1] that Gorakhnāth once visited Nepāl. Because he was not received with sufficient respect, he took the clouds, fastened them in one of his bundles and sat on them, remaining motionless, in meditation, for twelve years. During that time there was no rain in Nepāl. Finally, it chanced that Matsyendranāth passed by, and Gorakhnāth, unreflecting, arose, out of respect for his guru. The clouds escaped thereupon and the drought was broken.[2]

The illumination of the story, just related, is found in the following, in which his wish to have an interview with Matsyendranāth, who was in an inaccessible part of the mountains, supplies the motive. Gorakhnāth resorted to the device of confining the nine serpents who gave the rain, thereby causing a twelve-years' drought. At last Macchendranāth was obliged to come to Gorakhnāth to secure the release of the serpents and the return of rain.[3] Another version of the Nepalese legend[4] relates how Gorakhnāth attracted the nine Nāgas into a hillock, and sat down upon it, the twelve years' drought following. The people finally appealed to their king, who in turn sought Avalokiteśvara (Matsyendranāth) who lived in the Kāpōtal mountain. The rāja's old father's prayers were necessary for success. So he was called from retirement and the matter was talked over by the king and his father with a venerable teacher. Worship of a goddess (Jagāmbara Gñānaḍākini, one of the Śaktis) resulted in the release of one of the Nāgas. Taking this serpent with them they made the long and terrible pilgrimage to Kāpōtal.[5] After a long time, Macchendranāth was sufficiently aroused from his meditation to realize that Gorakhnāth, in Nepāl, wanted to see him, and was making trouble. Thereupon, he

---

[1] Levi, *Le Nepāl*, vol. I, pp. 352–57.

[2] See also Oldfield, *Sketches from Nepāl*, vol. II, pp, 325–26.

[3] Crooke, *Popular Religion and Folk-Lore of Northern India*, vol. II, pp. 129–30

[4] Wright, *History of Nepāl*, pp. 140–44.

[5] Kāpōtal lies beyond Kāmarūp, in the Eastern Himālayas (Levi, *Le Nepāl*, vol., I, p. 353). But, the place is evidently Kāmarūpa itself. See Kirkpatrick's account (1793), *Kingdom of Nepāl*, p. 190 f.

decided to go in person to release the Nāgas. Macchendranāth, in the form of a bee, was conveyed into Nepāl in an earthen pot and the drought was brought to an end.

Another version of the legends omits the confinement of the snakes and attributes the drought to Gorakhnāth's power of concentration.[1] Gorakhnāth, an eminent saint, a disciple of Macchendranāth, visited Nepāl. While there he did not receive reverent enough attention. He, therefore, sat immovable for twelve years on a mound, south of Debī Pātan.[2] A long drought ensued. It was felt that the only relief was to get Gorakhnāth to move. Consequently the king of Bhatgaon and an *āchārya* (a teacher) made a pilgrimage to Kāpōtal mountain where Macchendranāth resided, and, after much trouble, persuaded him to come to Nepāl. When Macchendranāth arrived in Nepāl, Gorakhnāth constrained by reverence for his spiritual superior, abandoned his posture and went to pay his respects. Thereupon rain fell copiously.[3]

It may be of interest to refer to the influence which Gorakhnāth was able to exercise over divine beings. This is illustrated by his persuading Brahmā, the 'God of Fate,' to change Vāchal's destiny in order to grant her a son (Gūgā legend).[4] Previously Bhagvān had refused the request, but Gorakhnāth hung from a tree, head downwards, swinging over a fire, until the smoke of his burning flesh attracted the notice of the god, who then granted Gorakhnāth's prayer.

To Gūgā's wedding he brought a divine company.

The occult powers of the Yogī are further revealed in his use of innocence tests and ordeals.

In one version of the story of Puran Bhagat[5] Gorakhnāth tests Puran's innocence by drawing him from the well by a thread spun by an unmarried virgin, using it in the name of Macchendranāth.[6] His innocence was proved by a further test of boiling oil. However, the king, Puran's

---

[1] Oldfield, *Sketches from Nepāl*, vol. II, pp. 325–26.

[2] *The Gurkhas*, p. 173.

[3] This account seems to combine elements of two stories related above.

[4] 'Legends of Gūgā,' *IA*, 1895, p. 51.

[5] *Temp.*, vol. II, no. 34.

[6] *Temp.*, vol. II, p. 433.

father, refused to believe this evidence and accepted the story told by his young queen, Lunan, claiming that Gorakhnāth, by magic, had saved Puran. Consequently, Puran was punished with the loss of hands, feet and sight, and was cast into a dry well.

When Mahitā accused Sīlā Dāī, his wife, of intrigue with Rasālū, the name of Gorakhnāth was called and she was proved innocent by dice.[1] In another ordeal by boiling oil she was likewise proved innocent. But Mahitā, insisting that Gorakhnāth had worked a charm to save her, straightway became a Yogī, i.e., turned celibate.

His superhuman powers found expression in other ways; for Gorakhnāth was able to do terrible things, and people were in fear of him and his curses. He sent a terrifying dream to Jewar (Gūgā legend) who then sent for Bāchal[2] his queen, whom he had driven from his palace. When he found Puran Bhagat in the well, the great Yogī threatened to sink the well to hell should Puran turn to be a wicked man, or an evil spirit.[3] And he threatened Rāñjha that he would cause the earth to sink and the Chenāb river to dry up, should the conch not be restored.[4]

Through prayer to Gorakhnāth, Gūgā was able to shoot an arrow into a Brāhmanī's pitcher and she was drenched. She had refused to give him water.[5]

In the legends of Gopicand,[6] Gorakhnāth contested the power and the place of his rival, Jālandharnāth, and sent a follower to break the cooking pots of his opponents, to break their boxes and 'to blow them away.' He set fire to their bodies.

Allusion has already been made to the humiliation of the women of Kārū.[7]

Popular descriptions of the Yogīs extend to departments of magic and to a knowledge of tenets of the Yoga.

---

[1] *Temp.*, vol. I, p. 243.
[2] *Temp.* vol. I, p. 158.
[3] *Temp.*, vol. II, no. 34.
[4] *Temp.*, vol. II, p. 551.
[5] *RTCP*, vol. I, p. 174. *Temp.*, vol. I, p. 167.
[6] Wright, *History of Nepāl*, pp. 140–44.
[7] See pp. 187, 188.

Gorakhnāth had a magic bag, or wallet, of wonderful potency, from which he drew gifts of various kinds. He took out of it the barley grains,[1] or the apple,[2] or the flowers,[3] or the ashes[4] which conferred the gift of sons; and also the ashes which he transmuted into gems, and supplies of goods and clothing for Gūgā's betrothal.[5] Similarly, he lent glory to the wedding in Assam.[6] From this bag came the wonderful ear-rings which Puran Bhagat received at his initiation,[7] and from the same sort of bag Puran Bhagat took the grapes and rice which Luman, his father's queen, swallowed whole in order to obtain a son.[8]

With his magic sandals he threatened Puran Bhagat, when he found him in the well, that, should he prove to be an horror or some dangerous being, he would strike the dry well and sink it into hell.[9] He threatened Rāñjha, who had hidden the conch-shell in the bank of the river Chenāb, that he would strike the bank with his shoe, make the earth sink and the river dry up.[10]

By means of a magic handkerchief one of Gorakhnāth's disciples restored sight to Puran's mother.[11]

His mat, or carpet, was so sensitive that a disciple at a long distance, needing help, thought of Gorakhnāth, and the carpet trembled,[12] thus gaining the attention of the Yogī. On this same carpet Gorakhnāth ascended to Bhagavān's heaven.[13]

Kabīr refers to Gorakhnāth's philosopher's stone in the following words:

> The cut mango will not blossom, the slit ear cannot be reunited; whose loss is it, if they apply not the philosopher's stone that Gorakhnāth had ?[14]

Ashes have magic powers, and with those from Gorakhnāth's sacred fire, in Pātāla, Viṣṇu created the world, by

---

[1] *IA*, 1895, p. 49. [2] *OCCS*, p. 67. [3] *Temp.*, no. 6.
[4] *RTCP*, vol. I, p. 184. [5] *IA*, 1895, p. 49.
[6] *Temp.*, no. 6. [7] *Temp.*, vol. II, p. 445.
[8] *Temp.*, vol. II, p. 454. [9] *Temp.*, vol. II, no. 34.
[10] *Temp.*, vol. II, p. 551. [11] *Temp.*, vol. II, p. 453.
[12] *IA*, 1895, pp. 51, 52. [13] *IA*, 1895, p. 50.
[14] *Wi.*, p. 87. Quoted from the *Bījak of Kabīr*. Philosopher's stone: Sanskrit, *Sparśamaṇi*; Hindi, *pāras patthar*. Some say that the philosopher's stone is still being sought for in Nepāl.

scattering them on the primeval waters.[1] Ashes were used in other wonderful ways, as in changing men into animals and back again, and as gifts with magical properties, as already mentioned.

Many allusions to the Yoga technique are found scattered through the legendary materials.

Whose breath is returning (through) the six [mystical] spheres [of the human body], (whose) thought is intent on vacuum.[2]

Jogīs meditate on God the Creator whom they call unseen, whose form is minute, whose name is the Bright One, and who is the image of their bodies.[3]

They know in ecstasy the experience of music heard in the head and call it *kiñjuri* (which is the name of a stringed musical instrument).[4]

Nānak gives a general description:

'To remain seated without support,
To collect and restrain the five evil passions,
To sleep little and to take scant food,
To keep guard over the saintly body,
To be constant in devotion, penance, self-restraint
 and remembrance of God—
Nānak saith, these are the marks of a Jogī.'[5]

And in the *Śākhīs* of Kabīr other aspects of Yoga are exhibited.

Gorakh, enamoured as he was of Rāma, is dead; his body was not burnt [the Jogīs bury their dead], the flesh has decayed, and is turned to clay, and such rank as the Kāuravas enjoy does he obtain [bodily annihilation].[6]

Accounts are given of Gorakhnāth and his followers and references are made to their modes of life and to their dress and equipment.

Gorakhnāth himself is described as a *parmhaṁs* (an ascetic of the highest order, one who has subdued all his senses by abstract meditation), mighty and devout.

---

[1] *CTC*, vol. III, pp. 153–4; *RTCP*, vol. II, p. 391.

[2] *Trumpp*, p. 472.

[3] *Mac.*, vol. I, p. 225, note 2 reads: 'The Yogīs, when in intensely deep meditation, close their eyes. On opening them and looking upward they suppose that they behold God in their own image in the firmament.'

[4] *Mac.*, vol. I, p. 274 and note 2.

[5] *Mac.*, vol. I, p. 160.

[6] *Wi.*, p. 86.

He is beloved of God and his worship has been accepted of the Almighty. You can ask what you please of him.[1]

Thus spoke Gorakhnāth's disciples of him to Puran Bhagat:

Very great is his beauty, say all men and women; no maid in India's court has greater beauty. He is like the swan of Sarwar.[2]

Viṣṇu described him as the greatest of saints, who only could supply patience.[3]

The Panjab legends frequently mention Siālkot and Ṭilla as favourite resorts of Gorakhnāth and of his followers.[4] Sometimes he was accompanied by four hundred disciples,[5] at other times by five thousand, two hundred visible, and five thousand, two hundred invisible, disciples.[6] To Gūgā's wedding in Assam, Gorakhnāth went gloriously with carriages, horses and palkis, a splendid retinue.[7]

This is not however, the austere picture brought out in the discourses that Yogīs carried on with candidates for the order.

At times his followers slept in tents;[8] or in huts.[9] Gorakhnāth said to Rāñjha, I sleep on the ground and have no bed coverings; and, again, I live among stones and potsherds.[10] Yogīs are penniless.[11]

The appearance of these Yogīs is incidentally described. They were evidently familiar persons everywhere. They wore very little clothing, as a rule, and covered their bodies with ashes.[12] If they wore a cloak, or robe, it was coloured with ochre.[13] Some wore a patched cloak;[14] others garments of deer-skins.[15] Rasālū asked for a deer-skin coat.[16] They carried

---

[1] *Swynn.*, no. 33; *Temp.*, no. 34.

[2] The Mansarowar Lake, the fabled dwelling of the Haṁsa on Mount Kailās in the Himālayas. Note, p. 130 in *Temp.*, vol. I; *Swynn.*, no. 33.

[3] Crooke, *Popular Religion and Folk-Lore of Northern India*, vol. II, p. 154.

[4] *IA*, 1895, pp. 49, 50, 53.

[5] *IA*, 1895, p. 53.

[6] *Temp.*, vol. II, p. 375.

[7] *Temp.*, no. 6.

[8] *Swynn.*, no. 33.

[9] *Temp.*, vol. II, no. 18.

[10] *Temp.*, vol. II. p. 549.

[11] *Temp.*, vol. II, p. 9.

[12] *Mac.*, vol. VI, p. 243.

[13] *Temp.*, vol. I, p. 60; vol. III, p. 265.

[14] *Mac.*, vol. VI, pp. 60, 168, 231, 243.

[15] *Temp.*, vol. I, p. 60; vol. II, p. 375.

[16] *Temp.*, vol. II, p. 548.

a patched quilt,[1] wore a black necklace[2] and a horn on a thread[3] and carried a conch,[4] a wallet of cloth,[5] a club,[6] and a staff.[7] Some had their heads shaved,[8] while others wore their hair in a knot,[9] or matted.[10] In initiating Puran Bhagat, Gorakhnāth cut off some of his hair.[11]

There are many references to the fact that these Yogīs had their ears split and wore great ear-rings.[12] Of Rāñjha it is recorded that his right ear-ring was of baked clay and his left one of unbaked clay.[13]

They practised control of the breath[14] and were concerned about the nāḍis.[15] Some were under a vow of silence.[16]

They sat cross-legged,[17] and in other postures,[18] and kept a sacred fire (dhūnī).[19]

In begging they called out '*Alakh*, *Alakh*'[20] and 'Gorakh, Gorakh.'[21]

They did not enter houses.[22] Some were so overbearing as to be described as warriors taking alms by force.[23] Accusations are made of hypocrisy,[24] and of bad habits, such as drinking[25] and the use of drugs.

---

[1] *Tr.*, pp. xl, 475.
[2] *Temp.*, vol. II, no. 18.
[3] *Mac.*, vol. VI, p. 169. *Tr.*, p. 475.
[4] *Temp.*, vol. I (Silā Dāī); vol. II, no. 34.
[5] *IA*, 1906, p. 213; *Temp.*, vol, II, no. 34; *Mac.*, vol. VI, pp. 199, 169, 243; *Tr.*, p. xl; *Mac.*, vol. I, p. 162; *Tr*, p. 475.
[6] *Mac.*, vol. VI, p. 231.
[7] *Tr.*, pp. xl, 475; *Mac.*, vol. I, p. 162.
[8] *Temp.*, vol. II, p. 548; *Mac.*, vol. p. 60; vol. VI, p. 167.
[9] *Temp.*, vol. I, p. 336.
[10] *Mac.*, vol. VI, p. 272.
[11] *Swynn.*, no. 33.
[12] *Mac.*, vol. VI, pp. 168, 231, 243; *Tr.*, p. xl; *Mac.*, vol. I, pp. 60, 162; *OMAS*, p. 267; *Wi*, p. 87; *Tr.*, p. 475.
[13] *Temp.*, vol. II, p. 55.
[14] *Mac.*, vol. VI, p. 168.
[15] *Mac.*, vol. VI, p. 194.
[16] *Temp.*, vol. I, p. 332.
[17] *Temp.*, vol. II, no. 34.
[18] *Mac.*, vol. VI, p. 168; vol. I, p. 41.
[19] *Temp.*, vol. II, no. 34.
[20] *Temp.*, vol. I, p. 332. *Alakh*, Sk. *Alakṣya* = unseen, invisible, without shape or form; 'the Imperishable Name;' the cry of mendicants, begging. Steele, *Tales of the Panjab*, pp. 252, 321.
[21] *Mac.*, vol. VI, p. 263.
[22] Swynn., no. 33.
[23] *Temp.*, vol. II, p. 435.
[24] *Mac.*, vol. I, pp. 314, 315, 350–2, 356–7; *Mac.*, vol. VI, p. 270.
[25] *Mac.*, vol. VI, pp. 154, 255.

The initiation of Yogīs attracts a good deal of attention and makes a deep impression. At the ceremony offerings were made.[1] Rāñjha brought five rupees and betel leaves when he asked Gorakhnāth for initiation.[2] When Gopicand was made a Yogī a great company was present. Gorakhnāth came on a chariot of flowers and the whole affair was on a grand scale. Gopicand made handsome presents. Both Vāiṣṇavites and Śāivites were present,[3] and Bālnāth also.[4] In fact, his mother, Mayanā, brought to the ceremonies 1,600 ascetics, and

In his chariot of flowers descended Gorakhnāth the Vidyādhāra (wizard) . . . there (was) no counting the number of *Hāḍīsiddhas* with theirs ears cut.[5]

The essential parts of the ceremony were the splitting of the ear, tonsure, the covering the body with ashes and the giving of the mantra. Gorakhnāth pierced Puran Bhagat's ears, put the mudrā (ear-rings) in them, and then whispered the mantra in his ear. (*Kānoṅ meṅ phuṅk lagāī*, 'blew into his ears.'[6])

Having shorn off some of his hair, he pierced his ears with his own hands and put the rings in them, and so Puran became a Yogī.[7]

Bhartṛhari said to Nānak:

The form of the *Jog* is the ear-ring, the patched quilt, the wallet, the staff and the horn, the sound of which is emitted in the Universe.[8]

The shaving of the head of Gopicand took one hundred days and the cut hair became a 'hairy Gaṅgā' and began to flow away.[9] In the rush to pierce the ears of Gopicand:

They snatched the razor from the hands of the *nāpit*, and gave it into the hands of the ear-cutter. Even as the ear-cutter took the razor in his hand, he cried, 'Rām, Rām,' and cut both the ears of the king. They fastened to the king's ear an ear-ring of crystal. They clothed

---

1 *Temp.*, vol. II, pp. 443, 444.
2 *Temp.*, vol. II, p. 547.
3 *JASBe*, vol. XLVII, pp. 221 ff.
4 *JASBe*, vol. XLVII, pp. 222, 223.
5 *JASBe*, vol. XLVII, pp. 222, 223.
6 *Temp.*, vol. I, p. 332.
7 *Swynn.*, no. 33.
8 *Tr.*, p. xl.
9 *JASBe*, vol. XLVII, p. 222.

him with a cloth covered with holy symbols. Five Vāiṣṇavas came and dressed the king in a laṅgoṭī. A laṅgoṭī with a string did they put upon him. They placed around his neck a Rāma rosary.

The case of Gopicand illustrates the degradation and poverty into which men of his class descended. His guru, Hāḍī, who was a sweeper (Ḍom), gave him food consisting of the leavings of his alms, and Gopicand says as he looked at it in dismay:

Rice which my dogs would turn aside from—such have I, a king, come to eat.

At initiation they put into his hands a gourd platter and they gave him a torn quilt and a torn laṅgoṭī.[1] He received a boon:

Thou shalt go to the three corners of the earth, but shalt not go to Yama's dwelling.[2]

Gopicand, the king, was reduced to great straits. He left his kingdom and wandered in the jungle, living on leaves of trees. One day he came to his mother's city. His mother recognized him and called to him. She said, 'You are my son; I am grieved at seeing you in this condition. You must be very verminous, let me clean you.' While removing the vermin she pulled out a hair. The king exclaimed, 'Are you removing vermin or pulling out my hair?' She said, 'Does it hurt you when a hair is pulled, or what?' He said, 'Yes.' Whereupon his mother replied, 'If you feel pain from getting one hair pulled, don't you think the trees from which you have been picking leaves must also have felt pain?' For this reason he gave up picking leaves to eat.[3] And Gopicand is reported as saying;

When I was lord of my kingdom, O my mother, then did I eat rice in many a golden dish. Now I am a beggar with not a single Kaoṛi; I cannot eat from a golden plate.

He took a plantain leaf and cut it. Thereon he placed a little rice. He took the shell of a broken gourd and from it drank a little water. He washed his face and hands with water.

---

[1] *JASBe*, vol. XLVII, p. 221.

[2] *JASBe*, vol. XLVII, pp. 223. There are references to his not having died.

[3] *Tuhfāt-ul-Karam*, quoted by Carter.

Then what did he do? He uttered the words 'Śrī Kṛṣṇa' and ate food. One mouthful, two mouthfuls, five mouthfuls he ate. Then he looked towards the water which was trickling out of the broken gourd. He put his face to the earth and sipped water.[1] His lot for many years was a hard one, in long journeys and heavy burdens at the direction of his guru, and years in prison in the house of a harlot. He finally collapsed carrying heavy burdens.[2]

There are many passages describing the difficulties and the utter renunciation that initiation entailed. To Rāñjha it was said:

> The taste of a Jogī is bitter and sour. You will have to dress as a Jogī, to wear dirty clothes, long hair, cropped skull, and to beg your way through life. You will have to meditate on your *guru* and hold your breath in your mid-most throat. You will have to give up the pleasures of birth, to cease to rejoice when friends come or grieve when they die. You will have to abstain from casting eyes on women. You will have to become divinely intoxicated by taking *kand, mul, post, opium* and other narcotic drugs.[3]
>
> You will have to think the world a mere vision. You will have to go on long pilgrimages to Jagannāth, the Godāvarī, the Ganges, and the Jumna. *Jog* is no easy task. You Jāṭs (*i.e.* luxury-loving princes) cannot attain *jog*.[4]

Thus the novice was warned against the difficulties of the ascetic life and discouraged from choosing the life of a Yogī.

---

[1] *JASBe*, vol. XLVII, pp. 223–4.

[2] *JASBe*, vol. XLVII, pp. 221 ff. Allison, *The Sadhs*, quotes a verse attributed to Gopicand.

[3] *Post, posta*, an infusion of opium poppy heads (Smith, *Oxford History of India*, p. 412). A preparation of laudanum, arrack, sugar and cardamoms, very evil in its effects. *Bhaṅg*, a drink made from hemp leaves. It is conducive to quarrelling. *Gāñja*, a narcotic and intoxicant traditionally consumed by the warrior caste. It is obtained from the hemp plant; the dried leaves being smoked in the form which is familiar to some as *cannabis indica* cigarettes. Another form is *caras*, which is the resinous extract from the stalk of the plant. The harmful effects of *gāñja* smoking are more obvious to the laymen than those of opium, as it is seen to upset the mental equilibrium more quickly and more permanently. The alternate stages of excitement and depression soon become more marked, till the confirmed *gāñja*-taker becomes useless for life's ordinary activities. (See *Indian Social Reformer*, November 20, 1926. See also *An Essay on Hasheesh*.)

[4] *IA*, 1921 (Hīr and Rāñjha), p. 32 and also the last page of the article.

Renunciation was complete. These warnings are a description of the ascetic life. Gorakhnāth said to Puran Bhagat:

> *Jog* you must not think of. The performance of *jog* is beyond you. You will have to suffer hunger and thirst, to bear trials with patience, and to renounce the world. You will have to leave behind all the pleasures of sense and to enter upon a life most difficult to pursue.[1]

To Rāñjha the question was put:

> What is the good of begging if a man has no belief? Only those in love with death can acquire *jog*. Good men subdue their passions by riding on the horse of patience and holding the reins of remembrance. *Jog* means to be dead while alive. One has to sing the song of nonentity using one's meagre body as a guitar. One's self has to be entirely absorbed. It is no child's play. You will never be able to undergo *jog*. What is the use of asking for it? Child, listen, God has made his abode in this body of dust. He is in everything as a thread runs through the beads. He is the breath of life in the living. He is, as it were, the spirit of *bhaṅg* and opium. He is in the life of the world as colour is in the *meṁhdi* (indigo). He permeates everything even as blood runs through all the body of men.[2]

Again:

> Who takes saintship renounces all the desires of his heart. The saintship is hard and difficult in the world. Put off the five desires and the twenty-five (lusts). Then canst thou be a Jogī disciple. Renouncing thy whole family and sons, live alone in the world. The point of a sword is a very difficult thing (to rest on). Imagine not this saintship to be easy.[3]

Gopicand forsook harem and throne and family ties.[4] The legend of *Rāja Gopicand* as played at Jagādhrī in the Ambāla District contains a long account of the persuasions of queens, daughter, sister and mother to induce him to break his vows.[5] He said,

> I put away rule, power, wealth, goods and greed.

And, as he was led from the palace door, he was told that earthly love, affections, desires and lust are as the shadow of a tree, the illusion of a dream.

Bhaṛitri had to bring alms from his queens, calling them

---

[1] *Swynn.*, p. 238. [2] *IA*, 1921, Supplement, p. 32.

[3] Advice to Mahitā in the legend of Sīlā Dāī. *Temp.*, vol. I, p. 327.

[4] *Temp.*, vol. II, no. 18.

[5] See also the account by Śāntināth of the Panjab. *Temp.*, vol. II, no. 18.

'mother' and was on probation for twelve years before Gorakhnāth would receive him.[1]

Puran Bhagat was told that he must treat every one, man and woman, alike.[2] To Rāñjha it was said:

> Call the young women 'sister' and the old women 'mother.'[3]

Rāñjha had to put away chieftainship. Still, he was allowed to think of Hīr and even to send his black crow to get news of her.

Sometimes the initiate had his resolution put to the test. Puran Bhagat was sent back to the palace and his sincerity was tested under the enticements of his stepmother, the queen.[4] He was finally sent with the queen to the palace to reign, but escaped.[5] Again he was sent to his father the king and his own mother and they endeavoured to get him to assume the kingship, but he refused,[6] and went back to Ṭilla.

Gorakhnāth spoke of the Yogī's vow as irrevocable:

> Whose clothes (Yogī's) are red and whose minds are clear, return not from the wilds. Is a Jogī every one's friend?[7]

There is the other side of the story, and the free life of the Yogīs is often depicted, wherein asceticism is used as a means of access to women of the harems. One of the Rasālū stories may be taken as an illustration.[8]

A popular 'fling' at the ascetic may be quoted in the words of another faith:

> You get your ears bored and put some ashes to your body and all the world reveres you as a saint. Without toil or labour you can be as eminent as Nādir Shāh. The mysteries of birth and the sadness of death have no concern for the *faqīr*. He sleeps in the mosque free from the care of this impure world and begs and eats. He can scold people and incur no blame. If you call yourself as *pīr* or a *faqīr* everybody is your servant.[9]

This quotation expresses the commonly held belief that not many who don the Yogī's garb are sincere.

---

[1] Note, to call his queen 'mother' was to renounce finally the conjugal relation. *RTCP*, vol. II, p. 404.
[2] *Swynn.*, p. 33.
[3] *Temp.*, vol. II, p. 553.
[4] *Temp.*, vol. II, p. 441.
[5] *Temp.*, vol. II, p. 447.
[6] *Temp.*, vol. II, p. 453.
[7] *Temp.*, vol. II, p. 447.
[8] *Tales of the Panjab*, pp. 250 ff.
[9] *IA*, 1921, p. 31 f.

CHAPTER TEN

THE FORERUNNERS OF THE GORAKHNĀTHĪS

DISSATISFACTIONS with life arose far back in India; and the ascetic[1] and the mechanisms of the austere life, are in evidence in the earliest literature. The *Dīkṣa* rite,[2] for example, includes elements which are already in the *Ṛig Veda* ascetic in form. And even then the contradiction of natural desire, mortification of the body by unnatural inhibitions of all its desires (the conception of *tapas*) occupies a large place. Early the term tapas, applies to ascetic practices in general. The efficacy of the endurance of discomforts and of the difficulties of performance are recognized. The enducement of ecstatic states, of hysteria, of trance and of excitements through drugs and sex stimulation likewise are then known. These point toward mystic union with Reality and the acquisition of unusual powers. Tapas engendered strength, great in the extreme, involving mystic and creative power. Creation itself had its rise in tapas.[3] In the *Brāhmaṇas* Prajāpati practices tapas in order to acquire creative powers. In those writings also is found the recognition of the efficacy of asceticism in the pursuit of knowledge. 'Heaven is established on the air, the air on the earth, the earth on the waters, the waters on truth, the truth on the mystic love (of the sacrifice) and that on tapas'.[4] In the *Śatapata Brāhmaṇa* and afterwards, the gods create the worlds through the power of tapas.[5] Further on, while some of the earlier

---

[1] On this and the two following sections, see *ERE*, vol. II, pp. 63 ff.

[2] Keith, *Religion and Philosophy of the Veda*, vol. I, p. 301.

[3] *Ṛig Veda*, 10, 129, 3.

[4] *Ait. Br.*, 11, 6, 4.

[5] *E.g.*, 6, 1, 13.

Upaniṣads express doubts on the matter,[1] in the later (verse) *Upaniṣads*, from the *Kena* on, its value for the attainment of knowledge is recognized and is often insisted upon.[2] The *Jābāla* upholds an extreme asceticism and asks that men root out all desires.[3] Rhys Davids says that the nearer we get to Buddhism, the greater the importance we see attached to tapas (self-torture). Nowhere else in the world, he says, has the art of pain been so much studied as in India.

In the *Epics* austerities have become longer and harder and self-mortification has become a permanent idea and practice in the religious life of India. In the *Rāmāyaṇa* are to be found pictures of hermitage after hermitage famous for their ascetics who have acquired powers and privileges through prolonged austerities. The *Mahābhārata* in like manner sets forth this strenuous life.

Again, in the *Upaniṣads*, asceticism is related to special stages in life.[4] The conception of the *Āśramas*, 'places of asceticism,' arose complicating the old rules of life.[5] In the the earliest *Upaniṣads* the ascetic ideal is scarcely more than an alternative way of life beside that of the student and householder; but, in the later *Upaniṣads* the four stages are ordered.[6]

The powers of tapas and meditation, those arising from putting one's self in rapport with creative force, are declared to be supernatural. In the old days the worshipper tried, through concentration on the hymns to Agni, to identify himself with the glowing world energy resident in all things. In tapas he expressed Agni's eternal essence and activity, as illumination broke over the *tapasvin*. Tapas became the final world power out of which appeared the darkness, the primeval ocean, the creation: 'From fervour kindled to its height eternal law and truth were born.'[7] And in *Manu*[8] we read,

---

[1] *Bṛh. Up.*, 3, 8, 10; 4, 4, 22.

[2] Keith, *Religion and Philosophy of the Veda*, vol. II, pp. 514 ff.; *Kena*, 33; *Praśna*, 1, 10; *Muṇḍ.*, 1, 2, 11.

[3] Radhakrishnan, *Indian Philosophy*, vol. I, p. 510.

[4] *Bṛh. Up.*, *Chānd Up.*, *IA*, 1923, p. 278.

[5] Keith, *Religion and Philosophy of the Veda*, vol. II, p. 587.

[6] *E.g.*, *Jābāla*. See Deussen, *The Philosophy of the Upanishads*. pp. 367 ff.

[7] See *Ṛig Veda*, 10, 190, 1.

[8] 1, 12.

'Just by means of his own fixed attention (*dhyānāt*) he splits the egg in two.' These attitudes, far apart in time, speak of the same view of extraordinary and creative power for man, and the means thereto.

In *Manu* the formal conditions and rules for the austere life are set forth.[1] Here the rights and privileges of the ascetic are confined to the twice-born. In the sixth lecture[2] are set forth in detail the third and fourth stages of life (Āśrama). While a considerable portion of the chapter is now obsolete, still, it exhibits the earlier ideal. In the third stage the individual lives a very strict life, but continues to perform certain ritualistic acts. His food is mostly wild stuffs, and he may restrict it greatly in well-known ways. Austerities such as the use of the five fires, uncomfortable clothes, and silence are described. In the fourth stage the man severs all family and social ties, takes to begging, eats little, meditates, is indifferent to every sort of condition, and looks upon life as unattractive.

The references given above will suffice to show how ascetic ideas developed and permeated the thought and life of ancient India. Such notions have prevailed continuously down to the present time.

If it be objected that the conceptions of asceticism alluded to above form a one-sided picture, it must be remembered that this study has to do with Yogīs whose practice is that of the Haṭha Yoga.[3]

Not only is there very early the presence of the ideas of asceticism, but also the figure of the ascetic himself, almost as he appears today, is found in the oldest literature. The 'mad' *muni* is described in the following hymn:[4]

> The hairy one supports the fire,
> The poison-fluid, and heaven and earth;

---

[1] And in other works on *Dharma* likewise. For references see *ERE*, vol. II, p. 89.

[2] *Manu*, vi, 1-87.

[3] See Kirtikar, V. J., *Studies in the Vedanta*, chap. eight, and especially p. 134.

[4] *Ṛig Veda*, 10, 136. The translation is from Griswold's *Religion of the Ṛig Veda*, pp. 338 ff. See *Marshall*, vol. I. pp. 53 ff. and plates XLVIII and C for evidence of posture and other elements characteristic of Indian asceticism in the Indus Civilization.

He is all sky to look upon,
The hairy one is called this light.

The Munis, girdled with the wind,
Wear garments soiled, of yellow hue;
After the wind's course follow they,
When once the gods have entered them.

Transported with the ecstasy
Of Munihood we mount the winds;
Ye, mortal men, are able now
To see our bodies and no more.

He flies through regions of the air,
Beholding all the various forms,—
The Muni, who was made a friend
Of every god for ministry.

The steed of Vāta, Vāyu's friend,
The Muni, by the gods impelled,
In both the oceans hath his home,
In eastern and in western seas.

Treading the path of sylvan beasts,
Gandharvas and Apsarases,
The hairy one knows every thought,
Sweet and most stimulating friend.

Vāyu has twirled for him; for him
He breaketh things most hard to bend;
When he, the hairy one, has drunk
With Rudra from the poison-cup.

Concerning this hymn Keith says:[1]

He differs entirely from the Brāhman student or the man undergoing consecration, for his ecstasy is not connected either with the sacrifice or with any of the rites ancillary to it or to the entry of the youth into the full life of the community. His mortal body men see, but he himself fares on the path of the Apsarases, the Gandharvas, the beasts of the wild, he dwells in the east and the western ocean, the steed of Vāta, the friend of Vāyu, inspired by the gods. He knows secret desires, he is the dearest friend, he supports Agni and both the worlds, he is the heaven and the light, and his ecstasy, it seems, is due to a potent draught which, with Rudra, he drinks from a goblet, perhaps a reference to the use of some poison to produce exhilaration or hypnosis. His hair is long, his soiled garments are of yellow hue.

Hauer, in *Der Yoga Als Heilweg*[2] expresses the opinion that in this hymn there are materials belonging to the Rudra-

---

[1] *Religion and Philosophy of the Veda*, vol. II, p. 402. [2] P. 12.

Śiva cycle. The hymn describes those primitive ecstatics who, under the intoxication of holy poisons, overcome all earthly difficulty, reach out to cosmic forces and become like the gods in possessing vision and unusual powers. They know the earthly fetters which bind men and know how to bring help to their fellows.

The fifteenth book of the *Atharva Veda* appertains to the Vrātya, a seeker after ecstatic trance, a dealer in the supernatural, a type of Yogī. These were Āryans outside the sphere of Vedic culture who were admitted into Brāhman circles by means of ceremonial. Certain of their hymns, apparently, constitute such a ritual. They practised neither agriculture nor commerce nor did they follow the rules of the Brahmacharya.[1]

Hauer[2] lays considerable emphasis upon the importance of this cult in the history of Yoga. The Vrātyas had intimate dealings with Prajāpati and were worshippers of Rudra-Śiva, holding an early form of the theistic Sāṅkhya-Yoga philosophy. He holds that they were ascetics, possessing a ritual, who later found their way into Brāhmanism. It is of interest to note that they laid emphasis upon the doctrine of the breaths, naming three, five, six, ten and even more, assimilating them to functions of the cosmic process. Among their severe practices (tapas) is mentioned that of standing for a year upright. They moved about the country in strange processions, using song and choral ceremonial, dealing out blessings and curses according as they were honoured or offended. Their clothing and ornaments were fantastic; their turban was peculiar and their white garments were marked with black figures. The Vrātya stood upon a cart drawn by horses and mules and carried a magic bowl and a spear. Before him went swift runners.

He was accompanied by a prostitute. The Vrātya represented the god and the prostitute the goddess. Their practices and ceremonial suggest the later Tāntric ritual in the use of

---

[1] See *Vedic Index*.

[2] *Der Yoga Als Heilweg*, pp. 8 ff. Keith, *Religion and Philosophy of the Veda*, vol. II, pp. 338, 402, does not follow Hauer with reference to the Vrātya.

intoxicating drink, flesh, and grain, and in the association of Rudra with the goddess. The Vrātya seems to have known the experiences of concentration, of soul expansion, of the enhancement of personality-consciousness similar to those described by Patañjali in connection with samādhi, experiences which occur when the man in trance is raised above his own narrow I, over time and space. He was the greatly honoured holy man, possessed of supernatural power, approximating divine personality, wandering about the country.

Probably before 800 B.C. the Vāikhānasa[1] appears. The *Parivrājaka*, *Bhikṣu*, the wandering beggar and the Vānaprastha, or anchorite, are familiar forms before the rise of Buddhism. And the *Upaniṣads* know the Sannyāsī, the renouncer striving for the knowledge of the Brahma-Ātman.[2] Realizing the Ātman, men, liberated, exalted in mind,

> gave up completely the life of the family and the world and became wandering, homeless, celibate ascetics, without possessions, without responsibilities, devoted altogether to the life of the Ātman.[3]

With the story of the Buddha we meet full-fledged familiar asceticism. While Gāutama turned aside for extremes in this, as in all things, still, Brāhman and Jāin laid emphasis upon such a life. The description of the company to which the Buddha joined himself, as set forth popularly in *The Light of Asia*,[4] is exact enough for illustration:

> Midway on Ratnagiri's groves of calm,
> Beyond the city, but below the caves,
> Lodged such as hold the body foe to soul,
> And flesh a beast which men must chain and tame
> With bitter pains, till sense of pain is killed,
> And tortured nerves vex torturer no more:
> Yogīs and Brahmachārīs, Bhikshus, all
> A gaunt and mournful band, dwelling apart.
> Some day and night had stood with lifted arms,
> Till—drained of blood and withered by disease—
> Their slowly wasting joints and stiffened limbs
> Jutted from sapless shoulders like dead forks
> From forest trunks. Others had clenched their hands
> So long and with so fierce a fortitude,

---

[1] See also *Gāutama Dharma Śastra*, vol. III, 26.
See Keith, *Religion and Philosophy of the Veda*, vol. II, pp. 589 ff.
FORL, p. 52. [4] Pp. 115, 116, 117.

The claw-like nails grew through the festered palm.
Some walked on sandals spiked; some with sharp flints
Gashed breast and brow and thigh, scarred these with fire,
Threaded their flesh with jungle thorns and spits,
Besmeared with mud and ashes, crouching foul
In rags of dead men wrapped about their loins.
Certain there were inhabited the spots
Where death-pyres smouldered, cowering defiled
With corpses for their company, and kites
Screaming around them o'er the funeral-spoils;
Certain who cried five hundred times a day
The names of Shiva, knit with hissing snakes
About their sun-tanned necks and hollow flanks,
One palsied foot drawn up against the ham.
So gathered they, a grievous company;
Crowns blistered by the blazing heat, eyes bleared,
Sinews and muscles shrivelled, visages
Haggard and wan as slain men's, five days dead;
Here crouched one in the dust who noon by noon
Meted a thousand grains of millet out,
Ate it with famished patience, seed by seed,
And so starved on; there one who bruised his pulse
With bitter leaves lest palate should be pleased;
And next, a miserable saint self-maimed,
Eyeless and tongueless, sexless, crippled, deaf;
The body by the mind being thus stripped
For glory of much suffering, and the bliss
Which they shall win—say holy books—whose woe
Shames gods that send us woe, and makes men gods
Stronger to suffer than Hell is to harm.

A description from the *Rāmāyaṇa*[1] runs as follows:

Vāikhānasas who love the wild,
Pure hermits Bālakhiyas styled,
Good Śaṁprakṣālas, saints who live
On rays which moon and daystar give:
Those who with leaves their lives sustain,
And those who pound with stones their grain:
And they who live in pools, and those
Whose corn, save teeth, no winnow knows:
Those who for beds the cold earth use,
And those who every couch refuse:
And those condemned to ceaseless pains,
Whose single foot their weight sustains:
And those who sleep neath open skies,
Whose food the wave or air supplies,
And hermits pure who spend their nights,

[1] Book 3, Canto 6. Griffith's translation.

On ground prepared for sacred rites:
Those who on hills their vigil hold,
On dripping clothes around them fold;
The devotees who live for prayer.
Or the five fires unflinching bear. . . .

There is no need to continue to set forth the presence of the ascetic in ancient India but it is interesting to read about the ascetics whom the Greeks met during Alexander's sojourn in India in 326 B.C.[1]

At Takshaçilā, so far as we know, the Greeks first noticed Indian ascetics. The report reached Alexander himself of a strange set of men who were to be seen naked somewhere near the city, 'practising endurance, men commanding a great reverence among the people. It was no use his sending for them, since they would certainly refuse to come: those who wished to learn their secret must go to them. Alexander, however, on his side, felt he could not go to them consistently with his dignity: so he chose an envoy, a Greek officer named Onesicritus, who had been a disciple of the Cynic philosopher, Diogenes a figure obviously akin to the Indian ascetics. Onesicritus, in the book he afterwards wrote, gave an account of his interesting mission, and we may still read it in Strabo's version. He found fifteen ascetics some ten miles from the city, sitting naked and motionless in a sun so burning that one could not even walk over the stones with bare feet. Onesicritus could only communicate with them through a series of three interpreters, but he made them understand that the Yavana king would like to learn their wisdom. The ascetic to whom he first addressed himself answered bluntly that no one coming in the bravery of European clothes—cavalry cloak and broad-brimmed hat and top-boots, such as the Macedonians wore—could learn their wisdom. To do that, he must strip naked and learn to sit on the hot stones beside them. Another answered more mildly that it was really very creditable for such a man as Alexander to desire to know something of the deeper wisdom, but one must remember that to attempt to convey their teaching through three interpreters, common men incapable of understanding more than the mere words, would be like trying to make water flow clear through mud. They seem however to have made an attempt, and then they asked Onesicritus whether among the Yavanas there was any teaching of this kind, and he told them about Pythagoras and Socrates and his old master, Diogenes. The ascetics seemed pleased, but expressed regret that the wise men of the Greeks had clung to such superfluities as clothes. One of these ascetics was ultimately persuaded by the rāja of Takshaçilā to accompany Alexander and return to clothes and a worldly life. His

[1] *The Cambridge History of India*, vol. I, pp. 358 ff. Quoted by permission of Macmillan and Company, Publishers.

companions considered it an apostasy, and followed him with reproaches. The name of this Indian, who remained a notable figure in Alexander's entourage, was one which Plutarch reproduces as 'Sphines,' but the Greeks, catching among the Indian words of greeting which he exchanged with his fellow-countrymen, the word, *kalyāṇa*, 'lucky,' came to call him Kalanos.

Lanman points out[1] that Onesicritus reported with great accuracy the interviews which he had with Hindu ascetics:

> That is the best doctrine, which rids the spirit not only of grief but also of joy; and again, that that dwelling-place is the best, for which the scantiest equipment or outfit is needed.

Alberuni describes practices of Yoga.[2]

Reference must be made to ancient notions concerning the aims, the powers and the privileges issuing from ascetic practices. In the *Rāmāyaṇa*, for example, the renowned superiors of hermit settlements were held in the highest reverence and talked of the greatness of the boons and rewards that they had won. And throughout Indian literature is found abundant testimony on these points. Among the aims of asceticism may be mentioned first the attainment of the ecstatic condition. Originally, perhaps, this department of experience was reserved for the medicine man; but, in the *Upaniṣads* at least, the sage seeks such states of soul. The figure already exhibited from the *Ṛig Veda* is in a frenzy. This muni is also addicted to poisons. And it is clear that from ancient time drugs and sex stimulations were used for the same ends of ecstasy and trance.

For the *Atharva Veda* Professor Radhakrishnan's summary will suffice:[3]

> We hear of great ascetics who obtain the mastery of nature by *tapas*. They reduce the elemental forces to their control by this asceticism. It was then well known that ecstatic conditions could be induced by the mortification of the body. Man can participate in divine power by the hidden force of magic. The professors of magic and witchcraft were accepted by the Vedic seers, and their calling was dignified, with the result that magic and mysticism soon became confused. We find people sitting in the midst of five fires, standing

---

[1] *Harvard Theological Review*, October, 1918, p. 358.

[2] *Alberuni's India*, vol. I, p. 69. His date is in the eleventh century. See p. 443.

[3] *Indian Philosophy*, by S. Radhakrishnan, vol. I, p. 121. Quoted by permission of Macmillan and Company, Publishers.

on one leg, holding an arm above the head, all for the purpose of commanding the forces of nature and subduing the gods to their will.

Reference has already been made to supernatural and creative powers engendered by asceticism. All sorts of marvellous things were won through protracted and extreme penance. And all down through India's past are to be found men who through asceticism have realized the impossible. Dhruva[1] is a famous example. Viśvamitra, the Kṣatriya, by most severe and protracted austerities compelled the gods to grant him the birth and rights of a Brāhman.[2] This story from the *Epic* belongs to an earlier period. Nahuṣa by tapas won for himself the rank of Indra.[3] From the other *Epic* two examples may be cited. Rāvaṇa acquired, through ascetic practices, invulnerability to death by gods or demigods, and Virādha secured immunity against all kinds of weapons. The *Rāmāyaṇa* is full of *mighty* saints, miracle-workers.

Manu recognizes the power of asceticism.

> Whatever is hard to be traversed, whatever is hard to be attained, whatever is hard to be reached, whatever is hard to be performed, all may be accomplished by austerities; for austerity (possesses a power) which it is difficult to surpass.[4]

Since the Yogīs are a monastic order, it may be of interest to look for a moment at the development of the monastic idea in India. The institution is old. The Buddha organized his followers and set up his characteristic institution, the Saṅgha. The establishments of the order flourished and became in later centuries great in size, importance and wealth. There may be a question as to whether the Buddha originated the institution.[5] Barth thinks that the organization of the Saṅgha was perfected before the time of Aśoka.[6] But, in the Jāin faith, evidences seem clear that Mahāvīra was the last of a long line (twenty-four in all) of leaders. Of these his immediate predecessor as *tīrtha-kara* died some 250 years

---

1 *Mahābhārata, Viṣṇu parvā*, 1, 11, 12. See Dawson, *Classical Dictionary of Hindu Mythology*, p. 91.

2 Muir, *Sanskrit Texts*, vol. I, pp. 388 ff.

3 Muir, *Sanskrit Texts*, vol. I, p. 307.

4 11, 239 ff.

5 See *ERE*, vol. VIII, p. 799.

6 *Religions of India*, p. 127.

before him. Farquhar[1] puts the order of Sannyāsīs before those of the Buddhists and Jains. Earlier organizations were probably much simpler and perhaps were only places of residence for the rainy season.[2] The Yātīs and the Cārvākas seem to have had a simple sort of monastic organization. The major ascetic orders of the present time, of all sects, have their *maṭhas*, or monasteries, and many of these institutions are old.

Since the Yogīs are one of the chief divisions of the Śāivite ascetics,[3] attention will now be drawn especially to the line of ascetic orders out of which they have come.

As reported in a previous chapter, Śiva is the ideal ascetic. He exhibits both the get-up, the austerities and the powers arising from the pursuit of such activities. Even in the hymn to the 'mad' muni are discernible attributes such as the master Yogī, Śiva, exhibits.

The Yogīs are the residue of ancient Śāivite sects which began as philosophies and became ascetic orders.[4] More particularly are they Pāśupata Śāivas. However, influences of decadent Buddhism are clearly indicated in the Nepalese traditions of the Gorakhnāthīs and both Buddhist and Tāntric characteristics in the legends from Bengal. The chief of the Śāivite sects which precede the Kānphaṭas were the Pāśupata, the Lakuliśa, the Kālāmukha and the Kāpālika (and the Aghorī?) all of which are Pāśupata. The Kānphaṭas share many things with the earlier orders and do not differ so very much from them. The Pāśupata sects, as such, have almost completely disappeared. A few Aghorīs may be seen now and then. They are old Kāpālikas and a few Aughars who are Kāpālikas reformed under the influence of Kabīr.[5]

The earlier name, *Maheśvara* is an equivalent of Pāśupata. Here Paśupati is represented as having used the five topics

---

[1] 'The Fighting Ascetics of India,' *Bulletin of the John Rylands Library*, vol. IX, No. 2, July, 1925. Oldenberg traces the institution to the Sannyāsī. (*Buddha*, p. 32.)

[2] See *ERE*, vol. VII, p. 214. It is difficult to conceive of schools or orders of ascetics without establishments of some kind. Cf. *Hindu Civilization*, by R. K. Mookerji, p. 220.

[3] In this section on Śāivite sects Bhandarkar's *Vāiṣhṇavism, Śaivism and Minor Religious Systems* has been freely used.

[4] Hopkins, *Religions of India*, p. 487.

[5] *FORL*, p. 347.

of the sect. This makes the god their original teacher, much as the Gorakhnāthīs make Ādinātha, as Śiva, the original teacher of the Yogīs. In South India Lakulin or Lakulīśa is said to be the original teacher of the order. Lakulīśa became a name for the schools of the Pāśupatas, at least after the eleventh century. Likewise the Kālāmukhas were called Lakulīśas. Bhandarkar concludes that these three names cover about the same period of time.

Lakula was a general term by which Śiva sects were called, another was Pāśupata. Later arose out of this original Lakulīśa-Pāśupata sect the three systems, Pāśupata, Kālāmukha and Kāpālika. These sects were more extreme and less rational than the other Śāivites. Bhandarkar says that from 934 to 1285, in inscriptions, Lakula was a general name designating sects of Śiva.[1]

One of the early references to Pāśupatas[2] is in the *Atharva Śiras* where their vow is recorded. They are enjoined to give up greed and anger; to realize forgiveness; to mutter the syllable *oṁ*; to practice the meditation which issues in perception. There the Pāśupata device of besmearing the body with ashes is used with the words:

> The ash is fire, the ash is water, the ash is earth, everything is ash, the ether is ash, the mind, the eyes and other senses are ashes.

The Pāśupata vow is enjoined for the removal of the noose with which the Paśu or individual soul is tied. This practice is calculated to effect deliverance from the trammels of life. The expression, '*Paśu-pāśa vimokṣa*', which means 'the loosening of the noose tied round the neck of beings,' is characteristic of the Pāśupata sect.

The *Mahābhārata* knows the Pāśupata[3]; and the sect, which is represented as open to all classes, is charged with subverting caste. Here perhaps the name is that of a new Śāivite school of theology.[4]

In the centuries around the Christian Era, perhaps two

---

[1] *Vāiṣṇavism, Śaivism and Minor Religious Systems*, p. 121. See Fleet, *JRAS*, 1907, pp. 419 ff.

[2] On the systems of the *Nakulīśa-Pāśupata* see *Sarva Darṣana Saṅghra*, pp. 103 ff.

[3] Hopkins, *The Great Epic*, p. 118.

[4] *E.g.*, 12, 285, 321-350; 13, 14-18, 160-161.

centuries before, the school was well known and contained many noted men.[1]

In the *Vāyu Purāṇa* (*c.* fourth century A.D.) is found a statement concerning the peculiar Yoga of the sect with its various forms of physical and intellectual discipline. A section of the *Purāṇa* introduces the Lakulīśa as a sub-sect of the Pāśupatas. They are known in inscriptions of the fifth century.[2] The sect entered Nepāl in the eighth century,[3] where the cult is still popular, as it is in other parts of the Himālayas. Śaṅkara (*c.* A.D. 850) criticized the teachings of the Pāśupatas, and in the twelfth century Rāmānuja did likewise, and named four classes of them, Kāpāla, Kālāmukha, Pāśupata and Śāiva.[4]

Śaṅkara[5] says:

> The Maheśvaras (Śāivas) maintain that the five categories, viz., effect, cause, union, ritual and the end of pain were taught by the Lord Paśupati (Śiva) to the end of breaking the bonds of the animal (i.e., the soul): Paśupati is according to them, the Lord, the operative cause.

Their famous statement is that Paśupati is the Lord (*Pati*) and man his creature (*paśu*) is bound by the fetter (*pāśa* of the world, and requires to be set free by the Lord. In more expanded form, the five categories may be set forth thus: (1) Effect (*kārya*), includes the evolution of *pradhāna* and the individual soul (*paśu*); (2) Cause (*kāraṇa*), Īśvara or Maheśvara (Pati) and pradhāna as efficient and material aspects of the whole creation, Pati possessing unbounded power of acting and knowing; (3) Union (Yoga), absorption in meditation or muttering the syllable *oṁ*, contemplation embracing both action and the cessation of action; (4) bathing in ashes, besmearing the body with ashes, sleeping in ashes, mutterings, absurd and obscene practices; (5) final deliverance (*dukhānta*), total destruction of misery and the acquirement of special powers.

---

[1] See Bhandarkar, p. 117.

[2] Hopkins, *Religions of India*, p. 482.

[3] Smith, *Catalogue of Coins in the Indian Museum, Calcutta*, pp. 280 ff.

[4] For this list see also Bhandarkar, *JASBy*, vol. XXII, p. 158.

[5] Thibaut, *The Vedanta Sutra with Sankara's Commentary*, pt. I, p. 453.

Rāmānuja[1] says:

> They maintain the general material cause to be constituted by Paśupati. They further hold the wearing of the so-called 'mudrā' badges and the like to be means to accomplish the highest end of man.

In Devendra's *Mahārāṣṭri Tales*, the Pāśupata ascetic, really a highway robber,

> Wears a diadem of long matted hair; his limbs are strewn with ashes; in his fist he holds a trident; he is encircled with evil-averting amulets; his fingers are busy with his hermit's token.[2]

Bloomfield[3] describes the Pāśupatas as persons who practice deceit and violence, as robbers and would-be murderers.

Even in the *Great Epic*[4] they are looked upon with disfavour. They bear the brand of the *liṅga* on forehead, arms, breast and navel. Farquhar[5] states that they laid emphasis on the worship of the liṅga, an aspect of Lakulīśa practice. Suggestive *Epic* expressions as recorded by him are: *ūrddhva-liṅga*, *sthīra-liṅga*, *ūrddhva-retas* and *mahāśepo-nagno*. Their marks are the necklace, the golden ornament, the ear-ring, the head-jewel, ashes and the sacred thread—'owning these one is not born again.'[6]

The Lakulīśa[7] are a sub-order of the Pāśupata. The word *Lakula* or *Nakula*, means 'club' and the reference is to the Lord-of-the-Club or the Lord-Bearing-a-Club. Probably the name belongs to a great religious teacher of the school of the Pāśupatas, who carried a club. He has been indentified with Śiva. There is an interesting note in the *Vāyu Purāṇa*,[8] and in the *Liṅga Purāṇa*[9], which in the form of prophecy states that Maheśvara in the *Kṛṣṇa Dvāipāyaṇa* would incarnate as a Brāhman by the name of Lakulin, entering a dead body thrown into a cemetery; and that he would have four disciples who would be Pāśupatas. Thus the movement

[1] Thibaut, *Vedanta Sutras with Ramanuja's Commentary*, p. 520.
[2] *Wi.*, p. 80. [3] *JAOS*, vol. XLIV, p. 232.
[4] 12, 285, 194–195. [5] *FORL*, p. 103.
[6] Thibaut, *Vedanta Sutras with Ramanuja's Commentary*, p. 521.
[7] See *Archæological Report*, 1906-7, pp. 179 ff. Here evidence shows the cult to be widespread.
[8] Chap. 21, vv. 204-212. [9] Chap. 24, vv. 124-137.

seems to have its beginning in Gujrāt. Or, as it is otherwise stated, Śiva through his Yogic powers, entered a dead body in a cemetery and became incarnated as Lakula at Kāyāvarohaṇa in the Lāṭa Country, Baroda. The inscription at Ekliṅgajī states that Śiva was incorporated in the country of Broach and that he carried a club. The place is located at Karwar in Baroda State and there is still there a temple to Lakulīśa.[1] The teaching of the sect can be traced to the first century of our era[2]. The great Harṣa was a disciple of the faith[3]. The sect spread also into Merwār and Rājputāna. During the period, 550–900 it spread into the south as well. The Pāśupatas were designated by the name Lakulīśa and were widely worshipped on the plains of India[4]. Lakula was reincarnated in Chilluka in South India in the tenth century[5]. This means evidently that a revival of the movement set in there at that time. It appeared in Melpāḍi, North Arcot, about 1020 and spread to the south. The Kālāmukhas, or 'Black Friars' were active in teaching the doctrine in the south in the eleventh, twelfth and thirteenth centuries.

Temples of the tenth century at Purāṇādhiṣṭhāna (near Śrīnagar in Kashmīr) and that of Pāyar Cave have figures of Lakula on them.[6] The Ekaliṅgaji inscription of the tenth century, written in Devanāgari, begins with an obeisance to Lakulīśa. The date of the temple is A.D. 791. Temples of the seventh to the tenth centuries, as for example, that at Jharapatan (seventh century) show Śiva with but two arms, holding a short club, *mahāśeponagno*.

The Nakulīśa-Pāśupatas are described by Mādhava in his *Sarva Darṣana Saṅgraha*.[7] Their system was the doctrine of the Pañcādhyāyi, the main source of the later Śiva systems. It aims at a union of the soul with Śiva by pious mutterings, meditation and the cessation of all action so that the state of mere feeling is attained. By Yoga practices they attained miraculous powers of assuming various shapes and forms, and received messages from the dead. According to

---

[1] *FORL*, p. 146. [2] *Bhandarkar*, *JASBy*, vol. XXII, p. 57.
[3] *ERE*, vol. VI, p. 702. [4] *Archæological Survey of India Report*, 1915–16, p. 50. [5] *ERE*, vol. XI, p. 68.
[6] *Archæological Survey of India Report*, 1915-16, p. 75.
[7] Chap. six.

them, the religious emotions were to be excited by song and dance, by laughter, by simulating the acts and gestures of one in love, by speaking wildly, by wearing ashes and flowers from images in the temples and by loud uttering of the sacred sound, *huṁ*, like the sound of *vasat*, an imitation of a sound ascribed to a bull. Some think that the obscene postures depicted in Hindu temples are traceable to their behaviour.[1] All of this is very like that praxis ascribed to the Pāśupatas and the Kālāmukhas. Texts of the Yogīs are not ignorant of the substance of them.

Special postures are attributed to them and bathing and sleeping in sand instead of ashes is mentioned. They dispensed charity to all comers at their institutions.

The Kālāmukhas are closely associated with the Lakulīśas, in fact they were the 'black friars' who, as exponents of the Lakulīśa doctrines were responsible for its spread in the south during the eleventh and twelfth centuries. An inscription of the twelfth century (1177) notes Lakulīśa and Kālāmukha as one and both as Pāśupata.[2] Technically they were more extreme in their practices than the Kāpālakas, but there was no *popular* distinction between them.

They were distinguished by a black streak on the forehead.[3]

The system is referred to in Rāmānuja's Commentary on the Vedānta Sūtra.[4] The passage is as follows:

> Kālāmukhas teach that the means of obtaining all desired results in this world as well as the next are constituted by certain practices —such as using a skull as a drinking vessel, smearing oneself with the ashes of a dead body, eating the flesh of such a body, carrying a heavy stick, setting up a liquor-jar and using it as a platform for making offerings to the gods, and the like. A bracelet made of Rudrākṣa-seeds on the arm, matted hair on the head, a skull, smearing oneself with ashes, etc. All this is well known from the Śaivas. They also hold that by some special ceremonial performance men of different castes may become Brāhmaṇas and reach the highest *āśrama*: by merely entering on the initiatory ceremony (*dīkṣa*) a man becomes a Brāhmaṇa at once; by undertaking the Kāpāla rite a man becomes at once an ascetic.

---

[1] Gopi Nath Rao, *Elements of Hindu Iconography*, vol. II, pt. 1, p. 23, note.

[2] Bhandarkar, *Vāiṣṇavism, Śāivism, etc.*, p. 120.

[3] *Indian Iconography*, vol. II, pt. 1, p. 25.

[4] See Thibaut's Translation in *SBE*, p. 521.

This sect is still active. The members seem to be extremely horrible in character. They worship Śiva as Mahākāla (the great destroyer) or as Kāpālabhṛt (skull-wearer). Kapālin is Bhāirava, the most terrible form of Śiva[1]. With these are sometimes associated the possibly more revolting Aghorī. The latter, at least, are cannibalistic. Some modern sections of the cult are of recent origin. The Aghorī Yogīs of the Panjab are somehow related to these orders and that some Aughars were cannibals was admitted to the author during inquiries in that region in the winter of 1924. These disgusting features of the cult are associated with tāntra and the east of Bengal and Assam, and are supposed to be conducive to the acquisition of supernatural powers. These persons are looked upon by the populace with feelings of abhorrence and fear. It is a horrible and demoniacal sect. They seem to be a specialization within the Pāśupata cult rather than a true sect; and are close to Vāmacāra Śāktas, for they offer licentious homage to Śakti and Bhāirava. (The practice of making no discrimination in food is an old Pāśupata one.)

However, the Kāpālikas ('wearers of skulls', they wore skulls around their necks) were known fairly early. They are mentioned in the *Daśa-Kumāra-Carita* (see below) of the sixth century, and as early as the seventh century in Mahārāṣṭhra. Hiuen Tsang (in India 630-645) saw them and described them as wearers of skulls.

One of the characters in Bhavabhūtī's (eighth century) *Mālatī-Mādhava* is a Kāpālika. (See below.) Śaṅkara, so Mādhava says, was in controversy with Kāpālikas. Ānandagiri describes them. Rāmānuja held them to be extreme in their practices and Moshan Fani (seventeenth century) mentions them.

A general description of them would be as follows: They went about naked, wore a cap while travelling, smeared their bodies with funeral ashes, were armed with a trident or sword, carried a hollow skull for a cup or begging bowl, were half-intoxicated with spirits which they drank from the hollow skull, were known to commit acts of violence; their

---

[1] *Vāiṣṇaivism and Śāivism, etc.*, p. 128.

garments (when they wore them) were of patch-work, they slept on the ground,[1] and wore a rosary of rudrākṣa seeds. They offered human sacrifices to Cāmuṇḍā in order to obtain magic powers, and often resorted to tricks to ensnare victims.[2] Dust from their feet was supposed to cure disease and water from the washing of their feet drove away demons.[3] The powers which they acquired included the ability to fly through the air. Their wits were sharpened by the use of wine, eating disgusting food, and the embrace of the Śakti of Bhāirava. They were always lewd, and on occasion carried off maidens.[4]

In Bhavabhūti's *Mālatī-Mādhava* appears Aghoraghaṇṭa, a Kāpālika, priest of Cāmuṇḍā and Kāpāla Kuṇḍalā (skull-ear-ring), a nun, devotee of Cāmuṇḍā and pupil of the ascetic, practising Yoga, enjoying magic powers, Śāktas, wearing necklaces of skulls, and carrying heavy rods from which hung strings of bells. The nun kidnaps the heroine of the play, in the dead of night, and places her before the image of Cāmuṇḍā in a temple near a cemetery, where she is to be killed and offered to the goddess by the ascetic. (But Mādhava rescues her and slays Aghoraghaṇṭa).

The description of the wizard, Kāpālika, in the *Daśa-Kumāra Carita* is as follows:[5]

> His body is ornamented with glittering pieces of skulls; he is smeared with ashes of the funeral fires; he wears braids that look like a streak of lightning; with his left hand he is sacrificing steadily into a fierce fire crackling sesame and mustard. In front of him stands one of the aforementioned servants with folded hands, saying: 'Issue your command; wherewith can I serve you?' He is told to fetch the princess, Kanakalekhā, and he does so. (She is rescued from becoming a human sacrifice in the nick of time).

Ānandagiri's description is found in the *Śaṅkara-vijaya* and shows the standard get-up of the Kāpālikas.

> His body is smeared with ashes from a funeral pyre, around his neck hangs a string of human skulls, his forehead is streaked with a black line, his hair is twisted into a matted braid, his loins are clothed with a tiger's skin, a hollow skull is in his left hand (for a

---

[1] *JAOS*, vol. XLIV, p. 208.
[2] *JAOS*, vol. XLIV, p. 213.
[3] *JAOS*, vol. XLIV, p. 203.
[4] *JAOS*, vol. XLIV, p. 218.
[5] *JAOS*, vol. XLIV, p. 212.

cup), and in his right hand he carries a bell which he rings incessantly, exclaiming aloud, 'Ho, Śambhu, Bhāirava,—Ho, Lord of Kālī.[1]

In the *Prabodha Chandrodaya*[2] are found the following statements:

My necklace and ornaments are of human bones; I dwell among the ashes of the dead and eat my food in human skulls. I look with eyes brightened with the antimony of Yoga, and believe that the parts of this world are reciprocally different, but that the whole is not different from God. . . . After fasting we drink liquor out of the skulls of Brāhmans; our sacred fires are fed with the brains and lungs of men mixed up with their flesh, and human victims covered with the fresh blood gushing from the dreadful wound in their throats, are the offerings by which we appease the terrible god (Mahā Bhāirava). . . . . I contemplate the Lord of Bhavānī, the powerful god who creates, preserves and destroys the fourteen worlds, whose glory is both revealed in the *Vedas* and displayed in his works. The might of our religion is such that I control Hari-Hara and the greatest and most ancient of the gods; I stop the course of the planets in the heavens; I submerge the earth in water, with it mountains and cities, and I again drink up the waters in a moment . . . He who resembles the gods, whose crest is the lunar orb, and who with delight embraces women beautiful as Pārvatī, feel supreme bliss.

Who has enjoyed happiness independent of visible objects? The soul that lives without spiritual abstraction is in a state of felicity. But why do you pray to become like stones?

Accompanying the Kāpālika is a Kāpālinī in attire similar to his, with heavy breasts, addicted to spirits, who with her companion, at the command of Bhāirava, dances. It is stated in this connection that,

without renouncing the pleasures derived through the organs of sense, the eight great *siddhis* may be obtained.

Among these powers are the following: whatever a man desires he may obtain; the laws of nature are under his control; the body's size may be diminished or enlarged at will; and he may transport himself in an instant to any part of the universe.

Rāmānuja in his Commentary[3] makes Kāpālas say:

He who knows the true nature of the six *mudrās*, who understands

---

[1] *JAOS*, vol. XLIV, pp. 206, 207; and *Wi.*, p. 264.

[2] Taylor's Translation, pp. 38 ff.

[3] Thibaut, *Vedānta Sūtras with Ramanuja's Commentary*, pp. 520, 521.

> the highest *mudrā*, meditating on himself as in the position called *bhagāsana*[1], reaches Nirvāṇa. The necklace, the golden ornament, the ear-ring, the head-jewel, ashes, and the sacred thread are called the six *mudrās*. . . . He whose body is marked with these is not born again.

In the *Dabistan*[2] is an account of Yogīs

> who know no prohibited food. . . . They also kill and eat men. . . . There are some of this sect who having mixed their excretions and filtered them through a piece of cloth, drink them, and say that such an act renders a man capable of great affairs, and they pretend to know strange things. They call the performance of this act *atilea* and also *akhon*. They have all originated from Gorakhnāth. The author of this work saw a man, who singing the customary song, sat upon a corpse, which he kept unburied until it came into a state of dissolution, and then ate the flesh of it; this act they hold extremely meritorious.

More recent references to these ascetics are numerous.[3]

Wilson[4] states that the Kāpālikas have merged into other sects, particularly into the Kānphaṭas, but that these must all have been contemporary sects for some time.

From the foregoing accounts it is clear that the sects have much in common. A composite picture drawn from these descriptions would exhibit many traits discernible today in the sect of the Kānphaṭas.

The question of the date of Goraknāth as the founder of the Kānphaṭa Yogīs now arises and becomes the subject of the following chapter.

---

[1] He meditates on himself as seated in the *pudendum muliebre*. See *Indian Buddhist Iconography, etc.*, by B. Bhattacharya.

[2] (*c.* 1670) vol. II, p. 129.

[3] See *ERE*, vol. I, p. 211.

[4] *Wi.*, p. 18.

CHAPTER ELEVEN

GORAKHNĀTH

HAVING considered at length the characters of the sects of Śiva in which the Kānphaṭas have their origin, it becomes necessary to review the various data which have a bearing on the time of the founder of the order.

Traditions and legends concerning Gorakhnāth are as already shown, widespread and extensive. Nepāl, the United Provinces, Bengal, Western India, Sind and the Panjab each has a large collection.

Kānphaṭas say that their sect existed before the world came into being. Their story is that when Viṣṇu emerged from the lotus at the creation of all things, Gorakhnāth was in Pātāla. Viṣṇu, terrified at the waste of waters, went to Pātāla and implored the aid of Gorakhnāth, who, in pity for the deity, gave him a handful of ashes from his eternal fire (dhūnī) and said to him that, if he would sprinkle the ashes over the waters, he would be able to create the world. It happened as Gorakhnāth had promised, and then Brahmā, Viṣṇu and Śiva became the first disciples of Gorakhnāth.[1]

In many places Gorakhnāth is looked upon as more than a human teacher, outside of the ordinary laws of time, who has appeared on the earth in different ages (*yuga*). He is said to have lived in the Panjab at Peshāwar, beyond Lahore, in the Satya (Kṛta) Yuga; at Gorakhpur in the Tretā Yuga; at Hurmuj, beyond Dwārakā, in the Dvāpara Yuga; and three months journey west of Gorakhpur, at Gorakhmari (Gorakhmandi) in Kāṭhiāwār in the Kali Yuga.[2] This is evidently an attempt not only to refer the origin of

---

[1] *CTC*, vol. III, pp. 153, 154.

[2] See *Martin*, vol. II, p. 484; *Gr.*, p. 329.

the sect to the distant past, but to incorporate in the record references to widely separated places where Gorakhnāth and his followers had headquarters and were well known. It is also reported that Gorakhnāth appeared in the Kali Yuga in the form of Śeṣa Nāga.[1]

His followers frequently refuse to give the time and place of his origin because they consider him as superhuman. Nevertheless, statements are made concerning his movements in this age. The Nepalese hold that he came to Kāṭhmāṇḍu from the Panjab, or at least from beyond the borders of their kingdom.[2] And he is said to have lived near the temple of Paśupatināth in Kāṭhmāṇḍu.[3] He is also claimed as a saint of Oudh.[4] The monks of Gorakhpur say that he came to the United Provinces from the Panjab, and that their chief seat is at Ṭilla, in Jhelum. Traditions in Kacch go back to the Panjab; their chief, Dharamnāth, a disciple of Gorakhnāth, having come from Peshāwar. At Nāsik Yogīs hold, on the other hand, that Gorakhnāth went from Nepāl to the Panjab and from thence to other parts of India. Judging from the preponderance of tradition and the relation of the monastery at Ṭilla to the others in India, it would seem best to hold that Gorakhnāth was a native of the Panjab. On the other hand, Bengal and Nepalese traditions point to the east. And, with communications as they were, it is possible that he came from the east into the Panjab. Moreover it seems that Gorakhnāth was originally a Vajrāyaṇa Buddhist, connected to Śāivism by Matsyendranāth. The legends of Gopicand show how easily men could move from place to place even in those days.

Before proceeding to the discussion of the spiritual descent of Gorakhnāth and of his place in the history of India, it may be well to refer to some less pertinent scraps of information about him.

In the *Dabistan* there is mention of Gorakhnāth and of Yoga practices. Both the writings of Gorakhnāth and of

---

[1] *RTCP*, vol. I, p. 191.
[2] See above, the story of his coming to Matsyendranāth.
[3] *Martin*, vol. II, p. 484.
[4] *BCI*, p. 1,235.

those who quote him are cited.[1] Moshan Fani, the author of the *Dabistan*, lived in the time of Har Gobind (1607–1644).[2]

Another tradition connects Gorakhnāth with Bābā Farīd who visited Girnār in 1244, and who died in 1266. Gorakhnāth is represented by an old shrine on Girnār.[3]

The famous monastery at Dhinodhar, in Kacch, is connected with the name of Dharamnāth. This famous saint, who was a Gorakhnāthī, came to Kacch in 1382.[4] It is with reference to this event that Grierson places, provisionally, the date of Gorakhnāth in the fourteenth century.[5] The *paramparās* put at least one disciple between Dharamnāth and his famous guru and these two Yogīs might not have been contemporaries.[6]

The spiritual descent of Gorakhnāth is recorded in several places.[7] All of these paramparās agree in placing before him two teachers, Ādināth and Matsyendranāth (Macchendernāth). Khakkar names five teachers preceding Ādināth[8]; and Svātmarāma states that six gurus intervened between Matsyendranāth and Gorakhnāth.[9] Of these Lakṣmīnārāyaṇa, commentator on the *Gorakṣa Śataka* identifies Mīnanātha with Matsyendranāth.[10] Current tradition makes Matsyen-

---

[1] *Dabistan*, vol. I, p. 127.

[2] Sita Ram Kohila, in *The Journal of Indian History*, February, 1922. The translators of the *Dabistan* place the death of Moshan Fani not far from 1670. (vol. I, p. 15.)

[3] See above, page 119.

[4] *IA*, vol. VII, p. 49.

[5] *Gr.*, p. 329. For an account of Dharamnāth, see pp. 116 ff.

[6] See chap. four. Appendix D.

[7] *Gorakhnāth kī Goṣṭhī* (See Price, *Hindu and Hindustani Selections*, vol. I, p. 141); Trump, *The Ādi Grantha*, p. 36, note 4; *The Haṭhayogapradīpika* of Svātmarāma, verse 5; *Report on the Architectural and Archæological Remains in the Province of Kacch*, p. 3; *Śrī Jñāneśvara-mahārāja Carita*, Pāṅgārkar, p. 47; and current traditions. See also *Wi.*, p. 214, note 2 and the reference to Weber.

[8] Niranjan Nirākār, Ādhika Somnātha, Chet Somnātha, Omkāranātha, and Achetnātha. *IA*, vol. VII, p. 47.

[9] Nātha, Sahara, Ānanda, Bhāirava, Gāuraṅgi, and Mīnanātha.

[10] With this Levi agrees: *Le Nepāl*, vol. I, p. 155. Śrī Nānāmahārāja Josi Sākhara, *Sārtha Jñāneśvarī*, 18, verse 1754, translates Mīna as Matsyendra. Both 'mīna' and 'matsya' mean 'fish.' Bengal tradition seems to make them two different Yogīs, with Matsyendra the Guru of Gorakhnāth and Mīna a follower.

dranāth the teacher of Gorakhnāth. In the *Gorakhnāth kī Goṣṭhī* of Kabīr Gorakhnāth speaks of himself as the son of Matsyendranāth and the grandson of Ādināth.[1]

Although Ādināth may have been a Yogī preceding Matsyendranāth, he is now identified with Śiva, and the name is used in an attempt to trace the origin of the sect to the greatest of Yogīs, the god Śiva.

Much human interest centres around Matsyendranāth, who is close to Gorakhnāth. He is the guardian deity of Nepāl,[2] presiding over the destinies of the kingdom.[3] He is considered as a Buddhist saint,[4] as an incarnation of Padmapāṇi, or as Avalokiteśvara, the fourth divine Bodhisattva.[5] He evidently belongs to some place outside of the kingdom, for he is said to have come to Nepāl at the command of the Buddha.[6] It is said that Aryavalokiteśvara Padmapāṇi Bodhisattva taught Śiva the Yoga. On his way home, after having received his instruction, Śiva explained the doctrines to Pārvatī, at the seaside. She fell asleep while Śiva was speaking, but Lokeśvar[7] heard it, disguised

---

[1] *Wi.*, p. 214. Price, *Hindu and Hindustani Selections*, vol. I, p. 141. Quoted by Trump, p. 36, note 4.

[2] Wright, *History of Nepāl*, p. 34; Oldfield, *Sketches of Nepāl*, vol. II, p. 117.

[3] Levi, *Le Nepāl*, vol. I, p. 352.

[4] Matsyendranāth is a much Hinduised form of Dhyāni Bodhisattva Padmapāṇi or Avalokiteśvara. Temple, *Hyderabad, Kashmir, Sikkim* and *Nepāl*, vol. II, p. 244.

[5] Barth says that he belonged to Nepalese Buddhism. *RI*, p. 213. Under the name Chen-re-zi, Avalokita is the patron deity of Tibet, belonging to the Tāntric Buddhist cycle. Bell, *The Religion of Tibet*, p. 30.

[6] Aitkinson, *The Himalayan Districts of the North-Western Provinces of India*, vol. II, p. 808.

[7] Avalokiteśvara is called Lokanāth and Lokeśvar. His cult may be traced back to the dawn of the Christian era. He is an ascetic and magician, demiurge and saviour. He became a great Yogī and possesses the great *mantra*, or spell, *Oṁ maṇi padme huṁ* which means 'Om, the jewel in the lotus.' (Thomas, *JRAS*, 1906, p. 464.) Tāntric literature gives this sentence an obscene interpretation. Tibetan forms of this god are reflections of the Hindu cults as early as the tenth and eleventh centuries. There is a Nepalese inscription which reads: 'The chiefs of the Yogīs call him King of Fishes (Matsyendra); the devotees of the female deities call him Śakti;

in the form of a fish. He is consequently known as Matsyendranātha.[1]

It is supposed that Matsyendranāth actually came from Assam, from the region of the Kāmarūpa. In the shrine at Kāmākhyā there is a drawing under one of the windows representing the waves of the sea.

Another legend tells how Matsyendra was brought into Nepāl from Kāpōtal Parbat in Assam, to save the country from a twelve years' drought which Gorakhnāth had brought on.[2] This story has been told above. In Pātan (Kāṭhmāṇḍu) in Nepāl is held an annual ceremony in Matsyendra's name, during which an idol is carried in procession.[3] The idol, which formerly belonged to the Buddhist cult, is very old. It was taken over into Śāivism when Buddhism was superceded.[4] Then a temple was built in honour of Matsyendra and the festival in his honour was introduced. The idol, which is very small, is painted red. The procession of Matsyendranāth brings the rain of the spring, and without his effectual help the heavens would withhold their waters.[5]

In the *Dabistan* it is stated that Matsyendranāth was Jonah.[6]

Buddhists call him Lokeśvar. All honour to this being whose true form is Brahman.' The date of this inscription is 1672 (792 Nepali Samvat), *IA*, p. ix, 192. Vallee Poussin, *ERE*, vol. II, pp. 256–261. Avalokita regulates transmigration and can produce ready entrance into Paradise and escape from hell. His mystical spell, *Oṁ maṇi padme huṁ*, wins his favour. Waddell, L. A., Article, 'Lamaism,' *ERE*, vol. VII, pp. 784–789; Gr., *ERE*, vol. VI, p. 329.

[1] Wright, *History of Nepāl*, pp. 140, 141. This story is found in the *Jñāneśvarī*, 18, 1752, and in the introduction to the *Gorakṣa-paddhati*.

[2] Oldfield, *Sketches from Nepāl*, vol. II, pp. 325, 326; Wright, *History of Nepāl*, pp. 140 ff.; Levi, *Le Nepāl*, vol. I, p. 349. Tradition is divided nevertheless, regarding the location of this mountain. (Waddell, *JRAS*, 1894, p. 54). And some place it in Ceylon, or South India. It seems, however, that Avalokiteśvara came to Nepāl in the guise of a Śāivite priest, a Pāśupata Śāivite. In either case he would represent Śāivite faith. Dr. Singh (*G.*, p. 73) suggests that Saṅgaldvīpa is really Sakaladvīpa or Shakadvīpa near Sialkot.

[3] Landon, *Nepāl*, vol. I, pp. 43, 212; vol. II, pp. 213, 217-18, gives an account of the festival. See above, chap. seven.

[4] Levi, *Le Nepāl*, vol. I, p. 356.

[5] Levi, *Le Nepāl*, vol. I, p. 356. See also, Oldfield, *Sketches from Nepāl*, vol. II, p. 327; and above, chap. seven.

[6] Vol. II, p. 137.

Matsyendranāth figures neither in the Brāhmanical nor in the Buddhist pantheon in India proper. He is, however, well-known in the traditions of the Yogīs, as one of their first teachers.[1] Gorakhnāth is represented as saying that Matsyendra was his teacher[2] and he is sometimes looked upon as the founder of the sect of Kānphaṭas. He is said also to have introduced Śāivism into Nepāl.[3]

There is a legend that gives Matsyendra a place in the Hindu social order. A Rāja, Udhodhar, who lived in the Satya Yuga was exceedingly pious. At his death, his body was cremated, but his navel did not burn. This unburnt portion of his body was cast into a river and was devoured by a fish, which later gave birth to Matsyendra. By reason of having been a good man in his previous life, he became a saint.[4]

In one legend Matsyendra is represented as going to Ceylon where he was enamoured of the queen of the land. When Gorakhnāth heard of the fall of his master, he went to Ceylon in search of him. He found his teacher in the halls of the court and called him to account. Matsyendra then left the queen, but took their two sons with him. They afterwards became Pārasnāth and Nīmnāth, founders of the Jain religion.[5]

In a Nepalese version of this story, Matsyendra, by means of his powers of Yoga, left his body in the care of his disciple, Gorakhnāth, and entered that of a king, just dead. In this situation he fell into temptation. Luckily, Gorakhnāth, who was watching over his body, recalled him to his senses and the teacher returned to his own body.

In Nāsik they say that Matsyendranāth came from Muktināth, which lies to the north of Nepāl. These references testify to contacts between Gorakhnāth and Matsyendranāth and to the struggle between Buddhism and Śāivism in Nepāl.[6]

---

[1] Levi, *Le Nepāl*, vol. I, p. 354.
[2] *Temp.*, 34; *Gorakhnāth kí Goṣṭhī*, quoted above.
[3] Wright, *History of Nepāl*, p. 142; *Wi.*, p. 214.
[4] *RTCP*, vol. II, p. 393.
[5] Kitts, *Report, Census of Berār*, 1881, p. 59. See, for variants of this legend, *RTCP*, vol. II, p. 393 and note.
[6] See also Tessitori, *ERE*, vol. XII, pp. 833 ff.

There is evidence from Bengal to show that Matsyendra was a guru of the Nāthamārga who converted Gorakhnāth from Buddhism to Śāivism (*Or*).

Concerning the other teachers preceding Gorakhnāth, as named by Khakkar and Svātmarāma, little can be said. Those listed by the latter must be nearly or quite contemporary with Matsyendra and Gorakṣa, for the weight of tradition, especially in the Panjab, Nepāl and in Western India, indicates that Matsyendra was the immediate teacher of Gorakṣa.

There are numerous lists of disciples of Gorakhnāth.[1] The names recorded by Svātmarāma[2] are:

Gorakhnāth, Virūpākṣa, Bileśyā, Manthāna, Bhāirava, Siddhibuddha, Kathadi, Karaṇṭaka, Surānanda, Siddhipāda, Carapaṭi, Kānerī, Pūjyapāda, Nityanātha, Nirañjana, Kapāli, Vindunātha, Kakacandeśvara, Allāma, Prabhudeva, Ghodā, Colī, Ṭiṇṭini, Bhānukī, Nāradeva, Khanda, Kāpālika, and others.

These are probably the names of gurus in some particular establishment. They do not seem to relate themselves to other available lists.

In the *Jñānesvarī*, the poet gives the following names: Mīnanāth, Gorakṣanāth, Gāininātn, Nivṛṭṭināth and Jñāneśvar; and the author says that his Yogī discipleship runs back through this line. As stated above, Mīnanāth is Matsyendranāth. Nivṛṭṭināth, also a poet,[3] is usually considered to be the brother of Jñāneśvar.[4]

By putting the list just given alongside that found in *Bahiṇā Bāī*[5] some light is thrown on the date of Gorakhnāth. The account is as follows:

(1) Adināth (Shiva) taught a mantra to Pārvatī (His wife). Matsyendra heard it from within the belly of a fish. (2) Thus through him the supreme mantra, that Shiva held in His mind, became effective through bhakti. (3) He (Matsyendra) showed his favour by passing the mantra on to Goraksha (Gorakhnath). Through him it became known to Gahini. (4) Gahini bestowed his favour on

---

[1] For the list of sub-sects, see pp. 62 ff.

[2] *Haṭhayogapradīpika*, I, 5, 6, 7, 8.

[3] Underhill, *The Hindu Religious Year*, p. 147.

[4] *Jñāneśvarī*, 18, 1752-4. This is in the Poona edition of 1915. See also V. L. Bhāve, *Mahārāṣṭra Sārasvat*, first edition, p. 39; R. L. Pāṅgārkar, p. 47.

[5] Translation by Abbott, p. 1.

Nivrittināth, even while he was a child, but yet a Yogi. (5) From him Dnyāneshvara received the favour of the mantra, and this made him famous at Alandi, the home of Siddhas. (6) Dnyāneshvara gave his blessing to Satchidānanda, the home of bhakti. (7) Further on Vishvambhara, in the beauty of his Shiva form, gave the mantra to Rāghava (Chaitanya). (8) He gave it to Keshava Chaitanya, and he to Babaji Chaitanya, who gave it to Tukobā (Tukārām). (9) Because Bahiṇi placed her undivided devotion at the feet of Tukobā, she received (the mantra through him).

There are evidently gaps in this list. The dates, so far as certain, in this list are: Bahiṇā Bāī, 1628–1700: Tukobā, 1608–1649; Viśvambhara (Kṛṣṇa Carianya), 1485–1533. The usual date given for Jñāneśvar is *c.* 1290.[1]

Turning now to a study of legend and tradition, an attempt will be made to determine the time when Gorakhnāth lived.

The richest field for legends in which Gorakhnāth plays an important part is the Panjab.[2] The several legends, concerning Gūgā, a disciple of Gorakhnāth, are related to events of varying date. One version, which makes him the son of Jewar, a chieftain of Bagar (about fifty miles from Sirsa), is connected with local ballads that represent him as having fought with Aurangzeb (1659–1707).[3] According to another,[4] Gūgā was killed in battle with Firoz Shāh (1351–1388) of Delhi. This would put the death of Gūgā towards the close of the fourteenth century. A more complete story puts him still earlier. Gūgā, who became a saint, is now considered as a snake godling and is well known and popular in the Panjab, in fact in all northern India. He is worshipped especially by the lower castes. Tod[5] gives him a substantial place as a Rājput hero who fell before Mahmud of Ghazni. The Ambāla version of the legend[6], together with Wynard's account of the Rāipur Rāos[7], support Tod. The Firozpur

---

[1] But see below.

[2] *Temp*; Swynn; Steele and Crooke in the *IA*; *Trump*; *Tod.* See pp. 183 ff.

[3] *IA*, 1881, pp. 32–43.

[4] *Temp.*, vol. III, pp. 261 ff.

[5] *Tod*, vol. II, p. 807. Compare Steele, *IA*, 1881, pp. 32 ff.

[6] *IA*, 1881, pp. 34, 35.

[7] *Amballa Settlement Report*, 1859.

version[1] makes Gūgā a Chāuhan by birth. The Bijnor version[2] places him in the reign of Prithvī Rāj, Chāuhan of Dehli, and makes him the son of a rāja. These various legends converge upon a definite era. Mahmud of Ghazni made numerous raids into India, the last of which was in 1024.[3] Prithvī Rāj fell before Muhammad of Ghor in 1192.[4] Near Gūgā's tomb, which is about two hundred miles south-west of Hissar, there is now a tribe of Muhammadan Chāuhans[5], Gūgā's descendants, the Gogawats. They were part of the force with Abhāi Singh in his struggle with Muzaffar.[6] At Mandor, the ancient seat of the Rāos of Jodhpur[7] there is a gallery of colossi, sixteen figures, knights errant of the desert, hewn out of a single, natural rock. Some are on horseback and others are unmounted. Among the former is Gūgā, the Chāuhan.[8] These colossi were erected during the reign of Abhāi Singh (1720–50). Gūgā is thus placed amongst the ancient heroes of Mārwār. Moreover, tradition says that he was a Chāuhan by birth and that he became a Muhammadan faqīr.[9] He is also known as Zahra Pīr. The most likely conclusion, then, from these data is that Gūgā belonged to the time of the struggle between the Rājputs and their Muhammadan conquerors, not later than the twelfth century.

The writings of Kabīr and of the Sikhs contain many references to Gorakhnāth.[10] In the time of Amar Dās (1552–1574) there was trouble between the Sikhs and the hitherto powerful Yogīs, and temples of the Gorakhnāthīs were defiled.[11] Gorakhnāth must have lived long before this evident defeat of his sect, for the famous legends of the Panjab picture him as a very powerful leader with a large following. But, earlier than this, as recorded in the Janam Śākhīs of

---

1 *IA*, 1881, p. 35. 2 *IA*, 1895, p. 49. 3 *Ox*, pp. xix, 11.
4 *Ox*, pp. 195, 197, 218–220; *Duff*, p. 277; *HIG*, vol. II, p. 312.
5 *ERNP*, vol. I, p. 255.
6 *Tod*, vol. II, p. 1,027.
7 *Tod*, vol. II, p. 951.
8 *Tod*, vol. II, p. 848; opposite this page (848) is a good picture of the figure. 9 *IA*, 1882, p. 35.
10 *Tr., Gorakhnāth kī Goṣṭhī, Mac.*
11 *Mac.*, vol. II, pp. 139, 140.

Bābā Nānak (1469–1538), Nānak is represented as talking with both Gorakhnāth and Matsyendranāth.[1] In these accounts Nānak is said to have visited many places. He is mistaken for Gorakhnāth in Ceylon.[2] In this third retirement from the world,[3] Nānak visited the northern region, and, in the fastnesses of the mountains, came to the residence of Mahādeva (Śiva). There he met Śiva, Gorakhnāth, Bhartṛhari, and others, all of whom were perfect Yogīs (*Siddhas*).[4] Nānak's fifth retirement was passed at Gorkhatari,[5] a quarter in the city of Peshāwar.[6] There he met eighty-four Siddhas (adepts) who performed many wonders for him. Later, he and Gorakhnāth had a talk together.[7] The setting of this account, and especially the third retirement of Nānak, shows that Gorakhnāth belonged to a much earlier period. Nānak seems to have known about the Yogīs of Gorakhnāth's order for, Bhartṛhari says to him:[8]

> The form of the Jōg is the ear-ring, the patched quilt, the wallet, the staff (and) the horn.

Nānak speaks about Gorakṣas and Siddhas.[9] He talks with ascetics at the temple of Gorakhmātā (at Pīlībhīt, U.P., now Nānakmātā;[10] he knows their teaching and their practices;[11] and he is acquainted with their hypocrisies.[12] Gorakhnāth pressed Nānak to become a Yogī![13] All of these references show familiarity with a well-established and well-known order, and not to a sect in the early process of its development.

---

1 *Tr.*, p. xxxvi.
2 *Tr.*, p. xxxvii; *Mac.*, vol. I, p. 156.
3 *Tr.*, p. xxxix.
4 See *Mac.*, vol. I, pp. 170, 171.
5 *Tr.*, pp. xlii, xliii.
6 *Mac.*, vol. I, p. 172.
7 *Tr.*, p. xliv.
8 *Mac.*, vol. I, pp. 133, 151, 60, 161–163; *Tr.*, p. xl.
9 *Mac.*, vol. I, p. 41;
10 *Mac.*, vol. I, pp. 59, 60, 309.
11 *Mac.*, vol. I, pp. 160, 161, 173, 174, 225, 274, 295, 338, 349, 350.
12 *Mac.*, vol. I, pp. 314, 315, 350–352, 356, 357.
13 *Mac.*, vol. I, p. 162.

Further, Kabīr (1440-1518), to whom Nānak was largely indebted for his teaching[1], is supposed to have been a contemporary of Gorakhnāth. In the *Gorakhnāth kī Goṣṭhī*[2] is recorded a controversy between Kabīr and Gorakhnāth. It was on the basis of this reference that Wilson assumed that Gorakhnāth belonged to the fifteenth century. This date has been followed for the most part since Wilson's time.[3] But the general attitude of the *Janam Śākhīs* of Kabīr point to an earlier age. Wilson[4] quotes the following verse in translation from the *Bījak of Kabīr:*

> Gorakhnāth, enamoured as he was of Rāma, is dead; his body was not burnt (the Jogīs bury their dead), and the flesh has decayed, and is turned to clay, and such rank as the Kāuravas enjoy, does he obtain (bodily annihilation).[5]

This verse conveys the impression that Gorakhnāth had been long dead, and that his name was so well known in common tradition that Kabīr could give point to his teaching by reference to him. The passages in the *Ādi Granth* bear out this contention. In this book Kabīr speaks of himself as having been a Yogī in previous births[6] and he knows something of Yoga doctrine.[7]

> (Whose) breath is returning (through) the six (mystical) spheres (of the human body), whose thought is intent on vacuum.[8]

Kabīr makes references to Yogīs;[9] the nine Nāthas;[10] some

---

[1] *Wi.*, p. 69.

[2] Price, *Hindi and Hindustani Selections*, vol. I, p. 140. The *Gorakhnāth kī Goṣṭhī* is one of the books in the collection of *The Book* at Chāura, the *Khass Grantha*. *Wi.*, p. 76. This dialogue (*goṣṭhī*) is published and translated by Dr. Singh (*G.*) as the *Gorakhbodh*.

[3] *Wi.*, p. 255. See also Alexander, *Statistical, Descriptive and Historical Account of the North-Western Provinces of India, Gorakhpur*, p. 371, 'Not earlier than the fourteenth century.' Winternitz, *WGIL*, vol. III, p. 258, note 1, says that he should be placed in the first half of the fifteenth century. See also *WGIL*, vol. III, p. 142.

[4] *Wi.*, p. 86.

[5] Verse 40.

[6] *Tr.*, p. 462; *Mac.*, vol. I, p. 149.

[7] *Mac.*, vol. VI, pp. 164, 167, 168, 169, 194, 199, 200, 285.

[8] *Tr.*, p. 472; *Mac.*, vol. VI, pp. 168.

[9] *E.g.*, *Tr.*, pp. 475, 654; *Mac.*, vol. VI, pp. 142, 154, 155, 198, 235, 240.

[10] *Tr.*, p. 696.

of the distinctive marks of the Yogī, such as the ear-rings,[1] the patched coat,[2] postures,[3] the horn,[4] ashes,[5] the wallet,[6] the club,[7] matted hair,[8] the cry, '*Gorakh*, *Gorakh*,'[9] and their faults of drinking[10] and hypocrisy.[11] It is evident that in Kabīr's time Gorakhnāth was a well-known person of the past.[12]

Another cycle of Panjab legends, those of Rāja Rasālū and his half-brother, Puran Bhagat, is intimately concerned with Gorakhnāth. Rasālū's name is famous from Afghanastān to Bengal, and Puran is one of the most famous saints of the Panjab. Both became followers of Gorakhnāth, and Puran, especially, became a renowned Yogī. The well where Puran was left for twelve years,[13] is still shown in Siālkot. Rasālū was the son of the famous Śālavāhan of Siālkot. If the date of this famous rāja could be fixed, much light would be thrown upon that of Gorakhnāth. In 1884, Temple[14] attempted to show that Rasālū belonged to the early eighth century. He traced Rasālū's ancestry through Jāṭ families in the Panjab in two main stocks, the Siddhus and the Saṁsīs. The former trace their line back to the Rājput prince, Jāisal, who founded Jāisalmeer[15] about 1156 A.D.,[16] and who died in 1168.[17] The Saṁsīs go further back, practically through the same descent, to Rāja Gaj, father of the great Śālavāhan.[18]

---

[1] *Mac.*, vol. VI, pp. 168, 231, 243.
[2] *Mac.*, vol. VI, pp. 168, 231, 243.
[3] *Mac.*, vol. VI, p. 168.
[4] *Mac.*, vol. VI, p. 169.
[5] *Mac.*, vol. VI, p. 169.
[6] *Mac.*, vol. VI, pp. 169, 243.
[7] *Mac.*, vol. VI, p. 231.
[8] *Mac.*, vol. VI, p. 272.
[9] *Mac.*, vol. VI, p. 263.
[10] *Mac.*, vol. VI, pp. 154, 255. [11] *Mac.*, vol. VI, p. 270.
[12] According to the traditions of the Sādhs (Allison, *The Sādhs*), Uda Das (early 17th cent.) was a disciple of Gorakhjī (p. 99) and the Bhandhara was established by Gorakhjī. (pp. 86, 116).
[13] See chapter on Legends, p. 199.
[14] *CR*, 1884, pp. 379–415. [15] See Griffin, *Rajas of the Panjab*, p. 2.
[16] *Tod*, vol. II, pp. 1,204, 1206; *Duff*, p. 290; *Rājputāna Gazetteer*, p. 171.
[17] *CR*, 1884, p. 390; Griffin, p. 2, says that he was driven from Jāisalmeer in 1180. Table of descent from Jāisal is found in Griffin, p. 9. [18] *CR*, 1884, p. 392.

Śālavāhan had many sons of whom Puran was the second and Rasālū the third. Tod[1] says that Rāja Gaj opposed the king of Khurasān at Ghazni, with great success at first, but was finally slain, and was succeeded by his son.[2] Śālavāhan retreated to the Panjab which he conquered. There he founded Siālkot. Later, he recovered Ghazni. Rāja Gaj is placed in the end of the seventh century.[3] This would put Rasālū early in the eighth century. This conclusion is confirmed by the account of the struggles of Hindu chiefs in Afghanastān from A.D. 697. Rasālū evidently had a considerable share in the early part of this struggle. There is reference to a very prominent character on the Hindu side whose name is variously written and who fought the Musalmans. He became the subject of many Arab stories in the holy wars on the frontiers of India and played a considerable part in events in the Kābul valley around the beginning of the eigth century. A Hindu chief by the name of Ranbal defeated Abdullah, governor of Seistān in 697 and played an important part in events that followed in 700–703.[4] In 712 a treaty was made, in Sind, by Muhammad Qasim with a Hindu king named Rasil. The name of the chief referred to above has been variously rendered Zantil, Zanbil, Ratbil, Retpeil, Ratbal, Raptil, Rantal, Rattiel, Ratbyl, Ratpeil[5] and Ranbal.[6] In modern legends Rasālū's name varies as Risalu, Salu, Rasal, and Risal.[7] If Risal is Rasālū, as Temple suggests, then Gorakhnāth must have belonged to a time not later than the eighth century. Some writers are inclined to place Rasālū still earlier. Princep[8] would say A.D. 400, and Mrs. Steele[9] would date Śālavāhan in A.D. 78. Dr. Hutchinson[10] who, in

---

[1] Vol. II, p. 1,179.

[2] *Tod*, vol, II, p. 1,180.

[3] *CR*, 1884, p. 393. See table on same page.

[4] *EHI*, vol. II, pp. 416, 417.

[5] *EHI*, vol. II, p. 417.

[6] *CR*, 1884, p. 393.

[7] But, is this man Rāī Sāl, who was destroyed in 1205? In this case the Rasālū legend would point to and strengthen the conclusion drawn on p. 236. See *Cambridge History of India*, vol. III, p. 47.

[8] *IA*, 1884, p. 183.

[9] *IA*, 1882, p. 347. Also *Gazetteer of Siālkot*, 1883–4, p. 20.

[10] In a personal letter to Dr. H. D. Griswold, of Lahore, dated June 20, 1925. See also *Siālkot Gazetteer*, 1921, p. 14.

his revision of the *Gazetteer of Siālkot* some years ago,[1] went into the question, holds that Rasālū was a Punwār Rājput, belonging to the Yadubaṁsi race, which had its seat at Rāwalpiṇḍī, then called Gajpur. They were expelled by Indu-Scythians and returned to the east of the Jhelum where Śālavāhan made Siālkot his capital. Rasālū succeeded his father, Śālavāhan, about the end of the first century A.D. He seems to have been succeeded by an Indu-Scythian by the name of Rāja Hudi.[2]

These data show that there are traditions, which supersede those of Kabīr, which point to an early date for Gorakhnāth. Whether the stories of the relations between Gorakhnāth and Puran Bhagat, which are very persistent, would allow a date as early as the eighth century A.D. for Gorakhnāth, as Temple would suggest, or still earlier, as Dr. Hutchinson's data would suggest, must depend upon corroborative evidence from other sources. At the lowest, the weight of the Punjab legends, Gūgā, Rasālū, Puran and Śālavāhana, point to the struggles between Musalmān and Hindu on the frontiers, before the end of the twelfth century.

The note made by Jñāneśvar in his famous paraphrase of the *Bhagavad Gītā* is of great importance, for the author states that he was a Yogī, a disciple of Gorakhnāth.[3]

Using tradition based on Nāmdev,[4] R. L. Pāṅgārkar, in his *Śrī Jñāneśvaramahārāja Carita*, Poona, 1912, states that Gorakhnāth came to the home of Govindpanth, the grand-

---

[1] 1921.

[2] Sials were also Punwār Rājputs. In the time of Hiuen Tsaing Sialkot was called Śakala. Kot is a modern addition. Śakala became Sala, Sal, Sial through phonetic modifications. Rāja Hudi, with whom Rasālū's name is associated in the legends, Princep (*IA*, 1884, pp. 182, 183) would put about A.D. 360.

Śālavāhan is also said to have been of the Nāga race of Takṣa (*JRAS*, 1891, p. 37; *Tod*, vol. I, p. 82). The name of Hudi, or Udi is associated with the caves at Hoda in Afghanastān, the largest being known as the Palace of Hoda Rājā. Khairābād, opposite Attock, is known as the stronghold of Hodi, or Udi (*JRAS*, vol. XIV, p. 323). Cunningham (*Archæological Survey of India*, vol. XIV, pp. 44–47) thinks that Hodi should be placed before the Christian era. Others (*IA*, 1884, p. 78) seem to think that his date is about A.D. 200.

[3] See above, pp. 311, 312.

[4] *Abhaṅgacī Gāthā*, Bombay, 1894, pp. 421 ff.

father of Jñāneśvar (p. 32) and that Gāininātha was the guru of Viṭṭhal, the father of Jñāneśvar (p. 32). Bhave repeats the tradition to show that there was an old connection between Gorakhnāth and Jñāneśvar's grandfather, Govindpanth. He says also that Govindpanth's father worked under Jāitrapāl of Bīṛa in 1207, and had his mind turned to religious things by Gorakhnāth.[1] The same author (Bhave)[2] holds that similes and arguments in passages from the *Gorakṣa-amar-samvād* and the *Jñāneśvarī* are sufficiently in agreement to belong to the same literary descent. The *Gorakṣa-amarsamvād* is attributed to Gorakhnāth. He, therefore, thinks that there were very close relations between Jñāneśvar's forebears for two or three generations and the Nātha sect.[3] Bhave also says that the Nātha sect was widely spread throughout Mahārāṣṭra about the twelfth century.[4]

There is thus found in the *Jñāneśvarī* a literary reference to Gorakhnāth, which gives him a definite place in history. If the usual date, 1290,[5] for the *Jñāneśvarī* be accepted, Gorakhnāth may be placed not later than 1225. There is, however, some uncertainty concerning the date of this work. While it may be said that the poem was written not later than 1290, it may have been written earlier. The late Dr. Justin E. Abbott, in an unpublished paper, reported four manuscripts of the *Jñāneśvarī* which are undated, indicating that the dates found in the others have been interpolated, and that there are manuscripts belonging to a recension which does not know this date, and, therefore, may be older. The language of the *Jñāneśvarī* is sufficiently archaic, he said, to allow for argument for an earlier date than 1290 for its composition. The date for Gorakhnāth might, therefore, on the argument from the *Jñānesvarī*, be placed as early as A.D. 1100.[6] Bhave would say the tenth or eleventh century.[7]

There is another cycle of legends, centering around Gopicand, Rānī Piṅglā, and Bhartṛhari (Bhartri), which is repeated from Bengal to Western India and Sind and which is not unknown in the Panjab.

---

[1] *Bhave*, vol. I, p. 30.
[2] *Bhave*, vol. I, pp. 38, 39.
[3] *Bhave*, vol. I, p. 41.
[4] *Bhave*, vol. I, p. 37.
[5] *BVS*, p. 92.
[6] His shrine is at Alandi.
[7] *Bhave*, vol. I, p. 37.

Gopicand is known in a famous legend of Sind as Pīr Patāo. This story goes back to the first decade of the thirteenth century, since the saint is said to have died in 1209.[1] Pīr Patāo lived in a cave, Pīr Arr, in an island hill near Ṭhaṭha in the delta of the Indus, about twenty miles from the present railway station of Jungshahi. By Hindus he is called Gopicand. The story of Gopicand as told in the East is found in *The Song of Manickchandra.*[2] Manikcand, a chief who lived in the neighbourhood of Rangpur, in Eastern Bengal, was a brother of Dharmapāla.[3] The Pāla dynasty came to an end in Bengal in 1095.[4] The Yogīs rose to power under the Pālas. Manikcandra's wife, mother of Gopicand, was a disciple of a sweeper, Hāḍī by name, a Yogī of the sect of Gorakhnāth. Gopicand's mother was herself a skilled magician. Grierson thinks that the Yogī Hāḍī represents the movement of the Kānphaṭa Yogīs eastward from Nepāl. Sen[5] conceives of the movement in the other direction. The Kānphaṭa Yogīs of the neighbourhood of Rangpur, today, who sing the song of Manikcandra, are Pāśupata Śiva worshippers who consider Gorakhnāth as their guru. Hāḍī, therefore, lived as early as the first half of the eleventh century. Gorakhnāth preceded Hāḍī.

Dinesh Chandra Sen[6] points out that in the *Dharma Mangala* there are frequent references to Mīnanāth, Gorakhnāth, Hāḍīpā and Kālupā, whom he terms Buddhist saints.[7] He says also that the ballads of the Pāla kings of Bengal have the distinct marks of Buddhism on them and indicate the marvellous powers wielded by Gorakhnāth and Hāḍīsiddha. They were popular. Hāḍī was a Ḍom.[8] Sen also states that

---

[1] Account furnished by E. L. Carter, Esq., I.C.S., and sent to the author by Dr. J. J. Modi, Hon. Secretary of the Anthropological Society of Bombay. The legend is found in the *Tufat ul Kiram.*

[2] *JASBe*, 1877, 1878, articles by Grierson.

[3] *JASBe*, 1878, p. 135.

[4] Kennedy, *Imperial Gazetteer, Indian Empire*, vol. II, p. 317.

[5] *History of Bengali Language and Literature*, p. 29.

[6] *History of Bengali Language and Literature*, p. 29.

[7] *History of Bengali Language and Literature*, p. 28.

[8] Sen, p. 29. Grierson held that Hāḍī was not a Ḍom and that Manikcandra was a Bania by caste; *JASBe*, 1878, p. 138; 1877, p. 186; not a Pāla (ibid., p. 135). But see below, p. 244.

the Dharma cult, to which these saints belonged, was expounded by Rāmāi Paṇḍit who was born at the end of the tenth century; that his contemporary, Dharma Pala V belonged to the early eleventh century; and that Manikcandra Pāla of the first half of the eleventh century is the Manikcandra of the song translated by Grierson.[1]

The mother of Gopicand, Manavatī, is spoken of as the sister of Bhartṛhari, who abdicated his throne in favour of his brother, Vikramāditya (Candragupta II) of Ujjāin, after the death of his queen, Rānī Piṅglā. Bhartṛhari (Bhartri) became a Gorakhnāthī.[2] One of the sub-sects of the Kānphaṭas is named after him. Vikramāditya ruled in Ujjāin from 1076 to 1126.[3] This would place the death of Rānī Piṅglā before the end of the eleventh century.

Another version of the Rānī Piṅglā story makes her the queen of Rāja Bhoj of Dhār (Mālwā), who reigned from 1018 to 1060.[4]

The references to Gopicand, Bhartri, Bhoja and Rānī Piṅglā all suggest a date not later than the early eleventh century for Gorakhnāth.

Moreover, there are historical data to support these Bengal traditions. The Pālas were plebeians elected to kingship (*Sāstrī*, p. 3), and their period runs from the eighth to the twelfth centuries (*Ban*). During the reign of the third king

---

[1] Sen, *History of Bengali Language and Literature*, pp. 407, 456.

[2] See Eknāth, *Ānanda Lahari*, edition of 1912, Poona, verse 95. A legend describing his acceptance of Gorakhnāth is as follows:

Bhartri happened to go into the forest where Gorakhnāth was practising asuterities, but he knew not that the saint was there. Soon after the disciples of Gorakhnāth met him and asked him to become one of them. He answered, 'What do I care for Gorakhnāth? If he wishes to learn the ways of the almighty let him come and hear from me.' Finally, Gorakhnāth said to Bhartri, 'If you give me a handful of patience, I will become your disciple.' So Bhartri, in search of patience, came to the gods, but they could not supply it. At last he went to Viṣṇu, who said, 'I cannot supply you with patience. If you want it, you must go to Gorakhnāth who is the greatest of saints.' Thus convinced, Bhartri accepted Gorakhnāth as his guru. *CTC*, vol. III, p. 154.

[3] *Ox*, p. 202.

[4] See *RTCP*, vol. II, p. 403; *Archæological Survey of Gujarat*, p. 3; *Ox*, p. 189; compare *HIG*, vol. II, p. 249. Forbes, *Rās Māla*, vol. I, p. 112, gives Bhoja Pramāra the dates 1010 to 1053.

of the line, the worship of Dharma as a god came into fashion through the influence of Rāmāi Paṇḍit. Devapāla's sister, Mayanā, actively encouraged the Paṇḍit. The next king but one of the line is known to have granted lands to Pāśupatas, whose temples he is said to have erected by the thousands (*Sāstrī*). Conflicts with the Pratīhāras would make possible the relationships suggested by the stories involving Bhoja and Bhartri. Mahīpāla (before 1020) saw vernacular literature developing and the admission of the Tāntric gods Bhāirava and Bhāiravī into popular Buddhist religion. Then too, the Nāthas were becoming objects of veneration. Rāmanavajra, of the Vajrayāna Buddhist development, became a disciple of Matsyendranāth (see above, p. 151 and below, p. 277), a Śāivite belonging to the Nāthamārga, taking the name of Gorakhnāth. (*Sāstrī*, p. 9.) And he only among the great Nāthas was considered as a heretic by the Buddhists (*Or.*). Govinda Chandra (Gopicand) was a contemporary of Mahīpāla and belongs to the eleventh century (*Sāstrī*).

There is, moreover, in Rājputāna, a tradition which associates Gorakhnāth with Bappa in the early eighth century. Bappa of Mewār grew up in the wilds of Udaipur. The story is that he met there, one day, a hermit, by name Gorakhnāth, who gave him the two-edged sword with which he opened the way to the throne of Mewār.[1] Tod relates[2] how Pushpavatī, daughter of a Pramār prince of Candravatī[3] was returning from a pilgrimage to her own country, from the shrine of Ambā Mātā when she heard of the sack of Vallabhī[4] at the hands of the Māitrikas.[5] Her lord, a prince of the Solar dynasty, perished. The queen took refuge in a cave in the hills of Malia. There she was delivered of a son. She gave him into the keeping of a Brāhmanī with instruc-

[1] *Tod*, vol. I, p. 265.

[2] *Tod*, vol. I, pp. 258–268.

[3] *Tod*, vol. I, p. 265. This place has disappeared. It was about twelve miles from the foot of Abu, at the junction of the Banās and the Śivālan. See *Archæological Survey of India*, 1903, pp. 96–99.

[4] Wala, eighteen miles north-west of Bhāunagar in Kāṭhiāwār. The Gahlotis took possession of this place about A.D. 470; *Archæological Survey of India*, New Series, vol. II, p. 80. Compare Forbes, *Rās Māla*, vol. I, p. 261.

[5] *Ox*, p. 164; *Tod*, vol. I, p. 255.

tions that he be brought up as a Brāhman, but that he be married to a Rājputnī. The queen then mounted the funeral pyre. The child's foster mother named him Goha, which is popularly rendered as 'Cave-born.' The word is derived, however, from 'Guha,' or 'Guhasena' the name of the fourth and probably the first great Vallabhī monarch, 559–567.[1] As he grew up, he became the friend of the Bhīls, and later, their king, ruling the Idar, south of Mount Abu. The ninth in the line from 'Goha' was Bappa, or Bāpa, who overthrew the Moris of Chitor, of whom he was a chieftain, in A.D. 728[2] and founded the dynasty of Mewār.

The sack of Vallahbī took place in 524.[3] This and the date 728 agree sufficiently to satisfy the chronological requirements of the tradition.

There is additional evidence concerning this tradition of Bappa and the Yogīs. The famous temple of Ekliṅgajī, north of Udāipur, was founded by Bappa.[4] While he was herding cattle in the neighbouring hills, Bappa followed, one day, one of the cows that was behaving strangely. In his curiosity about her he stumbled upon a phallic symbol of Mahādeva.[5] On this spot the temple was built. The sage whom Bappa found there became his teacher, and Bappa was initiated into the mysteries of Śiva. Śiva's consort invested Bappa with divine weapons and the sage made him invulnerable from weapons. An inscription, found in a store-room of the temple, and dated A.D. 971, and written in the Devanāgrī character of the tenth century, confirms the tradition and shows the earlier existence of the temple. The location of the temple above the ruins of Nāgahrada (Nāgda, Nāgendra) shows that Tod's legends concerning Bappa have some historical foundation.[6] This inscription would place

---

[1] *Tod*, vol. I, p. 259.

[2] *Tod*, vol. I, p. 269; *HIP*, vol. X, p. 229, says 734; *Duff*, p. 278, says 735. See *Tod*, vol. I, p. 265, note.

[3] *Tod*, vol. I, pp. 254, 251; Yates, *Rajputana Gazetteer*, vol. III, p. 15, accepts the date. *FHIEA*, vol. I, p. 24: 'From about A.D. 500, Kāthiāwār was held by the Māitrikas'. See also Cunningham, *Coins of Mediæval India*, p. 46; *Ox*, p. 164; *Archæological Survey of India*, vol. II, p. 70, says A.D. 523.

[4] *HIG*, vol. XXIV, p. 104.

[5] *Tod*, vol. I, pp. 263, 264.

[6] *Bhandarkar*, *JASBy*, vol. XXII, pp. 151 ff.

the time of the founding of the temple not far from that when Bappa took Chitor from the Moris. The store room was a temple of the Nāthas. The inscription confirms also the tradition of the Rānas of Udāipur as ministers in the temple. The hermit who met Bappa may have been Gorakhnāth. In that case his date would be not later than the early part of the eighth century.

An interesting coin of Bappa has been found and is described in a recent issue of the *Journal of the Asiatic Society of Bengal.*[1] On the *obverse* of this coin are found the words *Śrī Voppa*, in characters of the eighth century and figures of the trident, the liṅga of Śiva and the bull. Below these is the image of a man, prostrate, having large ears, pierced, the holes exaggerated. The *reverse* shows a cow. All of this is suggestive of the legend recorded above.

It is true that the prevailing Śāivite ascetics of that time in Rājputāna are usually considered to have been of the Lakulīśa sect.[2] But, the name of Gorakhnāth is mentioned, in an inscription recording a consecration of five liṅgas at Somnāth in 1287, along with that of the Lakulīśas.[3] Bhandarkar points out[4] that Lakulīśa was a general name by which Śāivite sects were called in inscriptions (i.e., from 943 to 1285). It is not improbable, then, that Gorakhnāth was known in Bappa's time.

Considerable attention has been given to Nepalese legends and the meeting of Matsyendranāth and Gorakhnāth at Pātan.[5]

Later traditions and coins[6] do not help to fix the date of Gorakhnāth. But the main tradition concerning Matsyendranāth and his disciple does. That the tradition goes back for some centuries is clear from an inscription cited by Valleé

---

[1] *Numismatic Supplement*, 1926–27, p. 14.

[2] Fleet, *JRAS*, 1907, p. 420, states that Ekliṅgajī is a temple of the Lakulīśas.

[3] In the *Cintra Praśasti* of the Reign of Sāraṅgadeva, *Epigraphia Indica*, vol. I, pp. 271 ff. The images, a Gorakṣaka, a Bhāirava, an Āñjaneya (Hanumān), a Sarasvāti and a Siddhi Vināyaka (Ganeśa) were placed in five temples.

[4] *Vaiṣhṇavism, Śāivism*, &c., p. 120.

[5] See pp. 231, 232, 233, above.

[6] See p. 179, note 4.

Poussin[1] which shows that Matsyendranāth, in his relations with Yogīs, as represented in the story of the fish, and as Lokeśwar, were traditional in 792; Nepāli Samvat, A.D. 1672. Matsyendranāth represents the union of Pāśupata Śāivism and Buddhism in Nepāl.[2]

In the *Vaṁśāvalī Pārbatiyā* it is stated that Matsyendranāth came to Nepāl to meet Gorakhnāth in the reign of Bardeva (Varadeva). This king lived not later than the middle of the eighth century.[3] According to Walsh[4] coins of the dynasty to which Bardeva belonged, ranging from 635 to 751, have been identified. Chronology based upon these coins would place Bardeva somewhere about 700, at least not later than the middle of the eighth century. Levi[5] puts Narendradeva, father of Bardeva, in the middle of the eighth century. The father, an old man, was living when Gorakhnāth came to Nepāl.

Besides literary and legendary sources, there are some archæological data which may help to fix the date of Gorakhnāth. There is a division of opinion amongst Yogīs as to who began the practice of splitting the ears and inserting the huge ear-rings. At any rate, the practice is closely associated with Matsyendranāth, and Gorakhnāth, and secondarily with Śiva.[6] In the Ellora Brāhmanical cave temple, Kāilāsa, there is a figure of Śiva as a Mahāyogī with the huge ear-rings.[7] This temple belongs to the early part of the eighth century.[8] There is a similar figure of Śiva as Jogeśvar on Salsette Island, belonging to the second half of the eighth century.[9] If this evidence be indefinite, there is other more exact.

---

[1] *ERE*, vol. II, p. 260.

[2] Tibetan tradition says that Gorakhnāth's Kānphaṭa disciples originally were Buddhists and that they became Śāivites in the twelfth century. Levi, *Le Nepāl*, vol. I, pp. 355 f.

[3] Wright, *History of Nepal*, p. 313. The list contains 5. Narendradeva, 8. Vara Deva, 9. Śaṅkaradeva.

[4] *JRAS*, 1908, pp. 669, 760.

[5] *Le Nepāl*, vol. I, p. 347.

[6] *WGIL*, vol. III, p. 258, note 1.

[7] *Archæological Survey of Western India*, 1883, plate xxi. These are not, however, worn as Kānphaṭas wear theirs.

[8] About A.D. 725. *Cave Temples*, pp. 400, 453.

[9] *Cave Temples*, p. 475. *Wi.*, p. 212, note: 'In the temples of Salsette, Elephanta, and Ellora the principal figure is mostly Śiva,

The builder of the temple of Paraśurāmeśvara in the North Arcot district, evidently had in mind the form of the liṅga, for the structure is built on that general plan. The liṅga in this temple is an exact phallus, and is the only one of its kind in South India. On the liṅga is carved an image of Śiva with two hands only. In his right hand he is carrying a ram by its hind legs, and in his left a water-bottle. He has a battle-axe on his left shoulder. His hair is matted and twisted and he is standing on a *rākṣasa*. The image shows the split ears and the rings characteristic of the Gorakhnāthīs. An inscription shows that the temple was rebuilt in 1126. T. A. Gopināth Rāo, who described the temple and liṅga,[1] insisted that the carved liṅga, which shows Śiva with the split ears and the huge ear-rings, should be dated not later than the second or third century. The image seems to be as early as the twelfth century, anyway.

The pertinent data for determining the date of Gorakhnāth has been assembled. The evidence may be grouped around four periods. First of all, there is the association of the name with those of Kabīr and Nānak; but it has been shown that this evidence really points Gorakhnāth to an earlier period.

There is, then, the period of the eleventh and twelfth centuries, before A.D. 1200, the era of the early Hindu-Moslem conflict, principally in the north-west. For this period there is the cycle of the Gūgā legend; the literary evidence from the Nāthas of Western India, including Jñāneśvar; the Bengal Śāivite-Buddhist tradition, including the *Dharma* cult; and the archæological fragment from South India. The destruction of the shrine at Gorakhpur in the thirteenth century would have its bearing on this date. This whole body of material seems to support a date not later than A.D. 1200; most of it would favour a date at least a century earlier.

---

decorated with ear-rings, such as are worn by the Kānphaṭa Jogīs; the walls are covered with ascetics in the various *āsanas* . . . in which the Yogī is to sit . . . and one of the caves of Salsette is named that of Jogīśvra, or Śiva, as the Lord of Yogīs.' Quoted from *Translation of the Literary Society of Bombay*, vols. I and II. See note 7, p. 248.

[1] *IA*, vol. XL, 1911, pp. 104 ff.

Then there is the third suggestion of the seventh–eighth century. For this there is the Buddhist-Śāivite tradition in Nepāl going back to the Narendradeva; Bappa of Udāipur; Rasālū and Hodi of the north-west; and scraps of references about Śaṅkara in the east and in Nepāl. While it may seem that this data is not clear enough to argue that Goraknāth lived so far back, still, in considering these sources it is well to bear in mind that the centuries, seven to twelve, mark the period of the decline of Buddhism and the rise of Śāivism, and that the latter was at its height in the tenth and eleventh centuries. The Śāiva movement was advancing powerfully in the days of Śaṅkara (788–850). The struggle between Buddhism and Śāivism was at its highest in South India in the seventh century. Śāivism was introduced into Nepāl early. In 627 there were seven Śāivite shrines in Nepāl.[1] There are traditions in the east to the effect that the Yogīs were Śāivites degraded by Śaṅkara for drunkenness.

Finally, there are bits of opinion, based upon a reference here and there, pointing to still earlier times.

Taking all of these data into consideration, it may be assumed that Goraknāth lived not later than A.D. 1200 in the second of the four periods suggested above. And it is not unreasonable to push back his date another century, since, if the conjecture about the date of the *Jñāneśvarī* be correct, Bengal literary and historical tradition would agree with that of Western India. This would be supported by the inscription at Somnāth (dated 1287), for the fact that Gorakhnāth could have a temple and an image so early would indicate that he had lived at least a century before.

Until further data are discovered, the conclusion must be that Gorakhnāth lived not later than A.D. 1200, probably early in the eleventh century, and that he came originally from Eastern Bengal.[2]

---

[1] Levi, *Journal Asiatique*, vol. II (1904), p. 225.

[2] Dr. Mohan Singh in his *Gorakhnāth and Mediaeval Hindu Mysticism*, argues from data chiefly found in vernacular sources, not noted above, that Gorakhnāth lived in the 9th–10th centuries.

CHAPTER TWELVE

THE LITERATURE

THERE seems to be little teaching of books and a limited practice of Yoga amongst the Kānphaṭas.[1] Inquiries at the principal centres of the Yogīs elicit very little knowledge of their texts, even of the names of their treatises on the Haṭha Yoga. Many of the Yogīs and some of their mahants are quite illiterate. There is, however, some oral teaching. Besides the cyclic songs already mentioned, there are a number of works which Goraknāthīs use, and others which are attributed to them, or which deal with the Haṭha Yoga. For convenience of record, these books are arranged in four groups and numbered consecutively.[2]

---

[1] At Ṭilla they reported no practice and very little teaching. Others claim that all Yogīs practise a little meditation in the night, at four in the morning and at nine in the evening. They fix their minds on Parameśwar.—The Āipanth at Hardwār.

[2] The works are numbered for convenience, not for suggested chronological order. The author's own lists are supplemented by references to the following writers against whom the works they cite are numbered.

Gr., Numbers 13, 14, 21, 36, 43, 45, 46, 47.
Wi., Numbers 24, 26, 31, 32, 35, 36, 41.
Hall (*An Index of the Indian Philosophical Systems*), 11, 12, 14, 25, 33, 35, 36, 45, 46, 47.
Farquhar (*FORL*), 11, 15, 19, 22, 23, 24, 25, 26, 28, 30, 33, 34, 35, 36, 41, 42, 45, 47.
Garbe (*Śāṅkhya und Yoga*), 34, 35.
Atkins (*Himalayan Gazetteer*, vol. II, p. 809), 26, 36, 41.
Jñāneśvara (Pāṅgārkar), 22, 26, 36, 41.
Aufrecht (*Catalogus Catalogorum*), 13, 14, 17, 20, 21, 26, 36, 37, 38, 43, 45, 46, 47.

Mitra, Rajendralala (*Yoga Aphorisms of Patañjali*, pp. 219 ff.; *Sanskrit Manuscripts of the Raja of Bikanir*, pp. 567 ff.; *Sanskrit*

I.

1. *Devī Bhāgavat.*
2. *Sapta Deva Stotra.*
3. *Bhagat Sāgar.*
4. *Sati Sāgar.*
5. *Durgā Pāṭ.*
6. *Bhāiroṁ Pāṭ.*
7. *Rāmbodh.*
8. *Gorakhbodh.* Written in an old form of Hindi, and reported to date from the fourteenth century.[1]
9. *Gyān Sāgar.*
10. *Brāhmaṇḍa sar Gītā.*
11. *Haṭha Yoga.* Attributed to Gorakṣanātha.
12. *Haṭha Saṁhitā.*
13. *Caturasītyāsana.*
14. *Yoga Cintāmani*, on *Haṭha Yoga* by Śivānanda Sarasvathi.[2]
15. *Yoga Māñjarī.*
16. *Yoga Saṁdhya.*
17. *Gorakṣa Saṁhitā.* Mitra says that this deals with details of performing Yoga Meditations.
18. *Yoga Saṁgraha*, by M. Sukla.[2]
19. *Gorakṣa Kāumudī.*
20. *Yoga Mārtaṇḍa.*
21. *Vivekamārtaṇḍa Yoga*, by Rameśvara Bhaṭṭa.
22. *Gorakṣa Gītā.*
23. *Gorakṣa Pañcaya.*

Manuscripts of the Raja of Bihar, pp. 11, 14, 17, 18, 25, 33, 34, 35, 36, 37, 39, 40, 43, 44, 45, 46, 47.

Besides these, he lists other secondary works on the *Haṭha Yoga*;
Haṭha Pradīpika-Ṭīka, by Rāmānanda Tirtha;
Haṭha-Pradīpika Ṭippaṇa, by Umāpati;
Jyotsnā, by Brahānanda;
Haṭha Ratṇavali;
Haṭha Yoga Dhīrāya by Śiva;
Haṭha Yoga Dhīrāya Ṭīka by Rāmānanda Tirtha;
Haṭha Yoga Viveka, by Vāmadeva;
Jñānamṛta Ṭippaṇa by Sadānanda;
Jñāna Yoga Khaṇḍa.

[1] Tessitori, *ERE*, vol. XII, p. 834. He also reports *Gorakhnāth ki vacan*, by Banārsī Dās, a Digambara Jain priest of the seventeenth century. Dr. Singh gives an English translation of this work and reproduces the text.

[2] *Mitra*.

24. *Śiva Gītā.*
25. *Haṭha Saṅketa Candrikā*, by Sundra Deva.[1]
26. *Gorakṣa Sahasranāma.* Mitra states that this is a book on the 1,000 names of Kṛṣṇa while he was employed as a shepherd in Vraja.

These books are of varying dates, some in Hindi, others in Sanskrit, and are not of primary significance.

II.

27. *Śiva Purāṇa.*
28. *Nirañjana Purāṇa.*
29. *Viṣṇu Sahasranāma.*
30. *Visvānanda Tantra.*
31. *Śiva Rahasya Tantra.*
32. *Rudra Yamala Tantra.*

The books of this list are general *Purāṇic*, *Tāntric* and sectarian works.

III.

33. *Haṭhayogapradīpika.* This is a *Tāntric-Haṭha-Yoga* treatise written by Cintāmani, who as a hermit took the name of Swātmarāma and attained the title, *yogīndra.*[1] He knows a long list of Yogīs who preceded him, more than twenty-four in all.[2] The book, therefore, is fairly late, and is sometimes assigned to the fifteenth century. It is certainly not earlier. It contains 382 verses arranged in four chapters. The verses in the *Gorakṣaśataka* are found, verbatim, or in substance, scattered in the *Haṭhayogapradīpika.* Portions of it are found in the commentary, as well as in the text of the *Gorakṣa Paddhati.* It may be considered, therefore, as an elaboration of earlier works of the school. The verses were translated into English in 1915 by Pañcam Sinh, and printed at Allahabad in the series known as 'The Sacred Books of the Hindus'. Herman Walter, in 1893, at Müncen, published a translation of the book, with commentary. In the same year Śrīnivās Jayangār published an English translation in Bombay, and in 1889 Brahmānanda Bhaba of Śrī Dhara, likewise published a translation at Bombay. It was translated by Yogī Śrīnivāsa Iyangār in 1893 and a

[1] *Mitra.* [2] See opening verses of the work.

second edition of this work was issued from the Theosophical Publishing House, Adyar, Madras, in 1933. The numbering of the verses in this edition does not always agree with that in Pañcam Sinh's edition.

34. The *Gheraṇḍa Saṁhitā* is a work very similar to the preceding, from which it borrows;[1] but it gives much attention to *dhāutī* and more details of personal hygiene. It was translated and an introduction was prepared for it by Richard Schmidt, at Berlin, second edition in 1921, under the title, *Faqiṛe und Faqirtum*. The work was edited by Bhuvanana Chandra Vasaka, at Calcutta, in 1877. There are English translations by Śrī Chandra Vasu, Bombay, 1895, and by Rai Bahadur Śrīs Chandra Vasu, Allahabad, 1914. This last belongs to the series entitled 'The Sacred Books of the Hindus.' It was re-issued in 1933 from the Theosophical Publishing House at Adyar. The author was an adept named Gheraṇḍa, a Vāiṣṇavite of Bengal. His pupil, to whom he addresses his teaching, was Caṇḍa-Kāpāli. This is an interesting name, in view of the origins of the sect of the Kānphaṭas.

35. The *Śiva Saṁhitā* is a Tāntric treatise on Yoga also, but much more difficult than the two preceding works and much longer, containing 517 verses. It is Vedantic in its philosophical outlook. Chapter Five seems to be of independent origin, its contents having been recited to Pārvatī by Śiva himself. In 1923 a second edition of an English translation by Rai Bahadur Śrīsa Chandra Vidyarnanda was published in the series 'The Sacred Books of the Hindus,' the first having been issued in Lahore in 1884.

These three treatises, especially the first and the third, are of considerable value for this study.

IV

36. *Gorakṣa Śataka.*

37. *Jñāna Śataka.*

38. *Jñānaprakāśa Śataka.*

39. *Gorakṣa Śataka Ṭīka*, a commentary on No. 36 by Śaṅkara.[2]

---

[1] *SBH*, vol. XV, pt. 4, p. 11.

[2] *Mitra.*

40. *Gorakṣa Śataka Ṭippaṇa*, notes on No. 36 by Mathuranāth Sukla.[1]

41. *Gorakṣa Kalpa.*

42. *Gorakṣa Paddhati.*

43. *Yoga Siddhānta Paddhati*, on the practice of Yoga by Gorakhnāth.[1]

44. *Siddhānta Paddhati*, rules of Yoga praxis by Gorakhnāth.[1]

45. *Siddhasiddhānta Paddhati*, or metaphysics according to Yoga doctrine, by Nītyānanda Siddha.[1] '*Siddhānta*' is demonstrated truth, i.e., what is proved by reason. The commentary on verse thirteen of *P*[2] attributes this work to Gorakhnāth.

46. *Yoga Mahimān.*

47. *Jñānamṛta*, poems on duties of Yogīs by Gorakhnāth.[3]

Of these works numbers 37, 38 are identified as the *Gorakṣaśataka* (No. 36).[4] Farquhar[5] states that the *Gorakṣa Kalpa* (No. 41) is translated into Hindi as the *Gorakṣa Paddhati* (No. 42). The latter consists, however, of the *Gorakṣaśataka* and one hundred other verses, all in Sanskrit, with a commentary in Hindi. This commentary contains quite a number of verses found in the *Haṭhayogapradīpika* (No. 33).

Numbers 39, 40, 41, 42, 43, 44 are commentaries (*ṭīka*, *ṭippaṇa*) and manuals, secondary or supplemental documents (*paddhati*) on the *Gorakṣaśataka* (No. 36). Mitra attributes numbers 43, 44, and 47 to Gorakhnāth, number 39 to Śaṅkara (788–850) and the others (numbers 40, and 45) to later writers.

In the foregoing lists there must be many duplicates of books, with names as variations of descriptive titles; so perhaps No. 26 and No. 29. This may be illustrated further. In the commentary on the *Gorakṣa Paddhati* (No. 42), the

---

[1] *Mitra.*

[2] Hereafter *P* refers to the 'Poona Text' of the *Gorakṣaśataka*; *B*, to the 'Benares' manuscript; *GP* to the *Gorakṣa Paddhati.*

[3] *Mitra.*

[4] Aufrect, *Catalogus Catalogorum*, p. 165; Mitra, *Aphorisms*, p. 219.

[5] *FORL*, p. 384.

first hundred verses, which are the *Gorakṣaśataka*, are spoken of as the *Gorakṣa Śāstra* and on page ninety-five the second hundred verses are often spoken of as the *Yoga Śāstra*. On pages ninety-four, ninety-five and ninety-six of the same work the text is referred to as *Gorakṣa Saṁhitā*. The Benares manuscript after verse 157 calls itself the *Gyān Prakāsh* and at the end speaks of the *Gorakṣaśataka* and of the whole 198 verses as *Yoga Śāstra* and at the very end of the '*Jñāna Śataka* composed by Gorakhnāth.'

Moreover, in verse four of the commentary to *P* the *Śataka* is called *Haṭha Grantha* and in the comment on verse fourteen the *Yoga Sāgar*; in that to verse fifty-four, *Yoga Cintāmani* (No. 14) and in that to verse forty-one, *Haṭha Yoga Chintāmani*.

The *Gorakṣa Paddhati*, on page four, calls itself *Gorakṣa Saṁhitā* (No. 17) where *P* has *Gorakṣaśataka* and on page twenty speaks of the *Śiva Yoga Śāstra*.

In the foregoing analysis of the titles of works attributed to the Yogīs it seems clear that the *Gorakṣaśataka* is a fundamental text of the sect.[1] It has, therefore, been selected for translation and exposition. The copies made use of for this purpose are three: The *Gorakṣaśataka* with commentary by Lakṣmi Nārāyāṇa, copied from a manuscript in the library of the Bhandarkar Oriental Institute in Poona, and one copied from a manuscript in the library of the Sanskrit College at Benares. Both of these were secured for the author by the late Dr. J. N. Farquhar. The third text is the *Gorakṣa*

[1] Gopi Nāth Kavirāj says that 'the *Gorakṣa Śataka* and the *Gorakṣa Paddhati* are two of the few Sanskrit works published, which profess to give an exposition of this teacher's (Gorakhnāth's) instructions. The *Haṭha Yoga Pradīpika* also belongs to this school.' *The Prince of Wales Sarasvati Bhavana Studies*, p. 85: Article, 'The System of Chakras according to Gorakhnāth.' Dr. Singh does not agree with this, but holds that the doctrines of Gorakhnāth belong to a period covered by some *Upaniṣads*, not the earliest, and tries to show by the literature he uses that left-hand śākta doctrine is foreign to Gorakhnāth's thought. Verses 131 and 132 of the *Gorakhbodh*, which he translates, however, show knowledge of the Haṭha Yoga framework. In his work, Dr. Singh (pp. 8 ff.) cites and translates quite a number of works, both in Sanskrit and in vernaculars, that are not listed in this chapter.

Paddhati, a book procurable in the bazaars from Hardwār to Bombay.

A word may be said concerning each of these works.

The 'Poona' text consists of one hundred and one verses together with a voluminous commentary called *Bālaprabodhinī* (for the use of beginners) by Lakṣmi Nārāyāṇa.

The 'Benares' manuscript consists of 157 verses with a supplementary series of forty-one verses. A comparison with the *Gorakṣa Paddhati* shows that it is essentially identical with that work.

The copy of the *Gorakṣha Paddhati* used in this study was purchased in the Bombay Bazaar. It consists of two series of one hundred verses each, the first hundred being the *Gorakṣaśataka*. The second hundred deals with six topics, *prāṇāyāma* (twenty-one verses), *pratyāhāra* (thirty verses), *dhāraṇā* (nine verses), *dhyāna* (twenty-four verses), *samādhi* (thirteen verses) and *mukti* (four verses). The commentary is in Hindi, and contains numerous quotations from the *Haṭhayogapradīpika*.

It is impossible to date this material. The *Śataka* is attributed to Gorakhnāth and the traditions and literary references all persist in connecting his name with this body of literature. The only datable reference, which is not modern, is that which assigns the *Gorakṣa Śataka Ṭīka* to Śaṅkara. The text of the *Śataka* with the commentary of Lakṣmi Nārāyāṇa is dated *guṇa-abdhi-aṅka-mahī*, which may be rendered Samvat 1143 *or* 1943 and in our calendar 1086 or A.D. 1886. The author states that he wrote the commentary while living in Benares.

There seems to be unanimous agreement that Gorakhnāth is the author of the *Śataka*; and, in that case, the work must be as old as the twelfth century.

The teaching contained in the *Gorakṣaśataka* is a mingling of Yoga and Tāntra doctrines.

CHAPTER THIRTEEN

YOGA AND TANTRA

YOGA is both a branch of Hindu philosophy[1] and a system of physical and mental discipline, 'a code of disciplinary practices.'[2] In this latter aspect it plays an important part in all the philosophical systems of India and in asceticism in general. Yoga was, undoubtedly, a praxis, a set-up of actions, long before it was a system of philosophy.[3] It is, undoubtedly, in this aspect of the Yoga that the *Gorakṣa-śataka* is chiefly interested, and in that text the philosophical implications of the Yoga system, or better, its background of systematic thought, is assumed rather than expounded. Without doubt the disciplines of the system, that is, performance, have been the dominating interest from the earliest times until now.

Even where the aim of 'knowledge' is to the front, the preparatory methods are not lost sight of.

> When the mind is once purged of all impurities, truths arrived at by philosophical discussions carry whole-hearted conviction. Yoga holds that discussions are not enough for the purpose, for in order to be assured that our minds would not be attracted by worldly temptations, certain psychological exercises should be undertaken in order to move the mind in a direction, the reverse of ordinary experience.[4] The (Yogī) looks to the Yoga practice for gaining a complete mastery over his mind.[5]

Interest in the Yogī was not only in his *knowledge* but also in his *powers*, superior powers.

---

[1] *Das G.*, p. 8.
[2] *Das G.*, p. 1.
[3] See Edgerton, *AJP*, vol. XLV, 'The Meaning of Sankhya and Yoga.'
[4] *Das G.*, pp. 11, 12.
[5] *Das G.*, p. 330.

Throughout all the epochs of Indian culture we find the highest reverence paid to the (Yogis) who were believed not only to possess a superior sense, by which they could know the highest truth beyond the ken of ordinary vision, but also to wield the most wonderful miraculous powers which Patañjali has described as the *vibhūtis* of Yoga, by which the (Yogī) showed his control not only over his mind and the minds of others, but also over inert external objects.[1]

Practices which are included in Yoga run very far back, and some of them may have had their origin in non-Aryan sources.[2] They antedate all systems of philosophy. Ascetic practices, by which it was believed that men could come into intimate relations with the spirit-world and obtain power to change the natural course of things, contributed to the origin of the praxis. And Yoga is associated with asceticisim and the acquirement of supernatural powers, and Yoga practices are very old,[3] even though they may not be much in evidence in the earliest literature.[4] The *Brāhmaṇas*[5] and the *Upaniṣads* are familiar with Yoga ideas. From early times the ascetic has been looked upon as a wonderful magician. Fasts, mortifications and ascetic disciplines generally fall within the province of Yoga practice. Bodily discipline became a means to further mental control.[6] Both Jains and Buddhists witness to the practice of Yoga, which, however antedates them both.[7]

The practices of Yoga, as found in the oldest textbook of the system, the *Yoga Sūtras* of Patañjali, contain much that in itself is a relic of very primitive conceptions of the value of psychic states of profound excitement.[8]

The *Sūtras* are at least 1,000 years later than the ideas.

---

[1] *Das G.*, p. 347. Vivekananda insisted that 'the Yogī proposes to himself no less a task than to master the whole universe, to control the whole of nature.' Quoted by Schmidt in *Faqire and Faqirtum*, p. 60.

[2] *GSY*, p. 34; *GPU*, pp. 18, 19. See *Marshall*, vol. 1, pp. 53, 54; Hauer, p. 1.

[3] 'Pre-Vedic, pre-Brahman.' *WGIL*, vol. III, p. 458.

[4] *E.g.*, in *Ṛig Veda*. See *GSY*, p. 34, and *Ṛig Veda*, 3, 27, 11; 4, 24, 4; 7, 67, 8; 1, 5, 3; 1, 30, 7; 1, 34, 9; 10, 30.

[5] See *Śat. Brāh.*, 14, 7, 1, 11.

[6] *GSY*, p. 35.

[7] *WGIL*, vol. III, p. 458; *MWB*, p. 228.

[8] *GSP*, p. 147.

There are traces of wider and wider recognition of these practices in each succeeding literary age, from the beginning. The *Ṛig Veda* knows the 'mad muni.[1] As early as *Pāṇini's* time (*c.* 500. B.C.) 'Yogī' meant a man who practised religious austerities; and these were much valued, and asceticism and the vow of celibacy and life-long study were regarded as great virtues and as being productive of the highest powers.[2] 'Yoga' was applied to the control of the senses.[3] Yoga doctrines appear in the second group of *Upaniṣads.*[4] In its technical sense Yoga appears for the first in the *Taittirīya*, *Kaṭha*, *Śvetāśvatara*, and *Māitrāyaṇa Upaniṣads.*[5] In the *Kena Upaniṣad* it is stated that

> The self cannot be known by him who has knowledge, but only by him who has no knowledge. Hence comes the effort to subdue all the activity of the senses and the mind, to empty the intellect and thus to make it ready for a new apprehension.[6]

Passages imply that Yoga is well known. For example:

> When cease the five
> (Sense-) knowledges, together with the mind (*manas*).
> And the intellect (*buddhi*) stirs not—
> That, they say, is the highest course.
>
> This they consider as Yoga—
> The firm holding back of the senses.
> Then one becomes undistracted.
> Yoga, truly, is the origin and the end.[7]

And further:

> An intelligent man should suppress his speech and his mind.
> The latter he should suppress in the Understanding Self (*jñāna ātman*).

---

[1] See above, p. 210, and *Ṛig Veda*, 10, 136.

[2] *DHIP*, p. 226. See *Cand. Up.*, 3, 17, 4; *Bṛh. Up.*, 1, 2, 6; 3, 8, 10; *Tait.*, 19, 1; 3, 2, 1; 3, 3, 1; *Tait. Br.*, 11, 2, 3; *Ṛig Veda*, 10, 129; *Śat. Brāh.*, 10, 5, 8, 1.

[3] *Kaṭha Up.*, 3, 4.

[4] *DHIP*, p. 227.

[5] *Tait.*, 2, 4; *Kaṭha*, 2, 12; 6, 11, 18; *Śvet.*, 2, 11; 6, 13; *Mait.*, 6, 18; *D.Up.*, p. 385.

[6] *KSS*, p. 54.

[7] *Kaṭha Up.*, 4, 10, 11. Translation by Hume, *Thirteen Principal Upanishads*, pp. 359–60. Note: 'The World' becomes created for the person who emerges from the Yoga-state, and passes away when he enters it.

The understanding he should suppress in the Great Self (*buddhi*, intellect),
That he should suppress in the Tranquil Self (*śānta ātman*).[1]

It is to be noted that here it is the Absolute Brahman upon which the mind is to be fixed.[2] Likewise in the *Māitrāyaṇa Upaniṣad* is attention directed toward the Supreme Brahma.[3]

The seer sees not death,
Nor sickness, nor any distress.
The seer sees only the All,
Obtains the All entirely.[4]

And again, it is by austerity that success in the knowledge of Brahman is won.[5]

'Brahma is!' says he who knows the Brahma-knowledge.
'This is the door to Brahma!' says he who becomes free of evil by austerity.[6]

Knowledge, however, probably refers to magical power, to the *Upaniṣadic*

belief in the inherent power of *knowledge*, as such . . . The reason why they (the *Upanishads*) seek the 'truth', any truth, is precisely this: that by *knowledge* of the truth they expect to master their destiny wholly or partly; and not by a course of action dedicated by knowledge, but directly, immediately, and by virtue of that knowledge in itself; in brief, we may say, magically.[7]

We are here in contact, not with philosophical speculation, but with means to practical ends. Or, it may be suggested that even metaphysical knowledge is viewed from the point of view of possessing or giving supernatural power.

In the *Māitrāyaṇa Upaniṣad* mention is made of a number of Yoga technical terms.

---

[1] *Kaṭha Up.*, 3, 13. Translation by Hume, *Thirteen Principal Upanishads*, pp. 352, 353.

[2] Hume, *Thirteen Principal Upanishads*, p. 360, note 2. *KSS*, p. 55.

[3] *KSS*, pp. 4, 17, 18.

[4] *Mait. Up.*, 7, 11, 6. Hume, *Thirteen Principal Upanishads*, p. 458.

[5] *Mait.*, 4, 3.

[6] *Mait.*, 4, 4. Translation by Hume, *Thirteen Principal Upanisads*, p. 421.

[7] 'The Upanishads; What do They Seek, and Why,' by F. Edgerton, *JAOS*, vol. XLIX (1929), pp. 97 f.

The precept for affecting this (unity) is this: restraint of the breath (*prāṇāyāma*), withdrawal of the senses (*pratyāhāra*), meditation (*dyāna*), concentration (*dhāraṇā*), contemplation (*tarka*), absorption (*samādhi*). Such are said to be the six-fold Yoga.[1]

And one long passage besides, deals with Yoga.[2]

In the *Śvetāśvatara Upaniṣad* Yoga practice is set forth at considerable length.[3] Concerning this *Upaniṣad* Dasgupta says:

Yoga has come to be regarded as a method of attaining salvation; here for the first time we hear of a meditative (*dhyāna*) Yoga and Sāṅkhya-yoga by which final truth could be known, and we find, with the description of Yoga, its posture, its breath-control and the different psychical states preceding the final illumination.[4]

And, he continues, there grew up a whole series of *Upaniṣads* which

dealt exclusively with Yoga discipline with little or no reference to Sānkhya metaphysics . . . all busy in describing the Yoga physiology and the practical methods of attaining concentration. In these the philosophical aspect has been largely subordinated to the elaborate physical processes of Yoga, which began to grow almost independently of Patañjali's treatment of the subject, and were accepted and assimilated later on by the sectarian schools of the Śāktas, Śāivas and also by some later schools of Buddhism.[5]

This is an important consideration as will appear later on.

It may be well to carry a little further the discussion of the meaning of the word 'Yoga.' The word is primarily a technical term with a specific general meaning. Professor Edgerton says[6] that it signifies a method or a way, a way of disciplined activity whereby an end is attained, usually *mokṣa*, or, more popularly, some power or skill or experience. It is not the end or aim that is referred to by Yoga, but the disciplined action or activity which leads to the end desired.

---

[1] *Mait.*, 6, 18. Translation by Hume, *Thirteen Principal Upanishads*, p. 435.

[2] *Mait.*, 4, 18–30.

[3] *Śvet.*, 2, 8-15. See also 1: 8 and chap. 3; also *D. Up.*, p. 386.

[4] *Das G.*, p. 39.

[5] *Das G.*, pp. 40, 41. This statement assumes the early date for Patañjali.

[6] 'The Meaning of Sankhya and Yoga,' in *AJP*, vol. XLV (1924), pp. 1 ff.

This is its use in important parts of the Great Epic, such as the *Bhagavad Gītā* and the *Mokṣadharma* section of Book XII.

It will clarify the discussion to follow Professor Edgerton's method and his argument for a moment, and study the words, 'Sāṅkhya' and 'Yoga,' together. From earlier times (see *Śvetāśvatara* and later *Upaniṣads*), Sāṅkhya and Yoga refer to two methods of reaching *mukti*, the one the method of knowledge, the other that of action. Sāṅkhya in the Gītā means the way of salvation by pure knowledge, the intellectual method, and it is understood as implying quietism, renunciation of action (*sannyāsa*, *vāirāgya*). Yoga, on the other hand, is understood as disciplined, unselfish activity. This method of unselfish or disciplined activity, with indifference to results, is what the *Gītā* always means by Yoga when it contrasts it with the Sāṅkhya, the (quietistic) way of knowledge. Yoga 'discipline,' is synonymous with *karma-yoga*, 'discipline of action.' Both Sāṅkhya and Yoga lead to salvation; but since the intellectual and inactive way is hard, the other is to be preferred. 'Yoga' means discipline of some kind and different schools use varying systems of activity, as that of the *Gītā*, for example, where the word Yoga means a disciplined course of procedure leading to emancipation, a method of salvation characterized by participation in action without interest in the fruits thereof. The argument which Kṛṣṇa advances to Arjuna is that in life action is inevitable, but that it must be brought under a rule of conduct (*dharma*) suitable to Arjuna's station in life, engagement in battle. Over against this Yoga of action is the *jñāna-yoga*, the discipline of knowledge with the abandonment of action (*sannyāsa*.) Yoga is always a way, a method of getting something, usually salvation, although sometimes, in popular usage, a lower goal is aimed at.

> The common denominator of all the epic definitions of Yoga is *disciplined activity, earnest striving*—by *active* (not rationalistic or intellectual) means.

The following verse from the *Gītā* (iii. 3), will serve as an illustration of this point of view:

> 'Loke 'smin dvividhā niṣṭhā purā proktā mayā 'nagha
> Jñānayogena sāṅkhyānāṁ karmayogena yoginām.'

Professor Edgerton's rendering is:

'In this world a twofold foundation (of religious salvation) (Śaṅkara's rendering is 'two kinds of fixed rule') has been expounded by me of old: by the discipline of *knowledge* of the followers of Sāṅkhya, and by the discipline of *action* of the followers of Yoga.'

In this connection it may be of interest to note that Professor Hiriyanna[1] says that the *Gītā* would lose its entire significance if action were not regarded as its essential lesson. And he holds that the central point of the teaching is activitism, *karma-yoga*. He goes on to define karma in terms of duties prescribed by custom and tradition, the *varṇa-dharmas* (the specific customary duties of the various orders of society). So that, for him, *karma-yoga* in the *Gītā* means 'harnessing' or 'applying oneself to' social obligations. The concern of the individual is solely with action, never with its fruits.

Professor Dasgupta in speaking of *samādhi* as a state of release (*kāivalya*), says that what the Sāṅkhya aims to gain by knowledge, the Yoga achieves through the perfected discipline of the will and psychological control of mental processes (states).[2]

Dr. Thomas points out[3] that the primary meaning of the word was 'discipline,' and that secondarily it referred to 'union' as the effect or end of yoga.

Another point of importance is that the word 'yoga,' is not used for 'union.' As Professor Edgerton says:

> In English we may describe the *goal* of Yoga (or of Sāṅkhya either) as 'union' (with Brahman or God). But it is a striking fact that the word *Yoga*, and its cognates are *not* ordinarily used of this. Instead, the emancipated soul 'goes to' (*adhigam*) 'attains' (*āp, prāp*), or 'sees' (*paś*) Brahman; or if he is said to attain 'oneness, sameness' with Brahman, the word used is not *yoga* but, e.g., *sāmyatā*.[4]

Attention is called to Hopkin's remark that the union-idea of the author of the *Muṇḍaka* (Upaniṣad) is expressed not by 'yoga' but by *sāmya*.

Professor Edgerton points out further that Carpentier

---

[1] *Outlines of Indian Philosophy*, p. 118. So also B. G. Tilak in his *Gita Rahasya*. See vol. I, p. 81. [2] *DHIP*, vol. I, p. 273.

[3] *History of Buddhist Thought*, p. 43, note 2. [4] Op. cit.

has shown[1] that not only in the Epic but even later the word yoga, does not mean 'union.' And Professor Radhakrishnan says[2] that in Patañjali Yoga means only effort, not union.

Yoga finds its classical expression in the *Sūtras* of Patañjali, written somewhere between A.D. 300 and 500.[3] The author was a compiler, a systematizer, rather than an original thinker. While the *Sūtras may* be interested in speculation as such, still, they are based upon methods of *action*, disciplined actions, with their concomitant supernatural powers associated with self-hypnotism and the like. The superior powers of the Yogī are simply those of attaining the highest goal, release,[4] such powers *as such* being viewed as unworthy of the struggle.

The aims of Yoga, in Patañjali's sense, may be spoken of as controls of various kinds, a graded series of disciplines, directed towards steadying the mind; gradually advancing stages of rigid control of body and mind; the stoppage of all movement and all thought—that the soul be absorbed in itself, loosing the sense of duality, of subject and object; immediate perception;[5] ultimately, prolonged, fixed attention to the point where the mental processes are stopped absolutely.[6]

But there is ancillary to the mental discipline, a long period of preparatory action, organized according to a well-developed, progressive plan. In the preliminary stages of the preparation for the fixing of the attention, there are purifying processes to be carried out, first with stress laid upon external means;[7] then, after these have been mastered, with recourse to the internal controls.

These disciplines, which are eight in number, may be classified as five indirect and three direct means to release.[8] They are *yama*, *niyama*, *āsana*, *prāṇāyāma*, *pratyāhāra*, *dhāraṇā*, *dhyāna* and *samādhi*.

First, there are certain restraints whose mastery is necessary before essential physical discipline may begin.

---

[1] *ZDMG*, vol. LXV, pp. 846 f.

[2] *Indian Philosophy*, vol. II, p. 337.

[3] Following Woods (*WYS*, pp. xvii, xix), Keith (*SS*, p. 56), Jacobi (*JAOS*), vol. XXXI, and others.

[4] See Edgerton, in article referred to above.

[5] *WYS*, p. 172. [6] *WYS*, p. 8. [7] See *D. Up.*, p. 384.

[8] *WYS*, 2: 28, 29.

They appear as five commands: abstinence from injuring anything (ahiṁsa); from falsehood or deceit; from theft; from sexual intercourse (continence, celibacy); and from covetousness. The last means accepting only what is absolutely necessary, and refusing to accumulate objects or riches.

A second set of rules that must be mastered consists of observances involving necessary religious duties and self-restraint, and are five in number. They include purificatory prescriptions, for the external cleanness of the body, which beget attitudes of disgust for the body, discourage intercourse with others and lead to asceticism,[1] to the subjugation of the senses. They conduce to inner cleanness of mind, contentment, moderation and frugality; to the habit of bearing all privations of cold and heat equally, keeping the body unmoved; silence; asceticism and restraint; to the study of philosophy; to the repetition of spells, words and syllables, amongst others that of the mystic oṁ; to the keeping of fasts and religious observances; and to meditation on Īśvara (*Īśvara pranidhāna*) which gives perfection of concentration, devotion to Cod, and resignation to his will.[2] These, it will be seen, include tapas, mantra and bhakti. If obstacles arise while practising niyama (or yama) resort should be made to *pratipakṣahāra*, the principle of using the opposite quality[3] and of thinking of the consequences as deterrents.[4] They are: the setting of good over against bad in thoughts and deeds; thinking of all beings as friends; kindly feeling for sufferers; feeling of happiness for the good of all; and feeling of equanimity and indifference for the vices of others, not taking note of vices of the vicious, conscious that nothing is worth striving for or desirable.[5]

Yama and niyama comprise all the active and passive virtues. Professor Radhakrishnan says:[6]

> A practice of these two favours the development of *vāirāgya*, or passionlessness or freedom from desire, either for things of the world or the pleasures of heaven.

When these two disciplines have been mastered, the Yogī

---

[1] *WYS*, 2: 40. [2] *WYS*, 2: 44, 45. [3] *WYS*, p.1 83.
[4] *WYS*, p. 185. [5] *WYS*, 1: 35.
[6] *Indian Philosophy*, vol. II, p. 354. Quoted by permission of Macmillan and Company, Publishers.

should pass in turn to other disciplines of Yoga and perfect them. These are āsana; prāṇāyāma and pratyāhāra. Practice begins with āsana.

Postures (āsana) have as their object the discipline of the body in stillness or rigidity. To this end the Yogī should choose a quiet place where, in comfort, he may carry out his practice. Steadiness of mind (fixed attention) is contingent, in the end, on bodily poise (and breath control). The ideal adept sits motionless as a stock or stone or as the flame of a lamp in a windless place. Later works, like those on Haṭha Yoga, state that there are an infinite number of postures, or eighty-four *lakṣa*, of which eighty-four are chief, while some reduce the essential or the most useful and all sufficient to two.[1] The *Gheraṇḍa* names thirty-one; the *Śiva Saṁhitā* considers four as chief.

Having mastered Āsana, the Yogī proceeds to the next discipline, the control, or the regulation, or the restraint of the breaths.[2] Because constant respiratory action has a disturbing, or obstructing effect upon the attainment of perfect concentration, breathing should be controlled and finally stopped. Prāṇāyāma consists in interruptions of the natural alternation of out and in breathing. The expulsion of the held-in breath is called *recaka* and is to be done with thought on Śiva; the inhaling of the breath is called *pūraka*, and this done with the mind on Viṣṇu. Retention of the breath is called *kumbaka* and is done with the thought of Brahmā.[3] Its central aim is in the holding of the in-breathed air.[4] The control of breathing is said to be carried to great extremes. 'With practice one may retain breath steadily for hours, days, months, even years.'[5] In the Haṭha Yoga breath control is esteemed for its great efficiency in producing occult powers.

---

[1] Compare *Gorakṣaśataka*, 9, 10. [2] See *D. Up.*, p. 384.

[3] But see below, where the process is joined to the recitation of the syllable *oṁ*. [4] Or, holding the lungs empty.

[5] *DHIP*, p. 272. Quoted by permission of Macmillan and Company, Publishers. *Das G.*, p. 334. The *Dabistan* (vol. II, pp. 137, 138) mentions several Yogīs famed in that time for the restraint of the breath. Baliknāth, who at the age of 120 years, was in full vigour, was one. Serudnāth could hold his breath for two days. Sāñjānāth, of the Āipanth, was seven hundred years old and not yet gray. The author of the book saw both Serudnāth and Sāñjānāth.

With the breathing thoroughly under control, after a considerable period of practice, the Yogī proceeds to the next discipline, described as the suppression of the organs of sense,[1] their subjugation or withdrawal from the objects of sense. The result of this practice is the limitation of the span of attention within the mind, the inhibition of the sensory systems, the serving of external contacts. It serves to keep the mind from wandering.

Pratyāhāra is based upon the Sāṅkhya and Yoga theories of sense perception.[2] It may be achieved by prāṇāyāma (and by the *khecarīmudrā*).

These, yama, niyama, āsana, prāṇāyāma and pratyāhāra, constitute the five external means preliminary to the higher stages which issue in samādhi, or release. In yama and niyama are laid the foundations for the beginnings of concentration of mind; in āsana and prāṇāyāma additional powers for the exercise of fixed attention are developed; and in pratyāhāra the mind cuts off external contacts thus completing preparation for the beginning of those *inner* exercises through which the end of Yoga, release, is achieved.[3]

The concluding (three) stages in the Yoga praxis deal with mind in its internal processes, the progressive stopping down of the mental activities until they cease altogether. This is achieved through increasing power in the fixing of the attention, at the same time making use of āsana and prāṇāyāma and the rest.

Together the three (directed to a single object) are called *samyama*, or conquest,[4] concentration, meditation, contemplative trance.[5] The three are *dhāraṇā*, *dhyāna*, and *samādhi*. The first two deal with illumination, the last with 'union.' Meditation is a process of restricting mental activity. When *samyama* is directed to external or internal objects extraordinary powers arise.

Dhāraṇā, fixed attention,[6] is the establishment of the mind in steadfastness, using some object or position, such as the navel, the nose, the tip of the tongue, the space between the

---

[1] *D. Up.*, p. 385. [2] See *DHP*, p. 25.
[3] *GSY*, p. 44. Pratyāhāra is often grouped with the next three.
[4] *GSY*, p. 44. [5] *SBH*, vol. IV, pp. ix, x; *WYS*, 2: 13.
[6] *WYS*, 3: 1.

eyebrows, Īśvara, or extended space. This 'one-point meditation,' made possible through the moral and physical restraints, is a step in the completion of all these. Dhāraṇā is directed to the fixing of the attention on one out of many objects in the mind. When the discipline is perfected the Yogī can, at will, keep the mind from wandering away from its object.

An extension and intensification of this principle of concentration of mind is called Dhyāna. It represents adeptness in prolonging the state of 'one-pointed' concentration. In this state one object is held in attention to the *exclusion* of all others.

The final phase in the stoppage of the mental processes is called samādhi. This state of mind is variously described as absorption,[1] concentration, fusion of knower and the process of knowing with the object to be known. It is the more or less prolonged experience of 'release.' Having come so far in rigorous discipline, the Yogī is now able to fix his mind on any object he chooses. It is preferable, however, that he choose Īśvara, for 'The Lord' then becomes a help to him in his final effort. He can, however, choose anything he likes for the 'unifying' concentration (samādhi) of his mind.[2] This stage may be described as a state where the object is fixed in attention in such a way that consciousness of the self or of the activity of the mind is lost.

Samādhi is described in its four successively progressive aspects: concentration on objects remembering their names and qualities; then on the five subtle elements (*tanmātras*) first remembering their qualities and then without any notion of their qualities; afterwards on the buddhi with its functions of the senses causing pleasure and then, leaving the feelings of joy behind; and upon pure substance divested of all modifications. Here memory is eliminated and mind (subject) alone is left.[3] In this whole process there are those stages called the *samprajñāta*, that samādhi in which there is consciousness of objects; and beyond these the *a-samprajñāta* or *nirodha samādhi*, in which the mind is without an object,

---

[1] *D. Up.*, p. 385. [2] *DHIP*, p. 271.
[3] *WYS*, p. 84; *DHIP*, p. 271.

a state of unconsciousness, at the same time that of isolation.[1] Here there is no actual mental state of any kind, but pure vacuity.[2] This is the end of the search; at first but fleeting experience of it; then, as Yoga is perfected, longer and longer tastes of it; and finally, in death, eternal release. It is isolation of soul according to the *Sāṅkhya* or the experience of Brahma, or 'union' with Brahma, according to the *Vedānta*.

So far the point kept in view, in sketching Patañjali's Yoga has been the goal, first formulated in the *Upaniṣads*, of the attainment of release (mukti). On the other hand, however, Yogīs, and others as well, have always evinced much interest in certain powers which have been associated with the process of samādhi (and austerities), and which precede final beatitude. While the books advise that men turn not aside to these, and even condemn them as harmful, still these supernormal powers (*vibhūti*), both physical and mental, have been by no means despised. The belief that such powers are attainable is very ancient, and has been held without a break down to the present day.

Concerning the belief in the powers which the Yoga may produce Professor Radhakrishnan says:

> They (the ancient thinkers of India) tell us that we can acquire the power of seeing and knowing without the help of the outer senses, and can become independent of the activity which we exercise through the physical senses and the brain. They assume that there is a wider world about us than we are normally able to apprehend. . . . There are laws governing the acquisition of this larger vision and manifestation of latent powers. By following the principles of the Yoga, such as heightening the power of concentration, arresting the vagaries of the mind, by fixing one's attention on the deepest sources of strength, one can master one's soul even as an athlete masters his body. The Yoga helps us to reach a high level of consciousness, through a transformation of the psychic organism, which enables it to get beyond the limits set to ordinary human experience. We discern in the Yoga those cardinal conceptions of Hindu thought, such as the supremacy of the psychic over the physical, the exaltation of silence and solitude, meditation and ecstasy, and the indifference to outward conditions, which make the traditional Hindu attitude to life appear so strange and fantastic to the modern mind.[3]

---

[1] *WYS*, p. 13. [2] *Das G.*, p. 341.

[3] *Indian Philosophy*, vol. II, pp. 336 f. Quoted by permission of Macmillan and Company, Publishers.

These powers my be classified as physical and psychical.[1]

The Yogī possesses supernatural control over the processes of nature. In the evolutionary series according to the Sāṅkhya (and the Yoga) the lowest level marks the limit of evolution, further development being merely changes at the moment in the arrangements of the atoms (*guṇa*). Ordinarily, change at this level follows a general but orderly course; but it is conceivable that one who knows the laws of change, from sheer insight, or by magical knowledge, might be able to direct and control nature.[2] Such is the claim of Yoga. Consequently the Yogī, they say, is able at will to become exceedingly small, or increase in size to enormous proportions; he may become very light or very heavy, he may reach to great distances over the earth, and travel through the air and through space at incredible speed; he may dive into the earth and up again as if it were water; and he may become very powerful, stronger than an elephant, bolder than a lion; and he may change the course of nature, having complete mastery of the elements, and authority over the states of existence. He is complete master of the body and of the inner organ. Besides, he may call up the dead and speak with them; he may enter the bodies of snakes, demons, men, women or deities, and return at will; and he may enter more than one body at a time, leaving his own. Simultaneously he may control[3] these several bodies while he retains his own individuality in his own body. So fine are his perceptions that he hears peculiar and subtle sounds and has super-sensual powers of touch, taste, sight and smell. For example, he can hear the sounds that are in distant worlds. He has great capacity for friendliness, passions and joy.

Since the Yogī is master of all processes in the evolution of *prakṛti*, having brought all under his control by practice of Yoga, he possesses supernatural or intuitive insight or knowledge. He sees all things, all processes, all time as an

---

[1] See *GSY*, p. 46. The whole list of powers may be found in *WYS*, 3: 16-52. See also Woods in *JAOS*, vol. XXXIV (1915), pp. 1 ff.; and Lanman, *Harvard Theological Review*, 1918.

[2] *WYS*, 3: 44; *DHIP*, p. 256.

[3] *WYS*, 3: 43.

inclusive, present whole without sequence.[1] Such powers are sometimes called *siddhis*. He has, therefore, insight into the past and the future, knows the cries, or speech, of all living beings, has complete knowledge of all his previous births, can look into the mind stuff of others, knows the law of death, understands the subtle, the obscure, that which is concealed, the remote; and both things and events even in other worlds are present in his mind, so that he understands all the mysteries of the universe.[2] He knows all cosmic spaces and the orders of the stars and their movements; knows the arrangements of the body; sees all things and is familiar with the processes of the mind. In short, the Yogī attains to clear vision, or extraordinarily penetrating wisdom. He obtains full *intuitive* knowledge of whatever he concentrates upon.

Even if the work of Patañjali and his commentators be viewed as systematized philosophy, still, it maintains interest in the chief emphasis of Yoga, activity, an interest which has continued from the earliest times down to the present. With the passage of time, specialized emphases appeared. Professor Dasgupta says:

> Thus, the *Yoga* practices grew in accordance with the doctrines of the Śāivas and Śāktas and assumed a peculiar form as the *Mantra-yoga*; they grew in another direction as the *Haṭha Yoga* which was supposed to produce wonderful bodily feats of breath-control and control of involuntary muscles and organs through constant practices of elaborate nervous, muscular and breath exercises which were also associated with art of healing diseases, keeping the body free from all kinds of diseases and supernatural powers. The *Yogatattva Upanishad* says that there are four kinds of *Yoga*, the *Mantra-Yoga*, *Laya-Yoga*, *Haṭha-Yoga* and *Rāja-Yoga*. In some cases we find that there was a great attempt to associate even Vedāntism with these mystic practices. The influence of these practices on the development of *Tāntra* and other modes of worship was also very great.[3]

In Rāja-Yoga (and Jñāna-Yoga) intellective processes are

---

[1] *WYS*, 3: 84, 3: 16, 17, 18, 19, 22, 25, 26, 27, 28, 30, 33 and 34; and p. 315.

[2] *DHP*, p. 117. For other details of powers see *Śiva Saṁhitā*, 3: 41 ff.

[3] *DHIP*, pp. 228, 229. Quoted by permission of Macmillan and Company, Publishers. Another known as *Kriya-Yoga* is mentioned. It aims to destroy the five evils, included under *Niyama*, i.e., the 'six works.' Haṭha-Yoga is sometimes called Karma-Yoga. Śiva-Yoga is called the highest, or spiritual Yoga. *SBH*, No. 68, p. 61.

the predominant, even where they are not the sole means employed.[1] It deals with the mind and psychic powers, also. Mantra-Yoga employs sacred texts, and syllables and consequently, enters the realm of magic. It is Yoga in the act of repetition. Laya-Yoga has to do with the quieting, one might almost say elimination, of the mental processes, issuing in trance (*laya*) or unconsciousness, such as the 'fourth' state, finally ending in permanent quiet of mind. Associated with Kuṇḍalinī-Yoga, it is considered as of the highest form by Śāktas, because, by its means, perfect samādi is gained by union with Śiva of both mind and body. The Laya-Yoga is elucidated in the *Gheraṇḍa Saṁhitā*. Haṭha-Yoga lays emphasis upon prāṇāyāma,[2] the object of which is to produce in the body voluntary suppression of the breath. It lays most stress upon physical methods for the attainment of various mental states. Haṭha-Yoga is spoken of in distinction from Laya-Yoga, but in a more general sense it includes the latter; and it involves also some practices that are used as auxiliaries in other 'Yoga'. Each Yoga employs some methods of the others and all are various modes of practice by which the feelings and the intellectual activities of the mind are brought into control and the Brahma, or the Puruṣa, realized in various ways.

All types of Yoga have in view in general the system of Patañjali, but each lays emphasis upon particular phases of discipline and brings into play other methods as well.

According to the *Haṭhayogapradīpika*, Haṭha and Rāja Yoga should both be used, and each is necessary to the success of the other.[3] The practicer of Haṭha Yoga gets his knowledge or realization of the Absolute, his union (*svarūpa*) with Śiva in the *Sahasrāra* through Kuṇḍalinī herself. This truth is illustrated in the *Gorakṣaśataka*, as the detailed study in the succeeding chapters will show.

---

[1] See *Serpent Power*, pp. 200 ff., from which the data for this paragraph are taken, mostly in quotation.

[2] According to *Gr.*, p. 26, the aim of this Yoga is said to be to transcend the lower self, which consists of the sexual power, the vital air and the mind, by a method in which the control of the breath is the key to the control of the other two.

[3] 2: 76. The *Śiva Saṁhitā*, 5: 9, mentions Mantra-Yoga, Haṭha-Yoga, Laya-Yoga and Rāja-Yoga.

The Yoga of the Kānphaṭas is called Haṭha. An interesting derivation for the word is given in the commentary to verse one of the *Gorakṣa Paddhati*, where it is stated that *ha* means the sun (*sūrya*) and *ṭha* the moon (*candarama*); and that their union is called Yoga. This symbolism is significant as will appear in later chapters. The word signifies, however, hard, or extreme, or strenuous discipline and the doctrines lay particular stress upon āsana, mudrā, prāṇāyāma, dhāutī, cakra, nāḍi and kuṇḍalinī,[1] and most of these receive a great deal of attention in Tāntric works. Laya Yoga is sometimes identified with *Kuṇḍalinī Yoga*. Again, two main lines of Yoga are set forth; Dhyāna, looking to ecstasy by mental processes (Rāja-Yoga); and Kuṇḍalinī Yoga, which requires the help of mantra. And it is pointed out that Kuṇḍalinī is that part of Haṭha-Yoga in which, though the intellectual is not neglected, the creative sustaining śakti of the whole body is actually and truly united with the Lord-consciousness.[2] As implied above, Yoga is one, but many diverse emphases are specialized in its practice.

The Tāntric element is prominent in the teaching of the Gorakhnāthīs. Both the Buddhist and the Śāivite Tantras have had their influence upon the beliefs and practices of the sect. These works have to do with the use of both magic and of the magic formulæ and of erotic ritual in the effort to get into touch with super-normal existences, with cosmic powers. Śāktism is closely allied with Tāntra, the ritual for which includes the *Pañcamakāra*. In fact, śākta is one of the chief elements in the system of Tāntra, and Śakti is, where these Yogīs are concerned, the consort of Śiva. If Śākta and Tāntra were to be discriminated one would refer specifically to the worship of the goddess, the other to magical and sacramental ritual. One of the bases of the latter is the assumption that man and the universe correspond as microcosm and macrocosm and that both are subject to the mysterious power of words and letters. Śākta as a system, as carried on in Assam and Bengal, is usually associated with the worship of the consort of Śiva with rites prescribed in the Tantras.

---

[1] For the meaning of these terms see the Glossary, and the following chapters. [2] *Śakti and Śakta*, p. 414.

Bhattacharyya says[1] that Tāntric culture presupposes Rāja and Haṭha Yoga. He also holds that historically the Buddhist preceded the Hindu Tantras; and that the latter are dependent upon the former. While, on the one hand, Rāja and Haṭha Yoga give control over the mind and body, Tāntric practices, on the other, confer various magic powers, contingent upon the deities worshipped and the mantras employed.

In recent years a good deal of attention has been given to both Buddhist and Hindu Tantras. For the former the works of Dr. B. Bhattacharyya may be mentioned. He has edited a number of Vajrayāna works[2] with valuable introductions and has published *Buddhist Esoterism*, based largely upon these editions and in which he has repeated a good deal from his introductions to the Sanskrit works. He has also written *Indian Buddhist Iconography*. T. G. Shastri has edited the *Āryamañjuśrīmūlakalpa* in three volumes.[3] These writings have not been translated into English. On the Hindu side interest, so far as translation is concerned, centres around the very extensive work of Arthur Avalon. Here again there are valuable studies of the subject in his *Serpent Power* (both editions) and in his *Shakti and Shakta*. Arthur Avalon has worked with Hindu *paṇḍits*.

A recent work by E. A. Payne[4] contains a very useful study of the Hindu cult, Śākta. It gives a survey of some of the literature.

Bhattacharyya says that the whole of the culture history of the eastern part of India from A.D. 700 to A.D. 1200 is locked up in the Tantras. Although the Buddhist cult disappeared under the Islamic advance, Hindu practice has continued down to the present time.

The Buddhist Tantra is essentially Vajrayāna. According to Bhattacharyya[5] this system, a development of the Mahā-

[1] *Buddhist Esoterism*, p. 166.

[2] Gaekwad's Oriental Series, Numbers, 26, 41, 44, 53, 61. Other works on Tantra issued in this series are Numbers, 24, 56.

[3] Trivandrum Sanskrit Series, Numbers, 70, 76 and 84 in the years 1920, 1922 and 1925.

[4] *The Śāktas of Bengal*, Calcutta, 1933.

[5] The account which follows is based primarily upon the introduction to his edition of the *Sādhanamālā*, Gaekwad's Oriental Series, Number 41.

yāna, contains certain elements which reach back to the Buddha himself. Certain concepts which found a place in original Buddhism, contain the seeds of Tāntra. These are mudrā, mantra, maṇḍala, dhāraṇī, yoga and samādhi, all of which contributed to the attainment of happiness and prosperity. He holds that there was a popular side to early Buddhism and that within the cult there were many who were unhappy under the extreme severity of the discipline enforced. These concepts, therefore, found fertile soil in which to develop both liberty and license, in the search for supernatural power and for enjoyment.

The immediate sources of the Vajrayāna are three: the introduction of the theory of *mahāsukha* in the conception of the Buddhist *nirvāṇa*; the reaction to the more strict and unnatural rules of discipline within the *Saṅgha*; and the weakening influence of the theory which required each individual Bodhisattva to sacrifice everything, himself, his happiness, his family and children, for the emancipation of suffering humanity—the doctrine of *Karuṇā*. In the face of this great vow, 'little' sins are comparatively nothing. The vow to emancipate others was reduced to a mere convention. Monks took shelter under its cover and found in it 'an excuse for committing acts of great sin and immorality.'[1] Later it was declared that there is nothing in the world that cannot be done by the Bodhisattva who has taken the vow to emancipate the world.

The teaching of this development was carried on for some three centuries in secret, through a series of gurus and disciples, before it came into the open as a well-established cult. Its questionable side is evidenced by its use of the so-called twilight language, a style which admitted of two interpretations, one refined, the other indecent. This was necessary because 'much of their work appears as indecent' (Bhattacharyya).

The teachings of the Vajrayāna have been handed down by a long line of persons, particularly in songs of the eighty-four Siddhas and their disciples. The greatest of these, the Mahāsiddhas, belong to the seventh, eighth and ninth centuries.

---

[1] Gaekwad's Oriental Series, No. 44, p. 9.

From the point of view of this study it is of interest to note in the lists of names that of Jālandharipā, whom Bhattacharya identifies with Hāḍipā of the *Dharammaṇgala* and of the Manikcand-Gopicand stories recounted in a previous chapter. One of these tells how he was buried in a hole in the ground by Gopicand, who later became a Yogī. In one of the *paramparās* attached to chapter four, it will be remembered that he is placed before Gorakhnāth. Bhattacharyya assigns Jālandharipā to the eighth century. If this date were established, it would move Gorakhnāth to a somewhat earlier time than that suggested in chapter eleven.

'The main point on which the Vajrayāna conception of the pantheon revolves' is that of the five Dhyāni Buddhas and the five Buddha families (*kula*). The deities are all voluntary manifestations of Śūnya, in forms dependent upon the *Bījas* uttered. They are also embodiments of the five *Skandhas* over each of which one of them presides. These deities are of distinctive colours, although their representations vary in colours, form and posture according to the rites in which they figure. Many of them are exceedingly terrific externally, even though they are compassionate internally (compassion is an essential character in the Mahāyāna). Mahā Kāla, however, does not show any but terrific aspects either externally or internally, having to do with the fate of the incorrigible only. Vajra-sattva is viewed as the priest of the Vajrayāna. Most of the gods belonging to these families are associated with terrible and gruesome rites and are of repulsive aspect. Goddesses have the same general characters as the gods.

According to this system the world is composed of five elements deified in the forms of the Dhyāni Buddhas. Vajradhara is by many considered as the highest deity, the *Ādi* or primal monotheistic god from whom the five Dhyāni Buddhas arise. Homage is paid to him in the shape of a flame of fire, considered as eternal, self-born and self-existent. He appears in two forms, single and in *yab-yum*.

In Vajrayāna three elements are involved, śunya, vijñāna and mahāsukha. The combination of these is called *Vajra*. Śūnya is *Nāirātmā*, a goddess in whose eternal embrace the individual mind (Vijñāna) is locked, and in which it remains in eternal bliss and happiness. Or, in another aspect, voidness (śūnyatā) and compassion (karuṇā) together constitute the individual mind, and like the deities, Heruka and Prajña, unite as the god, *advaya* (non-double). This union is *yab-yum*. The doctrine of karuṇā gave excuse, in the end, for the grossest forms of immorality and lawlessness. The regulation being that the *sādhaka* should not be attached to particular foods or women.[1] Śūnya is handled in compromise fashion under the assertion that 'it is better to take the world as real. . . . When the conception of unreality is abandoned, it gives rise to a state which is neither saṁsara nor nirvāṇa. The realization of voidness (śūnyatā) of all phenomena, after careful discrimination between knowledge and the object of knowledge, is what is known as the highest knowledge of the Prajñā. . . . Compassion is of the nature of affection (*rāga*) as it removes the sufferings (*rañjati*) which spring up from numberless causes. This compassion is called Upāya or "means." Because it always, like a boat, leads him towards the goal. The commingling of the two—Prajñā and Upāya—is the like commingling of water and milk whereby the duality is merged into one without distinction, and is called Prajñopāya. This . . . is the creative principle of the Universe and everything emerges and develops from this principle. This Prajñopāya is called Mahāsukha because it gives eternal happiness. . . . Vajrayāna is thunderbolt-knowledge. . . . It is known as mahāmudrā (great woman). . . The realization of this Vajrayāna leads to happiness and to the highest goal of Nirvāṇa or emancipation.'[2]

'By those identical actions by which mortals rot in hell for hundreds of crores of cycles, the Yogin is liberated.'[3]

While early Buddhism enforced unnatural and strict rules of behaviour and forbade all kinds of worldly enjoyments, such as wine, women, fish, meat and all kinds of exciting food, the Tāntrics embodied all these in their practice in the form

---

[1] *Sādhanamālā*, Introduction, p. xxxii.

[2] Introduction to *Two Vajrayāna Works*, Gaekwad's Oriental Series, No. 44, by B. Bhattacharyya, pp. xiv, xv, xix, xx.

[3] *Prajñopāyaviniścayasiddhi*, 1, 15. Translation by Bhattacharyya.

of the five *makāras*. The *Sri-samāya* is the cause of all happiness and divine perfection by *Mahāmudrā* and without her there is no emancipation. For them, to repeat, nirvāṇa is defined in terms of śūnya, vijñāna and mahāsukha and the conditions of the Bodhi-mind in nirvāṇa is as in the embrace of a woman. Union with their śaktis is termed by Tāntrics, 'Yoga.' The enjoyment of perfect truth, the *Prajña*, resides in all women, and they should be enjoyed without reservation. The highest class of Yoga-tāntra cannot be practiced without the assistance of śaktis.

In his *Sādhanamālā*[1] the editor writes: 'It is indeed a pity that Hindus and also the Jains, to a certain extent, could not throw off the worthless and immoral practices enjoined in the Tantras, even when Buddhism was stamped out in India.

In his *Indian Buddhist Iconography*, Mr. Bhattacharyya furnishes data from the following summary: the worship of female energy in connection with that of the male, the union of male and female energies, is the essence of Tāntra; purely Tāntric gods are invariably accompanied by their Śaktis, who are sometimes given a separate seat in representations of them while at other times are seated in the lap of the gods, but they are often depicted in the actual embrace of the gods; while most forms of Tāntra generally adopt the former types of illustrations, still, in the most thoroughgoing form of it the gods are worshipped in the embrace of, in union with, the Śaktis. He refers more especially to the Vajrayāna.[2]

Most of the Buddhist Tāntras are connected with Yoga. Their teaching is a mixture of mysticism, sorcery, and erotics, accompanied by disgusting orgies. These works inculcate the worship of Śāivite gods, of the liṅga, and of many female deities. Historically they represent the later age of the degeneration of Buddhism in India. Their only connection with Buddhism is their claim that their tenets were delivered by the Buddha himself.[3] It is in accordance with this assertion that a story is told in the *Brahmayāmala*, and in the

---

[1] Vol. II, p. 33.
[2] See pp. 209, 323.
[3] *India*'s *Past*, p. 64.

Rudrayāmala also (both Hindu Tāntric works)[1] that Vaśiṣṭha, after years of hard discipline, failing in his efforts to obtain success (*siddhi*) cursed Tārā. She then appeared to him and pointed out that perfection did not lie along that way and directed him to Tibet (Mahācīna), country of Buddhists and land of the *Atharva Veda*. There he found the Buddha indulging in all sorts of loathsome practices. Appalled at what he saw Vaśiṣṭha asked for light, and for help to attain perfection. He made inquiry of the Buddha about the use of wine and meat in the presence of naked women who were drinking blood and wine and behaving like drunkards. The Buddha's reply was an exposition of the duties of the Kāulas, explanation of their mysteries and their uses, and revelation of their secret rites and practices. Ultimately Vasiṣṭha found in the unrestrained use of the five makāras the siddhi which he sought.

The Hindu Tantras are the fifth Veda of Hinduism, the satisfactory scripture for this degenerate age, the *Kali Yuga*.[2] They are of two types, the *Niyamas* containing instructions from the Devī to Sadā Śiva and the *Āgamas* in which the latter teaches the Devī. The Āgamas are of particular interest in this study. Already references have been made to Śiva teaching the Yoga to Pārvatī. Here the Yoga doctrine of the Gorakhnāthīs is traced to Mīnanāth (Matsyendranāth) who obtained it from Śiva by taking the form of a fish and listening while that god was expounding the doctrine to Pārvatī as both stood on the shore of the sea.[3] Another version of the story declares how a fish remained immovable, mind concentrated, and heard all. So Ādināth (Śiva) perceiving this, sprinkled water upon him and he became a Siddha and was called Matsyendranāth.[4] The characters in these works are restricted almost entirely to these two divinities. These books are the texts of the Śāktas, dealing with

---

[1] Also in *Sādhanamālā*, Introduction. This is the Tārā Tantra, a secret Tantra belonging to the Yoga Tantra class which prescribes revolting practices. Bhāiravī asks Bhāirava the nature of the mantra by which the Buddha and Vaśiṣṭha obtained Siddhi.

[2] See Geden in *ERE*, vol. XII, pp. 192, 193.

[3] *GP*, p. 1.

[4] Iyangar, *HYP*, p. 15.

the left-hand worship of Śakti and with *Kāulācāra*. They are based upon the *Kāula Upaniṣad*[1] the most important being the *Rudrayāmala Tantra* of which the *Jātimāla* is an important section.[2]

Selections from the *Syāmārahasya* and the *Rudrayāmala* are found in the footnotes of Wilson's works.[3] Avalon[4] has translated a number of the *Tantras*. Dr. Ewing[5] analyzed the *Śārada Ṭilaka*, pointing out that it was full of sorcery, both in its beneficent and in its horrible aspects, and of the use of yantra and mantra, the latter in cases of black magic. It exhibits Kuṇḍalī and the cakras, and its doctrine is of the Pāśupata type.

As suggested above, these developed principles, associated with this specialized aspect of Yoga, are a late formulation. Amarakosa (*c*. A.D. 500) does not know Tantra as literature and the system does not appear in the *Mahābhārata*. Śaṅkara (ninth century) noted sixty-four *Tantras*, but few of these can be identified. Their traditional author is Dattatreya. They are found as early as the seventh sentury, and from the tenth century at least they are well-known works. Their philosophy is that of the Sāṅkhya (and Yoga), often elevated into Vedānta. The topics with which they deal are the creation and destruction of the universe; worship of gods; attainment of supreme power; and union with the Supreme Being. They are concerned with the magical and the mysterious and the use of mystic symbols and sounds (including syllables and sentences), thus involving a form of Yoga in which the essences of the mystical sacred syllables are called bīja.

It may be well to look further at the Hindu Tantric practice.[6] This is described as a short cut to ends otherwise

---

[1] *B* and *H*, p. 207.

[2] Other Tantras may be mentioned. *Śakti-saṅgama*, *Viśva-sâra*, *Mahānirvāṇa*, *Vīra*, *Kulārnava*, *Syāma-Rahasya*, *Śāradā-Ṭilaka*, *Uḍḍīsa*, *Kāmākhyā*, *Viṣṇu Yāmala*, *Kālikā*, *Tantratattva*, and *Yoginī*. Lists are given by A. Avalon, *Principles of Tantra*, vol. I, pp. lxv–lxvii. Tantra means rule, ritual. Dawson, p. 317.

[3] *Wi*., pp. 254 ff. [4] Sir John Woodroffe.

[5] *JAOS* (1902), pp. 65 ff.

[6] The summary here set down is based upon pertinent chapters in *The Philosophy of Hindu Sādhanā*, by N. K. Brahma.

difficult to achieve, a way which offers to its adherents easy and speedy attainment of enjoyment as well as final beatitude. In the end soul becomes identified with Śiva, there remaining no difference in essence between them. The identity is achieved through the Kuṇḍalinī, and the disciplines are used for her awakening and raising. This is through psychical and physical exercises.

Special emphasis is put upon mantra, an infallible means to liberation. Mantra is concentrated thought of great power. It is built upon *Śabda* (sound), *nāda* (sound), and prāṇa (breath), synonymous of cosmic energy. In gross form nāda supports the things of the universe as their soul, in subtle form it is represented by the Absolute Goddess. The subtle form is realized in the gross one. So, mantra, breathing, *japa*, generate vibrations of Nāda as soul of the universe. *Nāda sādhanā* (practice of nāda), all efficient, is the invaluable discovery of the Tantras. Nāda (vibration) and jñāna (illumination) are two parallel manifestations of Śakti. One leads to and awakens the other. Illumination may be realized through breath and sound (*dvani*, primal, inaudible vibrations that cause the Universe). Nāda which is dvani, is very powerful when joined with suṣumṇā (see following chapters). In this union is power, for Kuṇḍalinī is raised up. The gross body is harmonized through posture (āsana), the internal, vital powers by breath control (*prāṇāyāma*), the higher cerebral centres through regulated sounds (nāda with suṣumṇā), the mental, with meditation. Śabda has fifty radical elements of vibration, on the vocal side the fifty letters of the alphabet. The stages of the sādhanā are: (1) purification (by karma); (2) illumination (by bhakti); (3) unification (in jñāna).

There are three classes of practitioners (*sādhaka*): (1) *Paśu*, those seeking self-control, and desiring what adepts enjoy. They strive to master their passions and impulses. (2) *Vīra* (controlled), those who have attained complete self-control and do not forget themselves even in the most trying and tempting circumstances. They enjoy freedom. They are not only allowed but are definitely instructed to include such things as the five makāras in their offerings to god. The Paśu is not allowed even to touch or to see these things. Finally the method as prescribed for the Vīra is Kāula. (3) The Divya, free from the trials of the *Vīra* is allowed to take substitutes for all material things in his process of worship. In the highest stage of attainment, kāulācāra, the sādhaka does away with all rules and injunctions of the *Śāstras*. 'For the Kāula there is neither merit nor demerit, virtue nor vice.' The theory is that as poisons counteract poisons, so men must rise by those things through which they so often lose their manhood.

In the *Yoga Tantra* and *Anuttarayoga Tantra* all gods are represented as embracing their Śaktis and feeling the bliss of Nirvāṇa.[1]

---

[1] Introduction, *Sādhanamālā*, p. 147.

CHAPTER FOURTEEN

THE GORAKṢA ŚATAKA[1]

Oṁ Haṭhayoga Gorakṣaśataka prarambhaḥ

Oṁ, the beginning of the One Hundred of the Haṭha Yoga of Gorakṣa!

Śrīguram paramānandam vande śvānandavigraham.
Yasya sāmnidhyamātreṇa cidānandāyate tanuḥ. 1.

1. I bow down to the venerable *guru*[2] (who is) supreme bliss, embodiment of his own bliss; simply by means of proximity to whom the body becomes nothing but knowledge and bliss.

Antarniścallitātmadīpakalikāśvādhārbandhādibhiḥ
Yo yogī yugakalpakālakalanāt[3] *tvañja jegīyate;*
Jñānāmodamahodadhiḥ samabhavadyatrādināthaḥ svayam
Vyatkāvyakta guṇādhikam tamaniśam śrī mīnanātham bhaje. 2.

2. Who (= That Yogī) by reason of (his practice of) *ādhārbandha* and the other (postures), in the rays of the inner steady light of his soul is highly praised as a Yogī and as the essence of the reckoning of time (manifested) in the *yugas* and *kalpas* (or, as reality on account of his making time consisting of *yugas* and *kalpas*), in whom (= who) the primeval Lord himself, the ocean of the bliss of knowledge took form, who (= who above) is superior to qualities both manifest and unmanifest (*i.e.*, matter), him (= who, that *guru*) Śrī Mīnanath,[4] I revere continually.

---

[1] The text used is *P*; the commentary (*CP*), unless otherwise stated, is that of *P*. The references may be made to *GP*, and its commentary.

[2] Mātsyendranāth. [3] Read *Kalanā* with *B* and *CP*.

[4] Śrī Mīnanāth = Matsyendranāth.

Namaskṛtya gurum bhaktavyā gorakṣo jñānamuttamam
Abhīṣṭam yogīnām brūte paramānandakārakam. 3.

3. Having saluted his *guru* with devotion, Gorakṣa describes the supreme knowledge, desired by Yogīs, bringing about supreme bliss.

Gorakṣaḥ śatakam vakti yogīnām hitakāmyayā
Dhruvam yasyāvabodhena jāyate paramampadam. 4.

4. With desire for the benefit of Yogīs, Gorakṣa proclaims (the) One Hundred (verses) by the knowledge[1] of which is surely brought about the highest state.[2]

Etadvimuktisopānametatkālasya vañcanam
Yadvayāvṛttam manobhogādāsaktam paramātmani. 5.

5. This (by which) the mind is turned away from (sensual) enjoyments, and (is) attached to the supreme spirit, (is) a ladder to final release; this (is) a cheating of death.

Dvijasevita śākhasya śrutikalpataroḥ phalam
Śamanam bhavatāpasya yogam bhajata sattamāḥ. 6.

6. O excellent men![3] Practice Yoga, the fruit of the-tree-of-wishes, the sacred word whose branches (punning 'schools') are frequented by birds (punningly called Brāhmans, *dvīja*), (which) brings to an end the misery of the world.

Āsanam prāṇasamrodhaḥ pratyāhāraśca dhāraṇā
Dhyānam samādhiretāni yogāṅgāni vadanti ṣaṭ.[4] 7.

7. Postures, control of the breath, withdrawal of the senses from their external objects, fixing of the mind upon a single object, abstract meditation and identification of the self with

---

[1] *B* reads: 'By the knowledge of this surely all good fortunes are attained.'

[2] *CP* interprets this to mean *jīvanmukti*; and the commentary attached to *GP*, 'attaining knowledge of which the Yogī attains *jīvanmukti*.'

[3] Men of great attainment in Yoga, whose passions are ripe for destruction. *CP*.

[4] These are the technical Yoga terms. *Yama* and *niyama* are omitted; they must be mastered before the practice of Haṭha Yoga begins.

the object of meditation, these they say, are the six stages[1] of the Yoga.

Āsanāni ca tāvanti yāvantyo jīvajātayaḥ
Eteṣāmakhilānbhedānvijānāti maheśvaraḥ. 8.

8. (There are) as many postures as (there are) species[2] of living beings. The distinctions between them all Śiva (alone) fully understands.

Caturaśīti[3] *lakṣāṇāmekāikam samudāhṛtam*
Tataḥ śivena pīṭhānām ṣoḍāśonam śataṅkṛtam. 9.

9. Every single one of the 84,00,000 (of postures) has been described (by Śiva). From them eighty-four postures have been selected by Śiva.

Āsanebhyaḥ samastebhyo dvayametadudāhṛtam
Ekam siddhāsanam tatra dvitīyam kamalāsanam. 10.

10. From amongst all these (eighty-four) postures these two have been selected: the first, 'the perfect posture' (*siddhāsana*); the second 'the lotus posture' (*kamalāsana*).[4]

Yonisthānakamaṅghrimūla ghaṭitam kṛtvā dṛḍham vinyaset
Meḍhrepādamathāikameva niyatam kṛtvā samam vigraham
Sthāṇuḥ saṁyamitendrayo'caladṛśā paśyanbhruvoramtara[5]
Metanmokṣakapāṭabheda janakam siddhāsanam procyate.
11.

11. The Yogī should press firmly the heel of the (left) foot against the perineum and the right foot just above the male organ, keeping the body fixedly erect, immovable;[6] the senses under control; and with motionless gaze should look at the spot between the eyebrows. This (posture), which is the opener of the door of release,[7] is called the perfect posture (*siddhāsana*).

---

[1] Or aids (Woods), means (M.-Williams), methods.

[2] The *GP* reading would mean 'as many as there are men, or living beings.'

[3] The *ā* has been shortened to agree with *GP*. *PC* says that *a* was lengthened for metre.

[4] These names will be used freely in the exposition.

[5] *P* and *B* read *paśyan*.

[6] *GP* reads 'the chin pressing on the chest.'

[7] *Mokṣadvāra*, the way *suṣumṇā*, the channel of the spinal cord, closed by Kuṇḍalinī, is opened.

Vāmorūpari dakṣiṇamca caraṇam samsthāpya vāmamtathā
Dakṣorūpari paścimena vidhinā dhṛtvā karābhyām dṛḍham
Aṅguṣṭhāu hṛdayenidhāya cibukam nāsāgra mālokaye
Deta dvayādhivikāra nāśanakaram padmāsanam procyate. 12.

12. And having placed the right foot upon the left thigh, and likewise the left (foot) upon the right thigh, and having grasped firmly the great toes with the hands crossed from behind (and) fixing the chin on the chest, (the Yogī) should gaze at the tip of the nose. This (posture), the destroyer of diseases and mental and physical disturbances is called the lotus posture (*padmāsana*).

The *Haṭhayogapradīpika* gives a second padmāsana, which the commentary (*GP* 12) attributes to Matsyendranāth. 'Place the feet on the thighs, with the soles upwards, and place the two hands on the thighs, palms upwards. Gaze on the tip of the nose, keeping the tongue pressed against the root of the teeth of the upper jaw,[1] and the chin against the chest, and raise the air up slowly (pull the *apāna vāyu* gently upward.) This is called *padmāsana*, the destroyer of all diseases. It is difficult of attainment by everybody, but can be learned by intelligent people in this world.'

Ṣaṭacakram ṣoḍaśādhāram trilakṣam vyomapañcakam
Svadehe yeṅajānanti katham sidhyanti yoginaḥ. 13.

13. How can Yogīs, who do not know the six centres (*cakra*), the sixteen props (*ādhāra*)[2], the 3,00,000[3] ('channels,' *nāḍi*) (and) the five sheathes (*vyoma*) in their (own) body, attain perfection (in Yoga)?

Ekastambham navadwāram gṛham pañcādhidāivatam
Svadeham ye na jānanti katham sidhyanti yoginaḥ. 14.

14. How can those Yogīs who do not know their own body (as) a house[4] of one column (with) nine doors, and (as

[1] This is called *Jihvabandha* (*Jihva* = tongue).

[2] The commentary on *P* states that Gorakhnāth in his own work, the *Siddha Siddhānta Paddhati*, names the sixteen *ādhāras*.

[3] A note to *B*, verse eleven, substitutes 'three worlds' for *trilakṣa*; and the commentary to *GP* uses two *lakṣa*, stating that they are two classes of channels.

[4] *B* writes '*three guṇa*' for 'house,' in which case 'house' is understood.

presided over by) five tutelary divinities, attain perfection (in Yoga)?

Caturdalam syādādhāraḥ svādhiṣṭhānamca ṣaṭdalam
Nābhāu daśadalam padmam sūryasañkhydalam hṛdi. 15.

15. The four-leaved (lotus) should be the *ādhāra*, and the six-leaved the *svādhiṣṭhāna*. In the navel (is) the ten-leaved (lotus) and in the heart the twelve-leaved[1] (lotus).

Kaṇṭhesyāt ṣoḍaśadalam bhrūmadhye dvidalantathā
Sahasradalamākhyātam brahmarandhre mahāpathe. 16.

16. The sixteen-leaved (lotus) should be in the throat; similarly the two-leaved (lotus) between the eyebrows; in the hole-in-the-skull, in the great path, the one-thousand-leaved (lotus).[2]

Ādhāraḥ prathamam cakram svādhiṣṭhānam dvitīyakam
Yonisthānam dvayormadhye kāmarūpam nigadyate. 17.

17. *Ādhāra* is the first *cakra*; *svādhiṣṭhāna* the second; *yonisthāna*, between these two, is named *kāmarūpa*.[3]

Ādhārākhyam gudasthānam paṅkajamca caturdalam.
Tanmadhye procyate yoniḥ kāmākṣā siddhavanditā. 18.

18. And the *gudasthāna* (is) the four-leaved lotus called *ādhāra*. In the midst of it is said to be the *yoni*,[4] the 'eye of love,' praised by adepts.

Yoni madye mahāliṅgam paścimābhimukham sthitam
Mastake maṇivad bimbam yo jānāti sa yogavit. 19.

19. In the midst of the *yoni*, with its face towards the

---

[1] *Sūrya*, twelve months (Sūrya=sun).

[2] The *nīrbāṇa cakra*.

[3] The *Śiva-Śakti*, called *Kāmarūpa*, is in the *Yoniṣṭhāna*.

[4] The *Yoni* is situated in the middle leaf of the *mūlādhāra*, touching the triangular object with its face downwards, facing into the *suṣumṇā*. *CP*.
gudasthāna, the anus.
paṅkaja, mud-born, a name for lotus.
yoni, vulva.
kāmākyā, eye of love.
There is a place in Kāmarūp (Assam) called *Kāmākhyā*. See chap. eight.

back, there stands the great liṅga: Who knows the disk of light, like a luminous[1] jewel, in its head,[2] (is) an adept.

Tapta cāmīkarābhāsam taḍillekheva visphurat
Trikoṇam tatpuram vanheradhomeḍhrātpratiṣṭhitam. 20.

20. Flashing even like forks of lightning, looking like molten gold, the triangular place (yonisthāna) of fire (is) situated below the *membrum virile*.

Yatsamādhāu param jyotir anantam viśvatomukham
Tasmin dṛṣṭe mahāyoge yātāyātam na vidyate. 21.

21. Having seen that, the supreme light unending, shining in all directions, in samādhi, the adept does not experience (any more) transient existence.[3]

Svaśabdena bhavet prāṇaḥ svādhiṣṭhānam tadāśrayaḥ
Svādhiṣṭhānātpadādasmān meḍhram evābhidhīyate. 22.

22. By means of the word *sva*,[4] prāṇa[5] arises; the resting place of that prāṇa (is) svādhiṣṭhāna. For it is from this very place, the svādhiṣṭhāna (that) the meḍhra is named.

Tantunā maṇivatproto yatrakandaḥ suṣumṇayā
Tannābhimaṇḍalam cakram procyate maṇipūrakam. 23.

23. Where the kanda (uterus?) is strung on the suṣumṇā,[6] like a jewel on a thread, that region[7] of the navel is called *maṇipūrakam.*

Dvādaśāre mahācakre puṇyapāpavivarjite
Tāvajjīvo bhramatyeva yāvattatvam na vindati. 24.

24. The soul[8] wanders[9] only so long as it does not find the Real in the great twelve-spoked[10] cakra (where there is) freedom from (the fruits of) merit and demerit.

---

[1] Being very bright.
[2] According to *GP*, the head of the *mahāliṅga* is meant.
[3] That is, change, birth and death, coming and going.
[4] The commentator (*GP*) says that haṁsa has as its resting place the svādhiṣṭhāna, the liṅgamūlā.
[5] Prāṇa, the breath. For more exact definition see next chapter.
[6] The nāḍi or channel of the spinal cord.
[7] Circle (*maṇḍala*), the ten-petalled lotus.
[8] Jīva, is the bound soul, wandering soul.
[9] The reference is to saṁsāra.
[10] The lotus of the heart, where the three guṇas reside, and, therefore, merit and demerit.

Ūrdhvam meḍhrādadhonābheḥ kandayoniḥ khagāṇḍavat
Tatranāḍyaḥ samutpannāḥ sahasrāṇām dvisaptatiḥ. 25.

25. Below the navel and above the male organ (is) the *kandayoni*,[1] shaped like the egg of a bird. There (are) the origins of the seventy-two thousand nāḍis.

Teṣu nāḍīsahasreṣu dvisaptatirudāhṛtāḥ
Pradhānam prāṇavāhinyo bhūyastāsu daśasmṛtāḥ. 26.

26. Among these thousands of nāḍis seventy-two have been specially noted. Again, among these ten carriers of the praṇa are designated as the most important.

Iḍā ca piṅgalā cāiva suṣumṇāca tṛtīyikā
Gāndhārī, hastijihvāca pūṣā cāiva yaśasvinī. 27.

27. *Iḍā* and *piṅgalā* and also the third, *suṣumṇā*, *gāndhārī*, *hastijihvā*, *pūṣā* and also *yaśasvinī*.

Alambuṣā kuhūś cāiva śaṁkhinī daśamī smṛtā
Etannāḍīm ayam cakram jñātavyam yogibhiḥ sadā. 28.

28. *Almabuṣā*, *kuhūś*, and also *śaṁkhinī* the tenth are taught (authoritatively as the ten chief nāḍis). The centres containing these nāḍis should be known always by Yogīs.

Iḍā vāme sthitā bhāge piṅgalā dakṣiṇe sthitā
Suṣumṇā madhyedeśe tu gāndhārī vāmacakṣuṣi. 29.

29. Iḍā (is) situated on the left side, piṅgalā on the right, and suṣumṇā[2] in the mid region (*e.g.*, between them); and gāndhārī in the left eye;

Dakṣiṇe hasti jihvāca pūṣākarṇe ca dakṣiṇe
Yaśasvinī vāmakarṇe hyānane cāpyalambuṣā. 30.

30. And the *hastijihvā* in the right (eye) and *pūṣā* in the right ear, *yaśasvinī* in the left ear, and likewise the *alambuṣā* in the mouth:

Kuhūśca liṅgadeśe tu mūlasthāneca śaṁkhinī
Evam dvāram samāśritya tiṣṭhanti daśanāḍikāḥ. 31.

---

[1] Kanda=uterus? The body cosmically viewed contains both male and female characteristics.

[2] *GP* commentary says that the origin of these three is in the triangle of the mūlādhāra; and *B* states that they are said to be the way of the prāṇa.

31. And *Kuhuś* in the region of the liṅga and in the mūlādhāra the *śaṁkhinī*. Thus are the ten[1] nāḍis (each) attached to a door (of the body).

Iḍā piṅgālasuṣumṇāḥ prāṇamārge samaśritāḥ
Satatam prāṇavāhinyaḥ somasūryāgnidevatāḥ. 32.

32. Iḍā, piṅgalā and suṣumṇā in the path of the prāṇa are connected. (They are) always the conductors of the prāṇa. (Their) presiding deities are the moon, the sun and fire.

Prāṇo'pānaḥ samānaścodānavyānāuca vayavaḥ
Nāgaḥ kūrmo'tha kṛkaro devadatto dhanañjayaḥ. 33.

33. (The breaths[2] are) prāṇa (air of breathing), apāṇa (air of the rectum), samāna (digestive air), udāna (air in the throat), vyānā (air circulating through the body), nāga (air of eructation), kūrma (air of blinking), similarly kṛkara[3] (air of sneezing), devadatta (air of yawning) (and) dhanañjaya.

Hṛdiprāṇo vasennityam apāno gudamaṇḍale
Samāno nābhideśesyād udānaḥ kaṇṭhamadhyagaḥ. 34.

34. Prāṇa always lies in the chest (heart), apāna in the region of the rectum, samāna is in the region of the navel; udāna moves in the midst of the throat.

Vyāno vyāpī śarīretu pradhānam pañca vāyavaḥ
Prāṇādyāścātra vikhyātā nāgādyāḥ pañcavāyavaḥ. 35.

35. But the vyānā pervades the (whole) body. The five airs beginning with prāṇa are said to be chief; the other five airs are nāga, etc.

Udgāre nāgākhyātaḥ kūrma ūnmīlane smṛtaḥ
Kṛkaraḥ kṣutakṛjjñeyo devadatto vijṛmbhaṇe. 36.

36. Nāga is said to be the air (that functions in) eructation; kūrma in winking; kṛkara[4] (is) known as causing sneezing,[5] (and) devadatta in yawning.

---

[1] The nine doors together with the hole-in-the-skull. They are passages for the prāṇas.

[2] The breaths are really the functional or vital forces of the body all of which are dependent upon the prāṇa, of the respiratory system. Prāṇa is identified with jīva, the soul, which is, of course, the bound soul.

[3] Sometimes spoken of as the digestive air.

[4] *B* says that it arouses hunger.

[5] *B* says involuntarily.

Na jahāti mṛtam cāpi sarvavyāpi dhanañjayaḥ
Ete sarvāsu nāḍīṣu bhramante jīvarūpiṇaḥ. 37.

37. Dhanañjaya, pervading the whole (body) does not quit even the dead (body). These (prāṇas), vital functions[1], wander through all the nāḍīs.

Ākṣipto bhujadaṇḍena yathoccalati kandukaḥ
Prāṇāpānasamākṣiptastathā jīvo na tiṣṭhati. 38.

38. As a (wooden) ball struck by the hand-club flies up, so the jīva[2] struck (in turn) by prāṇa and apāna, does not rest[3] (is kept moving).

Prāṇāpāna vaśo jīvo hyadhaścordhvam ca dhāvati
Vāmadakṣiṇamārgeṇa cañcalatvān na dṛśyate. 39.

39. Because the soul is under the control of prāṇa and apāna, it moves up and down through the left and right paths (Iḍa and Piṅgalā). Because of restlessness it is not perceived (clearly).[4]

Rajjubaddho yathāśyenogato'pyākṛṣyate punaḥ
Guṇa baddhastathā jīvaḥ prāṇāpānena kṛṣyate. 40.

40. As a hawk tied with a string, even though it flies (away) is drawn back; so the jīva, bound by the guṇas, is controlled by prāṇa and upāna.

Apānaḥ karṣati prāṇam prāṇo'pānam ca karṣati
Ūrdhvādhaḥ saṁsthitāvetāu saṁyojayati yogavit. 41.

41. Apāna pulls prāna and prāṇa pulls apāna (alternately); an adept in Yoga causes the union[5] of these two, lower and upper (airs).[6]

Hakāreṇa bahiryāti sakāreṇa viśetpunaḥ
Haṁsahaṁsetyamuma mantram jīvo japati sarvadā. 42.

---

[1] Literally 'forms of life,' appearing as possessing life. Reference is to the doctrine of māyā, avidyā.

[2] Jīva is the soul in bondage in saṁsāra.

[3] Illusion is due to the moving of the prāṇa.

[4] Until one controls the prāṇa he cannot *see* clearly. *PC* : Jīva does not understand its own reality because disturbed.

[5] The commentary on *GP* calls this *prāṇāyāma* '*haṭha yoga,*' the union of sun and moon.

[6] The commentator quotes *Haṭha Yoga Cintāmani*: '*Prāṇāyāma* has been described by Yogīs as *Haṭha Yoga.*'

42. With the sound of '*ha*' jīva (in the form of prāṇa) goes out; with the sound of '*sa*' (in the form of apāna) it enters (the body) again. The jīva repeats continually that mantra '*haṁsa, haṁsa.*'[1]

Ṣaṭa Śatānitvahorātre sahasrāṇy ekaviṁśatiḥ
Etat saṁkhyānvitam mantram jīvo japati sarvadā. 43.

43. The jīva recites continually this mantra, twenty-one thousand six-hundred times in a day and a night.

Ajapā nāma gāyatrī yogīnām mokṣadāyinī
Asyāḥ saṅkalpamātreṇa sarvapāpaiḥ pramucyate. 44.

44. The gāyatrī called ajapā[2] (is) the giver of liberation to Yogīs; simply with the desire to recite this (gāyatrī) is he freed from all demerit.

Anayā sadṛśī vidyā anayā sadṛśo japaḥ
Anayā sadṛśam jñānam na bhūtam na bhaviṣyati. 45.

45. Knowledge like this, repetition like this, insight like this neither was nor shall be.[3]

Kuṇḍalinyāḥ samudbhūtā gāyatrī prāṇadhāriṇī
Prāṇavidyā mahāvidyā yastām vetti sayogavit. 46.

46. The gāyatrī is sprung from[4] Kuṇḍalinī and supports the prāṇa. Knowledge of the prāṇa is the great knowledge. Who knows this is an adept.[5]

Kandordhvam kuṇḍalī śaktiraṣṭadhā kuṇḍalākṛtī
Brahmadvāramukham nityam mukhenācchādya tiṣṭhati. 47.

47. Above the kanda *Kuṇḍali-śakti* forms an eight-fold coil. She remains there constantly with her mouth (face) covering the 'door of Brahmā.'[6]

Yenadvāreṇa gantavyam brahmasthānamanāmayam
Mukhenācchādya tatdvāram prasuptā parameśvarī. 48.

---

[1] Haṁsa, the chief mantra of the jīva, is gāyatrī. The first clause is according to *CP*.

[3] = Haṁsa, the mantra consisting only of exhalation and inhalation, not of vocal sound.

[3] The reference is to the gāyatrī and its efficiency. *PC* : It is Supreme Knowledge.

[4] *GP* uses locative: Gāyatrī arises in Kuṇḍalinī.

[5] Prāṇa is dependent upon Kuṇḍalinī.

[6] The entrance into Brahmā: the lower end of the suṣumṇa.

48. Having covered with her face that door by which (the soul), free from disease, should go to the seat of Brahmā, the goddess (Kuṇḍalinī) lies asleep.

Prabuddhā vahniyogena manasā marutā saha
Sūcīvad guṇamādāya vrajatyūrdhvam suṣumṇayā. 49.

49. By the mind aroused through the union of fire (buddhi) and prāṇa (Kuṇḍalinī) is drawn upward through the suṣumṇā as a needle draws a thread.

Prasphuradbhujagākārā padmatantunibhāśubhā.
Prabuddhā vahniyogena vrajaty ūrdhvam suṣumṇayā. 50.

50. Through the suśumṇā (she), aroused through union with fire, goes upwards, like a serpent, auspicious, gleaming like a filament of a lotus.

Udghaṭayetkapātantu yathā kuñcikayā haṭhāt
Kuṇḍalinyā tathā yogī mokṣadvāram prabhedayet. 51.

51. As one might open a door by force with a key, so the Yogī may break open the door of release by means of Kuṇḍalinī.[1]

Kṛtvā samputitāukarāudṛḍhataram badhvātu padmāsanam
Gāḍham vakṣasi sannidhāya cibukam dhyātvāca tat prekṣitam
Vāramvāram apānamūrdhvam anilam proccārayet pūritam
Muñcanprāṇamupāiti bodhamatulam śaktiprabodhānnaraḥ. 52.

52. Having closed the two hands firmly, having taken the lotus posture, having pressed down the chin on the chest, (and) it (Kuṇḍalinī) having been looked at; he should expel again and again the apāna breath after he (has filled) it in; he attains at the time of expelling the prāṇa unequalled knowledge through the awakening of Śakti.

Aṅgānām mardanam kuryācchramajātena vāriṇā
Kadvamlalavaṇa tyāgī kṣīra bhojanamācaret. 53.

53. One should rub his limbs with the perspiration that

[1] The commentary on *GP* says that the door here referred to is the mouth of the suṣumṇā, and the key the knowledge of Kuṇḍalinī.

results from (the above) effort. Let him drink milk and abstain from bitter, acid and salty (food).[1]

Brahmacārī mitāhārī tyāgīyogaparāyaṇaḥ
Abdādūrdhvam bhavetsiddho nātrakāryā vicāraṇā. 54.

54. (He should be) chaste, one who eats little, an abstainer from worldly pleasures, a practiser of Yoga. After a year he will have perfected this skill. One must have no doubt concerning this.[2]

Susnigdham madurāhāram caturthāṁśavivarjitam
Bhujyate surasamprītyāi mitāhāraḥ sa ucyate. 55.

55. One (by whom) very soft, sweet, good-tasting (food), leaving one fourth of it,[3] is taken with enjoyment, is called *mitāhāra.*

Kandordhvam kuṇḍalī śaktiraṣṭadhā kuṇḍalākṛtiḥ
Bandhanāya ca mūḍhānām yogīnām mokṣadā smṛtā. 56.

56. Kuṇḍalinī-śakti, coiled eight times above the kanda (is) said to be the giver of release to Yogīs[4] and of bondage to the uninitiated.[5]

Mahamudrām nabhomudhrām uḍḍīyānam jalandharam
Mūlabandhamcayovetti sayogī muktibhājanam. 57.

57. That Yogī is ready for release who knows *mahāmudrā, nabhomudrā,*[6] *uḍḍīyāna, jalandhara*[7] and *mūlabhanda.*

Śodhanam nādijālasya cālanam candra sūryayoḥ
Rasānām śoṣaṇam cāiva mahāmudrā 'bhidhīyate. 58.

58. The purification of the collection of the nāḍis, the

---

[1] Commentary on *GP* says that this is the perspiration arising from the practice of prāṇāyāma; and that it is for rousing Kuṇḍalinī. Thus, also, the *dhātus* or secretions of the body are preserved.

[2] Again the commentary to *GP* states that this assists in moving Kuṇḍalinī.

[3] Two parts (fourths) of the stomach should be filled with food; one part with water; and one part should be left empty for the passing of air.

[4] To the adept in moving *her.* [5] Literally 'fools.'

[6] The commentary to *GP* substitutes Khecarīmudrā; and states that through these exercises the Kuṇḍalinī is set in motion. These are *Śakti cālana mudrās.*

[7] *Jalam* means nectar (bindu) dropping from the-hole-in-the-skull.

moving of both the moon and the sun, and also the drying up of the liquids of the body, is called mahāmudrā.

Vakṣonyasta hanuḥ prapīḍya suciram yonimca vāmāṅghriṇā
Hastābhyāmanudhārayanprasaritam pādam tathā dakṣinam
Āpūryaśvasanena kukṣiyugulam[1] *badhvāśanāirecayed*
Eṣā vyādhivināśinī sumahatī mudrā nṛṇām kathyate. 59.

59. Having rested the chin on the chest, and pressing for a long time the yoni with the left great toe, with the two hands grasping the extended right foot, having filled with breath both sides of the abdomen and having held it, one should expel it slowly. This is said to be the very great mudrā, the destroyer of the diseases of men.

Candrāṅgena samabhyasya sūryāṅgeṇābhyasetpunaḥ.
Yāvattulyā bhavetsaṅkhyā tatomudrāmvisarjayet. 60.

60. Having practiced it first with the iḍā and then with the piṅgalā an equal number of times, he should discontinue the mudrā.[2]

Nahi pathyamapathyam vā rasāḥ sarve 'pi nīrasāḥ
Api muktam viṣamghoram pīyūṣamiva jīryate.[3] 61.

61. (There is) neither wholesome nor unwholesome (food). All tastes (are) indeed tasteless. Even deadly poison (food) (when) eaten is digested as if it were nectar.[4]

Kṣyakuṣṭha gudāvarta gulmā jīrṇapurogamāḥ.
Rogāstasya kṣayam yānti mahāmudrāmcayo 'abhyaset. 62.

62. His diseases, consumption, leprosy, constipation, enlargement of the spleen, decrepitude go to destruction who practices mahāmudrā.

---

[1] *P* reads *yugulam.*

[2] The breathing should be done an equal number of times with each nostril. *PC* reads:

'*OṀ*' should be repeated twelve times in inhaling, sixteen times in holding and ten times in expelling the breath. This is called prāṇāyāma.

There are three classes of prāṇāyāma. In the lowest begin with twelve times, in the middle with twenty-four times, in the highest with thirty-six times. In the lowest there is great perspiration, in the middle trembling, in the highest the Yogī floats in the air.

[3] *P* reads *jīryati.* But *B* and *GP* read *jīryate.*

[4] The effect of the mahāmudrā is to destroy the distinction in sense or effect.

Kathiteyam mahāmudrā sarvasiddhikarīṇṛṇām
Gopanīyā prayatnena na deyāyasya kasyacit. 63.

63. This mahāmudrā has been described, which secures all kinds of success[1] for men. It should be kept secret by all means. It (is) not to be revealed to all sorts of people (literally, 'any one').

Kapālakuhare jihvā praviṣṭā viparītagā
Bhruvorantargatā dṛṣṭirmudrā bhavati khecarī. 64.

64. By turning the tongue over backwards into the hollow above the throat and by fixing the sight between the eyebrows the khecarīmudrā is performed.[2]

Na rogo maraṇam tasya na nidrā na kṣudhātṛṣā
Naca mūrcchā[3] *bhavettasya yo mudrāmvetti khecarīm.* 65.

65. Neither disease nor death nor sleep nor hunger nor fainting[4] is there for him who knows the khecarīmudrā.

Pīḍyate nasa śokena lipyate na sakarmaṇā
Bādhyate na sa kālena yo mudrām vetti khecarīm. 66.

66. He is not troubled by affliction; he is not besmeared (bound) by the fruits of deeds, he is not troubled[5] by death who knows the khecarīmudrā.

Cittam carati khe yasmājjihvā carati khegatā
Tenāiva khecarīmudrā sarvasiddhāir namaskṛtā. 67.

67. The *citta* wanders in space (*khe*)[6] because the tongue having entered khe (the hollow above the throat) moves about. For that very reason the khecarīmudrā is highly valued by all adepts.[7]

---

[1] Mahāmudrā gains all perfections.

[2] This takes the place of nābhomudrā in the exposition. See verse 57. The commentary to *GP* explains that the tongue has first to be released from the cords which bind it to the floor of the mouth, and then to be elongated by repeated stretching and kneading.

[3] Better, *mūrchā*.

[4] Or, delusion.

[5] *HYP*: 'Not snared by death (time).'

[6] The space between the eyebrows characterized by freedom from the universe.

[7] *SCN*, Text, p. 87. (*The Serpent Power*), speaking of khecarī: 'As by this the *citta* roams in the Brahman (Kha = ether and space

Bindu mūlam śarīram tu śīrāstatra pratiṣṭhitāḥ
Bāvayanti śariram yā āpādatalamastakam. 68.

68. But the bindu[1] is the cause of the body.[2] In it (*tatra*) arise all the channels which together constitute the body, from head to foot.

Khecaryā mudritam yena vivaram lambikordhvataḥ
Na tasya kṣarate binduḥ kāminyāliṅgitasya ca. 69.

69. By whom the hollow in the top of the throat is sealed by khecarī, his bindu, even (though he be) embraced by a woman, does not fall.

Yāvad binduḥ sthito dehe tāvanmṛtyubhayam kutaḥ.
Yāvad baddhā nabhomudrā[3] *tāvad bindur nagacchati.* 70.

70. While the bindu remains in the body, there is no fear of death.[4] As long as the khecarīmudrā is continued, so long the bindu does not go down.[5]

Calito 'pi yadā binduḥ samprāptaśca hutāśanam
Brajaty ūrdhvam hṛtaḥ śaktyā niruddho yonimudrayā. 71.

71. Even if the bindu has reached the fire (yonisthānam), it straightway returns (goes up) arrested by Śakti, by the yonimudrā.

Sa punar dvividho binduḥ paṇḍuro[6] *lohitastathā*
Pāṇḍuram śukramityāhurlohitam tu mahārajaḥ. 72.

72. Further, the bindu (is) of two kinds, pale-white and blood-red. The pale-white they call *semen virile*, the blood-red menstrual fluid.

Sindūradrava saṅkāśam ravisthāne sthitam rajaḥ
Śaśisthāne sthito bindustayorāikyam sudurlabham. 73.

---

between the eyebrows, *ājñā*), and as the sound of unwritten words also roams in the ether (khe), therefore khecarīmudrā is honoured by all. Citta is *khecare*, what moves in the sky. This is the case where the *citta* is free from all attachments.

[1] *Semen virile. Candrāmṛta*, nectar of the crescent moon.

[2] *Mūla* = root.

[3] = Khecarīmudrā. See above.

[4] Or, 'Where (is) the fear of death?'

[5] The idea is that the bindu is distilled above the soft palate and proceeds *down* through the hollow above the throat and the suṣumṇā.

[6] The text reads *pāṇḍaro*; but following *B* and *GP*, *pānduro* is used here.

73. *Rajas* (menstrual fluid) secreted[1] in the place of the sun, resembling vermilion, and the bindu secreted in the place of the moon—the mingling of these two is very difficult to accomplish.

Binduḥ śīva rajaḥ śaktir bindum indū[2] *rajo raviḥ*
Ubhayoḥ saṅgamādeva prāpyate paramam padam. 74.

74. Bindu is Śiva, rajas (is) Śakti; bindu (*is*) the moon, rajas the sun; from the mingling of these two, verily, one obtains the highest state.

Vāyunā śakti cārena preritantu mahārajaḥ
Bindunāiti sahāikatvam bhaved divyam vapustadā. 75.

75. Then, by moving Śakti, by vayu the rajas (is) impelled and united with bindu. Then (the body) becomes divine,[3] wonderful in appearance.

Śukram candreṇa samyuktam rajaḥ sūryeṇa samyutam
Tayoḥ samarasāikatvam yojānāti sa yogavit. 76.

76. *Śukra* (bindu) is joined[4] with the moon, rajas is joined with the sun. One who knows (the means of) uniting[5] the two is an adept.

Uḍḍīnam kurute yasmād aviśrāntam mahākhagaḥ
Uḍḍīyānam tadevasyān mṛtyumātaṅgakeśarī. 77.

77. Even as a great bird is able to fly[6] without taking rest; so indeed *uḍḍīyāna* may become the lion (which is) the death[7] of the elephant.

Udarātpaścimebhāge hyadho nābhernigadyate
Uḍḍīyānasya bandhoyam tatrā bandho vidhīyate. 78.

78. This *bandha*[8] at the back of the abdomen and below the navel is called bandha of the uḍḍīyāna; there bandā (mudrā) is to be practised.

---

[1] *Sthitam, sthito* = 'whose natural place is,' or 'situated.'
[2] *GP* reads *candra.*
[3] *E.g.*, fire does not burn it, weapons do not pierce it, etc.
[4] 'Means,' or 'is equivalent to.'
[5] *GP* commentary says that the *union* of these two is Yoga.
[6] In space, in the heavens, ākāśa = *khe* of verse 67.
[7] *E.g.*, as the lion kills the elephant, so uḍḍīyāna destroys death.
[8] = mudrā.

Badhnāti hi śirajālamadhogāmiśirojalam
Tato jālandharo bandhaḥ kaṇṭhaduḥkhāughanāśanaḥ. 79.

79. Because the *jālandharabandha* closes the network of channels (all the nāḍis) and stops the water[1] from flowing down from the head; therefore, it destroys the host of disorders of the throat.

Jālandhare kṛte bandhe kaṇṭhasaṅkocalakṣaṇe
Pīyūṣam na patatyagnāu na ca vāyuḥ prakupyati. 80.

80. The jālandharabandha, characterized by the closing of the throat, having been performed, the nectar[2] does not fall into the fire, nor is the air disturbed.

Pārṣṇibhāgena sampīḍya yonimākuñcayed gudam
Apānamūrdhvam ākṛṣya mūlabandho vidhīyate. 81.

81. Having pressed the yoni[3] with the back of the left heel, one should contract the rectum; (and then), draw[4] the apāna upward—(thus) is the mūlabandha performed.

Apānaprāṇayorāikyāt kṣayānmūtrapurīṣayoḥ
Yuvā bhavati vṛddho 'pi satatam mūlabandhanāt. 82.

82. From the union of prāṇa and apāna, from the decrease of urine and fæces, even an old man becomes young by much (practice) of the mūlabandha.

Padmāsanam samāruhya samakāyaśirodharaḥ
Nāsagradṛṣṭirekānte japedoṁkāramavyayam. 83.

83. Having taken the lotus posture, holding the body and neck steady, fixing the sight on the tip of the nose, in a secluded place, one should repeat the unperishable oṁ.

Bhūr bhuvaḥ svarimelokāḥ somasūryāgnidevatāḥ
Yasyā mātrāsu tiṣṭhanti tatparamjyotir om iti. 84.

84. That supreme light, oṁ, is (that) in whose elements the worlds *bhūḥ*, *bhavaḥ* and *svaḥ* and the divinities moon, sun and fire exist.[5]

---

[1] *PC.* The nectar of the moon.
[2] Bindu.
[3] *PC.* Perineum = yonisthānam.
[4] Literally, having drawn.
[5] In oṁ you can meditate on all these.

Tryaḥ kālāstrayo vedāstrayo lokāstrayaḥ sverāḥ
Trayo devāḥ sthiṭā yatra tatparamjyotir om iti. 85.

85. In which the three times, the three *Vedas*, the three worlds, the three accents, and the three gods are situated, that, oṁ, is the supreme light.[1]

Kriyā cecchā tathā jñānābrāhmīrāudrīca vāiṣṇavī
Tridhāśaktiḥ sthitā yatra tatparamjotir om iti. 86.

86. In which action and desire and knowledge, *Brahmī*, *Rāudrī* and *Vāiṣṇavī*,[2] the threefold śakti, is contained, that, oṁ, is the supreme light.

Akāraścatathokāroṁakāro bindu saṁjñakaḥ
Tisromātrāḥ sthitāyatra tatparaṁjyotir om iti. 87.[3]

87. That oṁ, in which these three letters *A*, and likewise *U* and *M*, which has the bindu as its mark, exist, is the supreme light.

Vacasā tajjayed bījam vapuṣā tatsambhyaset
Manasā tatsmarennityam tatparamjyotir om iti. 88.

88. With the voice one should repeat that bījam;[4] one should practice it with the body[5]; with the mind one should remember it.[6] That, oṁ, is the supreme light.

Śucirvā'pyaśucirvāpi yo japet praṇavam sadā
Lipyate na sa pāpena padmapatram ivāmbhasā. 89.

89. Whether (he be) either pure or impure, one who recites oṁ continually is not besmeared by sin, even as the leaf of the lotus (is not wet) by water.[7]

Calevātecalo bindur niścale niścalo bhavet
Yogīsthāṇutvam āpnoti tatovāyum nirodhayet. 90.

---

[1] Three times, past, present, future. Three worlds, three kinds of beings. Three gods, Brahmā, etc.
[2] The consorts of the three gods.
[3] These verses describe groups of three to include *all* in oṁ.
[4] Literally *seed*; = oṁ.
[5] Using postures.
[6] With the mind, meditate on om. These acts should all be done continually.
[7] Water does not cling to the lotus leaf; so sin does not cling to the one who recites oṁ.

90. So long as the air moves, bindu[1] moves; (and) it becomes stationary (when the air) ceases to move. The Yogī should, therefore, control the air (and) obtain immovability.[2]

Yāvad vayuḥsthito dehe tāvajjīvona[3]mucyate.
Maraṇam tasya niṣkrāntistato vāyum nirodhayet. 91.

91. As long as prāṇa remains in the body, life (jīva) does not depart. Its departure (is) death. Therefore, one should become proficient in restraining the prāṇa.

Yāvad baddho maruddehe yāvaccittam nirāmayam
Yāvad dṛṣṭir bhruvor madhye tāvatkālabhayam kutaḥ. 92.

92. As long as prāṇa is held in the body[4], so long consciousness (cittam) (is) free from disease.[5] What cause is there for fear of death so long as the sight (remains fixed) between the eyebrows?

Ataḥ kālabhayād brahmā prāṇāyāmaparāyaṇaḥ
Yogino munayaścāiva tato vāyum nirodhayet. 93.

93. Therefore, from the fear of death, Brahmā (is) intent on prāṇāyāma, as are also Yogīs and sages. Therefore, one should restrain the prāṇa.

Ṣaṭ triṁśadaṅgulohaṁsaḥ prayāṇam kurute bahiḥ
Vāmadakṣiṇamārgeṇa tataḥ prāṇo 'bhidhīyate. 94.

94. The prāṇa[6] goes out to a distance of thirty-six fingers[7] through the left and right nostrils.[8] Therefore it is called prāṇa.

---

[1] *B* gives reading *cittam* as does *HYP*, 2: 2.

[2] Immovability, indifferent to heat and cold, etc.

[3] *B* reads *jīvo* and this has been substituted for *jīva* of *P*.

[4] Held in by kumbakha.

[5] So long is the mind undisturbed.

[6] *Haṁsa* is *prāṇa* + *apāna*.

[7] The degrees of distance are as follows:
naturally—twelve fingers;
sleeping—sixteen fingers;
eating—twenty fingers;
walking—twenty-four fingers;
sound sleep—thirty fingers;
cohabitation—thirty-six fingers. So the verse refers to vajrolī (see chap. sixteen).

[8] Iḍā and piṅglā.

Śuddhim eti yadā sarvam nāḍīcakram malākulam.
Tadāiva jāyate yogī prāṇa saṁgrahaṇe kṣamaḥ. 95.

95. When the whole group of nāḍis, full of secretions, is purified, then indeed the Yogī becomes capable of restraining the prāṇa.

Baddhapadmāsano yogī prāṇam candreṇa pūrayet.
Dhārayiṭvā yathāśakti bhūyaḥ sūryeṇa recayet. 96.

96. Assuming the lotus posture, the Yogī should fill in the prāṇa through the left nostril; then, having held it as long as possible, he should expel it through the right nostril.

Amṛtam dadhisaṅkāśam gokṣīrarajatopamam
Dhyātvā candramaso bimbam prāṇāyāmī sukhībhavet. 97.

97. Having meditated on the circular image of the moon, nectar as white as curds (and) cow's milk, (or) of the colour of purest silver, one practising prāṇāyāmā should find peace.[1]

Dakṣiṇo śvāsamākṛṣya pūrayet udaram śanāiḥ.
Kumbhayitvā vidhānena puraścandreṇa recayet. 98.

98. Having filled in the breath through the right nostril, one should fill the abdomen slowly; having held it according to the rules he should expel (it slowly) through the left nostril.

Prajvalajjvalanajvālāpuñjamādityamaṇḍalam
Dhyātvā nābhisthitam yogī prāṇāyāmī sukhībhavet. 99.

99. Having meditated on the circle of the sun, full of a mass of flame of fire burning very brightly in the navel, the Yogī who practices prāṇāyāma should find peace.

Prāṇam codiḍayā pibet parimitam bhūyo 'nyayārecayet.
Pītvā piṅgalayā samīraṇamatho badhvā tyajet vāmayā.
Sūryācandramasoranena vidhinā bimbadvayam dhyāyataḥ.
Śuddhā nāḍigaṇābhavanti yamino māsatrayādūrdhvataḥ. 100.

100. Meditating in turn on the two images, moon and sun, a (Yogī) should draw in the breath through the left nostril; he should expel it again through the other, according to the limit (of the times already explained): then having drawn in

[1] Meditation is with the breathing control outlined above.

the breath through the right nostril, and having held it, he should expel it through the left nostril. After three months the group of nāḍis of the practicer becomes pure.[1]

Yatheṣṭham dhāraṇam vāyoranalasya pradīpanam
Nādābhivyaktirārogyam jāyate nāḍiśodhanāt. 101.

101. By cleansing the nāḍis the prāṇa (is) restrained as desired, the digestive fire (is) kindled, internal sound[2] is heard (becomes manifest), (and) one becomes diseaseless.

Iti śrīgorakṣa śatakam sampūrnam.

Thus the completion of the one-hundred of Śrī Gorakṣa.

---

[1] This process of breathing is the chief means of cleansing the nāḍis.

[2] First, various kinds of loud sounds are heard, as of hammer, drum, the ocean; then as the practice proceeds, minute sounds are heard, musical, bell, blowing conch, bird, lotus-bee, flute, small bells and bamboo instrument, in the body.

CHAPTER FIFTEEN

MORE IMPORTANT PHYSIOLOGICAL CONCEPTS[1]

THE primary interest of the *Gorakṣaśataka* is with the major parts of the body, the trunk, neck and head.

How can those Yogīs who do not know their own (body) as a house of one column, (with) nine doors, and (as presided over by) five tutelary divinities, attain perfection (in Yoga)?[2]

The nine doors are the seven in the head and the two at the base of the trunk. To these is added as a tenth the hole-in-the-skull, and it is through this that the soul, liberated, escapes. The divinities are Brahmā, Viṣṇu, Rudra, Īśa and Sadāśiva, each of whom is assigned to a particular 'centre'.

More particularly, the system is concerned with the body from the standpoint of the two breaths, the six circles, the three channels, Śakti (Kuṇḍalinī) and Śiva.

The body is pervaded by ten[3] *airs* which are conceived of as vital powers, or functions of the human organism; specifically and particularly of the senses[4] and the involuntary processes, moving in channels, or paths, called nāḍi,[5] which are found in all parts of the body. Five of these airs are of more importance to the Yogī than are the others[6], and of the five two are of special interest; and, finally, prāṇa, as the function

---

[1] Many descriptions of the various physiological aspects of the system of tāntra are to be found. The works of Arthur Avalon give much more detailed accounts than are here set forth.

[2] *P*, verse 14.

[3] *P*, verses 34–37.

[4] Edgerton, *AJP*, 1924, p. 41.

[5] See below. [6] *SS*, 3: 6.

of breathing, is primary.[1] Prāṇa, vāyu and māruta seem to mean not merely air, or breath, but also vital force, the principal of life, vitality, the antithesis of physical or bodily inertness and death. The prāṇa is often identified with the individual soul (jīva). Thc airs are as follows:

1. The *prāṇa* is the breath,[2] having its chief seat in the region of the heart. It is always found in the mouth, the nose, the navel, the kanda and the great toe.[3] It is the most important of all the airs and its control (prāṇāyāma) is fundamental in the Haṭha Yoga. The *Upaniṣads* know a single vital principle (prāṇa) which derives its existence from the self and which superintends the other functions.[4]

2. *Apāna*, the air of the lower part of the trunk, has its chief seat in the rectum.[5] It functions in the voiding of faeces and urine[6] and in other vital forces operating in the various functions of the lower portion of the body. It is found in the rectum, male organ, thighs, knees, lower abdomen, waist, and navel.[7]

3. *Samāna* (*samavāyu*), whose chief seat is the region of the navel, is the function of digestion. This air, or intestinal fire, resides, also, in all the limbs and makes the body dry.[8]

4. *Udāna*, residing in the middle of the throat[9] is the function of speech. It is active also in the hands and feet and causes enlargement of the body.[10]

5. *Vyāna* pervades the whole body[11] and operates in the ears, lips, throat, nose, mouth, cheeks and the navel (*maṇi bandh*).[12]

The other airs are:[13]

Note: *P.* *Gorakṣaśataka*, Poona text. (*GS*)
PC. Commentary on *P.*
SCN. *Ṣaṭcakra Nirūpaṇa* (In *The Serpent Power*).
SP. *The Serpent Power.*
B. Benares manuscript of the *Gorakṣaśataka.*
GP. *Gorakṣa Paddhati.*
CGP. Commentary in *GP.*
HYP. *Haṭhayogapradīpika.*
SS. *Śiva Saṁhita.*

[1] See Keith, *Religion and Philosophy of the Veda*, vol. II, 453 ff.
[2] *P*, 33.
[3] *GP*, p. 20.
[4] See *Das G.*, p. 37.
[5] *P*, 34; *SS*, 3: 7.
[6] *CGP*, p. 34.
[7] *CGP*, p. 20.
[8] *GP*, p. 20.
[9] *P*, 34.
[10] *GP*, p. 20.
[11] *P*, 35.
[12] *GP*, p. 20.
[13] *P*, 35, 36.

6. *Nāga*, which causes eructation;
7. *Kurma*, which functions in winking;
8. *Kṛkara* which causes sneezing or hunger;[1]
9. *Devadatta*, yawning; and
10. *Dhanañjāya*; the air which remains in the body after death.[2] Is this the function of decay?

Prāṇa and apāna 'situated above and below'[3] the diaphragm, are the most important and receive the most attention in the system. They are 'joined' in the navel.[4] To the Yogī the navel is the centre of the body. Apāna is drawn up to the navel, by the prāṇa; and is there united with it (the prāṇa). Prāṇa and apāna alternately draw each other. In pronouncing '*ha*' apāna expels prāṇa; and in pronouncing '*sa*' prāṇa drives down apāna. Thus is described the breathing process and it is conceived of as an expelling and inhaling of the jīva, or soul, which, because of lack of clear insight, identifies itself with the process.[5] It is said that the final going out of prāṇa is the exit of jīva in death. The word, 'haṁsa', derived from the process of breathing (*ha*+*sa*) becomes a mantra, called the ajapa gāyatrī, the unmuttered gāyatrī. So the Yogī 'repeats' this mantra, of incalculable power, continually, twenty-one thousand six hundred times in a day and a night.[6]

In Yoga practice these two, prāṇa and apāna, are to be joined. The knowledge of how this is done is of great importance to Yogīs[7] and belongs to the highest knowledge,[8] delivering from old age and death.[9]

But the texts are more specific about the knowledge that is required of the body. The Yogī should add to his general knowledge (of the body), and of the prāṇas, that of the nāḍis, the six centres, and the sixteen supports (ādhāra).

The vital forces function through the nāḍis,[10] sometimes called channels, or arteries, or fibres. They are paths of power, not gross channels, but subtle lines.[11] They are spoken of as 72,000 in number[12] or as 3,00,000,[13] or as

---

[1] *B*, 33. [2] *P*, 37. [3] *P*, 42–44.
[4] See Brown, *JAOS*, vol. XXXIX, p. 108.
[5] *P*, 42. [6] *P*, 42–44. [7] *P*, 41.
[8] *P*, 45. [9] *HYP*, 2: 47. [10] *P*, 26.
[11] *SP*, p. 115. [12] *P*, 25; *HYP*, 4: 8. [13] *P*, 13.

2,00,000.[1] Among these seventy-two are of considerable importance,[2] but they are not named. The nāḍis are spoken of as a network pervading the body and having their origin in the kanda. They all have their ends (outlets) in the openings of the body. The ten chief nāḍis are *iḍā*, *piṅglā*, *suṣumṇā*, *gāndhārī*, *hastijihvā*, *pūṣā*, *yaśasvinī*, *alambuṣā*, *kūhūś* and *śaṁkhinī*.[3] They terminate respectively in the left nostril, the right nostril, the hole-in-the skull (anterior fontanelle), the left eye, the right eye, the right ear, the left ear, the mouth, the male organ and the anus.[4]

Of these nāḍis the first three are the most important and receive major attention as the paths of the prāṇa. They are of vital importance in prāṇāyāma and the raising of Kuṇḍalinī Śakti. The first two are subordinate to the third, through which, by Yoga, prāṇa is supposed to pass by way of the various centres out of the body through the brahmarandhra.

Iḍā, piṅglā and suṣumṇā are called respectively moon (candra, śaśī), sun (Sūrya, mihra) and fire (agni);[5] and Gaṅgā, Jumnā and Sarasvatī.[6] Iḍā is feminine, piṅglā is masculine. They both indicate *Kāla* (death) and suṣumṇā devours Kāla.[7] Iḍā was the universal mother, the mother Earth.[8]

Suṣumṇā is called also *brahmanāḍī* (The Brahma-channel),[9] *Śūnyapadavī* (path-of-non-existence, empty-path), *brahmarandhra* (hole-in-the-skull), *mahāpatha* (the-great-highway), *śmaśāna* (burial-ground), *śāmbhavī* (Durgā; sacred to Śiva), *madhyamārga* (middle-path), and *śaktimārga* (path of śaktī).[10] It is identified with the spinal cord,[11] and is said to extend from the mūlādhāra to the vacuum below the hole-in-the skull. It is the path of enjoyment, in which male and female unite.

Iḍā and piṅglā arising in the left and right scrotum (?) (kanda) ascend alternating from left to right, having thus gone around or through, all the centres ('proceeding spirally they meet the

---

[1] *GP*, 13. [2] *P*, 26. For other estimates see *SP*, p. 130. *Śiva Saṁsitā* speaks of fourteen as important.
[3] *P*, 27, 28. [4] *P*, 29, 30, 31. [5] *P*, 32; *SCN*, p. 4.
[6] *HYP*, 3: 51. [7] *SP*, p. 131.
[8] *JRAS* (1890), p. 344. Dr. G. W. Brown pointed out that *iḍā* is Dravidian for 'left.' [9] *CP*, *HYP*, 2: 46.
[10] *HYP*, 3: 4; *SCN*, p. 145. [11] So *DHIP*, vol. II, p. 354. *SS*, 5.121.

suṣumṇā in each cakra') and proceed to the space between the eyebrows, where they form a plaited knot with suṣumṇā and thence continue to the left and right nostrils. They also form a plaited knot with suṣumṇā in the kanda. They are pale, moon-coloured, and lustrous red, sun-coloured, respectively.'[1]

Suṣumṇā, the chief channel, lies between iḍā and piṅglā. It is the path of the Kuṇḍalinī.[2] The door at the lower end of the suṣumṇā is called brahmadvāra.[3] The suṣumṇā is threefold in its constitution; its inner fibre, very subtle, is the pale nectar-giving *citriṇīnāḍī*, the *brāhmānāḍī*.

The channels are conceived of as full of impurities or secretions.[4]

> The Nāḍis should be cleansed of their impurities by performing the mudrās, etc. (which are the the practices relating to the air) āsanas, kumbhakas and various curious mudrās.[5]

Other means also are used. For special persons, those in whose channels is an excess of fats and phlegm a special set of six duties (*ṣaṭkarmāṇi*) is enjoined.[6] In the cleaning of the paths prāṇāyāma is the chief agent.

When the channels have been cleansed the body becomes lean and of a glowing colour, the health is good, the appetite is strong,[7] divine sounds are heard (a most desirable state), and prāṇāyāma can be performed effectively, namely, Kuṇḍalinī can be raised (the aim of the Haṭha Yoga).[8]

The lotuses, circles, wheels, centres, vital stations (padma cakra, ādhāra) may be conceived of as positions or locations in the body where various aspects of vital force reside. They are often identified with the ganglia at various levels along the spinal cord; but this may not be accurate. They are not in the plexuses, but in the spinal column.[9] They are

---

[1] *SCN*, pp, 5, 6.
[2] *GP*, p. 19; *SCN*, p. 4.
[3] *HYP*, 4: 18. See below.
[4] *P*, 95.
[5] *HYP*, 1: 58.
[6] *HYP*, 2: 21, i; 2: 22.
[7] *HYP*, 2: 20.
[8] *HYP*, 2: 19; 2: 20.
[9] *SP*, p. 76. I find that Dasgupta, in the second volume of his *History of Indian Philosophy*, takes this position. He says:
'How far the *cakras* can themselves be called nerve-plexuses is very doubtful, since the nerve-plexuses are all outside the spinal aperture; but if the *kuṇḍalinī* is to pass through the aperture of the *citriṇī nāḍī* and at the same time pass through the *cakras*, the *cakras* or the lotuses (*padma*) must be inside the spinal cord. . . . A nerve-

most complicated in their symbolism and are not easy to describe. Conceived of as stations along the suṣumṇā, which passes through them, they are viewed in relation to the successive positions which Kuṇḍalinī reaches in her ascent to the place of Śiva. From the standpoint of creation, each padma may be conceived of as a place of union of Śakti and Śiva, each having within itself both male and female, divinities and forces. Each, except the last, may be viewed as a microcosm, containing all the forces of creation. Besides, each contains the union symbol of the yoni-liṅga, in triangle and liṅga, or letter and bindu, crescent and circle. They are described as lotuses (padma) with varying numbers of petals, each leaf having its letter, called bīja with bindu, and all drawn with symbolic use of colour, and mythical animals. The various figures, triangles, squares, and the like belong to yantra, the letters with their bindus to mantra. The latter as (mantras) are to be meditated upon in turn proceeding from right to left.

The circles, or lotuses, are a characteristic element in the Yogī's conception of the Haṭha Yoga. The lotuses, except the last are also called *Pīṭhas*,[1] and are seats of Śakti.

The names and locations of the various cakras, beginning with the lowest, are as follows:[2]

1. *Mūlādhāra*, at the base of the spinal column.
2. *Svādhiṣṭhāna*, at the root of the male organ, or the male organ.[3]
3. *Maṇipūraka*, in the region of the navel.
4. *Anāhata*, the heart lotus.
5. *Viśuddha*, in the throat.
6. *Ājñā*, between the eyebrows, within the skull.

Related to these most intimately are two other regions of the body, the kanda and the brahmarandhra; the former in the lower part of the abdomen, the source of all the nāḍis, the latter at the anterior fontanelle.

---

physical interpretation of them as nerve-plexuses would be unfaithful to the texts.' P. 356. Quoted by permission of Macmillan and Company, Publishers.

[1] See note under Devī Pātan in chap. five.

[2] The descriptions are based for the most part upon *P*, *SP*, *CGP* *CP* and *SP*.

[3] *P*, 22.

The lower five are counted as centres of the five forms of matter—earth, water, fire, air and ether, each with its appropriate letter with its bindu, known as its bīja mantra, and its colour. At the top of the head (brahmarandhra) is the blissful abode of Paramaśiva-Śakti.

As centres of characteristic vital forces, the cakras become the objects of concentration of thought or of fixed attention and in them are to be discovered the mysteries of creation and the psychic energies of Kundalinī. Not only does each centre contain a special form of substance and power but also of bliss or of ecstatic experience.

The mūlādhara,[1] is also called *ādhāra*, *gudādhra*, *gudasthāna*, *bhumaṇḍalā*, *mūlacakra*, and is described as located in the *gudadvāra*, 'the door of the anus.' Moreover it is attached to the mouth of the suṣumṇā thus being the lower doorway of the brahmarandra, or suṣumṇā. This ādhāra is the principal seat of the apāna. It consists of a lotus with four petals, red in colour, upon which are the golden letters वं, शं, षं, सं (v, ś, ṣ and s, with their bindus), which are objects for meditation.

In the centre of the lotus is a yellow square, surrounded by eight shining spears, the emblem of earth (*Pṛthivi*). The tips of the spears are shaped like a woman's breasts.

In the centre of the square is a red triangle resting on its apex, symbolizing the yoni, and called Kāmarūpa. It is described also as the triangular place of fire, looking like burnished gold, that by which kāma is felt. In the yoni stands the self-existent liṅga, with its disc of light like a jewel, around which is coiled eight times, and shining like lightning, Kuṇḍalinī. She is asleep closing with her mouth (head, face) the aperture of the liṅga. Here in particular is the brahmadvāra where she drinks nectar, and produces words, or is the source of sounds. She is to be meditated upon, here, as a girl of sixteen in full bloom (*Bālasūndarī*). Moreover, she is the support of the body as *Śeṣā* of the earth. On the triangle rests the bīja, or seed, or charm of the cakra, the letter ळं (*l*, *laṅg*), yellow in colour, the bīja-mantra

---

[1] *mūla*, root; *guda*, anus; *bhū*, earth; *dvāra*, door; *sthāna*, place; *maṇḍla*, circle.

of earth and also of Indra. The tip of the bīja rests on the elephant of Indra. In the bindu or dot of this letter is the four-headed, four-armed Brahmā, shining like 10,000,000 suns, seated on a haṁsa, or swan. By his side is Dākiṇī Śakti. She is a terrible form of Kālī, who feeds on human flesh; and who casts the evil eye upon children causing them to pine and die, by consuming their livers. She carries in her four hands a spear, a staff with a human skull, a sword and a cup of wine. She is fierce and plump, and is clad in a black antelope's skin. She is sitting on a lotus.

Svādhiṣṭhāna, is also called *jalamaṇḍala*, because its tattva or form of matter is water (*jala*). It is also known as *meḍhrādhāra*.[1] This centre is at the root of the male organ, some say that organ itself. The lotus consists of six petals of a reddish colour bordering on orange, upon which are written in gold the letters बं, भं, मं, यं, रं, लं (b, bh, m, y, r, and l each with its bindu). Within this cakra is a white half-moon, luminous as the autumn moon, and within this the watery region of Varuṇa. Some say that the moon has an eight-petalled lotus on each side of it. The central bīja is वं (*v vaṅg*), the bīja-mantra of Varuṇa, in white, resting on a *makara*, a legendary creature, a fabulous sea-monster, resembling an aligator, the vehicle of Kāma. In the bindu sits the four-armed Viṣṇu, luminous, blue-coloured, dressed in yellow, wearing the *svastika*, a garland, and the great jewel, both luminous. He holds the conch, discus, mace and lotus in his hands and is seated on Garuḍa. Within the circle of the moon, and associated with Viṣṇu, is the Goddess Śākinī[2] seated on a red, double lotus. She is a demon attendant of Kālī, blue in colour. In her four hands she holds a trident, a lotus, a drum and a battle axe. She is three-eyed, ferocious in aspect, showing her teeth (fangs), while a streak of blood issues from one of her nostrils. She is a wish-granter, and is exalted with the nectar. Prāṇa, which arises with the syllable *sva*, rests in this cakra and represents the *paraliṅga*.

Between the two cakras, the mūlādhāra and the svādhiṣṭhāna is the yonisthāna, spoken of as the image of desire. It is the

---

[1] *Meḍhra*, the liṅga.

[2] *GP*, p. 15. *Śiva Saṁhitā* says Rākiṇī.

four-fingered space between the anus and the root of the male organ, described as two fingers-breadth from each of them. It is further characterized as the place of Śiva-Śakti, the place of enjoyment, and as Kāmarūpa. In part, at least, this seems to be identified with the triangle of the mūlādhāra.[1] Its position, as here described, must involve the idea that the body contains within itself both aspects of the creative power, reminiscences of the thought of ardhanārī. The place is sometimes spoken of as the Gāurīpīṭha.

The *maṇipūraka*, also called *nābhiṣṭhana*, *ravisthāna*, *sūryasthāna*[2], is situated in the region of the navel. It contains ten blue petals, with the letters ḍं, ढं, णं, तं, थं, दं, धं, नं, पं, फं, (ḍ, ḍh, ṇ, t, th, d, dh, n, p, ph, also in blue, each with its bindu). It is the seat of the element fire, of the sun, and of the samāna. In the centre of the circle is a read triangle, bordered by three svastikas and containing the bīja-mantra रं (*r*, *raṅg)*[3] also in red. This centre is also viewed as the seat of rajas, the menstrual fluid,[4] and, as the sun, the cakra is said to soak up the nectar (bindu) from the moon. The bīja rests on a ram, radiant like the rising sun. Sitting above the triangle is Mahārudra, red in colour, but white with ashes, three-eyed, with hands extended to grant boons, or to dispel fear (*vara-* and *abhyamudrās*). He is the destroyer of creation. In one hand he holds a rudrākṣa rosary, in the other a weapon. He is seated on a bull. Beside him is Lākinī Śakti, blue in colour, four-handed, seated on a red lotus. She carries in her hands a thunderbolt, and a weapon of fire, while the other two hands are in gesture as are Rudra's. Her breasts are ruddy with blood and fat which drip from her mouth. She is fond of meat and of rice and of *dal* cooked and mixed with meat and blood.

The circle, or lotus, of the heart is called *anāhata*, *hṛdasthāna*.[5] Its name suggests the *sabdha brahma* (sound) which is heard, produced without striking two things together. It is the seat of the prāṇa, and the puruṣa or jīvātman, and includes,

---

[1] *PC* 18 so places it. [2] *Nābhi*, navel; *ravi*, sun; *sūrya*, sun.
[3] Raṅg is the seed-mantra of fire. [4] The kanda is conceived of as in the region described as the navel and is the place of fire symbolized by the yoni. [5] *Hṛda*, heart.

according to the *Upaniṣads*, both heart and lungs. Its element is air. The lotus consists of twelve petals of a golden colour, upon which are the letters, कं, खं, गं, घं, ङं·, चं, छं, जं, झं, ञं, टं, ठं (k, kh, g, gh, c, ch, j, jh, ñ, ṭ, ṭh, each with its bindu, and all painted red). The circle is bright-red in colour; within this is a double triangle, smoke-coloured, in the centre of which is a golden triangle containing a liṅga, bright like shining gold, with a white crescent in its head, above which is a bindu. The bīja-mantra of this cakra is यं (*y*, *yaṅg*), black, resting on an antelope. Above the double triangle, but within the circle sits Īśvara with hands in gesture for granting boons and dispelling fear. The god is three-eyed. With him is associated Kākinī Śakti with two hands as Īśvara, her other two containing a noose and a skull. She is yellow in appearance, happy (that is, in excited mood), auspicious, three-eyed, benefactress. Her heart is softened from drinking the nectar. She sits on a red lotus and wears the skin of a black antelope. This lotus is the seat of desires, of the *saṁskāras* or records of deeds, and of the egoizing faculty. It contains also the celestial wishing-tree bestowing more than the suppliant desires. (But below the *anāhata* is a small eight-petalled, red lotus containing the wishing-tree, considered also as the seat of the *iṣṭha devatā* wandering among trees laden with fruit, flowers, and birds. It is called the *ānandakanda*.)[1] When the *manas* is completely restrained or fixed in the heart, the Yogī attains consciousness of identity with Śiva.

In the throat, or at its base, is the cakra called *Viśuddha*, *kaṇṭhadeśa*,[2] *candrasṭhāna*, *jālandharpīṭha*, *bhāratiṣṭhāna*. Another name, derived from the fact that the *khecarimudrā* is performed there, is *vyomacakra*. It is also called the *nābhomaṇḍala*. It is the residence of udāna. Its element is ether. *It is the seat of* bindu. This lotus contains sixteen petals, of a smoky-purple colour, containing the crimson letters अं, आं, इं, ईं, उं, ऊं, ऋं, ॠं, ऌं, ॡं, एं, ऐं, ओं, औं, अं, अः (a, ā, i, u, ū, ṛ, ḷ, e, ai, o, au, and the two breathings a, ā, each with its bindu). These are all the vowels. Within the circle of the petals is

---

[1] *SCN*, pp. 58, 59.

[2] *Kaṇṭha*, throat; *deśa*, place; *candra*, moon.

the blue field of *ākāśa*, space, and within this, again, a crystal-white triangle, within which is a pure circle of the moon which contains a white elephant. Upon the beast rests the bīja-mantra of this cakra, हं (*h*, *haṅg*, the symbol of ether, ākāśa). In the bindu of the bīja is Sadāśiva,[1] with body half silver, half gold, seated on a bull. He is five-faced, three-eyed in each, covered with ashes, having a tiger's skin and a garland of snakes. He carries in his several hands a trident, an axe, a sword, a *vajra* (thunderbolt), dahana (fire?), a bell, a goad, a noose, and shows auspicious gestures. With him is Gāurī, Sadāgāurī, who is one-half of Śiva's body, with ten beautiful arms, five faces each with three eyes. She has a noose, a goad and a book, and is in auspicious gesture. She is seated on bones. (Or, he is accompanied by Śākinī, in yellow raiment, carrying in her four hands a bow, an arrow, a noose and a goad.) She is 'white.'

The ājñā is also called the uḍḍiyāṇa and the *jñāna*-lotus. It is situated between the eyebrows, and back of them, and consists of two white petals on which are the letters हं and क्षं (h, and kṣ variegated in colour and with their bindus). They are the bījas of kalās. *Kalā*, a digit or one-sixteenth of the moon's diameter, refers to Siva as bearing one-sixteenth of the moon. This cakra is the seat of the buddhi, ahaṁkāra, manas and the *indṛyas* (the sensory and motor functions), all in subtle state. It is the circle of command over movements. It is the place of uninterrupted bliss. The circle of this lotus is white and within it is a white triangle containing a white liṅga called *itara* liṅga. Here is Paramaśiva.[2] The bīja-mantra of this *cakra* is ॐ (oṁ). As the inner ātma this oṁ is pure mind, buddhi, like a flame. Above it is the crescent moon, above that the biṇdu from makāra (m) and still higher the half crescent moon. The goddess of this lotus is Hākinī, six-faced, like so many moons, with six arms bearing a book, a skull, a drum, a rosary and with two hands extending in auspicious gesture. She is seated on a white lotus, drinking ambrosia.

Each of these circles is described by Gheraṇḍa as a dhāraṇā and the characteristic effect of fixed attention on each is noted.

---

[1] *Sadā*, eternal. [2] *Parama*, the highest.

Two other centres are included in the scheme, the kanda and the *sahasrāra*.

The former, the kanda, is called also kandayoni and nāḍicakra. Descriptions are contradictory and do not make clear just what is meant and it has been suggested that it is the uterus, or the testes. It is spoken of as the meeting place, or the origin, of all the nāḍis, the place whence all the vital airs flow. It is shaped like an egg, and above it Kuṇḍalinī is coiled eight times and is asleep. It lies between the anus and the root of the *meḍhra* (male organ). And, again, it is said that it is strung on the suṣumṇā in the *maṇipūraka*. It is clearly close to the source of creative forces. Dr. Dasgupta says:

> Other accounts of these *nāḍīs* hold that the *iḍā* proceeds from the the right testicle and the *piṅglā* from the left testicle and passes on the left and right of the *suṣūmṇā* in a bent form (*dhanur ākāre*). The three, however, meet at the root of the penis, which is thus regarded as the meeting of the three rivers. . . .[1]

The final goal of the Kuṇḍalinī Yoga is the top of the head, the brahmasthāna, brahmarandhra, known as the hole-in-the-skull, the *nirvāṇacakra* (circle where release is achieved), *mahāpatha* (the great path of release). It is the place of final bliss (*brahmānanda*). It is situated above the end of the suṣumṇā. Because it is a lotus of 1,000 petals it is called *sahasrāra*. It has its head downwards, and its clustered filaments are tinged with the colour of the young sun. Each of the petals has upon it a letter of the alphabet, and they are recorded on the leaves and read from right to left, 50 × 20 = 1,000, one-thousand letters in all, each with its bindu; within this lotus is the full moon, resplendent as the clear sky, moist with nectar. And within this is a triangle, and in this the great void shines *Śūnya* (void) which is the subtle bindu, which is *para* bindu, which is Īśvara, having as its centre the abode of Brahma. Above the bindu, in the aperture is Saṁkinī, the goddess who creates, maintains and destroys. Within this lotus is the full moon, resplendent as the clear sky, moist

[1] *DHIP*, vol. II, p. 354. Quoted by permission of the Macmillan Company, Publishers.

with nectar. Here is experience of final union, *unmanī*, where the bond of attachment with the world is cut and the bliss of release is enjoyed. Here Śiva stands, free from all illusion, with Nirvāṇaśakti. In the triangle in the sahasrāra are three bindus; the हं (*haṅg*), the male, the other two in the form of *sa* which is *Prakṛiti.* The two bindus make up the third as *visārga* (:) so that their union is haṁsaḥ. The divine form here is one-half of Śiva (*Śivārdha*) united with nāda which calls or draws out bindu. Below this level are the forms of creative union in cakras down to mūlādhāra. But here is the undivided origin of all dual forms. This high place is, viewing the Kuṇḍalinī as she moves upwards, the level of dissolution. Śakti here is nirvāṇaśakti. The fruit of 'knowledge' of sahasrāra is final bliss.

The cakras which the Hindus mention are numerou but those already enumerated are the principle ones. Under the name of *ādhāras*, seats of vital functions, they are objects of meditation. The word is said to mean 'container.'[1] The list of sixteen as supplied by the commentary[2] to the Poona edition of the *Gorakṣaśataka*, together with their positions, which includes those already described is[3] as follows: (1) *Pādaṅgusthādhāra* (great toe); (2) *Mūlādhāra* (anus); (3) *Gudādhāra* (rectum); (4) *Meḍhrādhāra* (liṅga); (5) *Uḍḍiyānādhāra* (above the navel); (6) *Nābhyādhāra* (navel); (7) *Hṛdayādhāra* (heart); *Kaṇṭhādhāra* (throat); (9) *Ghaṇṭikādhāra* (soft palate); (10) *Tatvādhāra* (in soft palate); (11) *Jihvamūlādhāra* (root of the tongue); (12) *Urdhvadantamūlādhāra* (root of upper front teeth); (13) *Nāsāgrādhāra* (tip of the nose); (14) *Bhrumadhyādhāra* (a point between the eyebrows); (15) *Lalatādhāra* (forehead); (16) *Brahmarandhrādhāra* (top of head).[4]

---

[1] *SCN*, p. 80.

[2] To verse 13.

[3] They are supplied from the *Siddha-Siddhānta-Paddhati*.

[4] In the detailed accounts a number of cakras are described which occupy the space between these. Paṇḍit Gopi Nāth Kavirāj, in *The Princess of Wales Sarasvati Bhavana Studies* (in 1923), enumerates and describes a number which he found illustrated in an old coloured chart. The list agrees only in part with the ordinary ones.

A list with their names is given in *Haṭhayogapradīpika* (3: 72, note), and still another list is given in the *Gorakṣa-Paddhati* (comment on verse 13). In general, it may be said that these lists refer to the same portions of the body, the descriptive terms varying.[1]

The books give some attention to the dhātus or secretions of the body, whose removal, or drying up, or conservation is desired. They are seven in number, the skin, blood, flesh, fat, bone, marrow and seed. They include the five elements which co-operate to uphold the body.

The union of bindu and rajas is the aim of the Yoga; and, although it is difficult to achieve, its realization is the highest state. The place of union is of the highest importance. Bindu is of two kinds, pale-white and blood-red,[2] and is the root or cause of the body.[3] Its conservation is both the protection and the preservation of the body. Primarily bindu as pale-white is the semen virile,[4] the circular image of the moon, nectar, white as cow's milk, curds and silver. It is the product of the moon and is distilled to the left of the space between the eyebrows. Its seat is in the hollow above the throat, the *Vyoma* çakra, also described as the hole at the upper end of the suṣumṇā.[5] Thence it naturally proceeds down through the suṣumṇā to the place of fire, in the mūlā-dhāra, or in the nābhiṣṭhana, where it is consumed. For this reason the khecarīmudrā (see next chapter) is performed to hold the bindu in its native station; and other devices are used to cause it to return after it has actually gone down. It is Śiva. The conservation and control of the bindu is of great importance.

Rajas is the menstrual fluid. Its source, or station, is in the place of the sun, the circle of the sun full of a mass of flame, very bright, in the navel. It is Śakti.[6] It is rajas that drinks the *soma* (= bindu) falling from the moon. The symbolism of the descriptions represents the creative act according to the philosophy of the Śāktas, and the energy of the soul in the various levels or cakras, where the two principles are brought together.

---

[1] See also *SCN*, p. 80. [2] *P*, 72. [3] *P*, 68.
[4] *P*, 72. [5] *HYP*, 3: 51. [6] *P*, 71, 73, 74, 76, 99.

> *Kutilāṅgī* (crooked-bodied), *Kuṇḍalinī* (coiled), *Bhujaṅgī* (she-serpent), *Śakti*, *Īśwarī*, *Kuṇḍalī* (coiled), and *Arundhatī*—these words are synonymous.[1]

All the Yoga practice refers to Kuṇḍalinī.[2] She is described as coiled eight times around the liṅga, like a serpent, asleep, with her head (mouth) closing its aperture completely: Iyanger says three and one-half times. She is Śakti, Parameśvarī, the Infant Widow and Tapasvinī (female ascetic). Her place is between the guda and the liṅga. She is in all the mantras, *e.g.*, in all the letters, in all the lotuses, since the letters are her manifestations. She is the supreme Śakti active in both man and in the universe as prakṛti. She is best described in connection with her functions in the practice of Yoga which are set forth in the next chapter.

Importance is attached to the knots (*granthi*) the chief of which are the plaitings of the nāḍis in the kanda and in the ājñā. The total number is fourteen. The cakras contain some of them, Brahmā in the anāhata and Rudra in the ājñā. The knot in the ājñā is called *tribeṇī*.

Five sheaths (*vyoman*) are also mentioned. They are *ākāśā*, *prākāśa*, *mahākāśa*, *sattvākāśa*, and *sūryakāśa*. They refer to realms of experience. The commentary on verse thirteen of the Poona edition points out that the Yogī should know and meditate upon these. They are described in turns as freedom from impurities, like great darkness, like destroying fire, one's real form, and the sun shining like a thousand suns. They are also described from above down through the cakras to the mūladhāra. In this case the first is white, the second red, the third like fire, the fourth is blue and the fifth like lightning. By looking at these (vyoman) one becomes like the sky. Ākāśa in the viśuddha is the sheath of liberation. They (vyoman) are the substances of the cakras.

In recent times efforts have been made to relate the physiology of the Haṭha Yoga to that of present-day science. Notably, Dr. Brajendranath Seal, in his *The Primitive Science of the Ancients*,[3] has attempted, in the chapter on 'Hindu Physiology and Biology,' to identify the cakras with the

---

[1] *HYP*, 3 : 97. [2] *HYP*, 3 : 1.

[3] London, 1915.

plexuses of the human body. Previous to that[1] Major B. D. Basu, I.M.S., worked on the same problem. A recent, elaborate comparison of Haṭha Yoga physiology with modern anatomical science is found in the little book, *The Mysterious Kundalini*, by Dr. Vasant G. Rele.[2] This author, who is interested in explaining the effects or accomplishments of Yoga from the standpoint of modern physiology, identifies the prāṇas with the nervous energies, the five chief airs being the five important subsidiary nerve centres in the brain and spinal cord; the cakras with the plexuses, involving both spinal and cerebro-spinal automatic nervous systems; suṣumṇā, iḍā and pinglā with the sympathetic system; the nectar from the moon (bindu) with the cerebro-spinal fluid; the śaktis of the various cakras with the fibres connecting them with the spinal nervous system; and brahmarandhra with the cavity in the skull. Particularly does he connect the plexuses with the cerebro-cranial automatic nervous system and the Kuṇḍalinī with the right vagus nerve.[3] His position is that by means of the Yogic methods, prāṇāyāma, bandha and mudrā, the Yogī gains control of the automatic nervous system, especially that portion of it which controls the involuntary vital activities related to the plexuses. In this way does the author explain the voluntary control which the Yogī exercises over consciousness and his ability to produce trance and self-hybernation. Ecstatic experiences which occur, as plexus after plexus comes under control of the Yogī, are described by Dr. Rele as follows:[4]

A Yogī when he develops his automatic nervous system, becomes so engrossed in it that the somatic functions of his *Suṣumṇā nāḍi* and the knowledge of the relation with the eternal world are held in abeyance and he sees his own self which pervades the whole universe and becomes one with it. . . . When this *Kulakuṇḍalinī* is awakened or made active, it forces a passage through the different

[1] See *Guy's Hospital Gazetteer*, London, 1889, and Foreword to *SBH*, vol. XV, pt. 4, 1915.

[2] Bombay, 1927 (Third Edition, 1931).

[3] Pp. 39, 47, 101, 110. Dr. Dasgupta (*DHIP*, vol. II, p. 356) says: '*Kuṇḍalinī* itself cannot be called a nerve and it is distinctly wrong to call it the vagus nerve, as Mr. Rele does.' Quoted by permission of Macmillan and Company, Publishers.

[4] Pp. 39, 47, 101, 110.

cakras and excites them to action, and as it rises step by step, the mind becomes opened and all visions and wonderful powers come to the Yogī, when it reaches the brain. The Yogī then is perfectly detached from the body and the mind, and the soul finds itself free in all respects. . . . When a Yogī becomes a perfect adept in the control of *Kuṇḍalinī* . . . the soul is free to move out of the Brahmarandhra, in which it was kept in captivity, and occupies a bigger cavity surrounding the brain and the spinal cord known as *Ākāśa,* and becomes absorbed in the infinite intelligence from which it emanated. The Yogī, when in this state of *Nirvikalpa-samādhi,* identifies himself with that which he contemplates, and acquires certain supernatural powers. . . . I would, therefore, define *Kuṇḍalinī-Yoga* as a science of physical and mental exercises of a particular form by which an individual establishes a conscious control over his automatic nervous system, to be in tune with the Infinite.

CHAPTER SIXTEEN

CHIEF AIMS AND METHODS[1]

THE Kuṇḍalinī Yoga makes large use of the doctrine of the union of Śiva and Śakti; that is, it swings around the idealization of the experience of the ecstasy that arises in creative union. From the lowest centre (the mūlādhāra) to the place of final bliss (in the sahasrāra), each level, conceived of as a place of enjoyment, is symbolically the station of a god and a goddess; and at each of the stages in her ascent, the Śakti drinks the nectar of the crescent moon. Back and above this dual concept is that of the ardhanārī. The discipline of the Yoga, in so far as it concerns the lifting of Kuṇḍalinī from her place in the mūlādhāra to the region of the bindu, the nectar of the moon, which lies in the hollow above the throat, may be described as a series of manipulations of bodily functions, physical exercises and with accompanying mental concentrations, whose physical and psychical reactions are interpreted in supernatural terms as enjoyment of the Lord (Śiva) by Śakti. The thrills, or ecstasies, engendered by excitations all along the suṣumṇā, are regarded as religious experiences.[1] In this aspect of the system the female creative energy is raised to higher and higher levels in the body and experiences of union in succeeding cakras become more and more subtle.

Since the analogy is that of the union of Śakti with Śiva, the physical union of man and woman, when the former, at least, is a Yogī of advanced powers, becomes of great significance. The disciplines of the Haṭha Yoga enable the adept to reverse the process of nature, so as to detain the bindu in

---

[1] In this chapter descriptions of the various processes are limited to the more important details, sufficient only to illustrate the method and the results of Haṭha Yoga.

its original receptacle, or to draw it back, along with rajas, after the actual union. The former aspect of the case is illustrated by the following statement.

By whom the hollow *in the top* of the throat is sealed by *Khecari*, his *bindu*, even (though he be) embraced by a woman, does not fall.[1]

And the other aspect of the discipline may be considered from the point of view of *vajrolī* and similar practices as described below. There is here either a stoppage of the natural function or its ultimate reversal.

So, while there is a discipline which concerns itself simply with the body of the adept, there is also the method of some aspect or other of the vāmacāra. The union of male and female may be of equal significance with the more subtle discipline for the ends of the Yoga, and may symbolize the union of Śiva and Śakti. But, in this case, adepts are careful to point out that for the truly prepared alone is this form of the ritual profitable for the highest experience; for they only are able to retain the bindu or to draw up the bindu-rajas so that the act of coition becomes not a procreative act but an experience in the seat of Śiva. As will appear later, special disciplines look to this reversal of nature. In other words, this discipline is for those only who are ripe for release, for men of great attainments, useful and deserving.[2] Furthermore, so exacting is this process, that it is impossible for the Yogī to work out the whole of the discipline in a single incarnation. Consequently, those who are actually carrying out the practices are adepts who have already arrived at its final stages through the practice of Haṭha Yoga in a series of lives lived under conditions favourable to ultimate success in Yoga.[3] Undisciplined, untaught men perform these acts to their own degradation and ultimate destruction.

Āsana, mudrā and bandha may be looked upon as types of physical exercise whose aim is a healthful development of the body and the proper stimulation of the seminal (or ovarian)

---

[1] *GŚ*, 69. [2] *PC*, 9.

[3] *HYP*, p. ii. In the *Garuḍa Purāṇa* it is stated that the stages in the development of the Yoga are: being born a woman; then, as a Śūdra, a Vāiṣya and a Brāhman devoid of mercy; then, gradual improvement to the stage of Yogī and jñānī.—Iyangar, *HYP*, p. 73.

glands. Always it must be rememberd that *loss of the bindu* leads to disease, old age and death. It is claimed that these disciplines contribute to the retention and assimilation of bindu, yielding both vitality and victory over death itself.

The system rests, further, upon the conception of the female principle, or power, as ultimately the formative, or creative, energy of the universe; and upon the interpretation of physical and psychical experiences as the realization of the divine creative union. The trance, or unconsciousness, which is the outcome of prolonged effort, is the samādhi which transcends duality. The ecstasy bordering on samādhi is often sheerly sensual. In fact, there is plenty of authority for the statement that physical union is the way to release.

In the accounts in the text-books of the Haṭha Yoga, the two aspects of the discipline, that which deals wholly with matters within the physical frame, and that which involves two individuals are so interwoven, and the shifting from one to the other is so frequent and abrupt, that it is sometimes difficult to separate them.

In the terminology of the Haṭha Yoga, the two elements whose union is sought are the sleeping, female serpent (Kuṇḍalinī) resting with her head in the aperture of the male organ and the bindu lodged in the hollow of the throat. *She* drinks the nectar where she is, or is to be, drawn upwards (by means of prāṇāyāma and other disciplines) through this, the brahmadvāra, to higher centres, finally to the seat of bindu. She may enjoy the nectar at any of the stations along the suṣumṇā although the aim is union in the highest place. But, in all cases she drinks the nectar of the moon. In order that Kuṇḍalinī may appropriate the bindu she must be aroused and moved, and, for this purpose, āsana, prāṇāyāma, mudrā, bandha and the other exercises are employed.

It is further to be noted that behind all this is the age-long Indian view of the misery of the world, involved in all creation, which is to be removed in the final achievement of samādhi.[1]

---

[1] J. Ghosh, in *A Study of Yoga*, p. 330, says: 'The Yogī seeks elimination of misery and that alone.' Does he not seek *bliss* also?

And again, as the various levels of union are reached, as Kuṇḍalinī is lifted, supernormal powers of differing kinds are attained. But the higher and more subtle forms both of power and of experience are the aim of the adept.

Before proceeding with details of the discipline, it may be well to state in another form its aims and methods:

A. Aims:

(1) Immobility of body and of mental processes by āsana, mudrā, bhanda and prāṇāyāma.

(2) Retention of the breath.

(3) Retention of the bindu.

(4) The ecstatic experiences of the union of rajas (Kuṇḍālinī) and bindu (Śiva) at various levels in the body.

(5) Supernormal powers.

(6) Final release.

B. And to these ends:

(1) Cleansing of the nāḍis.

(2) Breath control.

(3) Āsana, mudrā and bhanda.

(4) Miscellaneous practices.

In the first place, the strenuous (haṭha) physical exercises of this system aim at health and vigour of body, without which the Yogī would be unable to carry out the whole of the difficult discipline and arrive at success. Consequently, attention is given to food and environment. Diet should be sparing.[1] Food should be very soft, sweet, good tasting,[2] and the Yogī should drink milk and abstain from bitter, acid and salty food.[3] He should limit his meal to three-fourths of a stomach-full, leaving one-fourth of the space for the passing of the prāṇa (in the exercise of prāṇāyāma). The books go into considerable detail about 'good' and 'bad' food. The former should be well-cooked with ghi, rice, wheat, barley, sugar, butter, white-honey, ginger-root and some fruits and vegetables. On the other hand foods to be avoided are those highly spiced, some green vegetables, fermented and oily food, those mixed with till and rape seed, intoxicating liquors, fish, meat, curds, *chassa*, pulses, plums,

[1] *P*, 54. [2] *P*, 55. [3] *P*, 53.

oil-cake, asafœtida, garlic, onions and so forth;[1] also foods heated a second time, dry foods, minor grains and vegetables that cause a burning sensation.[2]

The Yogī should choose a small room, in a solitary place, comfortable and clean, 'in a secluded place, in a country governed by a dutiful rāja, in a land of plenty and free from disturbance.'

He must be chaste and a renouncer of worldly pleasures; fire, women, travelling, and so forth should be shunned;[3] likewise the society of evil men.[4] He should avoid also early rising, the cold bath, fasting and bodily exertion;[5] and he must have a guru, or spiritual guide. As the *Śiva Saṁhitā* puts it, only the instruction imparted by a guru by word of mouth is of use (3: 11).

In considering the details of this Yoga it is necessary to note in all cases the bearing of the practices upon physical and mental excitements and upon the reactions to them. The immobility of mind and body is sought through high tension.

The chief postures (āsanas) are kamalāsana (padmāsana) and siddhāsana. The second is often spoken of as the best, the only necessary one, and is as its name implies, 'the perfect' āsana. Of these the first two are described in turn as follows:

(The [Yogī] should press firmly the heel of the (left) foot against the perineum (and) the (right) heel just above the male organ, keeping the body fixedly erect, immovable; the senses under control; and with motionless gaze should look at the spot between the eyebrows. This (posture), which is the opener of the door of release, is called siddhāsana.

And having placed the right foot upon the left thigh and likewise the left (foot) upon the right thigh, and having grasped firmly the great toes with the hands crossed from behind (and) fixing the chin on the chest (the Yogī) should gaze at the tip of his nose. This (posture), the destroyer of disease and mental and physical disturbances, is called padmāsana.[6]

This latter is described in the *Haṭhayogapradīpika* as follows:

---

[1] *HYP*, 1: 61.
[2] *HYP*, 1: 62.
[3] *HYP*, 1: 62, 63.
[4] *HYP*, 1: 63.
[5] *HYP*, 1: 63. Further details concerning things to use and to avoid are found in *Śiva Saṁhitā*, 3: 33, 35.
[6] *GŚ*, 11, 12. In the former, the *Śiva Saṁhita* suggests pressure upon the yoni and liṅga respectively.

Having placed the feet, bottoms up, firmly upon the thighs, and similarly having the hands, palms upwards, between the thighs; having the eyes directed to the tip of the nose, the [Yogī] should press the roots of the upper front teeth with the tongue; and, having rested the chin upon the chest, he should expel the breath slowly. This, styled the padmāsana, is the destroyer of all diseases. It is difficult to master, (but) may be perfected in (this) world by a wise man (by a man properly taught).[1]

An interesting list of āsanas is given in the *Haṭhāyoga-prādīpika*,[2] and there their bearing upon health and the eradication of disease is recorded. One of these, because of its reference to Gorakhnāth, may be of special inteterest:

[The Yogī] should place the ankles (heels) on either side of the seam below the scrotum, the left heel on the left, the right on the right. (He should) hold the feet firmly with the hands, immovable. This is the *bhaḍrāsana*, eradicator of all diseases. Adepts denominate this one *Gorakṣāsana*. By merely taking this posture, the eminent Yogī becomes fatigue-free.[3]

The bearing of these practices upon the awakening of Kuṇḍalinī is perfectly plain when ancillary means are noted, such as that in the padmāsana, where the left heel is placed upon the meḍhra, and the right upon the left.[4] This is called the 'thunder-bolt' (*vajra*) āsana, and also the 'liberating' and the 'secret' āsana.[5] Gorakhnāth was, to begin with, a Vajrâyāna Buddhist. The word vajra has an esoteric meaning. And it is maintained further that other postures are of no use when success has been achieved in this. Elements of āsana are found in mudrā and bandha,[6] and are combined with forms of prāṇāyāma.

There is an intimate relation between āsana and prāṇāyāma. But, in order that the breath, which is the jīva, may be controlled, it is necessary that the prāṇa and apāna move freely through the iḍā-pinglā system, and in turn that Kuṇḍalinī be moved upward. Consequently, the paths of such movements, the nāḍis, which are conceived of as obstructed with impurities

---

[1] *HYP*, 1: 47, 48, 49.
[2] 1: 21–34.
[3] *HYP*, 1: 55-57.
[4] *HYP*, 1: 38.
[5] *HYP*, 1: 39.
[6] The *Tantra* suggests special seats for certain āsanas; skulls for the mundāsana, the funeral pyre for the citāsana, a corpse for the savāsana, with the purpose of acquiring fearlessness and indifference. These āsanas are not included in the lists given above.

and secretions, must be cleansed by drying up and removing the substances accumulated in them. Moreover, with the purification of the nāḍis, the breath can be held for longer periods of time. While prāṇāyāma is a general means serving for this purpose, special devices, known as the six duties, or acts (*saṭkurmāni*), are employed. They are: *dhāutī*, *basti*, *neti*, *trātaka*, *nāuli* and *kapāla bhāti*. *Gajkaraṇi* may be added. These serve also for the acquisition and the preservation of health.

A wetted cloth four fingers wide and fifteen cubits long should be swallowed slowly, under the direction of a teacher, and then drawn back. This is called *dhāuti karma*. The novice begins by swallowing a cubit the first day, two the second, and so on, until he can manage the whole strip. After swallowing the whole of the tape, he should give his stomach a rotary motion from left to right and then draw the cloth slowly up. Without doubt cough, asthma, enlargement of the spleen, leprosy, and the twenty diseases are cured by the practice of dhāuti karma.[1]

Squatting in water reaching to the navel, with a tube inserted in the anus, one should contract the ādhāra (anus). (This) washing is the basti karma.

This is explained as the use of a half-inch tube about six inches long by means of which the bowels are flushed through contraction and expansion of the abdominal muscles.

Enlargement of the spleen and dropsy and also all of the disorders arising from wind, bile and phlegm are brought to an end. The basti karma, performed with water makes calm the (these) humours, the sensory and motor faculties and the seat of thought and feeling; gives glow and lustre (to the body) and good digestion. All accumulations of vitiated humours are destroyed.[2]

A very soft cord, about nine inches long, should be drawn (up) through the nostril and taken out through the mouth. By adepts this is called neti. This is indeed the cleanser of the skull (cranial passages) and the giver of divine sight. The multitude of diseases which arise in the upper portion of the chest is quickly destroyed.[3]

Having the thoughts fixed (in meditation), one should look fixedly at a small object (mark) until the eyes are suffused with tears. (This) by adepts is called trātaka. It destroys the diseases of the eyes and also removes exhaustion. Trātaka is a (door) that should be guarded (kept secret) as a gold (treasure) casket.[4]

---

[1] *HYP*, 2: 24, 25 and note in *HYP*, to verse 24.
[2] *HYP*, 2: 26–28.
[3] *HYP*, 2: 29, 30. [4] *HYP*, 2: 31, 32.

With shoulders bent, one should rotate the belly with an active, violent turning from left to right. This adepts call nāuli. This nāuli, excellent Haṭha exercise, removes dyspepsia, restores digestion and so forth and ever causes joy. It dries up all disorders.[1]

The performance of inhalation and exhalation, agitatedly like a blacksmith's bellows, is known as kapāla bhāti. It dries up phlegm disorders.[2]

Lifting the lower air (apāna) one vomits the contents of the stomach. By degrees the nāḍis and cakras are brought under control. (This act) is called gajkarṇi by those who know the Haṭha (Yoga).[3]

The *Gheraṇḍa Saṁhitā* gives a more elaborate and differently analyzed account of the elements of dhāuti.

It seems clear that the physical reactions to these practices may be interpreted in terms of religious experience. Physical and psychical effects of these exercises are inevitable.

The (system) of nāḍis and cakras having been cleansed by the control of the prāṇa according to rule (then) the air (*mārutā*), having opened the door of the suṣumṇā, enters (it) with ease. When the air moves in the middle (suṣumṇā), fixity of mind is induced. The mind (thus) fixed is verily in the condition of *manonmanī*.[4]

When the whole group of nāḍis, full of secretions, is purified, certainly then, the Yogī becomes capable of constraining the prāṇa.[5]

Chief reliance for the cleansing of the channels is placed, however, upon prāṇāyāma; and it is said that this is the only means needed.[6] Moreover, this control serves to arouse Kuṇḍalinī, and to lift her from centre (cakra) to centre. By using iḍā and piṅglā in the breathing process prāṇa, jīva, Kuṇḍalinī, may be directed into the suṣumṇā.

Some methods of prāṇāyāma are as follows:

Assuming the lotus posture (padmāsana), the Yogī should fill in the prāṇa through the left nostril; then, having held it as long as possible he should expel it through the right nostril.[7]

Iḍā is the left nostril, piṅglā the right.

Having meditated on the circular image of the moon, nectar as white as curds (and) cow's milk (or) of the colour of purest silver, one practising prāṇāyāma should find peace.[8]

---

[1] *HYP*, 2: 33, 34. [2] *HYP*, 2: 35. [3] *HYP*, 2: 38.

[4] *HYP*, 2: 41, 42. A state of mind in which there is no movement of thought. [5] *P*. 95.

HYP, 2: 37. An interesting statement about the functions of īdā and piṅglā for prognostication may be found in *The Secrets of the Kāula Circle*, by Elizabeth Sharp, 1936, pp. 76 ff. [7] *P*, 96. [8] *HYP*, 97.

Having filled in the breath through the right nostril, one should fill the abdomen slowly; having held it according to the rules, he should expel (it slowly) through the left nostril. Having meditated on the circle of the sun, full of a mass of flame of fire burning very brightly in the navel, the Yogī who practises prāṇāyāma should find peace.[1]

Meditating in turn on the two images, moon and sun, (a Yogī) should draw in the breath through the left nostril; he should expel it again through the other, according to the limit (of the times already explained). Then, having drawn in the breath through the right nostril, and having held it, he should expel it through the left nostril. After three months the group of nāḍis of the practitioner become pure.[2]

Naturally, the breathing process, as has been pointed out, involves the use of mantra (haṁsa) which adds to its own effectiveness. In the practice of prāṇāyāma, inhaling and exhaling of the breath are important, but the chief aim is the holding of 'the breath filled in,' *kumbhaka*. And it may be held for longer and longer periods. This process is regulated by the use of mantra also, oṁ being recited in a triple form ā-u-ṁ. The commentator on verse sixty-one of the *Gorakṣa-śataka* says that with the drawing in of the prāṇa (*pūraka*) oṁ should be recited mentally twelve times, sixteen times while it is being held (kumbhaka) and ten times during its expulsion (*recaka*). This is the lowest class of prāṇāyāma. In the middle class, the times are twenty-four, thirty-two and twenty; and in the highest thirty-six, forty-eight and thirty. This is a strenuous exercise. In the lowest level there is great perspiration; in the middle, trembling; and in the highest the Yogī 'rises up.' Reference here is probably to the sense of lightness. This exercise is joined with the mahāmudrā.[3]

[The Yogī] should practice holdings of the breath *kumbhakān* four times a day; at dawn, in the middle of the day, at evening and at midnight, gradually up to eighty times (320 for the twenty-four hours).[4]

But there are many variations in the use of mudrā, āsana, bandha and other exercises with the prāṇāyāma.[5]

When the adept is able to deal with kumbhaka without infilling or expelling the air, he has reached the point of

---

[1] *GŚ*, 98, 99. [2] *GŚ*, 100. [3] For this mudrā, see below.
[4] *HYP*, 2 : 11. [5] *HYP*, see chap. two.

mastery where 'there is nothing whatsoever in the three worlds difficult for him to attain, for he is able to keep the breath (*vāyu*) confined at will.[1] In the process the mind is caused to swoon.[2] This leads to *anāhata nāda* (certain internal sounds), and success may be achieved within a year.[3] The air is directed into the suṣumṇā and steadiness of mind is a result of the free movement of the prāṇā in the middle path (suṣumṇā). That is the manonmanī state which is attained when the mental processes are brought to a standstill.[4] Prāṇa is also bindu and jīva; and its relation to Kuṇḍalinī is referred to its origin in the svādhiṣṭhāna and in the mantra haṁsa.

The lifting of Kuṇḍalinī involves the understanding of the functions of the various cakras; that is, a knowledge of the peculiar kinds of experience referred to each of them. Since they are all strung on the suṣumṇā, they all lie in the path of Kuṇḍālinī. The same control of the breath, prāṇāyāma, which retards the bindu, arouses Kuṇḍalinī, and thus opens the door to release. When the skill in raising her is perfected and she is led to enjoy bindu, or Śiva, in the brahmarandhra, release is achieved. Each cakra symbolizes a type of reality and specific experiences; and the fixation of the attention upon each in turn secures reactions which are interpreted in terms of degrees of the realization of union of the individual with the Supreme Soul. Kuṇḍalinī enjoys Śiva in each cakra in her form peculiar to that lotus, and finally reaches the eternal One in the sahasra. In the ājñā she is Śakti on the mental plane; in the sahasra, on the spiritual plane. From this high place she should be brought back to the mūlādhāra. In fact she returns again and again in spite of the Yogī's efforts, and it is only after long practice that she takes up her more prolonged abode in the sahasra.

It is not necessary, apparently, that the Yogī follow the whole course through, since short-cuts to the end are suggested. And, further, he may seek such ends as are afforded by particular centres. In the mūlādhāra reside physical powers, and here is

---

[1] *HYP*, 2: 74. [2] *HYP*, 2: 69.

[3] *HYP*, 1: 59. [4] Dr. Singh (p. 51) calls the *unmam*, the state of self-transcendence.

found the sleeping Kuṇḍalinī. Here, also, is enjoyment on the physical plane. Knowledge and powers of experience are joined here. Meditation upon the svādhiṣṭhana yields power over the hindrances to success in Yoga, sexual feelings are aroused and mysterious, or divine, sounds are heard. In the maṇipūraka reside powers of destruction and recreation. Some describe the powers here obtained as twelve-fold. The cakra lies on the dividing line of the body and the adept who is able to raise Kuṇḍalinī above this centre passes into more subtle types of experience. Here insight arises. Anāhata (the heart) is the seat of desire, of the egoising faculty, of manas (mind), and of the records of deeds. Consequently the soul finds freedom here. While meditating upon this lotus, with the use of the *prānava* (oṁ) the mind (and the prāṇa) is brought to complete rest, like unto the state of the flame of a wick in a windless place. There arise, also, supernormal powers, such as ability of the soul to enter other bodies, to wander, the power to identify the self with the gods (both as to function and power) who create, preserve and destroy. Mystic light arises also as Kuṇḍalinī is established here. An illustration of the method of meditation on the cakra is to be found in the *śāmbhāvimudrā*.

> The aim (attention) inward (Iyangar, *HYP*, says, 'in any *cakra*'), the sight outward without winking—this is the śāmbhavīmudrā, hidden in the Vedas and Śāstras. When the Yogī remains with the prāṇa and citta (breath and thoughts) unmoving, the attention inward, the gaze immovable, looking outside, below, (yet) seeing nothing, the śāmbhavīmudrā, learned by the favour of a guru, is (performed) and the state of emancipation that is without marks of distinction, that which in reality is the highest Śiva, bursts forth.[1]

Its result is similar to that secured by the khecarīmudrā which is performed in the viśuddha. This last named cakra is the place of ambrosia and concentration here enables the Yogī to become a great sage, eloquent, wise, peaceful, a benefactor of all, free from disease, long-lived. Divine sounds, subtle tones, are heard. With the breath confined here, the Yogī, in his wrath, could move the three worlds. He becomes invincible. Thus, the union of bindu and rajas

---

[1] *HYP*, 4: 35–36.

in the throat yields supernatural powers. This is the *gateway* to the great liberation, which is opened by the khecarīmudrā. Still higher, as the jīva reaches the ājñā, it beholds light in the form of a lustrous flame, and becomes immortal. Here is the final approach to the highest bliss of the union in the sahasrāra. Between ājñā and sahasrāra are gradations of subtle experience, or ecstasy, approaching more and more to the bliss of union in the highest or final sense. The mind is dissolved, unconsciousness follows. At the last, after repeated experiences of this bliss, *final release* is reached. The sahasrāra is said to be the *satya-loka*, the true, or real, world, and to exude the stream of nectar which has its origin in the blissful *Union*. Here is the fountain head of all creation, where Kuṇḍalinī enjoys *Paramātman*, both being One, and pain, misery, birth and death are dissolved. It is the place of Brahmānanda, the Bliss of the Absolute.

It is to be noted that as Kuṇḍalinī moves upward, from cakra to cakra, the bodily regions below each successive stage become cold. In hypnotic trance, or in the trance of hybernation (as induced in khecarīmudrā, for example), only the region at the top of the head remains warm; and the Yogī in this state has to be guarded lest he be taken for dead and be buried.

Under excitation in the mūlādhāra simple, gross desire is experienced. Within the yonisthāna there is union of bindu and rajas. The bindu descends from its place of origin ; and the true Yoga requires that it be returned thither. Adepts, it is claimed, are able to do this at will, even drawing up after the act of coition both rajas and bindu. This is essential to the highest bliss.

Methods for the recovery of the bindu are set forth in the *Haṭhayogapradīpika* and in the *Gorakṣa Paddhati*. One of these is the *vajrolī*.

Even a Yogī who lives as he pleases (and) neglects the restraints prescribed by the Yoga, if he practises vajrolī, (is) a Yogī indeed and fit for beatitude (siddhi). For this (vajrolī) a couple of things difficult for the average man to obtain is prescribed. The first is milk and the second an obedient woman. One should draw back up again (should practice drawing back . . .) with the meḍhra slowly (the bindu discharged in *māithunā*). Whether a man or a woman, one should attain mastery of vajrolī. Carefully, with (through) a proper tube[1]) inserted) in the passage of the medhra (the Yogī) should blow air very slowly. By practice the bindu fallen into the yoni may be drawn back. Having drawn up his own discharged bindu [the Yogī] can preserve (it). The adept (the one skilled or physically able in Yoga), who can thus save his bindu, conquers death. By the loss of bindu (comes) death, from its retention, life. Through the preservation of the bindu a pleasant odour arises in the body of the Yogī. Where is the fear of death so long as the bindu remains in the body? The bindu of man (is) dependent upon mind (and) life upon bindu. Therefore both bindu and manas are to be protected in every way.

Sahajolī and *amarolī* are of one and the same kind as vajrolī. Ashes of burnt cow-dung should be mingled with water. After *vajrolī-māithunā*, seated comfortably, pervaded with freedom (thoroughly relaxed) the pair should both rub it on their bodies. This sahajolī is ever proclaimed by Yogīs as worthy of confidence. This fortune-granting practice (Yoga) gives both release (mukti) and enjoyment (bhoga) at the same time. This is *the* Yoga of merit-endowed, resolute, really perceiving men, who are without passion. But it can not be accomplished by the lust-filled.

According to the teaching of the Kāpālikas, amarolī is the enjoyment (sexually) of the passionless midstream; the first, excessive in bile and the last, the water stream, neglected are rejected. He who drinks amarolī constantly and snuffs it daily and practises vajrolī is said to be actually practising amarolī.

[The Yogī] should mix with the ashes of cow-dung the bindu (cāndrī) discharged in this practice. It should be rubbed on the most honorable parts of the body. Magic sight (seeing things divine) arises.[2]

Sahajolī gives both bhoga (enjoyment) and mokṣa (release).

Another practice based upon the same physiological concepts is as follows: Two men, *cela* and guru, pupil and teacher, retire to a secret place. The guru inserts a lead wire into the passage of the male organ to a distance of twenty-three fingers. It penetrates the suṣumṇā. Great powers are supposed to arise through this practice.

It may be noted that not only do the books speak of these matters, but also that the Yogīs themselves are familiar with them. At Devī Pātan these practices were described to the author by Yogīs.

---

[1] At Devī Pātan they said that this tube should be of silver and that milk should be used.

[2] *HYP*, 3: 82-96. The translator of the *Śiva Saṁhitā* omits the section on 'Vajroṇḍī' as 'an obscene practice indulged in by low-class Tāntrists'; p. 51.

The relation of prāṇāyāma to these devices is in the fact that the stabilizing of the bindu depends also upon the holding of the breath.

There are other exercises for holding the bindu in its place of origin, such as the jālandharabandha and the khecarīmudrā, which will be described below.

If the bindu, on the one hand, is to be kept secure in its original position, the Kuṇḍalinī, on the other, is to be aroused and caused to move upwards. This is called *Śakticālana.* For the union of these two is essential to ecstatic experience or bliss in varying degrees to final beatitude. For this reason the playing of one breath (prāṇā) against the other (apāna) is resorted to and pressure and mudrā are enjoined. For example, from the pressure of the heels in padmāsana and the alternate in filling of prāṇa and apāna for a considerable time both morning and evening, the Kuṇḍalinī begins to move. Likewise kumbhaka, the holding of the breath, incites her to motion. She then moves upwards through the channel (suṣumṇā) which extends from the aperture of the liṅga to the hollow above the throat.

The mudrās and bandhas are similar to āsanas in their action and efficacy. The Gheraṇḍa names twenty-five, including vajrolī and Śakticālana among them.

The gazing taught in some of these induces hypnotic sleep; and the bandhas, by closing all the exits of air, produce a tension within the system, generating thereby a sort of electric current, or force, called Kuṇḍalinī Śakti. It is this Śakti which is the helpmate of the Yogīs in performing their wonders.[1]

The description of the *mahāmudrā* is as follows:

That Yogī is ready for release who knows mahāmudrā, nabhomudrā, uḍḍīyāna, jālandhara and mūlābanda. The purification of the collection of the nāḍis, the moving of both the moon and sun, and also the drying up of the liquids of the body, is called mahāmudrā. Having rested the chin on the chest, and pressing for a long time the yoni with the left great toe, with the two hands grasping the extended right foot, having filled with breath both sides of the abdomen and having held it, [the Yogī] should expel it slowly. This is said to be the very great (mahāmudrā), the destroyer of the diseases of men.[2]

[The Yogī] should press the heel of the left foot against the

---

[1] *SBH*, No. 68, p. iv. [2] *GŚ*, 57, 59.

yonisthānam, and then place the right foot upon the left thigh (and) having drawn in the breath (and) having pressed the chin upon the chest, and having held the breath, he should fix his attention in the middle (between the eyebrows). Having held it as long as possible, he should expel the breath slowly. Having been performed (thus) on the left side, it should be practised on the right. However, the opinion of some is that the closing of the throat may be neglected, since an excellent stoppage is made by pressing the tongue against the roots of the upper front teeth. Moreover, this stops the upward movement in all the nāḍis; and, further, this mahābandha (great stoppage) bestows magical powers. Mahābandha is a clever means for loosening the snares of death. Triveni-union is given and the mind should reach *Kedār* (the seat of Śiva between the eyebrows).[1]

The effect of this exercise is to remove the sense and effect of differences.

(There is) neither wholesome nor unwholesome (food). All tastes (are) indeed tasteless. Even deadly poison (food) (when) eaten is digested as if it were nectar.[2]

And it removes diseases.

His diseases, consumption, leprosy, constipation, enlargement of the spleen and decrepitude go to destruction, who practises mahāmudrā.[3]

The *Yonimudrā* is described as follows:

Place left heel against the anus; the right heel on the left foot; sit erect with body, the neck and the head in a straight line. With the lips formed to resemble a crow's beak, draw in the air and fill the belly. Close the ear-holes with the thumbs, the eyes with the index fingers; the nostrils with the middle fingers; the mouth with the remaining fingers. Hold the air, and with the senses controlled, meditate on the mantra haṁsa.[4]

According to Iyangar, yonimudrā is another name for vajrolī (p. 52). In the *Śiva Saṁhitāā*, page forty-one, it is described as the sacred drink of the Kāulas, the worshippers of Śakti according to the vāmacāra.

The mūla-, uḍḍīyāna- and jālandhara- bandhas find their completion in the *siṁhāsana* which is described as follows:

[The Yogī] should place the heels on the sides of the seam below the scrotum, the left heel on the right and the right heel on the left

---

[1] *HYP*, 3: 19–24. Mahāmudrā, mahābandha and mahavedha (not described in this account) confer magic powers and perfection. *HYP*, 3: 30 (Iyangar). [2] *GŚ*, 61.
[3] *GŚ*, 62. [4] Based upon *SCN*, p. 87.

(of it); and having placed the hands on the knees, and having extended one's fingers, with the mouth open, and with the mind intently fixed, he should gaze at the tip of the nose. This siṁhāsana should be held sacred by adepts.[1]

The *mūlabandha* is thus described:

Having pressed the yoni with the back of the left heel [the Yogī] should contract the rectum; (and thus) draw the apāna upward. Thus is the mūlabandha performed.[2]

Although its (normal) course is downward, the Yogī should draw the apāna up forcibly by contracting (the anus). This Yogīs call mūlabandha. And having pressed firmly the anus with the heel [the Yogī] should draw the air forcibly upward. Little by little the air (apāna) goes up. By means of the mūlabandha prāṇa and apāna, nāda and bindu becoming one, the end of the Yoga is surely attained. (With) the union of prāṇa and apāna (results) the diminution of fæces and urine. Even an old man always regains his virility by practising mūlabandha.[3]

This brings about the 'union' of prāṇa and apāna as they enter the suṣumṇā; it decreases certain secretions and invigorates the body. Minor sounds are heard. If the thoracic and yoni regions are simultaneously contracted prāṇa is forced down and apāna upwards, and vāyu enters the suṣumṇā. This may become the yonimudrā.[4]

Mahāmudrā and mahābandha (and mahāvedha) confer magic powers.

This most sacred triad, destroyer of old age and death, increases the digestive fire, and even grants magic power such as becoming automatically small and so forth. They should be performed eight times a day, watch by watch. They ever add to the store of merit and deplete the stock of demerit at the same time. The practice of the three, under instruction, should be for short intervals at first.[5]

The *uḍḍiyāna* is a well-known bandha.

In the abdomen, above the navel [the Yogī] should make a contraction toward the spinal column. This is, verily, the uḍḍiyāna, a lion for the elephant of death. Of all the bandhas uḍḍiyāna is indeed the best. Stoppage (bandha) being fixed by the uḍḍiyāna, deliverance comes naturally (spontaneously).[6] Even as a bird is able to fly without taking rest, so indeed uḍḍiyāna may become the lion which is the death of the elephant.[7]

---

[1] *HYP*, 1: 52, 54a. [2] *GŚ*, 81. [3] *HYP*, 3: 61-64.
[4] *Śiva Saṁhitā*, 4: 42. [5] *HYP*, 3: 30, 31. [6] *HYP*, 3: 56, 59.
[7] *GŚ*, 77. It overcomes death, the death-dealing elephant. Manas, like a wild elephant is hard to control.

Again, the *jālandhara*:

Because jālandharabandha closes the network of channels (all the nāḍis) and stops the water from flowing down from the head, therefore, it destroys the host of disorders of the throat. The jālandharabandha, characterized as the closing of the throat, having been performed, the nectar does not fall into the fire, nor is the air disturbed.[1]

Having closed the passages with the jālandhara, at the end of an infilling of the breath [the Yogī] should expel it slowly. This is called *mūrchā* because it gives joy and swoon (*manomūrchā*).[2]

This bandha contracts the throat and prevents the nectar from falling into the fire, that is, bindu is restrained, and the air is not disturbed. The region of the heart is affected and the vital centres are stopped down.

The two bandhas just described are of use in rousing Kuṇḍalinī and, at the same time, in stabilizing the bindu. Of the three bandhas just cited it is written:

These three bandhas, the very best, have been practised by great adepts. These means of attaining the ends set forth in all the treatises on Haṭha Yoga are known to all (real) Yogīs.[3]

The *khecarīmudrā* is one of the most famous of all. And this is in many ways the chief[4] mudrā whose continued practice produces Yoga trance, the state resembling hybernation. Apparently this is the practice which is used in the exhibitions of suspended animation which have been reported to the West, for the practice of this mudrā results in the suppression of the breath and in insensibility, so that the Yogī may be buried in the ground without air, food or drink.

By turning the tongue over backwards into the hollow above the throat, and by fixing the sight between the eyebrows, is the khecarīmudrā performed.[5]

As fire cleaves to the wood and as a light to oil and wick, so the soul does not leave the body full of the drops of *soma* (bindu).[6]

Preliminary to the practice, the frænum of the tongue has to be cut. This is done a little at a time with a bamboo sharp edge or some other sharp instrument. Then the tongue

---

[1] *GŚ*, 79, 80. [2] *HYP*, 2: 69. [3] *HYP*, 3; 75.

[4] *HYP*, 1: 45: 'There is no āsana equal to the siddhāsana; no stoppage of the breath superior to the *kevala*; no mudrā equal to the khecarī; no *laya* (absorption) equal to the (anāhata) nāda.'

[5] *GŚ*, 64. [6] *HYP*, 3: 45.

is kneaded and stretched so as to permanently increase its length. Then the practice can be carried out.

[The Yogī] should stretch the tongue little by little, stretching and cutting the *frænum linguæ*. When it (the tip of the tongue) touches the space between the eyebrows (when it is folded back against the soft palate), khecarīmudrā is perfected. Having grasped a very sharp, smooth, clean instrument the shape of a *snuhi* (*Euphorbia*) leaf [the Yogī] should cut with it a hair's breadth (at a time). Then he should rub it with powdered rocksalt and myrobolan (*Terminalia Chebula*). Again, on the seventh day, he should cut it a hair's breadth. Thus over a period of six months he should do this regularly. By that time the whole of the frænum linguæ will be cut away. Having turned the tip of the tongue upward [the Yogī] closes the three passages (œsophagus, trachea and nostrils or (?) the three nāḍis). This is the khecarīmudrā and it is called the vyoma cakra. The Yogī, who remains even for a moment with his tongue turned upwards thus, is saved from poisons, diseases, death, old age, and so forth. He who knows the khecarīmudrā is without disease, death, lassitude, sleep, hunger, thirst or swooning. He who knows khecarīmudrā is neither beset by disease nor tainted by karma nor snared by death.

This mudrā, khecarī by name, has been desired by adepts because, when it is practised, the mind goes to ākāśa (khe)—(when) the tongue reaches khe.[1]

Above the throat is the space, ākāśa, or vacuum (khe), where limitation of sense is removed. It is here that bindu has its native seat and that union of Śiva and Śakti is on the subtle plane. The mudrā effectively binds bindu.

By whom the hollow in the top of the throat is sealed by khecarī, his bindu, even (though he be) embraced by a woman, does not fall.[2]

Here, then, is ecstatic experience which is beyond the range of the senses and which does not entail death.

While the bindu remains in the body, there is no fear of death. So long as the khecarīmudrā is continued, so long the bindu does not go down.[3]

Karma is inoperative in this state. Mind and tongue reach ākāśa.[4] Its unusual power and value are emphasized in the expression,

---

[1] *HYP*, 3: 33-41. Iyangar records, p. 50, that the Yogīs are prohibited the use of salt. Salt can be used only before beginning the practice of the Haṭha Yoga. Afterwards, only the burnt powder of the wood (cassia, *khādira* = acacia catechu). Khe = ākāśa; car, to move. Khecarī = 'whose movement is in space.'

[2] *GŚ*, 69. [3] *GŚ*, 70. [4] *HYP*, 3: 41. See just above.

The stream flowing visibly from soma (candra) is dear to Śiva. [The Yogī] should close (fill) the unequalled, divine suṣumṇā in the back of the mouth (by means of the khecarīmudrā).[1]

The Śāmbhavīmudrā differs from the khecarīmudrā only in the object looked at. Śiva (Śambhu) is viewed as formless; i.e., the Yogī is really seeing nothing.

The exercise of this (khecarī) mudrā enables one to *enjoy*. In performing this mudrā it is possible to neglect the other cakras in the path and to lift Kuṇḍalinī directly by the back path to the place of bindu. This mudrā is prescribed with the vajrāsana.[2]

Āsana, mudrā and bandha are clearly forms of exercise which contribute both to the increase of bodily health and to the stimulating and conservation of vital energy essential to success in Haṭha Yoga.

A further word may be written about mantra. The repetition of sacred formulæ is of great importance[3] and its results are essentially magical; it enhances the effectiveness of physical practice.

Already the place of om in the Yoga has been repeatedly illustrated; and its symbolical significance has been set forth in chapter eight.

With the voice [the Yogī] should repeat that bīja; he should practise it with the body; with the mind he should remember it. That, oṁ, is the supreme light.[4]

Haṁsa is related directly to the breath and has its rise in the place of origin of sexual desire; it is the chief mantra of jīva (life, or soul). It is the ajapa gāyatrī.

---

[1] *HYP*, 4: 45. The *Śiva Saṁhitā*, 3: 57, says that prolonged holding of the breath is pratyāhāra; and Śriśa Chandra Vidyarṇava, in his Introduction to this work (p. iv) insists that the trance of khecarīmudrā is not samādhi, but pratyāhāra. However, the exposition given above agrees with the other works cited.

[2] *Śiva Saṁhitā*, 4: 31.

[3] From one point of view mantra is the background of Tāntra. This derives in part from the dhāraṇī or spell, which is a shortened scripture-text, essentially a string of words without meaning, in form designed for repetition as containing the whole of the original passage. It may be reduced to a pregnant syllable or bīja. When applied according to rule, the bīja is endowed with enormous power.

[4] *GŚ*, 88.

Gāyatrī has a great reputation and has a very long history.

Knowledge like this, repetition like this, insight like this neither was nor shall be.[1]

Even the will to recite it gives freedom from sin. It originates in Kuṇḍalinī and from the restraint of the breath. Knowing (in the magical sense) this mantra renders one an adept.[2] Its repetition engenders hypnotic sleep. It serves to stop the breath. Its ajapa form is haṁsa.

The secretions of the body, controlled by the prāṇāyāma and bandha methods, should be preserved.[3] This is clear from the passages dealing with bindu, vajrolī, sahajolī and amarolī. Furthermore, the perspiration exuding from the exertion of the practice of prāṇāyāma should be rubbed into the body and not wiped off.

Out of these various, strenuous practices come some effects which are noted as indicative of success in the Yoga. Amongst these are certain sounds and colours, some of which have been mentioned already.

Great store is laid by anāhata nāda, or the sound (nāda) in the heart lotus.

Anāhata nāda is awakened by the exercise of prāṇāyāma. A couple of week's practice with eighty prāṇāyāmas in the morning and the same number in the evening will cause distinct sounds to be heard; and, as the practice goes on increasing, varied sounds become audible to the practiser. By hearing these sounds attentively (i.e., fixing the attention on them) one gets concentration of the mind, and thence *sahaja samādhi*. When Yoga-sleep is experienced, the student should give himself up to it and make no efforts to check it. By and by, these sounds become subtle and they become less and less intense, so the mind looses its waywardness and becomes calm and docile; and, on this practice becoming well-established, samādhi becomes a voluntary act. This is, however, the highest stage and is the lot of the favoured and fortunate few only.[4]

The following is the method for inducing trance, propounded by Gorakṣanātha:[5]

The Yogī, his mind single, sitting in muktāsana, having formed the śāmbhavīmudrā, ought to hear in his right ear inner sound. The ears, eyes, nostrils and mouth should be closed.[6]

---

[1] *GŚ*, 45. [2] *P*, 46. [3] *Śiva Saṁhitā*, 3: 40.
[4] *HYP*, (*SBH*) Introduction, p. iv. [6] *HYP*, 4: 66, 67a.
[5] *HYP*, 4 : 64.

The effects are very definite.

In the cleansed suṣumṇā-path pure, clear, sound is heard.[1]

Four states are recognized:

Joy arises in the void (in the heart), (and) in the body various anāhata sounds, like the beating of a drum. [In the first (stage)] the Yogī becomes divine of body, radiant, fragrant of body and free from disease; and his whole heart (becomes) a void. In the second period the air moves in the middle channel (suṣumṇā), the posture becomes fixed and the Yogī becomes wise like a god. From the piercing of the Viṣṇu Knot (in the throat) in this manner, the highest bliss is experienced. And, in the hollow in the throat, a tumult like the beating of a kettle drum is heard. In the third, in the space between the eyebrows the sound of a drum is recognized. Then the air goes to the great void, the refuge of all the adepts. Then, having overcome the joys of the mind, without evil, misery, old-age, disease, hunger or sleep, joy itself (ultimate joy) is experienced. The Rudra Knot having been pierced and the air having gone to the seat of Śiva, a sound like that produced by a flute, arises. Then there is the unity of consciousness called Rāja Yoga. (And) the Yogī, equal to Śiva, becomes a creator and a destroyer. Whether there be release or not, here is indeed unbroken peace. This felicity arising from absorption (laya) is obtained in Rāja Yoga.[2]

Concerning colours it is said:

During contemplation one sees, not with his eyes, as he does the objects of the world, various colours, which the writers on Yoga call the colours of the five elements.[3] Sometimes stars are seen glittering, and lightning flashes in the sky. But these are all fleeting in their nature. At first these colours are seen in greatly agitated waves which show the unsteady condition of the mind; and, as the practice increases and the mind becomes calm, these colour-waves become steady and motionless and appear as one deep ocean of light. This is the ocean in which one should dive and forget the world and become one with his Lord—which is the condition of highest bliss.[4]

It may be well, now, to quote a verse, with its note, in Pañcam Sinhi edition as summarizing the effects of the use of the mudrās and as verifying what was said above, in chapter thirteen, about supernormal powers (*āiśvarya*).

---

[1] *HYP*, 4: 67b.
[2] *HYP*, 4: 69-77.
[3] See description of the cakras in the preceding chapter.
[4] *HYP*, (*SBH*) Introduction, p. iv. Fixing attention on these phenomena is the point.

These, which bestow the eight magic powers, have been explained by Ādi Nātha, and are greatly prized by all adepts. (They) are difficult even for Mārutas (sons of Śiva) to acquire.

The eight Āiśvaryas are: *Animā*, becoming small, like an atom; *Mahimā*, becoming great, like ākāś, by drawing in atoms of Prakṛti; *Garimā*, light things, like cotton becoming very heavy like mountains; *Prāpti*, coming within easy reach of everything, as touching the moon with the little finger, while standing on the earth; *Prākāmya*, non-resistance to the desires, as entering the earth like water; *Īśatā*, mastery over matter and objects made of it; *Vaśitvā*, controlling the animate and inanimate objects.[1]

The signs of (success in) Haṭha Yoga are purification of the nāḍis, a lean body, tranquility in the face, manifestation of nāda (anāhata sounds), very clear eyes, freedom from disease, bindu under control (and) good digestion.[2]

The end of the Haṭha Yoga is the Rāja Yoga, ecstacy and trance of the experience of Brahma.

I will now describe the best course (leading up) to samādhi (that which) destroys death, induces peace and produces brahmānanda.[3]

Rāja Yoga, samādhi, unmanī, manonmanī, amaratvā, laya, tatva, śūnya, aśūnya, paramapada, *amanaska*, *advāita*, *nirālamba*, *nirañjana*, *jīvanamukti*, *sahajā* and *turiyā* denote the same state of being. Just as with salt in water all becomes salty, so the mingling of ātma and manas is denominated samādhi. When the breath (prāṇa) becomes exhausted and the mental processes (manas) are destroyed (*pralīyate*), then their being equal (union) is called samādhi. And this equality, (this) oneness of the two, the living self and the absolute self, when all desire (*sāñkalpa*) is destroyed is called samādhi.[4]

It is of interest to note how intimately the processes of the Kuṇḍalinī Yoga are related to the attainment of bliss.

By practice through various postures (āsana) and holdings of the breath, Kuṇḍalinī being aroused, the prāṇa is dissolved (pralīyate) in śūnya (samādhi).

(This) state of union (samādhi) of Yogīs who experience the aroused Śakti, and all of whose actions are renounced, is achieved even of its own accord. When the prāṇa moves in the suṣumṇā and mental action (mānasa) is absorbed in śūnya (samādhi), then the adept uproots all effects of works. When the mind has reached tranquillity (ceases to act) and the breath moves in the middle channel (suṣumṇā) amarolī, vajrolī and sahajolī are accomplished. How can there be knowledge (samādhi) as long as the brain works here, as long as prāṇa moves, before mental activity is dead? He alone who can lead these two, his prāṇa and manas, to dissolution (*vilayam*) achieves mokṣa (release, samādhi).[5]

---

[1] *HYP*, 3: 8. [2] *HYP*, 2 : 78. [3] *HYP*, 4: 2.
[4] *HYP*, 4: 3-7. [5] *HYP*, 4: 10, 11, 12, 14, 15.

The heart of the practice is made clear, as outlined above, in the following verses.

Only when the prāṇa moves in the suṣumṇā is manonmanī perfected, but no other discipline (or efforts) of Yogīs whatever (avail). Who has brought his breath to a stop has, at the same time, brought his mental activities to rest; who has brought his mental activities to rest has stopped down his breath. As mental activity is dissolved, the breath is stilled. As the prāṇa is stopped, the mind is brought to dissolution. As milk and water unite (and become one), likewise do these two, manas and prāṇa. As (does) the breath (mārutas) so (does) the mind (manas) behave. As the mind so the breath acts. From the suppression (lit. destruction) of the one that of the other follows. When both are active the *indriyas* (faculties of sense and volition) perform their functions; both disappearing the state (level) of mokṣa (samādhi) is achieved. When the mind is fixed and the breathing ceases, the bindu is retained (unmoved); from the stabilization of the bindu always true fixity of the body is produced. Mind (manas) is the master of the faculties of sense and volition; and breath is master of the mind; the master of the breath is laya (dissolution) and laya depends upon nāda (anāhata, sound). This itself (laya) is what is called mokṣa or, if you are of another opinion, —no matter. When mind and breath have been absorbed, a sort of ecstasy (ānanda) is experienced. With the ceasing of respiration, with the destruction of the range of the senses, and with the mind inactive and changeless, one wins the laya of Yogīs. For [the Yogī] all of whose effects of deeds are destroyed, and whose actions have ceased, laya, self-engendered and indescribable, is won.[1]

The state, induced by khecarīmudrā, is described at length and is identified with various technical expressions.

Between the eyebrows is the seat of Śiva and there the mind (manas) is absorbed. This condition (*padam*) should be recognized as *turiyā* (samādhi). Then death is not known. One should practise the khecarī until Yoga-nidra (sleep) (samādhi) is (induced). Under no circumstances is there death for [the Yogī] who has reached (is in) Yoga-nidra. Freeing the mind from all contacts, (the Yogī) should meditate on nothing at all. Like a pot in space (vyoman) (with ether) both without and within one should remain fixed. When the air outside the body is absolutely still like that within, the mind with the breath becomes fixed in its own place (? in the top of the skull). Consequently [the Yogī] should practise day and night in the way of breath-control. The breath is dissolved and the mind is absorbed. One should smear the body from head to foot with

---

[1] *HYP*, 4: 20, 21, 23-25, 28-32. Laya may be rendered 'dissolution' of mind or 'absorption' in, or identity with, Being. Dr. Singh says that laya and Kuṇḍalinī Yoga are identical (*Gr.*, p. 14).

amṛta. Great stature, that is great strength, and courage are surely perfected.[1]

And again:

Concentrating the mind in Śakti (Kuṇḍalinī) and the Śakti within the mind, and looking upon the mind with the mind [the Yogī] should reach the highest state. Hold the ātman within kha (Ākāśa) and the kha within the ātman, and making all this kha (this is union above the throat), [the Yogī] should think of nothing whatsoever. [The Yogī] should become void within, void without, void like a pot in space; full within, full without, full like a pot in space. There is to be thought neither upon things external nor upon things internal; having abandoned all thought [the Yogī] should think upon nothing whatsoever. (This) entire world (is) but a creation within the brain; (all) mental enjoyments are simply formed within the brain. Abandon (all) these (merely) mental creations utterly. Resolutely refusing to resort (to these), O Rāma attain peace. As camphor in fire, (as) salt in water, so the mental acts commingled are absorbed in Reality. The mind takes delight in knowledge, all that is known and that to be known. What is known and what is to be known are equally to be destroyed. There is no other, no second way. All this which is seen, whatever moves and that which is immovable, is merely mental. He whose mind ceases to act (*unmanī bhāvat*), knows no duality whatsoever.[2]

Returning now to the experience of nāda and its relation to samādhi, the following verses are of interest:

For reaching the unmanī (state) quickly concentration (of thought) upon the space between the eyebrows is, in my opinion, the best: for the gaining of the level of Rāja Yoga it is an easy method for people of little (irresolute) minds. The absorption (laya) produced from nāda wins immediately the firm assurance of union. Upon the sound of a drum which the Yogī hears when he closes his ears with his fingers (hands) the attention should be held fixedly until the state of inaction is reached. By the practice of this nāda external sounds [gradually] are shut out. Within the space of half a month, having become completely victorious, the Yogī ought to attain peace.

When practice first begins the nāda gives a great variety of very loud (sounds). Then, as the discipline continues, more and more subtle sounds are heard. In the first (stage) the (sounds) produced are like the rolling (thunder-cloud sound) of kettle drums and the *jharjhara* (a drum). In the second (stage) they are like those arising from the shaking of small bells, the conch and the *mṛdaṅga* (a drum). But, finally, they sound like those of the (buzzing of) the black bee, the vīna (flute) and small bells. These various sounds are heard as arising within the body. Even though listening for loud (sounds) like the rolling sounds of kettle drums, still [the Yogī] should seek

[1] *HYP*, 4: 47–52. [2] *HYP*, 4: 53–60.

(practise) (to hear) also the most subtle ones. Dispensing with the heavier ones for the subtle, or the subtle for the heavier, even the mind distracted with pleasure should not wander anywhere else. Anywhere where the mind first comes in contact with the nāda, right there becoming fixed it is absorbed with it. As the black bee, drinking the honey, does not notice the perfume (of the flower) so likewise when the mind is joined with nāda (is intent or listening to nāda), other objects are desired not at all. The mind, wandering in the garden of the objects of sense, like a rutting elephant, can be brought under control by the sharp elephant goad of this (anāhata) nāda. For the mind, taken in the snare of the nāda, having abandoned all fickleness (unsteadiness) becomes steadfast immediately, as a bird whose wings have been clipped. Having abandoned all anxieties (thoughts), with the mind collected [Yogīs], who are desirous of the dominion of Yoga, should consider this nāda worthy of investigation. Nāda becomes a snare for binding the mind, like the spotted antelope; and it can also slay it, as the (snared) antelope is slain.[1]

The final state is described.

From continuous practice of the nāda, the whole store of demerit is wiped out, and the breath and the mind are surely absorbed in the Passionless Being (nirañjana). [The Yogī] hears neither the conch nor the drum at all. Being fixed in the state of unmanī (mental inaction) (his) body becomes a piece of wood. Free from all states, exempt from all anxiety, that Yogī is as one dead, verily not other than liberated. He is neither consumed by death nor snared by (his) deeds. The Yogī, lost in samādhi, is not overcome by anything. The Yogī, who is lost in samādhi is conscious of neither smell nor taste nor form (or colour), nor feeling (touch) nor sound, nor himself nor the Highest. [The Yogī], whose mind is neither sleeping nor waking, remembering nor avoiding remembering, sitting down nor rising up, is indeed a liberated man. The Yogī who is lost in samādhi does not distinguish cold from heat, misery from comfort, honour from dishonour. He is verily free, who being himself really awake, appears like one sleeping, and who is without in- and out-breathing. The Yogī engaged in samādhi cannot be controlled by charms (yantra) and spells (mantra), is beyond the power of all corporeal beings and is immune from all weapons.

Just as long as the moving air does not enter the suṣumṇā, just so long the bindu is not stable, because the prāṇa is not stopped; as long as in dhyāna (fixed attention) spontaneously the form of Brahma (tattva) does not appear, so long, he who speaks of knowledge is a babbler of that 'knowledge' which is both futile and deceptive.[2]

Ecstatic experience, due to bodily manipulation, occupies a large place in this system, and the Hindu seems to understand fully the methods by which the ecstasy bordering on

[1] *HYP*, 4: 79, 81–93. [2] *HYP*, 4: 104–115.

trance may be induced. When certain internal sounds are heard, the desired end is known by the adept to be close at hand.

While tapas (hard discipline, austerity) are not without place in the system, most of the practice is based upon ideas of sex functions and experiences. There is a further method which induces similar ecstatic results, the use of drugs. The Yogīs are notorious as drug addicts. Some drugs, such as hemp, stimulate the imagination along the line of the experiences outlined above.[1] The use of drugs to induce ecstasy and vision plays a large part in religious experience the world over. Take the *peyote* (*mescal*) cult of the American Indians as an illustration. Another is the use of *hasheesh* (*carnabis-indica*) by the 'Assassins.' Both of these drugs produce hallucinations of colours as well. The Hindu knew these matters early. The muni in the *Ṛig Veda* is under the excitement of drugs. Patañjali is aware of this method for inducing samādhi for he says:

> Perfections proceed from birth or from drugs or from spells or from self-castigation or from concentration.[2]

And the commentator adds:

> He describes the perfection which proceeds from drugs. A human being, when for some cause or other he reaches the mansions of the demons (*asura*), and when he makes use of elixirs of life brought to him by the lovely damsels of the demons, attains to agelessness and to deathlessness and to other perfections. Or (this perfection may be had) by the use of an elixir-of-life in this very world. So for instance the sage Mandavya, who dwelt on the Vindhyas and who made use of potions.[3]

Again and again emphasis is put upon the fact that this Yoga staves off death. And one of the interpretations of the practice of vajrolī is that the woman serves to insure extension of life to the Yogī. On this point Miss Elizabeth Sharp's book, *The Secrets of the Kāula Circle* may be consulted.[4]

---

[1] See *An Essay on Hasheesh*, by Victor Robinson, M.D.

[2] *WYS*, p. 299. [3] *WYS*, p. 300.

[4] London, 1936.

BY THIS YOGA ŚIVA APPEARS AS THE VAST OCEAN OF BLISS AND KNOWLEDGE, DESTROYING THE MISERY OF THE WORLD; AND THE END IS THE STATE OF THE UNMOVING FLAMES OF LIGHT IN THE INNER SOUL, A BODY OF BLISS AND KNOWLEDGE.

CHAPTER SEVENTEEN

CONCLUSION

THE physical basis of this Yoga is apparent. And a healthy body is essential. The Yogī finds in his system both enjoyment (bhukti) and liberation (mukti). The essence of the Haṭha Yoga is physical exercise and manipulation, quite mechanical. And the symbolism is that of the sex functions. If it is charged against the exposition found in the preceding pages that it is overburdened with interpretations on too low a plane, it must be said in reply that both the practice and the outlook of the Yogīs confirm this point of view. The author has tried to follow their views and their explanations. Frenzy, or thrill, or ecstasy, seems to be the aim all the while; and these experiences are interpreted in terms of union with the divine. Divinity has to be sought within the body of the Śākta. Moreover, the historical background of the cult of Gorakhnāth points in the same direction. During many centuries preceding the fourteenth of our era, late Buddhist practice, especially in Bengal, was affecting the whole religious outlook. Both Śaivite and Vaiṣṇavite movements were profoundly influenced by it. The high religious value of intercourse with women was more and more insisted upon. Romantic love for beautiful women was viewed as a path to release. The post Cāitanya-Sahajiyā movement confirms this point, as does Gorakhnāth's early affiliation with the Vajrāyāna.[1] While the Vaiṣṇavite movement emphasizes love in the consort of the divine, the Śaivite lays stress upon her

[1] See *The Post Cāitanya Sahajiyā Cult in Bengal*, by M. M. Bose, 1930. This cult is based upon the idea of the Parakiya, denounced in ordinary society, but in religion adopted as the symbol of intense love. Here bhakti lies wholly in the sphere of emotion and is illustrated in the life of Kṛiṣṇa associated with Rādhā at Brindaban. See also *Śāstri*, *Or*, and *Bhattacharyya*.

power or energy. The Śrī-cakra and the whole Śākta symbolism enforce this interpretation. The paṇḍits, with whom the author read the literature of the Yogīs, had no other interpretations to offer. For example, no one ever suggested any other meaning for bindu than that used in this work. Arthur Avalon protested in his work on Tantra against the tendency to rate the teachings of these works too realistically,[1] but Sir John Woodroffe, in his introduction to Dr. Rele's *The Mysterious Kundalini*, says:

> What may be its value is another question, a matter upon which I am not so sure as I once was. . . . To me the Yogas of certain worth are those of Karma, Bhakti and Jñāna. There are, however, apparently some to whom Kuṇḍalinī Yoga makes special appeal and who receive satisfaction therefrom. In any case the test is that of Āyurveda, namely, results. If I deal with this matter here it is because, on further consideration, I am disposed to think that I underrated in my *Serpent Power* the value of some adverse criticism of this Yoga which I, in the volume mentioned, quoted.

This Yoga has wide acceptance in India today.[2]

Undoubtedly there is a higher interpretation of Śakti and of Śākta which may be given in metaphysical terms;[3] and there is as good a reason for the view that the female energy is the creative, formative power in the universe as there is for the male. But nowhere in the world has such symbolism been able to keep itself for long on a high plane. And, as elsewhere, here, emotional experiences of bhakti have given a large place for license and debauchery. Bhoga (enjoyment) as a means of liberation, of enlightenment, is here held as a tenet of faith. The adept acts and enjoys as manifest creation. Alberuni, a thousand years ago, made the following observation on the Yoga:

> He who wants God, wants the good for the whole creation without a single exception for any reason whatever; but he who occupies himself exclusively with his own self, will for its benefits neither inhale breath nor exhale it. When a man attains to this degree, his

[1] *Serpent Power*, pp. 25, 29.

[2] *Serpent Power*, p. 24. See also *The Śāktas*, by E. A. Payne.

[3] Dr. Singh (*Gr.*, p. 26) says that the aim of Gorakhnāth is to transcend the lower self, which consists of sexual power, vital air and the mind. But the method, he says, is the control of the breath which is the key to the control of the other two.

spiritual power prevails over his bodily power and then he is gifted with the faculty of doing eight different things by which detachment is realized; for a man can only dispense with that which he is able to do, and not with that which is outside his grasp.[1]

The foregoing remarks are not to be construed as to suggest that there is not a higher interpretation possible for the doctrines of the Śākta, but to show that so far as this group of Yogīs is concerned, and those who believe in them as well, the lower is the practical interpretation. Everywhere well-thinking Hindus express themselves unfavourably towards them.

The fact need not be ignored, however, that this kind of interpretation of the divine, the cult of female divinities, has been of world-wide distribution, and that it has found expression in every age. Neither should it be forgotten that tendencies of this kind find sympathy at the present time outside of India; still, nowhere else is this aspect of religion so persistently vital. Mr. Payne has pointed out that in India there has been, in recent times, a tendency to lay emphasis upon this horrible and revolting side of awe, which represents itself in worship of the Devī, during periods of economic and political depression. And he thinks that the view of God as Destroyer, the worship of Force and the use of a ritual essentially magic, portend the downfall of Śaktism. The history of religion in India would seem to throw doubt upon such expectation.

The Yogī is not to be judged altogether adversely. Behind this faith is the philosophy which deserves sympathetic study and an impulse, the age-long search for the experience of the Real, Sadāśiva, in this particular sect.

Some recent Western psychology seeks to understand experiences which lie outside ordinary self-consciousness.[2]

There stands out in asceticism as a whole that which the Yogī emphasizes in particular—the great seeker after truth, reality, with the supreme experience of the religious life. And, in the pursuit of this end, he exhibits both courage and persistence. Nowhere else in the world have men been

---

[1] Sachau's Translation, vol. I, p. 69.

[2] See K. T. Behanan, *Yoga: A Scientific Evaluation.* (1937).

found who have endured more in the way of physical pain or who have carried tapas through so long a discipline. The great Gorakhnāth is referred to as *the* embodiment of patience, that is, one able to carry *tapasya* through. He was quick tempered and terrible, but also *patient*.

Bhartri happened to go into the forest where Gorakhnāth was practising austerities, but he knew not that the saint was there. Soon after, the disciples of Gorakhnāth met him and asked him to become one of them. He answered, 'What do I care for Gorakhnāth? If he wishes to learn the ways of the Almighty let him come and hear from me.' Finally, Goraknāth said to Bhartri, 'If you give me a handful of patience, I will become your disciple.' So Bhartri, in search of patience, came to the gods, but they could not supply it. At last he went to Viṣṇu, who said, 'I cannot supply you patience. If you want it you must go to Gorakhnāth who is the greatest of the saints.' Thus convinced, Bhartri accepted Gorakhnāth as his guru.[1]

The penances of such men as Dharamnāth have become famous.

Perhaps the point with reference to members of the order which needs most emphasis is that of their relation to society. The Yogī cannot live as other men do. Unless he is untrue to his vows, he must live apart from society, but dependent upon it for a living: seeking only his own religious satisfactions and those of his few disciples. He bears no social responsibilities towards his fellow men. The Indian's concept of āśrama, the search for release alone at the last and for himself, is the fundamental error of the system.

The element of bhakti, or emotionalism, deserves a word. This Yoga movement, even in its earliest manifestations, looks to Rudra, to Śiva, the terrible; and the aspect of Śakti which the Yogī worships is everywhere that of Kālī, of Bhāiravī, and of fiendish female forms. With this is coupled realistic experiences on the plane of eroticism. Characteristically, horrible, abominable and revolting practices and license go together. It is because the ends achieved by restraint are also attainable by symbolic participation in a drama of divine joy where full play is given to indulgence, through sex stimulus and the use of drugs, that their whole system of religious devotion has to be revolutionized. Present

[1] See chap. eleven, p. 244, note 2.

day attitudes of Hindus insisting upon decency and strict conduct show how necessary this is. This has always been recognized with extreme forms of vāmacāra, in vajrayāṇa and in kāulācāra. The illegal has been the norm of the extreme. But the ideals and practices of the Yogīs are, consequently, not open to public gaze as they once were, and many are reluctant to admit that they indulge in them.

Finally, it is possible to question whether the end which follows ecstatic experience, that is, unconsciousness, or pure subjectivity, or the absence of self-conscious personality, is any more satisfactory as the solution of the problems of life, or as a view of the ultimate goal of man, than is the anti-social character of the whole movement. As meeting the demands of the new day in India itself, both the experience and the goal are insufficient.

GLOSSARY

Ādhāra. A 'support'; a centre of vital power or of specialized function in the body; a *cakra.* A ground or support for meditation.

Ahiṁsa. The doctrine of non-injury.

Akhāṛā. A monastery.

Ardhanārī. The half-male-half-female form of the Brahman.

Āsana. Posture. Sometimes involves exercises.

Avadhūta. Liberated. Gorakhnāth is often so designated. The word is a general term for 'non-Brāhman' ascetics who were freed from all ties, particularly of caste, and who accepted Yoya or yoga and bhakti, whether they were Śāivas (Sannyasīs or Jogīs), or Vāiṣṇavas (Vāivagīs).

Bandha. A binding; a stoppage. Often involved in physical exercises. The Bandhas are those devices which serve to close all exits of air and to produce tension in the body.

Çaran. Footprint of a divinity, of a saint, or of some other person; *pāduka.*

Ciṁtā. Fire tongs.

Cūrmā. A sweetmeat made of sugar, butter and crumbled bread.

Cuṭiya. Scalp-lock.

Devī. The Goddess.

Dhūnī. Yogī's sacred fire.

Ḍoli. A sort of chair, or palanquin for carrying people.

Dundubhī. A mystical drum; *dund*, a large kettle-drum.

Gaddī. A cushion, a throne.

Gaṅja. Hemp-plant preparation for smoking.

Gāurī. The Goddess.

Gāurīpīṭha. The *yoni*, *yonisthāna*.

Gotra. A sub-division of a caste.

Hom. A kind of burnt offering. An offering of ghi in fire.

Indriya. Motor or sensory function.

Jogī. Yogī.

Kachcha (*kacca*). (Food); uncooked food.

Kafni. A garment resembling a shroud, worn by Musulman *faqīrs*.

Kaṅgan. A bracelet or armlet of threads.

Kāuṛī. A shell used as money, of very little value.

4 kāuṛīs	=	1 gaṇḍa
20 gaṇḍas	=	1 paṇ
4 paṇ	=	1 ana
4 anas	=	1 kāhan (about ¼ rupee).

Ketkī. 'A sweet-scented flower.' *Ketaka*: the tree *pandonus odoratissimus*.

Khichṛī. A dish made of pulse and rice cooked together.

Khīr. Rice boiled in milk.

Kuṇḍal. Ear-ring; coil.

Laḍḍu. A ball of sweatmeat.

Laṅgotī. A loin cloth.

Laya. 'Union'; unconsciousness. A state where the mind ceases to function. A return to the undifferentiated state. Samādhi.

Liṅga. The Phallus of Śiva (in text the word is often used for *yoni-liṅga* and is so intended unless otherwise specified).

Mahant. Head of a monastery; a chief teacher.

Makāra. The letter *M*.

Manasā. A serpent goddess.

Maṇḍala. A circle. A *cakra*. A lotus.

Manonmanī. A state in which the mind is unmoving.

Mantra. A sacred text; a spell. An instrument of thought, when rightly used, embodying supernatural power.

Maṭha. A hut; a cottage; especially the retired hut or cell of an ascetic (student); cloister, college (especially for young Brahmans); a temple.

Meḍhra. Liṅga.

Mela. A religious fair.

Meṁdhī. A plant. Myrtle, *Lawsonia alba.*

Mīna. Fish.

Mokṣa. Release; 'salvation'.

Mṛdaṅga. A small drum.

Mudrā. Ear-ring worn by a Yogī.

Mudrā. A manipulation of the body, a posture, an attitude, a contortion. Often a kind of exercise. The word as applied to one of the five *M's* is usual rendered 'parched grain,' but 'gesture' or 'attitude' is probably correct.

Mukti. Release, *samādhi*, 'salvation'.

Nād. A whistle worn by Yogīs; more particularly, sound.

Nāda. Sound.

Nāḍi, Nāḍī. A channel, or a nerve, a path for vital force; one of the elements in the physiological theory of the Yoga.

Padma. Lotus; a *chakra.*

Pāduka. A foot-print. *Caran.*

Pakāurī. A dish made of peas meal.

Pakhal. A large leather bag such as is borne by bullocks.

Palāo. Rice cooked with mutton.

Pañcamakāṛa. The five *M*'s.

Panth. A sect, or a division of a sect.

Paramparā. Succession. A table of succession.

Pilāo. Rice cooked with mutton.

Pīr. A saint, a synonym for *mahant.*

Pradakṣiṇa. Going around an image, a shrine, or an object, with the right hand towards it.

Prasād. Food that has been offered to an idol or of which a spiritual teacher has partaken.

Pūjārī. One who conducts worship at a temple, or a shrine.

Rākṣasa. Fiend, ogre.

Śākta. A worshipper of Śakti.

Śakti. The female power or principle, often personified; the Goddess.

Śāligrām (*Sālagrāma*). A black stone found in the Ghandaki river, and worshipped by Hindus; sacred to Viṣṇu or Kṛṣṇa. Some say that it should be an amonite.

Samādh (*Samādhi*). Tomb of a saint. As a technical term the final state in the Yoga process; 'release'.

Saṁkalpa. Will, desire.

Satī. The true wife; a name of Śiva's consort.

Sattu. Parched grain reduced to meal and made into a paste.

Śelī. A necklace of threads, worn by mendicants.

Siddhis. Perfections; supernormal powers.

Siṅg. Horn.

Śrāddha. Religious rites for the dead.

Śrīcakra. A mystic circle of the Tāntra.

Sthān. A place or location; a small shrine.

Śūnya. Void.

Tāntra. For Tāntric.

Ṭhākur. An idol, a temple.

Ṭīkā. A sect mark made on the forehead or between the eyebrows.

Tīrṭha. A place of pilgrimage.

Tripuṇḍ. A sectarian mark of Śiva made with horizontal lines drawn with ashes or other substance on the forehead, arms or trunk.

Urd. A pulse.

Vāmacāra. Left-hand practice, or ritual.

Virakta. Dispassionate.

Yab-Yum. The state of union of the god and his consort.

Yantra. A symbol or magic figure.

Yoni. Womb, uterus, vulva, female organs of generation; source; origin, with the *liṅga* a typical symbol of the divine procreative energy.

BIBLIOGRAPHY

(Since, in the body of the text, the footnotes contain very full references to sources, it has been decided, for economy of space, to list here an abridged list of the works consulted in the preparation of *Gorakhnāth and the Kānphaṭa Yogīs*.

A. GOVERNMENT PUBLICATIONS AND WORKS OF OFFICIALS

The Census of India, both Imperial and Provincial Reports and Tables, 1882, 1891, 1901, 1911, 1921, 1931.

The Gazetteers, both Imperial and Provincial Series. The older works are of more value for students of culture.

ALEXANDER, E. B., *Statistical Description and Historical Account of the North-Western Provinces of India. Gorakhpur* (Gazetteer, North-Western Provinces). Vol. IV. Allahabad, 1881.

BCI BALFOUR, EDWARD, *The Cyclopædia of India and of Eastern and Southern Asia*. London, 1885.

CONYBEARE, H. C., *Statistical and Historical Account of the North-Western Provinces of India*. Bareilly. Allahabad, 1879.

CTC CROOKE, WILLIAM, *The Tribes and Castes of the North-Western Provinces and Oudh*. 4 Vols. Calcutta, 1896.

ERNWP ELLIOT, SIR H. M., *Memoirs on the History, Folklore and Distribution of the Races of the North-Western Provinces of India*. 2 Vols. Revised by JOHN BEAMES. London, 1869.

ENTHOVEN, R. E., *The Tribes and Castes of Bombay*. 3 Vols. Bombay, 1920, 1922.

MARTIN, MONTGOMERY, *The History, Antiquities, Topography and Statistics of Eastern India*. 3 Vols. London. 1838. (Contains DR. F. M. BUCHANAN'S work.)

NCS NESFIELD, J. C., *Brief View of the Caste System of the North-Western Provinces and Oudh, Together with an Examination of the Names and Figures Shown in the Census Report of 1882*. Allahabad, 1885.

RTCB RISLEY, H. H., *The Tribes and Castes of Bengal. Ethnographic Glossary*. 2 Vols. Calcutta, 1891.

RISLEY, H. H., *Census of India, 1901*. Vol. I. *India Ethnographic Appendix*. Calcutta, 1903.

RTCP ROSE, H. A., *A Glossary of the Tribes and Castes of the Punjab and North-West Frontier Province*. (Based on the Census Report for the Punjab, 1883; by the late SIR DENZIL IBBETSON, K.C.S.I., and the Census Report for the Punjab, 1892, by THE HONORABLE MR. E. D. MACLEGAN, C.S.I., and compiled by H. A. ROSE, Lahore. 3 Vols. 1914.

RTCCP RUSSELL, E. V., and RAI BAHADUR HIRA LAL, *The Tribes and Castes of the Central Provinces of India*. 4 Vols. London, 1916.

SHTC SHERRING, M. A., *Hindu Tribes and Castes as Represented in Benares*. London, 1872.

TCTSI THURSTON, E. and RANGACHARI, K., *Castes and Tribes of South India*. Vol. II. Madras, 1909.

THURSTON, E., *A Gazetteer of the Territories under the Government of the Viceroy of India*. Revised and Edited by SIR ROBERT LETHBRIDGE and ARTHUR N. WALLASTAN. London, 1886.

B. OTHER WORKS YIELDING ETHNOGRAPHIC DATA

BAINES, SIR ATHELSTANE, *Ethnography*, in Grundriss der Indo-Arischen Philologie und Altertumskunde. Vol. II, Pt. 5. Strassburg, 1912.

BHCS BHATTACHARYA, JOGENDRA NATH, *Hindu Castes and Sects*. Calcutta, 1896.

BRIGGS, GEO. W., *The Chamārs*. Calcutta and London, 1920.

ENTHOVEN, R. E., *Folklore of Bombay*. Oxford, 1924.

Gr GRIERSON, G. A., Article, 'Goraknāth', in *ERE*. Vol. VI.

KHAKHAR, DALPATRAM PRANJINAN, Article, 'The History of the Kanphatas of Kachh.' In *IA*. 1878.

NORTHEY, MAJOR W. BROOK, M.C. and MORRIS, CAPT. J. C., *The Gurkhas*. London, 1928.

POSTANS, L. T., Article, 'An Account of the Kanphatas of Dhinodhar in Cutch with the Legend of Dharamnath, their Founder.' In *JRAS*. 1839.

RAGHUNATHJI, Article, 'Bombay Beggars and Criers.' In *IA*, Vol. X.

SYED, SIRAJ UL HASSAN, *The Castes and Tribes of H. E. H. The Nizam's Dominions*. Vol. I. Bombay, 1920.

TEMPLE, RICHARD, C., *Punjab Notes and Queries*. Allahabad, London. Vol. IV. 1883–87.

C. LITERARY SOURCES

ABBOTT, J. E., *The Poet Saints of Mahārāṣhṭra*. Series, 10 Vols. Poona, 1926–34.

BHATTACHARYYA, B., (Editor) *Sādhanamālā*. 2 Vols. Baroda, 1925, 1928.

BHATTACHARYYA, B., *Two Vajrayāṇa Works*. Baroda, 1929.

GRIERSON, G. A., Article, 'The Song of Manik Chandra.' In *JASBe*. 1878.

GRIERSON, G. A., Article, 'The Versions of the Song of Gopi Chand.' In *JASBe*. 1885.

GRIERSON, G. A., *The Modern Vernacular Literature of Hindustan*. Calcutta, 1889.

HUME, E. R., *The Thirteen Upanishads, Translated from the Sanskrit, with an Outline of the Philosophy of the Upanishads and an Annotated Bibliography*. Oxford, 1921.

IYANGER, S., *Haṭhayogapradīpika*. Second Edition. Adyar, 1933.

Mac MACAULIFFE, MAX ARTHUR, *The Sikh Religion, Its Gurus, Sacred Writings and Authors*. 6 Vols. Oxford, 1909.

MITRA, RAJENDRALALA, *The Yoga Aphorisms of Patañjali, With the Commentary of Bhoja Raja and an English Translation*. Calcutta, 1883.

PANCHAM SINH, *Haṭhayogapradīpaka. Translation into English. Sacred Books of the Hindus*. Allahabad, 1915.

PANGARKAR, R. L., *Śrī Jñāneśvaramahārāja Carita*. Poona, 1912.

RAMA PRASADA, *Patañjali's Yoga Sūtras with the Commentary of Vyāsa and the Gloss of Vāchaspati Misra* Allahabad, 1912.

Śāstri ŚĀSTRI, MAHĀMAHOPĀDHAYA HAREPRASĀD, Editor. *Rāmacārita*, by Saṅdhyakāra Nandi. Memoirs of the Asiatic Society of Bengal. Vol. III (1910–14). Calcutta, 1914.

SMITH, R., *Faqire und Faqirtum.* Berlin. Second Edition. 1921.

STEELE, MRS. F. A., *Tales of the Punjab.* London, 1917.

Swynn SWYNNERTON, CHARLES, *Romantic Tales from the Punjab, with Indian Nights Entertainment.* New Edition in one volume. London, 1906.

TAYLOR, J., *Prabodha Chandrodaya, or Rise of the Moon of Intellect,* by KRISHNA-MISRA. Bombay, 1886.

THIBAUT, GEORGE, *The Vedānta Sūtras with the Commentary of Rāmanuja. SBE.* London, 1904.

THIBAUT, GEORGE, *The Vedānta Sūtras with the Commentary of Shaṅkarācārya. SBE.* 2 Vols. London, 1904.

Tr TRUMP, ERNEST, *The Ādi Granth.* London, 1877.

VASU, S. C. (Translator), *The Gheraṇḍa Saṁhitā.* Adyar, 1933. First printing, Allahabad, 1895.

VIDHYARAVASA, S. C. (Translator), *Śiva Saṁhitā.* Allahabad, 1923.

WOODROFFE, SIR JOHN (Arthur Avalon), *Principles of Tantra.* 2 Vols. London, 1916.

WOODROFFE, SIR JOHN (Arthur Avalon), *Tantra of the Great Liberation.* London, 1913.

WYS WOODS, JAMES HOUGHTON, *The Yoga System of Patañjali.* Cambridge, 1914.

BHAVE, V. L., *Mahārāṣṭra Sārasvat.* 2 Vols. New Edition. Poona, 1925.

FORL FARQUHAR, J. N., *Outlines of the Religious Literature of India.* London, 1920.

HODGSON, B. H., *Essays on the Languages, Literature and Religion of Nepal and Tibet.* London, 1874.

HGE HOPKINS, E. W., *The Great Epic of India, Its Character and Origin.* New York, 1901.

MACDONELL, A. A., and KEITH, A. B., *Vedic Index of Names and Subjects.* 2 Vols. London, 1912.

SEN, DINESH CHANDRA, *History of Bengali Language and Literature.* Calcutta, 1911.

SEN, DINESH CHANDRA, *Sati, A Mystical Story.* Calcutta, 1916.

CFD SHEA, DAVID, and FRAZER, ANTHONY, *The Dabistan or School of Manners.* Translated from the Original Persian with Notes and Illustrations. 3 Vols. Paris, 1843.

Temp TEMPLE, RICHARD C., *The Legends of the Punjab.* 3 Vols. London, 1884–1900.

WGIL WINTERNITZ, DR. M., *Geschichte der Indischen Literature.* 3 Vols. Leipzig, 1913, 1920.

D. WORKS ON PHILOSOPHY AND RELIGION INCLUDING TANTRA AND CULT

BEHANAN, K. T., *Yoga: A Scientific Evaluation.* New York, 1937.

BRAHMA, N. K., *The Philosophy of Hindu Sādhanā.* London, 1932.

BROWN, G. W., *The Human Body in the Upanishads.* Jubbulpore, 1921.

COWELL, E. B., and GOUGH, A. E., *The Sarva Darṣana Saṁgraha or Review of the Different Systems of Hindu Philosophy*, by MADHAVA ACHARYA. Translated by E. B. COWELL and A. E. GOUGH. Second Edition. London, 1894.

ELIOT, SIR CHARLES, *Hinduism and Buddhism.* 3 Vols. London, 1921.

DHIP DASGUPTA, SURENDRANATH, *A History of Indian Philosophy.* Vol. I, Cambridge, 1922.

DHIP(II) Vol. II, 1932.

Hindu Mysticism. Chicago, 1927.

Das G. *Yoga Philosophy* (In relation to other systems of Indian Thought). Calcutta, 1930.

DHP DAVIES, JOHN, *Hindu Philosophy, The Sāṁkhya Kārikā of Īśvara Kṛṣṇa.* London, 1894.

D.Up. DEUSSEN, P., *The Philosophy of the Upanishads.* English Translation by A. S. GEDEN. Edinburgh, 1906.

GSY GARBE, RICHARD, *Sāṁkhya und Yoga.* Grundriss der Indo-Arischen Philologie und Altertumskunde. Strassburg, 1896.

GSP GARBE, RICHARD, *Die Sāṁkhya Philosophie.* Leipzig, 1894. New Edition, 1917.

GHOSH, JAJNESWAR, *A Study of Yoga.* Calcutta, 1933.

HALL, FITZ-EDWARD, *A Contribution Towards an Index to the Bibliography of the Indian Philosophical Systems.* Calcutta, 1859.

HAUER, J. W., *Der Yoga als Heilweg.* Vol. I. Stuttgart. 1932.

KSS Keith, A. B., *The Sāṁkaya System. A History of the Sāṁkhya Philosophy.* Calcutta, 1916.

Keith, A. B., *The Religion and Philosophy of the Veda.* 2 Vols. Cambridge, Mass., 1925.

Radhakrishnan, S., *Indian Philosophy.* 2 Vols. New York, 1922, 1927.

SBH Rai Bahadur Śrīsa Chandra Vasu, *An Introduction to the Yoga Philosophy.* Allahabad, 1915.

Rele, Vasant G., *The Mysterious Kuṇḍalinī.* Bombay, 1927 (Third Edition, 1931).

Mohan Singh, *Gorakhnāth aud Mediaeval Hindu Mysticism.* Lahore, 1937.

Thomas, E. J., *The History of Buddhist Thought.* New York, 1933.

Arthur Avalon, *The Serpent Power.* London, 1919.

Arthur Avalon, *Shakti and Shakta, Essays and Addresses on the Shakta Tantra Shastra.* Second Edition. London, 1920.

BRI Barth, A., *The Religions of India.* London, 1882.

BVS Bhandarkar, R. G., *Vāiṣṇavism, Śāivism, and Minor Religious Systems.* Grundriss der Indo-Arischen Philologie and Altertumskunde. Strassburg, 1913.

Bhattacharya, B., *Introduction to Buddhist Esoterism.* Oxford, 1932.

BRV Bloomfield, M., *The Religion of the Veda.* New York, 1908.

Bose, M. M., *The Post-Cāitanyā Sahajiyā Cult of Bengal.* Calcutta, 1930.

Crooke, William, *An Introduction to the Popular Religion and Folklore of Northern India.* Allahabad, 1894. Revised and Illustrated Edition. 2 Vols. London, 1896. New Edition prepared for the press by R. E. Enthoven. Oxford, 1926.

Davids, Mrs. Rhys, *Outlines of Buddhism.* London, 1934.

Griswold, H. D., *The Religion of the Ṛig Veda.* Oxford, 1923.

HRI Hopkins, E. W., *The Religions of India.* Boston, 1895.

Judgment in the case of Mahant Brahm Nāth vs. Baba Gokul Nāth, Court of the Subordinate Judge of Gorakhpur of 1926.

MVM MACDONELL, A. A., *Vedic Mythology* (Grundriss der Indo-Arischen Philologie und Altertumskunde). Strassburg, 1897.

MWB MONIER-WILLIAMS, M., *Brahmanism and Hinduism*. London, 1891.

OBTM OMAN, JOHN CAMPBELL, *The Brahmans, Theists and Muslims of India*. Philadelphia.

OCCS *Cults, Customs and Superstitions of India*. London, 1908.

OMAS *The Mystics, Ascetics and Saints of India*. London, 1903.

TARANATH, *Geschichte des Buddhismus in Indien aus dem Tibetischen ubersetzt von Anton Schiefner*. St. Petersburg, 1869.

UNDERHILL, M. M., *The Hindu Religious Year*. Calcutta, 1921.

Or VASU, NAGENDRA NATH, *Modern Buddhism and Its Followers in Orissa*. Calcutta, 1911.

VON GLASENAPP, H., *Der Hinduismus*. München, 1922.

WARD, W., *View of the History, Literature and Religion of the Hindus*. 4 Vols. 1817–20.

WILKINS, *Hindu Mythology*. Calcutta, 1913.

Wi WILSON, HORACE HYMAN, *Essays and Lectures Chiefly on the Religion of the Hindus. A Sketch of the Religious Sects of the Hindus*. London. Edition. 1861. Vol. I. Edited by REINHOLD ROST. Also Vol. II. Was first published 1828, 1832.

E. ICONOGRAPHY, INSCRIPTIONS, SCULPTURE, ETC.

BHATTACHARYYA, B., *The Indian Buddhist Ikonography, Mainly Based upon the Sādhanamālā and other Cognate Tantric Texts*. Oxford, 1924.

BIDYABINOD, PANDIT B. B., *Supplementary Catalogue of the Coins in the Indian Museum, Calcutta, Non-Muhammadan Series*. Vol. I. Calcutta, 1923.

BROWN, C. J., *The Coins of India*. Calcutta and London. 1922.

BURGESS, JAMES, *Report on the Antiquities of Kathiawar and Kachh* (Archæological Survey of Western India). London, 1876.

BURGESS, JAMES, *Archæological Survey of Western India*, Vol. V. London, 1883.

BURGESS, JAMES, and COUSENS, HENRY, *Revised List of Antiquarian Remains of the Bombay Presidency (Archæological Survey of India)*. New Imperial Series, Vol. XVI. 1897.

CUNNINGHAM, SIR A., *Coins of the Indu-Scythians*. Calcutta. 1892.

CUNNINGHAM, SIR A., *Coins of Mediæval India. From the Seventh Century down to the Muhammadan Conquests*. London, 1894.

FHIEA FERGUSSON, JAS., *History of India and Eastern Architecture*. Revised and Edited by JAMES BURGESS and R. PHENE SPIERS. 2 Vols. London, 1910.

FRANCKE, A. H., *Antiquities of Indian Tibet*. Calcutta. Vol. I, 1914; vol. II, 1926.

FRENCH, J. C., *The Art of the Pala Empire of Bengal*. Oxford, 1928.

GOPI NATH RAO, T. A., *Elements of Hindu Iconography*. 4 Vols. Madras, 1914-16.

KHAKHAR, D. P., *Report on the Architectural and Archæological Remains in the Province of Kachh*. With five papers on Kachh Antiquities, by the late SIR ALEX. BURNES. With a Prefatory Note by J. BURGESS, Archæological Surveyor and Reporter to Government, 1879.

RAPSON, E. J., *Indian Coins* (Grundiss der Indo-Arischen Philologie und Altertumskunde). Strassburg, 1897.

SMITH, VINCENT A., *A History of Fine Art in India and Ceylon*. Oxford, 1911.

SMITH, VINCENT A., *Catalogue of the Coins in the Indian Museum, Calcutta, Including the Cabinet of the Asiatic Society of Bengal*. Oxford, 1906.

VOGEL, J. PH., *Indian Serpent Lore*. London, 1926.

WALSH, E. H., Article, 'The Coinage of Nepāl.' In *JRAS*, 1908.

F. HISTORY, DESCRIPTION

Ban BANERJI, R. D., *The Palas of Bengal*. Memoirs of the Asiatic Society of Bengal. Vol. V. Calcutta, 1915.

BURNES, LIEUT. ALEXANDER, *Travels into Bokhara*. 3 Vols. London, 1834.

BURTON, R. F., *Sciende: or The Unhappy Valley*. 2 Vols. London, 1851.

Duff DUFF, C. MABEL (MRS. W. R. RICKMERS), *The Chronology of India. From the Earliest Times to the Beginnings of the Sixteenth Century.* London, 1899.

EHI ELLIOT, SIR H. M., *The History of India as Told by Its Own Historians.* The Muhammadan Period. Edited by PROF. JOHN DAWSON. 2 Vols. London, 1867–69.

FORBES, A. K.. *Rās Mālā.* Edited by H. G. RAWLINSON. London, 1924.

GAIT, E. A., *History of Assam.* Second Edition. Calcutta, 1926 (First Edition, 1906).

GRP GRIFFIN, SIR L. H., *The Rajas of the Punjab.* London, 1873.

GRIFFIN, SIR L. H., *The Panjab Chiefs.* New Edition by C. F. MASSEY. 2 Vols. Lahore, 1890.

HAMILTON, F. (formerly Buchanan), *An Account of the Kingdom of Nepal and of the Territories Annexed to this Dominion by the House of Gorkha.* Edinburgh, 1819.

HART, CAPT., Article, 'Some account of a Journey from Kurrachee to Hinglaj in the Lus territory, descriptive of the intermediate country and of the port of Soumeanee.' *JASBe*, 1840, pp. 134 ff.

HOLDICH, SIR THOS. H., *The Gates of India.* London, 1910.

JARRET, COL. H. S., and BLOCHMANN, H., *Ain i Akbari by Abdul Fazl i Allami.* 3 Vols. Calcutta, 1894.

KIRKPATRICK, COLONEL, *An Account of the Kingdom of Nepal* (in 1793). London, 1811.

KITTOE, LIEUT. M., Article, 'Notes on a Journey to Girnar, etc.' *JASBe*, (1838), Vol. VII, pp. 865 ff.

LANDON, P., *Nepal.* 2 Vols. London, 1928.

LÉVI, SYLVAIN, *Le Nepal* (Annals du Musée Guimet). Paris, 1905.

MARSHALL, SIR JOHN, *Mohenjo-Daro and the Indus Civilization.* 3 Vols. London, 1931.

MASSON, CHARLES, *Narrative of Various Journeys in Balochistan, Afghanistan, and the Panjab.* 4 Vols. London, 1842–44.

OLDFIELD, H. O., *Sketches from Nepal.* 2 Vols. London, 1880.

RAPSON, E. J., *The Cambridge History of India.* Vol. I. Cambridge, 1922.

SACHAU, EDWARD C., *Alberuni's India, an Account of the Religions, Philosophy, Literature, Geography, Chronology, Astronomy, Customs, Laws and Astrology of India about A.D. 1030*. An English Edition with Notes and Indices. 2 Vols. London, 1910.

SHERRING, M. A., *The Sacred City of the Hindus* (*Benares*). London, 1868.

Tod TOD, JAMES (LT.-COL.), *Annals and Antiquities of Rajasthan*, or *The Central and Western Rajput States of India*. Edited with an Introduction and Notes by WILLIAM CROOKE, C.I.E. 3 Vols. London, 1920.

VASU, N. N., *The Social History of Kamarupa*. 2 Vols. Calcutta.

WRIGHT, DANIEL, *History of Nepal, Translated from the Vaṁśavalī Parbatiyā, by Munshi Shew Shunkar Singh and Pandit Shri Gunanand, with Introductory Sketch of the Country and People of Nepal by the Editor*. Cambridge, 1877.

G. OTHER SOURCES

EB *Encyclopædia Britannica*. 13th Edition (also 14th Edition).

CR *Calcutta Review*.

EI *Epigraphia Indica*.

ERE *Encyclopædia of Religion and Ethics*.

IA *Indian Antiquary*.

JAOS *Journal of the American Oriental Society*.

JAnth S. By *Journal of the Anthropological Society of Bombay*.

JASBe *Journal of the Asiatic Society of Bengal*.

JASBy *Journal of the Asiatic Society of Bombay*.

JASJ *Journal of the Asiatic Society of Japan*.

JRAS *Journal of the Royal Asiatic Society*.

PNQ *Punjab Notes and Queries*.

Archæological Survey of India.

American Journal of Philology.

Journal Asiatique.

Asiatic Researches.

INDEX

PLATES

CAVE OF GORAKHNĀTH IN NEPAL

Plate II

WIDOW WITH SPLIT EARS AND VARIOUS SORTS OF BEADS

PLATE III

RECENTLY INITIATED YOGĪS

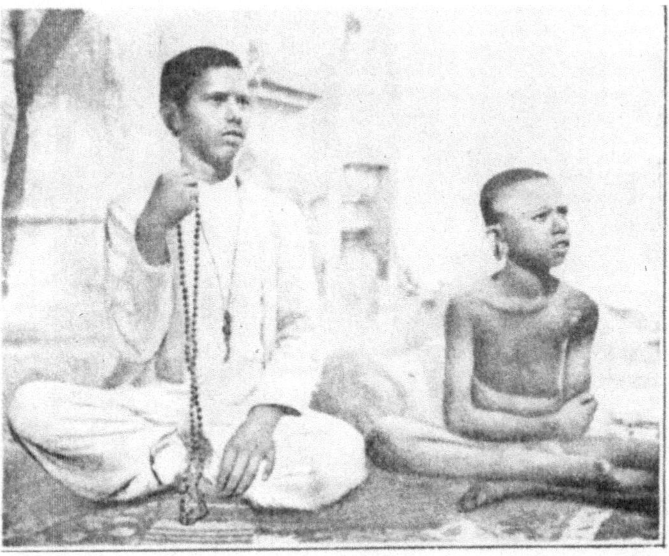

BOY INITIATES

Plate IV

MAHANT OF ṬILLA (1924)

MAHANT OF GORAKHPUR (1924)
(In his robes of office)

PLATE V

MAHANT OF PURĪ (1924)
With *Sudarṣan*, rings of copper and patch-work garments

MAHANT OF DHINODHAR (1924)

PLATE VI

GṚHASTHA AND WIFE

MAHANT OF KĀMA (1924)

(Turban of black wool threads)

PLATE VII

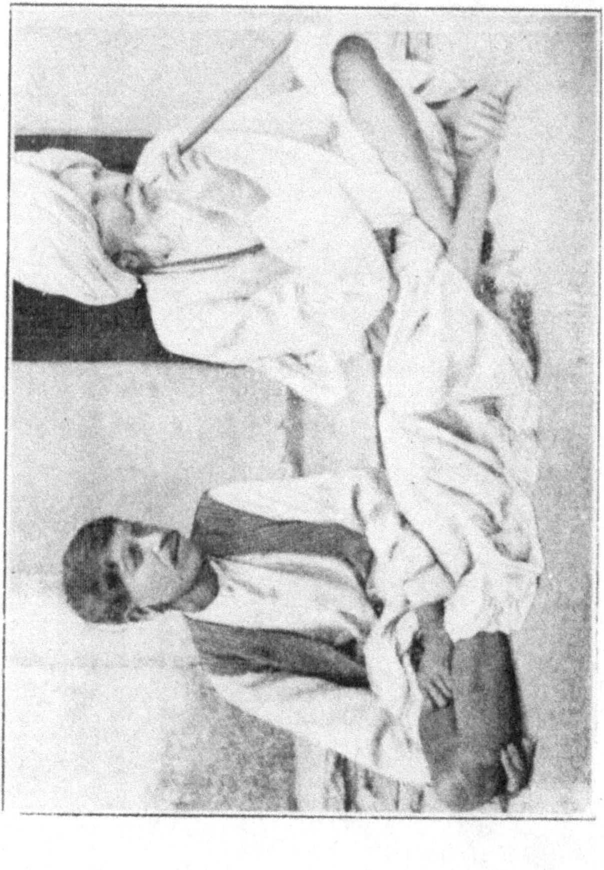

FATHER AND SON

GORAKHPUR SHRINE
(Before Reconstruction in 1924)

GORAKHPUR SHRINE
(After Reconstruction in 1924)

Plate IX

ṬILLA

TOMB OF DHARAMNĀTH

PLATE X

YANTRAS

SAMĀDHS OR TOMBS OF YOGĪS AT GORAKHPUR

SAMĀDH AT PURĪ
(The *Liṅga* is of wood)

PLATE XII

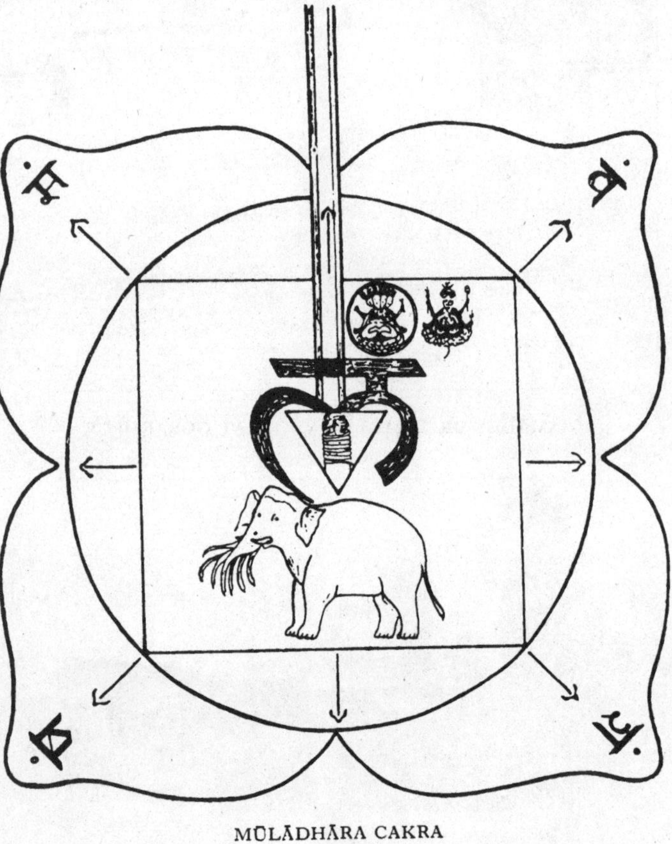

MŪLĀDHĀRA CAKRA

PLATE XIII

ĀSANA

(Showing bracelets of rhinoceros leather and rings of rhinoceros horn)

PLATE XIV

TRIŚŪLS AT GORAKHPUR